NYSTCE

LAST LIBERAL ARTS AND SCIENCES TEST 001

By: Sharon Wynne, M.S.

XAMonline, INC.
Boston

XAMonline, Inc.
25 First Street, Suite 106
Cambridge, MA 02141
Toll Free 1-800-509-4128
Email: info@xamonline.com
Web: www.xamonline.com
Fax: 1-617-583-5552

Library of Congress Cataloging-in-Publication Data

Wynne, Sharon A.
NYSTCE LAST Liberal Arts and Sciences Test 001 / Sharon A. Wynne. 3rd ed
ISBN 978-1-60787-019-7
1. NYSTCE LAST Liberal Arts and Sciences Test 001
2. Study Guides
3. NYSTCE
4. Teachers' Certification & Licensure
5. Careers

Disclaimer:
The opinions expressed in this publication are the sole works of XAMonline and were created independently from the National Education Association, Educational Testing Service, or any State Department of Education, National Evaluation Systems or other testing affiliates.

Between the time of publication and printing, state specific standards as well as testing formats and Web site information may change and therefore would not be included in part or in whole within this product. Sample test questions are developed by XAMonline and reflect content similar to that on real tests; however, they are not former test questions. XAMonline assembles content that aligns with state standards but makes no claims nor guarantees teacher candidates a passing score. Numerical scores are determined by testing companies such as NES or ETS and then are compared with individual state standards. A passing score varies from state to state.

Printed in the United States of America œ-1

NYSTCE LAST Liberal Arts and Sciences Test 001
ISBN: 978-1-60787-019-7

Table of Contents

DOMAIN II

COMPETENCY 10

COMPETENCY 11

DOMAIN III

COMPETENCY 12

COMPETENCY 13

COMPETENCY 14

COMPETENCY 15

COMPETENCY 16

DOMAIN IV

ASSESSMENT OF TEACHING SKILLS—PERFORMANCE (ATS-P)

BONUS SAMPLE TEST

NYSTCE
LAST LIBERAL ARTS AND SCIENCES TEST 001

SECTION 1
ABOUT XAMONLINE

XAMonline—A Specialty Teacher Certification Company

Created in 1996, XAMonline was the first company to publish study guides for state-specific teacher certification examinations. Founder Sharon Wynne found it frustrating that materials were not available for teacher certification preparation and decided to create the first single, state-specific guide. XAMonline has grown into a company of over 1,800 contributors and writers and offers over 300 titles for the entire PRAXIS series and every state examination. No matter what state you plan on teaching in, XAMonline has a unique teacher certification study guide just for you.

XAMonline—Value and Innovation

We are committed to providing value and innovation. Our print-on-demand technology allows us to be the first in the market to reflect changes in test standards and user feedback as they occur. Our guides are written by experienced teachers who are experts in their fields. And our content reflects the highest standards of quality. Comprehensive practice tests with varied levels of rigor means that your study experience will closely match the actual in-test experience.

To date, XAMonline has helped nearly 600,000 teachers pass their certification or licensing exams. Our commitment to preparation exceeds simply providing the proper material for study—it extends to helping teachers **gain mastery** of the subject matter, giving them the **tools** to become the most effective classroom leaders possible, and ushering today's students toward a **successful future**.

SECTION 2
ABOUT THIS STUDY GUIDE

Purpose of This Guide

Is there a little voice inside of you saying, "Am I ready?" Our goal is to replace that little voice and remove all doubt with a new voice that says, "I AM READY. **Bring it on!**" by offering the highest quality of teacher certification study guides.

Organization of Content

You will see that while every test may start with overlapping general topics, each is very unique in the skills they wish to test. Only XAMonline presents custom content that analyzes deeper than a title, a subarea, or an objective. Only XAMonline presents content and sample test assessments along with **focus statements**, the deepest-level rationale and interpretation of the skills that are unique to the exam.

Title and field number of test

→Each exam has its own name and number. XAMonline's guides are written to give you the content you need to know for the specific exam you are taking. You can be confident when you buy our guide that it contains the information you need to study for the specific test you are taking.

Subareas

→These are the major content categories found on the exam. XAMonline's guides are written to cover all of the subareas found in the test frameworks developed for the exam.

Objectives

→These are standards that are unique to the exam and represent the main subcategories of the subareas/content categories. XAMonline's guides are written to address every specific objective required to pass the exam.

Focus statements

→These are examples and interpretations of the objectives. You find them in parenthesis directly following the objective. They provide detailed examples of the range, type, and level of content that appear on the test questions. **Only XAMonline's guides drill down to this level.**

How Do We Compare with Our Competitors?

XAMonline—drills down to the focus statement level.
CliffsNotes and REA—organized at the objective level
Kaplan—provides only links to content
MoMedia—content not specific to the state test

Each subarea is divided into manageable sections that cover the specific skill areas. Explanations are easy to understand and thorough. You'll find that every test answer contains a rejoinder so if you need a refresher or further review after taking the test, you'll know exactly to which section you must return.

How to Use This Book

Our informal polls show that most people begin studying up to eight weeks prior to the test date, so start early. Then ask yourself some questions: How much do you really know? Are you coming to the test straight from your teacher-education program or are you having to review subjects you haven't considered in ten years? Either way, take a **diagnostic or assessment test** first. Also, spend time on sample tests so that you become accustomed to the way the actual test will appear.

This guide comes with an online diagnostic test of 30 questions found online at *www.XAMonline.com*. It is a little boot camp to get you up for the task and reveal things about your compendium of knowledge in general. Although this guide is structured to follow the order of the test, you are not required to study in that order. By finding a time-management and study plan that fits your life you will be more effective. The results of your diagnostic or self-assessment test can be a guide for how to manage your time and point you toward an area that needs more attention.

After taking the diagnostic exam, fill out the **Personalized Study Plan** page at the beginning of each chapter. Review the competencies and skills covered in that chapter and check the boxes that apply to your study needs. If there are sections you already know you can skip, check the "skip it" box. Taking this step will give you a study plan for each chapter.

Week	Activity
8 weeks prior to test	Take a diagnostic test found at www.XAMonline.com
7 weeks prior to test	Build your Personalized Study Plan for each chapter. Check the "skip it" box for sections you feel you are already strong in. SKIP IT ☐
6-3 weeks prior to test	For each of these four weeks, choose a content area to study. You don't have to go in the order of the book. It may be that you start with the content that needs the most review. Alternately, you may want to ease yourself into plan by starting with the most familiar material.
2 weeks prior to test	Take the sample test, score it, and create a review plan for the final week before the test.
1 week prior to test	Following your plan (which will likely be aligned with the areas that need the most review) go back and study the sections that align with the questions you may have gotten wrong. Then go back and study the sections related to the questions you answered correctly. If need be, create flashcards and drill yourself on any area that you makes you anxious.

SECTION 3
ABOUT THE NYSTCE LIBERAL ARTS AND SCIENCES TEST 001 (LAST)

What Is the NYSTCE Liberal Arts and Sciences Test 001 (LAST)?

The NYSTCE Liberal Arts and Sciences Test 001 (LAST) is meant to assess mastery of the basic skills required to teach students in New York public schools. It is administered by Pearson Education on behalf of the New York Department of Education.

Often **your own state's requirements** determine whether or not you should take any particular test. The most reliable source of information regarding this is your state's Department of Education. This resource should have a complete list of testing centers and dates. Test dates vary by subject area and not all test dates necessarily include your particular test, so be sure to check carefully.

If you are in a teacher-education program, check with the Education Department or the Certification Officer for specific information for testing and testing timelines. The Certification Office should have most of the information you need.

If you choose an alternative route to certification you can either rely on our website at *www.XAMonline.com* or on the resources provided by an alternative certification program. Many states now have specific agencies devoted to alternative certification and there are some national organizations as well, for example:

National Association for Alternative Certification
http://www.alt-teachercert.org/index.asp

Interpreting Test Results

Contrary to what you may have heard, the results of the NYSTCE Liberal Arts and Sciences Test 001 (LAST) are not based on time. More accurately, you will be scored on the raw number of points you earn in relation to the raw number of points available. Each question is worth one raw point. It is likely to your benefit to complete as many questions in the time allotted, but it will not necessarily work to your advantage if you hurry through the test.

Follow the guidelines provided by Pearson for interpreting your score. The web site offers a sample test score sheet and clearly explains how/whether the scores are scaled and what to expect if you have an essay portion on your test.

What's on the Test?

The NYSTCE Liberal Arts and Sciences Test 001 (LAST) consists of approximately 80 multiple-choice questions and 1 constructed-response essay. The breakdown of the questions is as follows:

Category	Approximate Number of Questions	Approximate Percentage of the test
I: Scientific, Mathematical, and Technological Processes	18	23%
II: Historical and Social Scientific Awareness	15	19%
III: Artistic Expression and the Humanities	15	19%
IV: Communication and Research Skills	15	19%
V: Written Analysis and Expression	16 & 1 constructed response essay	20%

Question Types

You're probably thinking, enough already, I want to study! Indulge us a little longer while we explain that there is actually more than one type of multiple-choice question. You can thank us later after you realize how well prepared you are for your exam.

1. Complete the Statement. The name says it all. In this question type you'll be asked to choose the correct completion of a given statement. For example:

The Dolch Basic Sight Words consist of a relatively short list of words that children should be able to:

A. Sound out

B. Know the meaning of

C. Recognize on sight

D. Use in a sentence

The correct answer is A. In order to check your answer, test out the statement by adding the choices to the end of it.

2. Which of the Following. One way to test your answer choice for this type of question is to replace the phrase "which of the following" with your selection. Use this example:

Which of the following words is one of the twelve most frequently used in children's reading texts:

A. There

B. This

C. The

D. An

Don't look! Test your answer. _____ is one of the twelve most frequently used in children's reading texts. Did you guess C? Then you guessed correctly.

3. Roman Numeral Choices. This question type is used when there is more than one possible correct answer. For example:

Which of the following two arguments accurately supports the use of cooperative learning as an effective method of instruction?

I. Cooperative learning groups facilitate healthy competition between individuals in the group.

II. Cooperative learning groups allow academic achievers to carry or cover for academic underachievers.

III. Cooperative learning groups make each student in the group accountable for the success of the group.

IV. Cooperative learning groups make it possible for students to reward other group members for achieving.

A. I and II

B. II and III

C. I and III

D. III and IV

Notice that the question states there are **two** possible answers. It's best to read all the possibilities first before looking at the answer choices. In this case, the correct answer is D.

4. **Negative Questions.** This type of question contains words such as "not," "least," and "except." Each correct answer will be the statement that does **not** fit the situation described in the question. Such as:

> **Multicultural education is not**
>
> A. An idea or concept
>
> B. A "tack-on" to the school curriculum
>
> C. An educational reform movement
>
> D. A process

Think to yourself that the statement could be anything but the correct answer. This question form is more open to interpretation than other types, so read carefully and don't forget that you're answering a negative statement.

5. **Questions that Include Graphs, Tables, or Reading Passages.** As always, read the question carefully. It likely asks for a very specific answer and not a broad interpretation of the visual. Here is a simple (though not statistically accurate) example of a graph question:

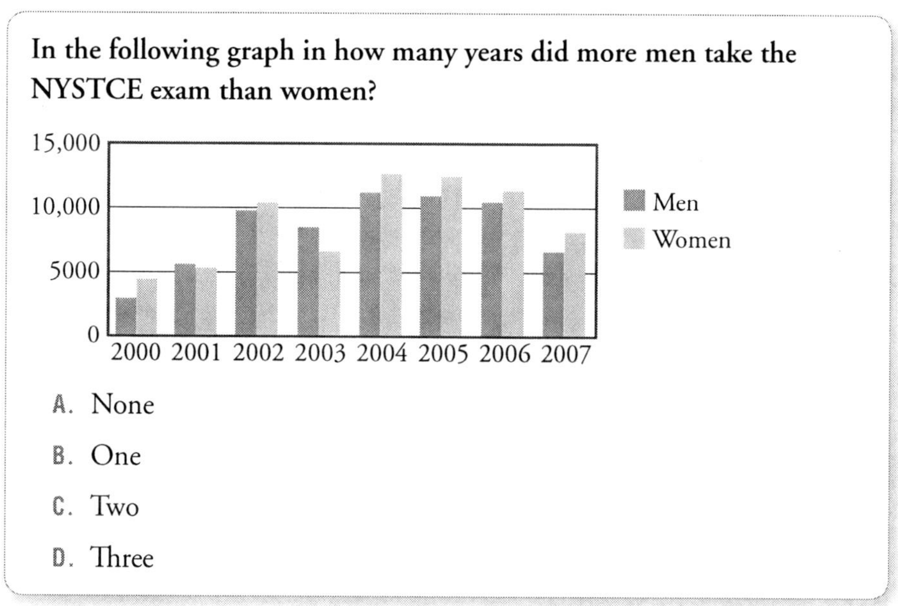

It may help you to simply circle the two years that answer the question. Make sure you've read the question thoroughly and once you've made your determination, double check your work. The correct answer is C.

SECTION 4
HELPFUL HINTS

Study Tips

1. You are what you eat. Certain foods aid the learning process by releasing natural memory enhancers called CCKs (cholecystokinin) composed of tryptophan, choline, and phenylalanine. All of these chemicals enhance the neurotransmitters associated with memory and certain foods release memory enhancing chemicals. A light meal or snacks of one of the following foods fall into this category:

   - Milk
   - Rice
   - Eggs
   - Fish
   - Nuts and seeds
   - Oats
   - Turkey

   The better the connections, the more you comprehend!

2. See the forest for the trees. In other words, get the concept before you look at the details. One way to do this is to take notes as you read, paraphrasing or summarizing in your own words. Putting the concept in terms that are comfortable and familiar may increase retention.

3. Question authority. Ask why, why, why? Pull apart written material paragraph by paragraph and don't forget the captions under the illustrations. For example, if a heading reads *Stream Erosion* put it in the form of a question (Why do streams erode? What is stream erosion?) then find the answer within the material. If you train your mind to think in this manner you will learn more and prepare yourself for answering test questions.

4. Play mind games. Using your brain for reading or puzzles keeps it flexible. Even with a limited amount of time your brain can take in data (much like a computer) and store it for later use. In ten minutes you can: read two paragraphs (at least), quiz yourself with flash cards, or review notes. Even if you don't fully understand something on the first pass, your mind stores it for recall, which is why frequent reading or review increases chances of retention and comprehension.

5. Get pointed in the right direction. Use arrows to point to important passages or pieces of information. It's easier to read than a page full of yellow highlights. Highlighting can be used sparingly, but add an arrow to the margin to call attention to it.

6. The pen is mightier than the sword. Learn to take great notes. A by-product of our modern culture is that we have grown accustomed to getting our information in short doses. We've subconsciously trained ourselves to assimilate information into neat little packages. Messy notes fragment the flow of information. Your notes can be much clearer with proper formatting. ***The Cornell Method*** is one such format. This method was popularized in *How to Study in College*, Ninth Edition, by Walter Pauk. You can benefit from the method without purchasing an additional book by simply looking up the method online. Below is a sample of how *The Cornell Method* can be adapted for use with this guide.

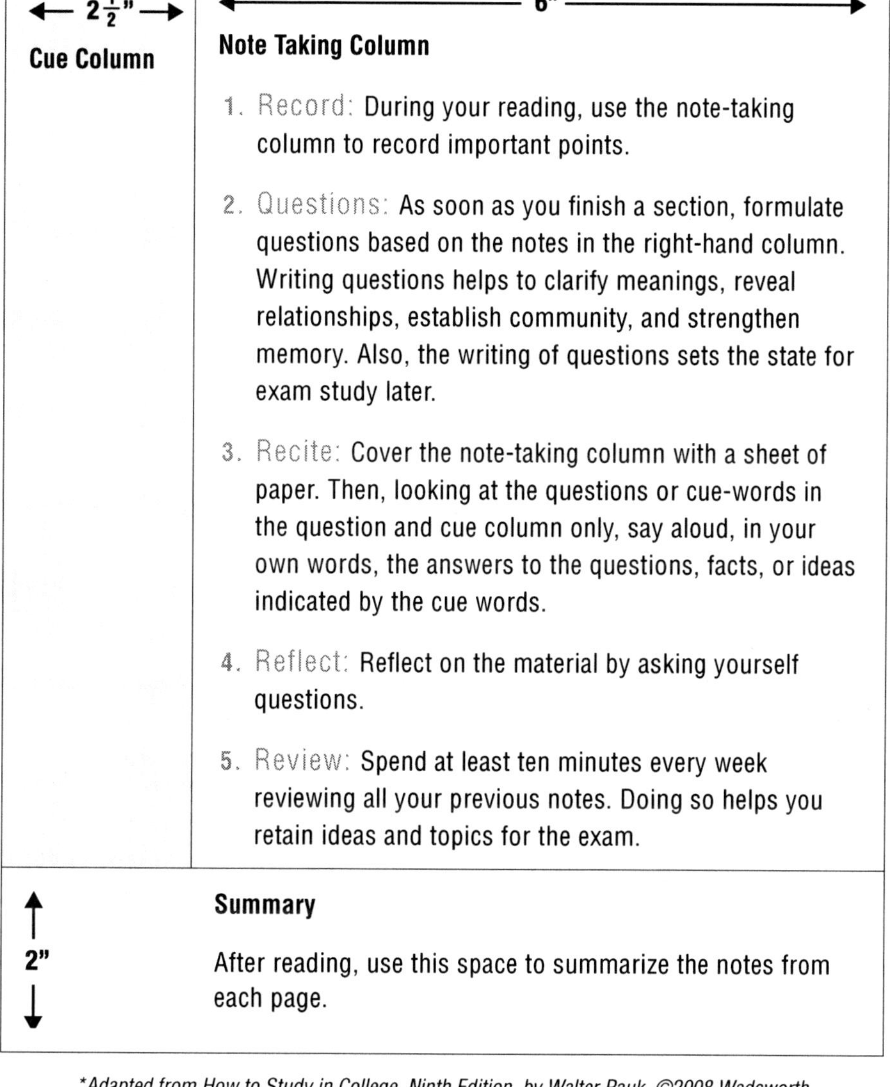

← $2\frac{1}{2}$" →
Cue Column
← 6" →
Note Taking Column
1. Record: During your reading, use the note-taking column to record important points.
2. Questions: As soon as you finish a section, formulate questions based on the notes in the right-hand column. Writing questions helps to clarify meanings, reveal relationships, establish community, and strengthen memory. Also, the writing of questions sets the state for exam study later.
3. Recite: Cover the note-taking column with a sheet of paper. Then, looking at the questions or cue-words in the question and cue column only, say aloud, in your own words, the answers to the questions, facts, or ideas indicated by the cue words.
4. Reflect: Reflect on the material by asking yourself questions.
5. Review: Spend at least ten minutes every week reviewing all your previous notes. Doing so helps you retain ideas and topics for the exam.
↑ 2" ↓
Summary
After reading, use this space to summarize the notes from each page.

**Adapted from How to Study in College, Ninth Edition, by Walter Pauk, ©2008 Wadsworth*

7. **Place yourself in exile and set the mood.** Set aside a particular place and time to study that best suits your personal needs and biorhythms. If you're a night person, burn the midnight oil. If you're a morning person set yourself up with some coffee and get to it. Make your study time and place as free from distraction as possible and surround yourself with what you need, be it silence or music. Studies have shown that music can aid in concentration, absorption, and retrieval of information. Not all music, though. Classical music is said to work best

The proctor will write the start time where it can be seen and then, later, provide the time remaining, typically fifteen minutes before the end of the test.

8. **Check your budget.** You should at least review all the content material before your test, but allocate the most amount of time to the areas that need the most refreshing. It sounds obvious, but it's easy to forget. You can use the study rubric above to balance your study budget.

Testing Tips

1. **Get smart, play dumb.** Sometimes a question is just a question. No one is out to trick you, so don't assume that the test writer is looking for something other than what was asked. Stick to the question as written and don't overanalyze.

2. **Do a double take.** Read test questions and answer choices at least twice because it's easy to miss something, to transpose a word or some letters. If you have no idea what the correct answer is, skip it and come back later if there's time. If you're still clueless, it's okay to guess. Remember, you're scored on the number of questions you answer correctly and you're not penalized for wrong answers. The worst case scenario is that you miss a point from a good guess.

3. **Turn it on its ear.** The syntax of a question can often provide a clue, so make things interesting and turn the question into a statement to see if it changes the meaning or relates better (or worse) to the answer choices.

4. **Get out your magnifying glass.** Look for hidden clues in the questions because it's difficult to write a multiple-choice question without giving away part of the answer in the options presented. In most questions you can readily eliminate one or two potential answers, increasing your chances of answering correctly to 50/50, which will help out if you've skipped a question and gone back to it (see tip #2).

5. **Call it intuition.** Often your first instinct is correct. If you've been studying the content you've likely absorbed something and have subconsciously retained the knowledge. On questions you're not sure about trust your instincts because a first impression is usually correct.

6. Graffiti. Sometimes it's a good idea to mark your answers directly on the test booklet and go back to fill in the optical scan sheet later. You don't get extra points for perfectly blackened ovals. If you choose to manage your test this way, be sure not to mismark your answers when you transcribe to the scan sheet.

7. Become a clock-watcher. You have a set amount of time to answer the questions. Don't get bogged down laboring over a question you're not sure about when there are ten others you could answer more readily. If you choose to follow the advice of tip #6, be sure you leave time near the end to go back and fill in the scan sheet.

Do the Drill

No matter how prepared you feel it's sometimes a good idea to apply Murphy's Law. So the following tips might seem silly, mundane, or obvious, but we're including them anyway.

1. Remember, you are what you eat, so bring a snack. Choose from the list of energizing foods that appear earlier in the introduction.

2. You're not too sexy for your test. Wear comfortable clothes. You'll be distracted if your belt is too tight or if you're too cold or too hot.

3. Lie to yourself. Even if you think you're a prompt person, pretend you're not and leave plenty of time to get to the testing center. Map it out ahead of time and do a dry run if you have to. There's no need to add road rage to your list of anxieties.

4. Bring sharp number 2 pencils. It may seem impossible to forget this need from your school days, but you might. And make sure the erasers are intact, too.

5. No ticket, no test. Bring your admission ticket as well as **two** forms of identification, including one with a picture and signature. You will not be admitted to the test without these things.

6. You can't take it with you. Leave any study aids, dictionaries, notebooks, computers, and the like at home. Certain tests **do** allow a scientific or four-function calculator, so check ahead of time to see if your test does.

7. Prepare for the desert. Any time spent on a bathroom break **cannot** be made up later, so use your judgment on the amount you eat or drink.

8. Quiet, Please! Keeping your own time is a good idea, but not with a timepiece that has a loud ticker. If you use a watch, take it off and place it nearby but not so that it distracts you. And **silence your cell phone**.

To the best of our ability, we have compiled the content you need to know in this book and in the accompanying online resources. The rest is up to you. You can use the study and testing tips or you can follow your own methods. Either way, you can be confident that there aren't any missing pieces of information and there shouldn't be any surprises in the content on the test.

If you have questions about test fees, registration, electronic testing, or other content verification issues please visit *www.nystce.nesinc.org*.

Good luck!

Sharon Wynne
Founder, XAMonline

DOMAIN I
SCIENTIFIC, MATHEMATICAL, AND TECHNOLOGICAL PROCESSES

PERSONALIZED STUDY PLAN

PAGE	COMPETENCY AND SKILL		KNOWN MATERIAL/ SKIP IT
5	**1:**	**Use mathematical reasoning in problem-solving situations to arrive at logical conclusions and to analyze the problem-solving process**	☐
	1.1:	Analyze problem solutions for logical flaws	☐
	1.2:	Examine problems to determine missing information needed to solve them	☐
	1.3:	Analyze a partial solution to a problem to determine an appropriate next step	☐
	1.4:	Evaluate the validity or logic of an argument that is based on statistics or probability	☐
11	**2:**	**Understand connections between mathematical representations and ideas, and use mathematical terms and representations to organize, interpret, and communicate information**	☐
	2.1:	Analyze data and make inferences from two or more graphic sources	☐
	2.2:	Restate a problem in mathematical terms	☐
	2.3:	Use mathematical information to present relationships	☐
	2.4:	Select an appropriate graph or table summarizing information presented in another form	☐
16	**3:**	**Apply knowledge of numerical, geometric, and algebraic relationships in problem solving and mathematical contexts**	☐
	3.1:	Represent and use numbers in equivalent forms	☐
	3.2:	Apply operational algorithms	☐
	3.3:	Use scales and ratios to interpret maps and models	☐
	3.4:	Use geometric concepts and formulas	☐
	3.5:	Solve problems using algebraic concepts and formulas	☐
	3.6:	Apply appropriate algebraic equations to the solution of problems	☐

PERSONALIZED STUDY PLAN

PAGE	COMPETENCY AND SKILL		KNOWN MATERIAL/ SKIP IT
39	**4:**	**Understand major concepts, principles, and theories in science and technology, and use that understanding to analyze phenomena in the natural world and to interpret information presented in illustrated or written form**	☐
	4.1:	Use an appropriate illustration, graphic, or physical model to represent a scientific theory, concept, or relationship	☐
	4.2:	Relate a major scientific principle, concept, or theory to a natural phenomenon	☐
	4.3:	Use design processes and procedures to pose questions and select solutions	☐
	4.4:	Apply technological knowledge to evaluate which products and systems meet human and environmental needs	☐
	4.5:	Analyze excerpts describing scientific advances in relation to underlying scientific principles	☐
57	**5:**	**Understand the historical development and cultural contexts of mathematics, science, and technology, the relationships and common themes that connect mathematics, science, and technology, and the impact of mathematics, science, and technology on human societies**	☐
	5.1:	Analyze the historical, societal, or environmental effects of given developments in science and technology	☐
	5.2:	Recognize how mathematical models can be used to understand scientific, social, or environmental phenomena	☐
	5.3:	Evaluate how historical and societal factors have affected developments in science and technology	☐
	5.4:	Analyze how developments in scientific knowledge may affect other areas of life	☐
64	**6:**	**Understand and apply skills, principles, and procedures associated with inquiry and problem solving in the sciences**	☐
	6.1:	Apply scientific methods and principles to investigate a question or problem	☐
	6.2:	Formulate questions to guide research and experimentation	☐
	6.3:	Infer the scientific principles or skills that contribute to a scientific development	☐
	6.4:	Demonstrate familiarity with electronic means for collecting, organizing, and analyzing information	☐
	6.5:	Analyze the components of an experimental design	☐
	6.6:	Demonstrate an understanding of the nature of scientific inquiry and the role of observation and experimentation in science	☐

COMPETENCY 1

USE MATHEMATICAL REASONING IN PROBLEM-SOLVING SITUATIONS TO ARRIVE AT LOGICAL CONCLUSIONS AND TO ANALYZE THE PROBLEM-SOLVING PROCESS

SKILL 1.1 Analyze problem solutions for logical flaws

DEDUCTIVE REASONING is the process of arriving at a conclusion based on other statements that are known to be true.

A symbolic argument consists of a set of premises and a conclusion in the format of *if* [premise 1 and premise 2], *then* [conclusion].

An argument is **VALID** when the conclusion follows necessarily from the premises. An argument is **INVALID** or a fallacy when the conclusion does not follow from the premises.

DEDUCTIVE REASONING: the process of arriving at a conclusion based on other statements that are known to be true

VALID: an argument is valid when the conclusion follows necessarily from the premises

INVALID: an argument is invalid when the conclusion does not follow from the premises

FOUR STANDARD FORMS OF VALID ARGUMENTS		
Law of Detachment	If p, then q p Therefore, q	premise 1 premise 2
Law of Contraposition	If p, then q not q Therefore, not p	premise 1 premise 2
Law of Syllogism	If p, then q If q, then r Therefore, if p, then r	premise 1 premise 2
Disjunctive Syllogism	p or q not p Therefore, q	premise 1 premise 2

Example: Can we reach a conclusion from these two statements?

A. All swimmers are athletes.
All athletes are scholars.

In "if-then" form, these would be:
If you are a swimmer, *then* you are an athlete.
If you are an athlete, *then* you are a scholar.

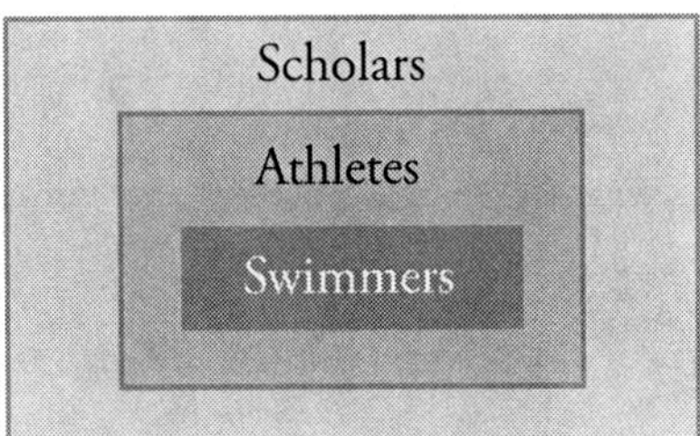

Clearly, if you are a swimmer, then you are also an athlete. This includes you in the group of scholars.

B. All swimmers are athletes.
All wrestlers are athletes.

In "if-then" form, these would be:
If you are a swimmer, *then* you are an athlete.
If you are a wrestler, *then* you are an athlete.

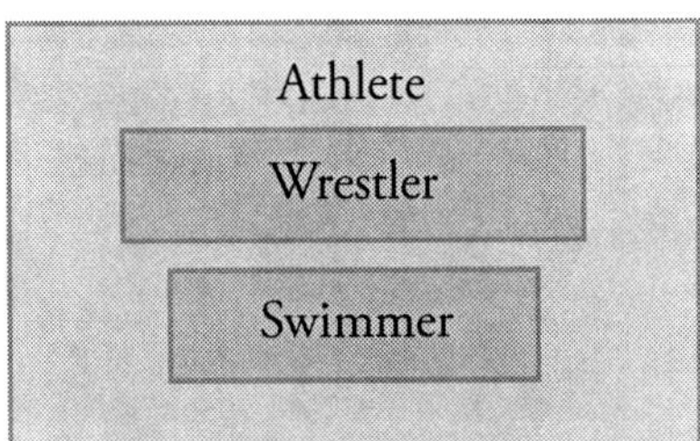

If you are a swimmer or a wrestler, then you are also an athlete. This does *not* allow you to come to any other conclusions.

A swimmer may or may *not* also be a wrestler. Therefore, *no conclusion is possible.*

Example: Determine whether statement A, B, C, or D can be deduced from the following:

(i) If John drives the big truck, then the shipment will be delivered.
(ii) The shipment will not be delivered.

A. John does not drive the big truck.

B. John drives the big truck.

C. The shipment will not be delivered.

D. None of the above conclusions is valid.

Let p: John drives the big truck.
q: The shipment is delivered.
Statement (i) gives $p \rightarrow q$. Statement (ii) gives $\sim q$ (not q). This is the Law of Contraposition.
Therefore, the logical conclusion is $\sim p$ (not p), or "John does not drive the big truck." The answer is A.

Example: Determine which conclusion can be logically deduced from the following information:

(i) Peter is a jet pilot or Peter is a navigator.
(ii) Peter is not a jet pilot.

A. Peter is not a navigator.

B. Peter is a navigator.

C. Peter is neither a jet pilot nor a navigator.

D. None of the above is true.

Let p: Peter is a jet pilot.
q: Peter is a navigator.
So we have $p \vee q$ (p or q) from statement (i)
$\sim p$ (not p) from statement (ii)
The answer is B.

Example: What conclusion, if any, can be reached? Assume each statement is true, regardless of any personal beliefs.

1. If the Red Sox win the World Series, I will die.
   I died.
   The Red Sox won the World Series.

2. If an angle's measure is between 0° and 90°, then the angle is acute.
   Angle B is not acute.
   Angle B is not between 0° and 90°.

3. Students who do well in geometry will succeed in college.
   Annie is doing extremely well in geometry.
   Annie will do well in college.

4. Left-handed people are witty and charming.
   You are left-handed.
   You are witty and charming.

SKILL 1.2 Examine problems to determine missing information needed to solve them

Some problems do not contain enough information with which to solve them.

Example: During one semester, a college student used 70 gallons of gas driving back and forth to visit her family. The total cost of gas was $225. What was the average number of gallons of gas used per trip?
This question cannot be answered because you do not know the number of trips the student made.

SKILL 1.3 Analyze a partial solution to a problem to determine an appropriate next step

Example: A fish is 30 inches long. The head is as long as the tail. If the head was twice as long and the tail was the same length, then the body would be 18 inches long. How long is the body?
Partial solution: Let x represent the head.

$$2x + x + 18 = 30$$
$$3x = 12$$
$$x = 4$$

We now create an equation to solve for the body of the fish with y representing the body.

$$x + x + y = 30$$
$$2x + y = 30$$

Substitute 4 for x.

$$2(4) + y = 30$$
$$8 + y = 30$$
$$3y = 30$$
$$y = 22$$

In this example, we are able to substitute the partial solution to solve for the variable in the problem's actual question.

Example: How many squares must be added to a 10-by-10 square to create an 11-by-11 square?

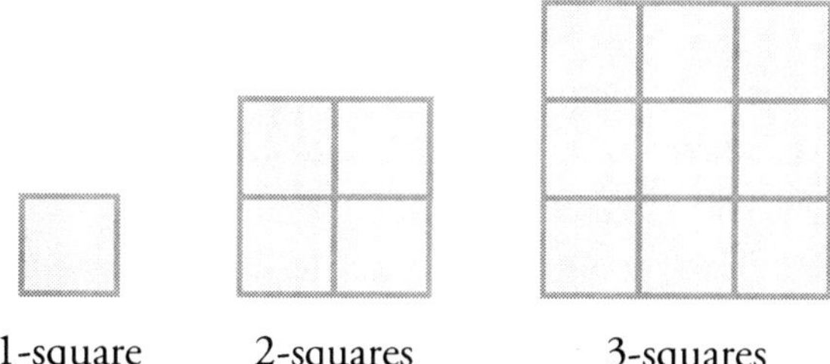

1-square 2-squares 3-squares

Partial solution: We determine that a 3-by-3 square has 5 more squares than a 2-by-2 square, which has 3 more squares than 1 square.

By examining the pattern, we can answer the question by adding the dimension of the previous square (in this case, 10) to the dimension of the current square (in this case, 11). Twenty-one squares must be added to a 10-by-10 square to create an 11-by-11 square.

SKILL 1.4 Evaluate the validity or logic of an argument or advertising claim that is based on statistics or probability

Statistics and probability deal with inherently uncertain situations where it may not be possible to evaluate whether a hypothesis is completely valid or completely invalid. There are mathematical constructs, however, that can be used to assign a certain degree of validity to a statistical result.

Random sampling is the process of studying an aspect of a population by selecting and gathering data from a segment of the population and making inferences and generalizations based on the results. Sample statistics such as mean, median, mode, range, and sampling error (standard deviation) are important generalizations about the entire sample. Various factors affect the accuracy of sample statistics and the generalizations made from them about the larger population. Sample size is one important factor in the accuracy and reliability of sample statistics. As sample size increases, sampling error (standard deviation) decreases.

Sampling error is the main determinant of the size of the **confidence interval**. Confidence intervals decrease in size as sample size increases. A confidence interval gives an estimated range of values, which is likely to include a particular population parameter. The **confidence level** associated with a confidence interval is the probability that the interval contains the population parameter. For example, a poll reports that 60% of a sample group prefers candidate A with a margin of error of ±3% and a confidence level of 95%. In this poll, there is a 95% chance that the preference for candidate A in the whole population is between 57% and 63%.

Apart from mathematical calculations of validity, there are other factors that influence the validity of a statistical result that must be taken into account when deciding whether an argument or advertising claim is valid. One question to ask is what the sampling procedure is and how bias-free it is. If an advertiser claims that a survey of 5,000 people shows that a particular toothpaste is preferred by most people, it makes sense to ask how that sample of 5,000 was selected. Is it an accurate representation of the general population? Exactly what questions were they asked? Is there any inherent bias in the kind of questions asked?

If the results of a study are shown in graphical form, what are the scales used on the axes? Graphical results can look very different with different choices of scales. If an average is quoted, is this average the mean, median or mode? The average of a data set does not include information about the data spread. Is the data spread normal or skewed in some way?

For instance, if the average salary at a company is $40,000, does everyone make an amount that is close to that number or do a few management people earn millions and the rest of the people a lot less than the stated number? If a percentage is quoted, it is necessary to ascertain what that percentage is relative to. For example, if an advertiser claims that the quantity of a bottle of detergent is increased by 33%, this does not mean that the price is reduced by 33%. The necessary calculations may show that price is reduced by only 25%. Other questions to ask include whether the figures given are too precise given the study methods or whether correlation is being confused with causation.

COMPETENCY 2

UNDERSTAND CONNECTIONS BETWEEN MATHEMATICAL REPRESENTATIONS AND IDEAS, AND USE MATHEMATICAL TERMS AND REPRESENTATIONS TO ORGANIZE, INTERPRET, AND COMMUNICATE INFORMATION

SKILL 2.1 Analyze data, and make inferences from two or more graphic sources *(e.g., diagrams, graphs, equations)*

To make a **BAR GRAPH** or a **PICTOGRAPH**, determine the scale to be used for the graph. Then determine the length of each bar on the graph, or determine the number of pictures needed to represent each item of information. Be sure to include an explanation of the scale in the legend.

BAR GRAPH: a graph that compares various quantities

PICTOGRAPH: a graph that compares quantities using symbols where each symbol represents a number of items

Example: A class had the following grades: 4 As, 9 Bs, 8 Cs, 1 D, and 3 Fs. Graph these on a bar graph and a pictograph.

Bar graph

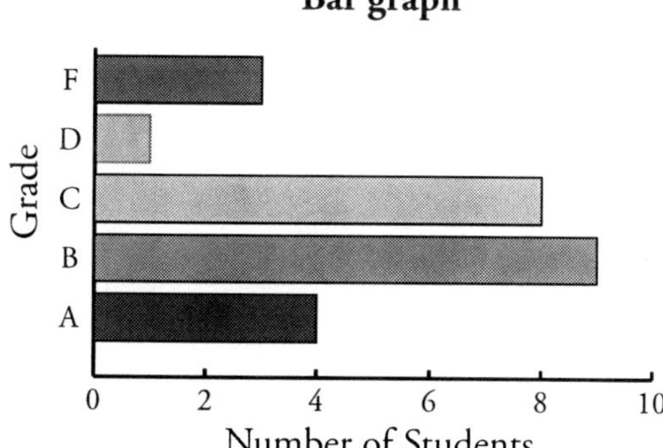

Pictograph

Grade	Number of Students
A	☺☺☺☺
B	☺☺☺☺☺☺☺☺☺☺
C	☺☺☺☺☺☺☺☺☺
D	☺
F	☺☺☺

LINE GRAPH: a graph that shows trends, often over a period of time

To make a **LINE GRAPH**, determine appropriate scales for both the vertical and horizontal axes (based on the information to be graphed). Describe what each axis represents, and mark the scale periodically on each axis. Graph the individual points of the graph and connect the points on the graph from left to right.

Example: Graph the following information using a line graph.

The number of National Merit Scholarship finalists per school year

	90–91	91–92	92–93	93–94	94–95	95–96
Central	3	5	1	4	6	8
Wilson	4	2	3	2	3	2

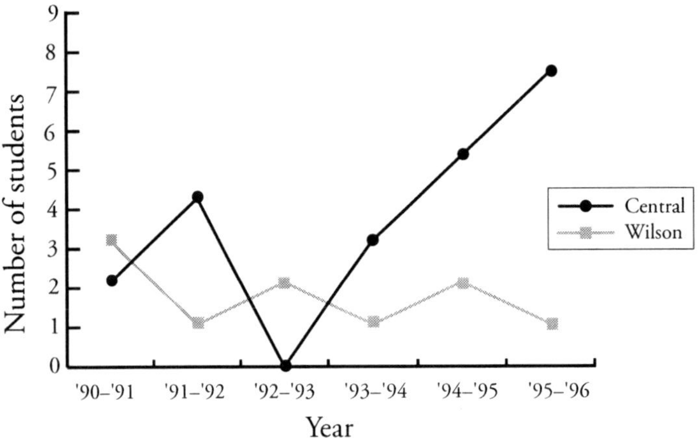

CIRCLE GRAPH: also called a pie chart, this graph shows quantities in proportional sectors

To make a **CIRCLE GRAPH**, total all the information that is to be included on the graph. Determine the central angle to be used for each sector of the graph using the following formula:

$$\frac{\text{information}}{\text{total information}} \times 360^{\circ} = \text{degrees in central } \measuredangle$$

Lay out the central angles to these sizes, label each section, and include each section's percent.

Example: Graph the following information about monthly expenses using a circle graph.

MONTHLY EXPENSES					
Rent	**Food**	**Utilities**	**Clothes**	**Church**	**Misc.**
$400	$150	$75	$75	$100	$200

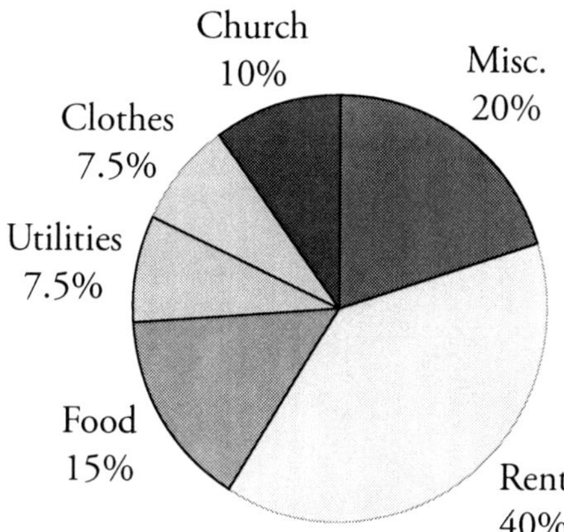

Scatter plots compare two characteristics of the same group of things or people and usually consist of a large body of data. They show how much one variable affects another. The relationship between the two variables is their CORRELATION. The closer the data points come to forming a straight line when plotted, the closer the correlation.

CORRELATION: the relationship between the two variables in a scatter plot

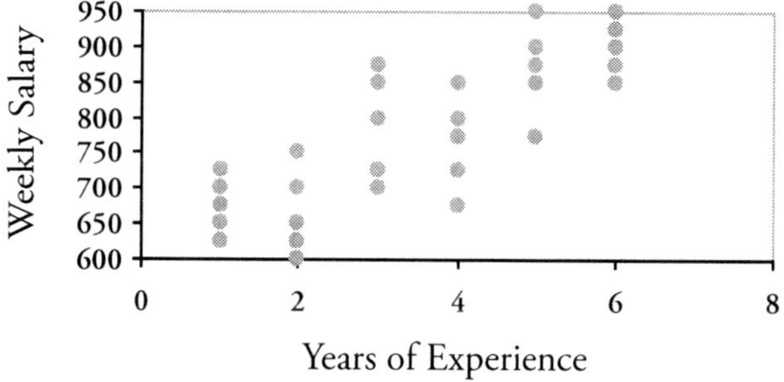

Stem-and-leaf plots are visually similar to line plots. The stems are the digits in the greatest place value of the data values, and the leaves are the digits in the next greatest place value. Stem-and-leaf plots are best suited to small sets of data and are especially useful for comparing two sets of data. The following is an example using test scores:

4	9
5	4 9
6	1 2 3 4 6 7 8 8
7	0 3 4 6 6 6 7 7 7 7 8 8 8 8
8	3 5 5 7 8
9	0 0 3 4 5
10	0 0

HISTOGRAM: a graph that summarizes information from large sets of data that can be naturally grouped into intervals

FREQUENCY: the number of times any particular data value occurs

FREQUENCY OF THE INTERVAL: the number of data values in any interval

TREND: a line on a line graph that shows the correlation between two sets of data

INFERENCE: a statement that is derived from reasoning

HISTOGRAMS are used to summarize information from large sets of data that can be naturally grouped into intervals. The vertical axis indicates **FREQUENCY** (the number of times any particular data value occurs), and the horizontal axis indicates data values or ranges of data values. The number of data values in any interval is the **FREQUENCY OF THE INTERVAL**.

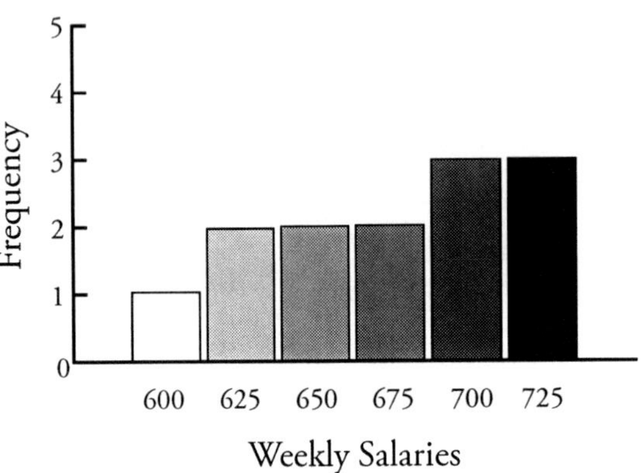

A **TREND** line on a line graph shows the correlation between two sets of data. A trend may show positive correlation (both sets of data get bigger together), negative correlation (one set of data gets bigger while the other gets smaller), or no correlation.

An **INFERENCE** is a statement that is derived from reasoning. When reading a graph, inferences help us interpret the data that is presented. From this information, a conclusion and even predictions about what the data actually mean are possible.

Example: Katherine and Tom were both doing poorly in math class. Their teacher had a conference with each of them in November. The following graph shows their math test scores during the school year.

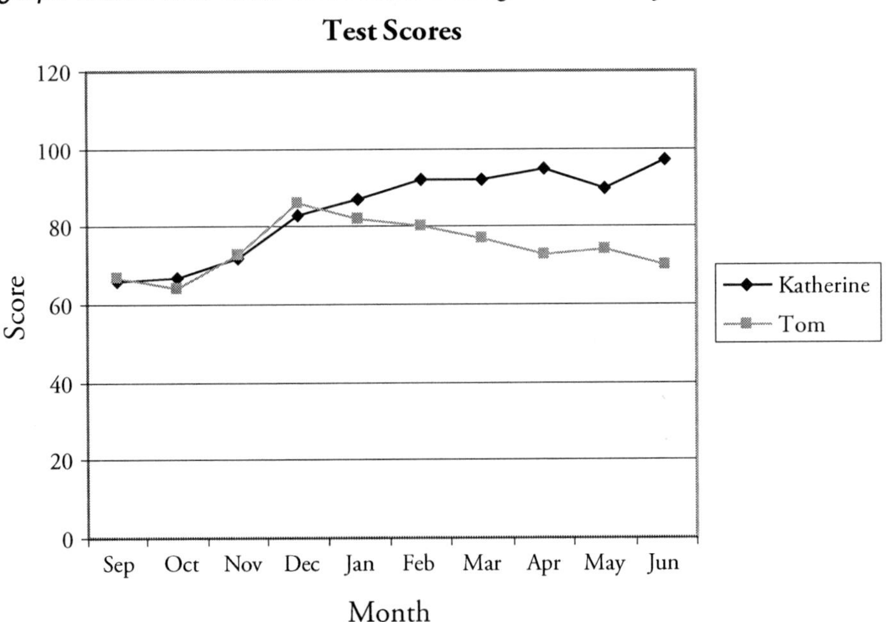

What kind of trend does this graph show?

This graph shows that there is a positive trend in Katherine's test scores and a negative trend in Tom's test scores.

What inferences can you make from this graph?

We can infer that Katherine's test scores rose steadily after November. Tom's test scores spiked in December but then began to fall again and trended negatively.

What conclusion can you draw based on this graph?

We can conclude that Katherine took her teacher's meeting seriously and began to study in order to do better on the exams. It seems as though Tom tried harder for a bit, but his test scores eventually slipped back down to the level at which they began.

SKILL 2.2 Restate a problem related to a concrete situation in mathematical terms

Example: The YMCA wants to sell raffle tickets to raise at least $32,000. If they must pay $7,250 in expenses and prizes out of the money collected from the tickets, how many tickets worth $25 each must they sell?

Since they want to raise at least $32,000, that means they would be happy to get $32,000 *or more*. This requires an inequality.

Let x = number of tickets sold.

Then $25x$ = total money collected for x tickets.

Total money minus expenses must be greater than $32,000.

$$25x - 7250 \geq 32000$$
$$25x \geq 39250$$
$$x \geq 1570$$

If they sell 1,570 tickets or more, they will raise at least $32,000.

For more examples see, Skill 3.5.

SKILL 2.3 Use mathematical modeling/multiple representations to present, interpret, communicate, and connect mathematical information and relationships

See Skill 2.1

SKILL 2.4 Select an appropriate graph or table summarizing information presented in another form *(e.g., a newspaper excerpt)*

See Skill 2.1

COMPETENCY 3

APPLY KNOWLEDGE OF NUMERICAL, GEOMETRIC, AND ALGEBRAIC RELATIONSHIPS IN PROBLEM SOLVING AND MATHEMATICAL CONTEXTS

SKILL 3.1 Represent and use numbers in a variety of equivalent forms *(e.g., integer, fraction, decimal, percent)*

RATIONAL NUMBERS: numbers that can be expressed as the ratio of two integers, $\frac{a}{b}$, where b ≠ 0

INTEGERS: the positive and negative whole numbers and zero

WHOLE NUMBERS: the natural numbers and zero

NATURAL NUMBERS: the counting numbers

RATIONAL NUMBERS are numbers that can be expressed as the ratio of two integers, $\frac{a}{b}$, where $b \neq 0$. For example, $\frac{2}{3}$, $-\frac{4}{5}$, and $5 = \frac{5}{1}$ are all rational numbers.

The rational numbers include integers, fractions and mixed numbers, and terminating and repeating decimals. Every rational number can be expressed as a repeating or terminating decimal and can be shown on a number line.

INTEGERS are the positive and negative whole numbers and zero.

...−6, −5, −4, −3, −2, −1, 0, 1, 2, 3, 4, 5, 6...

WHOLE NUMBERS are the natural numbers and zero.

0, 1, 2, 3, 4, 5, 6...

NATURAL NUMBERS are the counting numbers.

1, 2, 3, 4, 5, 6...

IRRATIONAL NUMBERS are real numbers that cannot be written as the ratio of two integers. They are infinite, nonrepeating decimals.

$\sqrt{5} = 2.2360$, pi $= \pi = 3.1415927...$

A **FRACTION** is an expression of numbers in the form of $\frac{x}{y}$, where x is the numerator and y is the denominator. The denominator cannot be zero.

$\frac{3}{7}$ 3 is the numerator; 7 is the denominator

If the fraction has common factors in the numerator and denominator, divide both by the common factors to reduce the fraction to its simplest form.

$$\frac{13}{39} = \frac{1 \times 13}{3 \times 13} = \frac{1}{3}$$

Divide by the common factor 13.

A **MIXED NUMBER** has an integer part and a fractional part.

$2\frac{1}{4}, -5\frac{1}{6}, 7\frac{1}{3}$

PERCENT means per 100 (written with the symbol %). Thus, $10\% = \frac{10}{100} = \frac{1}{10}$.

DECIMAL means deci or part of ten. To find the decimal equivalent of a fraction, use the denominator to divide the numerator, as shown in the following example:

Find the decimal equivalent of $\frac{7}{10}$.
Because 10 cannot divide into 7 evenly,
$\frac{7}{10} = 0.7$

The **EXPONENT FORM** is a shortcut method to write repeated multiplication. The basic form is b^n, where b is called the **BASE** and n is the **EXPONENT**. b and n are real numbers. b^n implies that the base b is multiplied by itself n times.

Examples:

$$3^4 = 3 \times 3 \times 3 \times 3 = 81$$
$$2^3 = 2 \times 2 \times 2 = 8$$
$$(-2)^4 = (-2) \times (-2) \times (-2) \times (-2) = 16$$
$$-2^4 = -(2 \times 2 \times 2 \times 2) = -16$$

Caution: The exponent does not affect the sign unless the negative sign is inside the parentheses and the exponent is outside the parentheses.

$(-2)^4$ implies that -2 is multiplied by itself 4 times.

-2^4 implies that 2 is multiplied by itself 4 times, and then the answer becomes. negative.

KEY EXPONENT RULES: FOR 'a' NONZERO AND 'm' AND 'n' REAL NUMBERS	
Product Rule	$a^m \times a^n = a^{(m+n)}$
Quotient Rule	$\frac{a^m}{a^n} = a^{(m-n)}$
Rule of Negative Exponents	$\frac{a^{-m}}{a^{-n}} = \frac{a^n}{a^m}$

IRRATIONAL NUMBERS: real numbers that cannot be written as the ratio of two integers; they are infinite, nonrepeating decimals

FRACTION: an expression of numbers in the form of $\frac{x}{y}$, where x is the numerator and y is the denominator

MIXED NUMBER: a number that has an integer part and a fractional part

PERCENT: means "per 100;" ten percent is 10 parts out of 100

DECIMAL: a number written with a whole-number part, a decimal point, and a decimal part

EXPONENT FORM: a shorthand way of writing repeated multiplication; the basic form is b^n, where b is the *base* and n is the *exponent*

BASE: the number to be multiplied as many times as indicated by the exponent

EXPONENT: tells how many times the base is multiplied by itself

When 10 is raised to any power, the exponent tells the numbers of zeros in the product.

Example:

$10^7 = 10{,}000{,}000$

SCIENTIFIC NOTATION: a convenient method for writing very large and very small numbers

SCIENTIFIC NOTATION is a convenient method for writing very large and very small numbers. It employs two factors. The first factor is a number between 1 and 10. The second factor is a power of 10. This notation is considered "shorthand" for expressing very large numbers (such as the weight of 100 elephants) or very small numbers (such as the weight of an atom in pounds).

Recall that:

10^n	=	Ten multiplied by itself *n* times
10^0	=	Any nonzero number raised to the zero power is 1
10^1	=	10
10^2	=	$10 \times 10 = 100$
10^3	=	$10 \times 10 \times 10 = 1000$
10^{-1}	=	$\frac{1}{10}$ (deci)
10^{-2}	=	$\frac{1}{100}$ (centi)
10^{-3}	=	$\frac{1}{1000}$ (milli)
10^{-6}	=	$\frac{1}{1,000,000}$ (micro)

Example: Write 46,368,000 in scientific notation.

1. Introduce a decimal point and decimal places.
   46,368,000 = 46,368,000.0000

2. Make a mark between the two digits that give a number between -9.9 and 9.9.
   4 $\wedge$ 6,368,000.0000

3. Count the number of digit places between the decimal point and the $\wedge$ mark. This number is the *nth* power of ten.
   So, $46{,}368{,}000 = 4.6368 \times 10^7$.

Example: Write 0.00397 in scientific notation.

1. Decimal point is already in place.
2. Make a mark between 3 and 9 to obtain a number between -9.9 and. 9.9.
3. Move decimal place to the mark (three hops).
   0.003 ∧ 97
   Motion is to the right, so n on 10^n is negative.
   Therefore, $0.00397 = 3.97 \times 10^{-3}$.

Converting decimals, fractions, and percents

A **decimal** can be converted to a **percent** by multiplying it by 100 or by merely moving the decimal point two places to the right. A percent can be converted to a decimal by dividing it by 100 or by moving the decimal point two places to the left.

Examples:

0.375 = 37.5%	84% = 0.84
0.7 = 70%	3% = 0.03
0.04 = 4%	60% = 0.6
3.15 = 315%	110% = 1.1
	$\frac{1}{2}\% = 0.5\% = 0.005$

A percent can be converted to a **fraction** by placing it over 100 and reducing to simplest terms.

Example: Convert 50% to a fraction.

$$50\% = \frac{50}{100} = \frac{1}{2}$$

A *decimal* can be converted to a fraction by multiplying by a number that will remove the decimal point and reducing the result to its simplest terms.

Example: Convert 0.056 to a fraction.

Multiply 0.056 by $\frac{1000}{1000}$ to get rid of the decimal point:

$$0.056 \times \frac{1000}{1000} = \frac{56}{1000} = \frac{7}{125}$$

Example: Convert 6.25% to a decimal and to a fraction.

$$6.25\% = 0.0625 = 0.0625 \times \frac{1000}{1000} = \frac{625}{10000} = \frac{1}{16}$$

An example of a type of problem involving fractions is the conversion of recipes. For example, if a recipe serves eight people and we want to make enough to serve only four, we must determine how much of each ingredient to use. The conversion factor, or the number we multiply each ingredient by, is:

$$\text{Conversion Factor} = \frac{\text{Number of Servings Needed}}{\text{Number of Servings in Recipe}}$$

Example: Consider the following recipe.

3 cups flour
1/2 tsp. baking powder
2/3 cups butter
2 cups sugar
2 eggs

If this recipe serves eight, how much of each ingredient do we need to serve only four people?

First, determine the conversion factor.

Conversion Factor $= \frac{4}{8} = \frac{1}{2}$

Next, multiply each ingredient by the conversion factor.

$3 \times \frac{1}{2} =$ $1\frac{1}{2}$ cups flour
$\frac{1}{2} \times \frac{1}{2} =$ $\frac{1}{4}$ tsp. baking powder
$\frac{2}{3} \times \frac{1}{2} = \frac{2}{6}$ $\frac{1}{3}$ cup butter
$2 \times \frac{1}{2} =$ 1 cup sugar
$2 \times \frac{1}{2} =$ 1 egg

PROPERTIES: rules that apply for addition, subtraction, multiplication, or division of real numbers

SKILL 3.2 Apply operational algorithms to add, subtract, multiply, and divide fractions, decimals, and integers

PROPERTIES are rules that apply for addition, subtraction, multiplication, or division of real numbers. These properties are:

Commutative	You can change the order of the terms or factors as follows. **For addition:** $a + b = b + a$ **For multiplication:** $ab = ba$ Since addition is the inverse operation of subtraction and multiplication is the inverse operation of division, no separate laws are needed for subtraction and division. *Example:* $5 + 8 = 8 + 5 = 13$ *Example:* $2 \times 6 = 6 \times 2 = 12$

Continued on next page

Associative	You can regroup the terms as you like. **For addition:** $a + (b + c) = (a + b) + c$ **For multiplication:** $a(bc) = (ab)c$ This rule does not apply for division and subtraction. *Example:* $(2 + 7) + 5 = 2 + (7 + 5)$ $9 + 5 = 2 + 12 = 14$ *Example:* $(3 \times 7) \times 5 = 3 \times (7 \times 5)$ $21 \times 5 = 3 \times 35 = 105$
Identity	Finding a number so that when added to a term results in that number (additive identity); finding a number such that when multiplied by a term results in that number (multiplicative identity). **For addition:** $a + 0 = a$ (zero is additive identity) **For multiplication:** $a \times 1 = a$ (one is multiplicative) *Example:* $17 + 0 = 17$ *Example:* $34 \times 1 = 34$ The product of any number and one is that number.
Inverse	Finding a number such that when added to the number, it results in zero; or when multiplied by the number, it results in 1. **For addition:** $a - a = 0$ **For multiplication:** $a \times (\frac{1}{a}) = 1$ $(-a)$ is the additive inverse of a; $(\frac{1}{a})$, also called the reciprocal, is the multiplicative inverse of a. *Example:* $25 - 25 = 0$ *Example:* $5 \times \frac{1}{5} = 1$ The product of any number and its reciprocal is one.
Distributive	This technique allows us to operate on terms within parentheses without first performing operations within the parentheses. This is especially helpful when terms within the parentheses cannot be combined. $a(b + c) = ab + ac$ *Example:* $6 \times (4 + 9) = (6 \times 4) + (6 \times 9)$ $6 \times 13 = 24 + 54 = 78$ To multiply a sum by a number, multiply each addend by the number, then add the products.

Addition of Whole Numbers

Example: At the end of a day of shopping, a shopper had $24 remaining in his wallet. He spent $45 on various goods. How much money did the shopper have at the beginning of the day?

The total amount of money the shopper started with is the sum of the amount spent and the amount remaining at the end of the day.

$$\begin{array}{r} \$\ 24 \\ +\ 45 \\ \hline \$\ 69 \end{array}$$

The original total was $69.

Example: A race took the winner 1 hr. 58 min. 12 sec. on the first half of the race and 2 hr. 9 min. 57 sec. on the second half. How much time did the entire race take?

1 hr	58 min	12 sec	
+ 2 hr	9 min	57 sec	Add these numbers.
3 hr	67 min	69 sec	
+	1 min	− 60 sec	Change 60 sec. to 1 min.
3 hr	68 min	9 sec	
+ 1 hr	−60 min		Change 60 min. to 1 hr.
4 hr	8 min	9 sec	Final answer.

Subtraction of Whole Numbers

Example: At the end of his shift, a cashier has $96 in the cash register. At the beginning of his shift, he had $15. How much money did the cashier collect during his shift?

The total collected is the difference between the ending amount and the starting amount.

$$\begin{array}{r} \$\ 96 \\ -15 \\ \hline \$\ 81 \end{array}$$

The total collected was $81.

Multiplication of Whole Numbers

Another way of conceptualizing multiplication is to think in terms of groups.

PRODUCT: the answer to a multiplication problem

Multiplication is one of the four basic number operations. In simple terms, multiplication is the addition of a number to itself a certain number of times. For example, 4 multiplied by 3 is equal to 4 + 4 + 4 or 3 + 3 + 3 + 3. Another way of conceptualizing multiplication is to think in terms of groups. For example, if we have 4 groups of 3 students, the total number of students is 4 multiplied by 3. We call the solution to a multiplication problem the **PRODUCT**.

The basic algorithm for whole number multiplication begins with aligning the numbers by place value, with the number containing more places on top.

$$\begin{array}{r} 172 \\ \underline{\times\ 43} \end{array}$$

Note that we placed 172 on top because it has more places than 43 does.

Next, we multiply the ones place of the bottom number by each place value of the top number sequentially.

$$\begin{array}{r} (2) \\ 172 \\ \underline{\times\ 43} \\ 516 \end{array}$$

$\{3 \times 2 = 6, 3 \times 7 = 21, 3 \times 1 = 3\}$

Note that we had to carry a 2 to the hundreds column because $3 \times 7 = 21$. Note also that we add carried numbers to the product.

Next, we multiply the number in the tens place of the bottom number by each place value of the top number sequentially. Because we are multiplying by a number in the tens place, we place a zero at the end of this product.

$$\begin{array}{r} (2) \\ 172 \\ \underline{\times\ 43} \\ 516 \\ 6880 \end{array}$$

$\{4 \times 2 = 8, 4 \times 7 = 28, 4 \times 1 = 4\}$

Finally, to determine the final product, we add the two partial products.

$$\begin{array}{r} 172 \\ \underline{\times\ 43} \\ 516 \\ \underline{+\ 6880} \\ 7396 \end{array}$$

The product of 172 and 43 is 7,396.

Example: A student buys 4 boxes of crayons. Each box contains 16 crayons. How many total crayons does the student have?

The total number of crayons is 16×4.

$$\begin{array}{r} 16 \\ \underline{\times\ 4} \\ 64 \end{array}$$

The total number of crayons is 64.

Division of Whole Numbers

Division, the inverse of multiplication, is another of the four basic number operations. When we divide one number by another, we determine how many times we can multiply the **divisor** (number divided by) before we exceed the

QUOTIENT: the answer to a division problem

number we are dividing (dividend). For example, 8 divided by 2 equals 4 because we can multiply 2 four times to reach 8 ($2 \times 4 = 8$ or $2 + 2 + 2 + 2 = 8$). Using the grouping concept we used with multiplication, we can divide 8 into 4 groups of 2 or 2 groups of 4. We call the answer to a division problem the QUOTIENT.

If the divisor does not divide evenly into the dividend, we express the leftover amount either as a remainder or as a fraction with the divisor as the denominator. For example, 9 divided by 2 equals 4 with a remainder of 1, or $4\frac{1}{2}$.

The basic algorithm for division is long division. We start by representing the quotient as follows.

$14\overline{)293} \rightarrow$ 14 is the divisor and 293 is the dividend.
This represents $293 \div 14$.

Next, we divide the divisor into the dividend, starting from the left.

$$\begin{array}{r} 2 \\ 14\overline{)293} \end{array} \rightarrow \text{ 14 divides into 29 two times with a remainder.}$$

Next, we multiply the partial quotient by the divisor, subtract this value from the first digits of the dividend, and bring down the remaining dividend digits to complete the number.

$$\begin{array}{r} 2 \\ 14\overline{)293} \\ -28\downarrow \\ \hline 13 \end{array} \rightarrow 2 \times 14 = 28,\ 29 - 28 = 1, \text{ and bringing down the 3 yields 13.}$$

Finally, we divide again (the divisor into the remaining value) and repeat the preceding process. The number left after the subtraction represents the remainder.

$$\begin{array}{r} 20 \\ 14\overline{)293} \\ -28 \\ \hline 13 \\ -0 \\ \hline 13 \end{array} \rightarrow$$

The final quotient is 20 with a remainder of 13. We can also represent this quotient as $20\frac{13}{14}$.

Example: Each box of apples contains 24 apples. How many boxes must a grocer purchase to supply a group of 252 people with one apple each?

The grocer needs 252 apples. Because he must buy apples in groups of 24, we divide 252 by 24 to determine how many boxes he needs to buy.

```
     10
 24)252
  − 24
     12 → The quotient is 10 with a remainder of 12.
   − 0
     12
```

Thus, the grocer needs 10 boxes plus 12 more apples. Therefore, the minimum number of boxes the grocer can purchase is 11.

Example: At his job, John gets paid $20 for every hour he works. If John made $940 in a week, how many hours did he work?

This is a division problem. To determine the number of hours John worked, we divide the total amount made ($940) by the hourly rate of pay ($20). Thus, the number of hours worked equals 940 divided by 20.

```
     47
 20)940
  − 80
    140
   −140
      0 → 20     Divides into 940 a total of 47 times with no remainder.
```

John worked 47 hours.

Addition and Subtraction of Decimals

When adding and subtracting decimals, we align the numbers by place value as we do with whole numbers. After adding or subtracting each column, we bring the decimal down, placing it in the same location as in the numbers added or subtracted.

When adding and subtracting decimals, we align the numbers by place value as we do with whole numbers.

Example: Find the sum of 152.3 and 36.342.

```
  152.300
+  36.342
  188.642
```

Note that we placed two zeros after the final place value in 152.3 to clarify the column addition.

Example: Find the difference of 152.3 and 36.342.

```
      2 9 10        (4)11(12)
  152.300         152.300
−  36.342       −  36.342
       58         115.958
```

(In the first column the digits "300" of 152.300 are struck through; in the second, "52.300" is struck through.)

Note how we borrowed to subtract from the zeros in the hundredths and thousandths places of 152.300.

Multiplication of Decimals

When multiplying decimal numbers, we multiply exactly as with whole numbers and place the decimal in from the right the total number of decimal places contained in the two numbers multiplied. For example, when multiplying 1.5 and 2.35, we place the decimal in the product 3 places in from the right (3.525).

Example: Find the product of 3.52 and 4.1.

$$\begin{array}{r} 3.52 \\ \times\ 4.1 \\ \hline 352 \\ +\ 14080 \\ \hline 14.432 \end{array}$$

Note that there are three decimal places in total in the two numbers.

We place the decimal three places in from the right.

Thus, the final product is 14.432.

Example: A shopper has 5 one-dollar bills, 6 quarters, 3 nickels, and 4 pennies in his pocket. How much money does he have?

$5 \times \$1.00 = \$5.00$

$$\begin{array}{r} {\scriptstyle 1\,3} \\ \$0.25 \\ \times\ 6 \\ \hline \$1.50 \end{array} \qquad \begin{array}{r} {\scriptstyle 1} \\ \$0.05 \\ \times\ 3 \\ \hline \$0.15 \end{array} \qquad \begin{array}{r} \$0.01 \\ \times\ 4 \\ \hline \$0.04 \end{array}$$

Note the placement of the decimals in the multiplication products. Thus, the total amount of money in the shopper's pocket is:

$$\begin{array}{r} \$5.00 \\ 1.50 \\ 0.15 \\ +\ 0.04 \\ \hline \$6.69 \end{array}$$

Division of Decimals

When dividing decimal numbers, we first remove the decimal in the divisor by moving the decimal in the dividend the same number of spaces to the right. For example, when dividing 1.45 into 5.3, we convert the numbers to 145 and 530 and perform normal whole-number division.

Example: Find the quotient of 5.3 divided by 1.45.

Convert to 145 and 530.

Divide.

$$\begin{array}{r} 3 \\ 145\overline{)530} \\ \underline{-435} \\ 95 \end{array} \qquad \begin{array}{r} 3.65 \\ 145\overline{)530.00} \\ \underline{-435} \\ 950 \\ \underline{-870} \\ 800 \end{array}$$

Note that we insert the decimal to continue division.

Because one of the numbers divided contained one decimal place, we round the quotient to one decimal place. Thus, the final quotient is 3.7.

Operating with Percents

Example: 5 is what percent of 20?

This is the same as converting $\frac{5}{20}$ to percent form.

$\frac{5}{20} \times \frac{100}{1} = \frac{5}{1} \times \frac{5}{1} = 25\%$

Example: There are 64 dogs in the kennel. 48 are collies. What percent are collies?

Restate the problem.	48 is what percent of 64?
Write an equation.	$48 = n \times 64$
Solve.	$\frac{48}{64} = n$

$n = \frac{3}{4} = 75\%$

75% of the dogs are collies.

Example: The auditorium was filled to 90% capacity. There were 558 seats occupied. What is the capacity of the auditorium?

Restate the problem.	90% of what number is 558?
Write an equation.	$0.9n = 558$
Solve.	$n = \frac{558}{.9}$

$n = 620$

The capacity of the auditorium is 620 people.

Example: A pair of shoes costs $42.00. The sales tax is 6%. What is the total cost of the shoes?

Restate the problem.	What is 6% of 42?
Write an equation.	$n = 0.06 \times 42$
Solve.	$n = 2.52$
Add the sales tax to the cost.	$42.00 + $2.52 = $44.52

The total cost of the shoes, including sales tax, is $44.52.

Addition and Subtraction of Fractions

Key points

1. You need a common denominator in order to add and subtract reduced and improper fractions.

   Example:
   $\frac{1}{3} + \frac{7}{3} = \frac{1+7}{3} = \frac{8}{3} = 2\frac{2}{3}$

   Example:
   $\frac{4}{12} + \frac{6}{12} - \frac{3}{12} = \frac{4+6-3}{12} = \frac{7}{12}$

2. Adding an integer and a fraction of the same sign results directly in a mixed number.

   Example:
   $2 + \frac{2}{3} = 2\frac{2}{3}$

   Example:
   $-2 - \frac{2}{3} = -2\frac{2}{3}$

3. Adding an integer and a fraction with different signs involves the following steps.

   - Get a common denominator
   - Add or subtract as needed
   - Change to a mixed number if possible

   Example:
   $2 - \frac{1}{3} = \frac{2 \times 3 - 1}{3} = \frac{6-1}{3} = \frac{5}{3} = 1\frac{2}{3}$

   Example:
   Add $7\frac{3}{8} + 5\frac{2}{7}$
   Add the whole numbers, add the fractions, and combine the two results:
   $7\frac{3}{8} + 5\frac{2}{7} = (7 + 5) + (\frac{3}{8} + \frac{2}{7})$
   $= 12 + \frac{(7 \times 3) + (8 \times 2)}{56}$ (LCM of 8 and 7)
   $= 12 + \frac{21 + 16}{56} = 12 + \frac{37}{56} = 12\frac{37}{56}$

   Example: Perform the operation.
   $\frac{2}{3} - \frac{5}{6}$
   We first find the LCM of 3 and 6, which is 6.
   $\frac{2 \times 2}{3 \times 2} - \frac{5}{6} \rightarrow \frac{4-5}{6} = \frac{-1}{6}$ (Using method A)

Example:

$-7\frac{1}{4} + 2\frac{7}{8}$

$-7\frac{1}{4} + 2\frac{7}{8} = (-7 + 2) + (\frac{-1}{4} + \frac{7}{8})$

$= (-5) + \frac{-2 + 7}{8} = (-5) + (\frac{5}{8})$

$= (-5) + \frac{5}{8} = \frac{-5 \times 8}{1 \times 8} + \frac{5}{8} = \frac{-40 + 5}{8}$

$= \frac{-35}{8} = -4\frac{3}{8}$

Divide 35 by 8 to get 4, remainder 3.

Example:

Caution: A common error would be

$-7\frac{1}{4} + 2\frac{7}{8} = -7\frac{2}{8} + 2\frac{7}{8} = -5\frac{9}{8}$

It is correct to add -7 and 2 to get -5, but adding $\frac{2}{8} + \frac{7}{8} = \frac{9}{8}$ is wrong. It should have been $\frac{-2}{8} + \frac{7}{8} = \frac{5}{8}$. Then, $-5 + \frac{5}{8} = -4\frac{3}{8}$ as before.

Multiplication of Fractions

Using the following example: $3\frac{1}{4} \times \frac{5}{6}$

1. Convert each number to an improper fraction

   $3\frac{1}{4} = \frac{(12 + 1)}{4} = \frac{13}{4}$ $\qquad$ $\frac{5}{6}$ is already in reduced form.

2. Reduce (cancel) common factors of the numerator and denominator if they exist

   $\frac{13}{4} \times \frac{5}{6}$ $\qquad$ No common factors exist.

3. Multiply the numerators by each other and the denominators by each other

   $\frac{13}{4} \times \frac{5}{6} = \frac{65}{24}$

4. If possible, reduce the fraction to its lowest terms

   $\frac{65}{24}$ $\qquad$ Cannot be reduced further.

5. Convert the improper fraction back to a mixed number by using long division

   $$\frac{65}{24} = 24\overline{)65} \quad \text{quotient } 2;\ \ 65 - 48 = 17 \qquad = 2\frac{17}{24}$$

Summary of sign changes for multiplication

1. $(+) \times (+) = (+)$
2. $(-) \times (+) = (-)$
3. $(+) \times (-) = (-)$
4. $(-) \times (-) = (+)$

Example: $7\frac{1}{3} \times \frac{5}{11} = \frac{22}{3} \times \frac{5}{11}$

Reduce like terms (22 and 11).

$= \frac{2}{3} \times \frac{5}{1} = \frac{10}{3} = 3\frac{1}{3}$

Example: $-6\frac{1}{4} \times \frac{5}{9} = \frac{-25}{4} \times \frac{5}{9}$

$= \frac{-125}{36} = -3\frac{17}{36}$

Example: $\frac{-1}{4} \times \frac{-3}{7}$

A negative times a negative equals a positive.

$= \frac{1}{4} \times \frac{3}{7} = \frac{3}{28}$

Division of Fractions

1. Change mixed numbers to improper fractions
2. Change the division problem to a multiplication problem by using the reciprocal of the number after the division sign
3. Find the sign of the final product
4. Cancel if common factors exist between the numerator and the denominator
5. Multiply the numerators together and the denominators together
6. Change the improper fraction to a mixed number

Example: $3\frac{1}{5} + 2\frac{1}{4} = \frac{16}{5} + \frac{9}{4}$

$= \frac{16}{5} \times \frac{4}{9}$ The reciprocal of $\frac{9}{4}$ is $\frac{4}{9}$.

$= \frac{64}{45} = 1\frac{19}{45}$

Example: $7\frac{3}{4} + 11\frac{5}{8} = \frac{31}{4} + \frac{93}{8}$

$= \frac{31}{4} \times \frac{8}{93}$ Reduce like terms.

$= \frac{1}{1} \times \frac{2}{3} = \frac{2}{3}$

Example: $(-2\frac{1}{2}) + 4\frac{1}{6} = \frac{-5}{2} + \frac{25}{6}$

$= \frac{-5}{2} \times \frac{6}{25}$ Reduce like terms.

$= \frac{-1}{1} \times \frac{3}{5} = \frac{-3}{5}$

Example: $(-5\frac{3}{8}) + (\frac{-7}{16}) = \frac{-43}{8} + \frac{27}{16}$

$= \frac{-43}{8} \times \frac{-16}{7}$ Reduce like terms.

$= \frac{43}{1} \times \frac{2}{7}$ A negative times a negative equals a positive.

$= \frac{86}{7} = 12\frac{2}{7}$

SKILL 3.3 Use scales and ratios to interpret maps and models

A **RATIO** is a comparison of two numbers. If a class had 11 boys and 14 girls, we can write the ratio of boys to girls in three ways:

RATIO: a comparison of two numbers

- 11:14
- 11 to 14
- $\frac{11}{14}$

The ratio of girls to boys is:

- 14:11
- 14 to 11
- $\frac{14}{11}$

We should reduce ratios when possible. A ratio of 12 cats to 18 dogs reduces to 2:3, 2 to 3, or $\frac{2}{3}$.

Note: Read ratio questions carefully. Given a group of 6 adults and 5 children, the ratio of children to the entire group would be 5:11.

Students need to understand that ratios and proportions are used to create scale models of real-life objects, to understand the principles of ratio and proportion, and to understand how to calculate scale using ratio and proportion.

Scaled drawings (maps, blueprints, and models) are used in many real-world situations. Architects make blueprints and models of buildings. These drawings and models are then used by contractors to build the buildings. Engineers make scaled drawings of bridges, machine parts, roads, airplanes, and many other things. Maps of the world, countries, states, and roads are also scaled drawings. Landscape designers use scaled drawings and models of plants, decks, and other structures to show how they should be placed around a building. Models of cars, boats, and planes made from kits are scaled. Automobile engineers construct models of cars before the actual assembly is done. Many museum exhibits are actually scaled models, because the items themselves are too large to be displayed.

Examples of real-world problems that students might solve using scaled drawings include:

- Reading road maps and determining the distance between locations by using the map scale
- Creating a scaled drawing (floor plan) of the classroom to determine the best use of space
- Creating an 8.5-by-11-inch representation of a quilt to be pieced together
- Drawing blueprints of their rooms and creating models from them

SKILL 3.4 Use geometric concepts and formulas to solve problems *(e.g., estimating the surface area of a floor to determine the approximate cost of floor covering)*

PERIMETER: the sum of the lengths of the sides of a polygon

AREA: the number of square units covered by the figure; the space a figure occupies

The **PERIMETER** of a polygon is the sum of the lengths of the sides.

The **AREA** of a polygon is the number of square units covered by the figure.

FIGURE	AREA FORMULA	PERIMETER FORMULA
Rectangle	LW	$2(L + W)$
Triangle	$\frac{1}{2}bh$	$a + b + c$
Parallelogram	bh	sum of lengths of sides
Trapezoid	$\frac{1}{2}h(a + b)$	sum of lengths of sides

Perimeter

Example: A farmer has a piece of land shaped as shown below. He wishes to fence this land at an estimated cost of $25 per linear foot. What is the total cost of fencing this property, to the nearest foot?

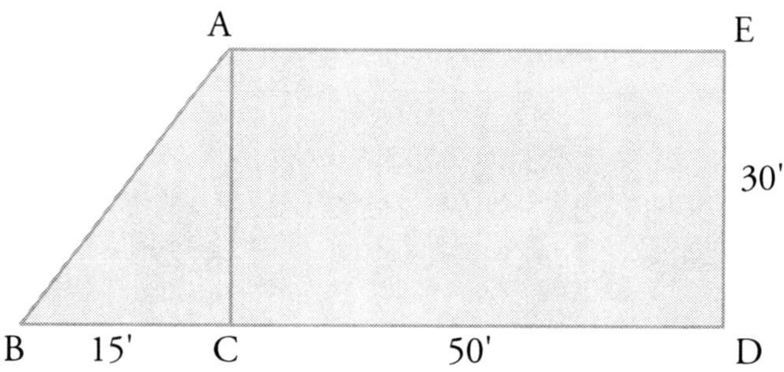

For the right triangle ABC, $AC = 30$ and $BC = 15$.

Since $(AB)^2 = (AC)^2 + (BC)^2$

$(AB)^2 = (30)^2 + (15)^2$

So feet $\sqrt{(AB)^2} = AB = \sqrt{1125} = 33.5410$ feet

To the nearest foot, $AB = 34$ feet.

Perimeter of the piece of land =

$34 + 15 + 50 + 30 + 50 = 179$ feet

Cost of fencing = $\$25 \times 179 = \$4{,}475.00$

Area

Area is the space that a figure occupies.

Example: What will be the cost of carpeting a rectangular office that measures 12 feet by 15 feet if the carpet costs $12.50 per square yard?

The problem is asking you to determine the area of the office. The area of a rectangle is $length \times width = A$.

Substitute the given values in the equation $A = lw$.

$A = (12 \text{ ft})(15 \text{ ft})$

$A = 180 \text{ ft}^2$

You must determine the cost of the carpet at $12.50 per square yard.

First, you need to convert 180 ft^2 into yd^2.

$1 \text{ yd} = 3 \text{ ft}$

$(1 \text{ yd})(1 \text{ yd}) = (3 \text{ ft})(3 \text{ ft})$

$1 \text{ yd}^2 = 9 \text{ ft}^2$

Hence, $\frac{180 \text{ ft}^2}{1} = \frac{1 \text{ yd}^2}{9 \text{ ft}^2} = \frac{20}{1} = 20 \text{ yd}^2$

The carpet costs $12.50 per square yard; thus, the cost of carpeting the office is $\$12.50 \times 20 = \$250.00$.

Example: Find the area of a parallelogram whose base is 6.5 cm and the height of the altitude to that base is 3.7 cm.

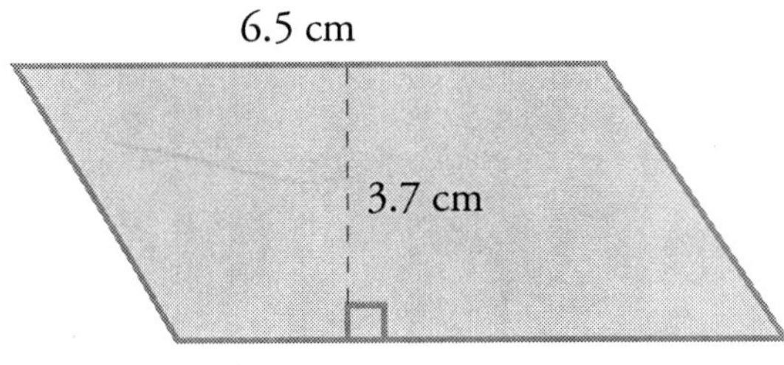

$A_{parallelogram} = bh$

$A_{parallelogram} = (3.7)(6.5)$

$A_{parallelogram} = 24.05 \text{ cm}^2$

Example: Find the area of this triangle.

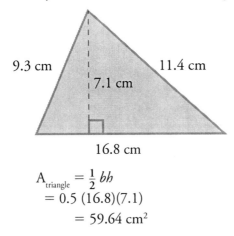

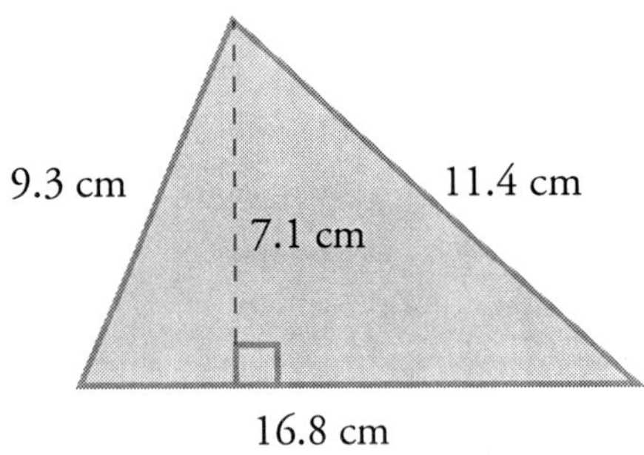

$A_{triangle} = \frac{1}{2} bh$

$= 0.5\ (16.8)(7.1)$

$= 59.64 \text{ cm}^2$

Example: Find the area of this trapezoid.

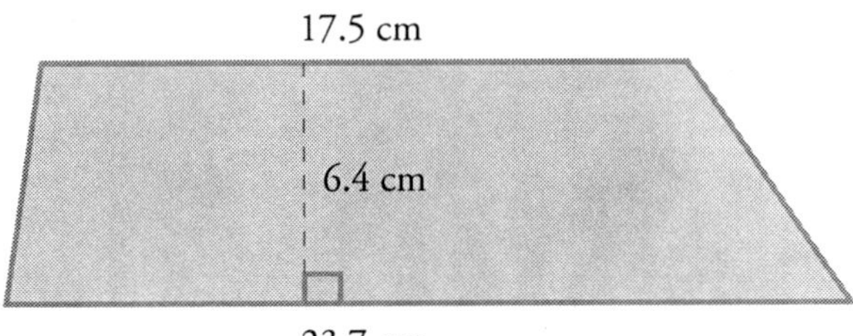

The area of a trapezoid equals one-half the sum of the bases times the altitude.

$$\begin{aligned} A_{\text{trapezoid}} &= \tfrac{1}{2}h(b_1 + b_2) \\ &= 0.5\,(6.4)(17.5 + 23.7) \\ &= 131.84 \text{ cm}^2 \end{aligned}$$

The distance around a circle is called the **CIRCUMFERENCE**. The Greek letter pi (π) represents the ratio of the circumference to the diameter.

$\pi \approx 3.14 \approx \frac{22}{7}$.

CIRCUMFERENCE: the distance around a circle

The circumference of a circle is found by the formula $C = 2\pi r$ or $C = \pi d$, where r is the radius of the circle and d is the diameter.

The area of a circle is found by the formula $A = \pi r^2$.

Example: Find the circumference and area of a circle whose radius is 7 meters.

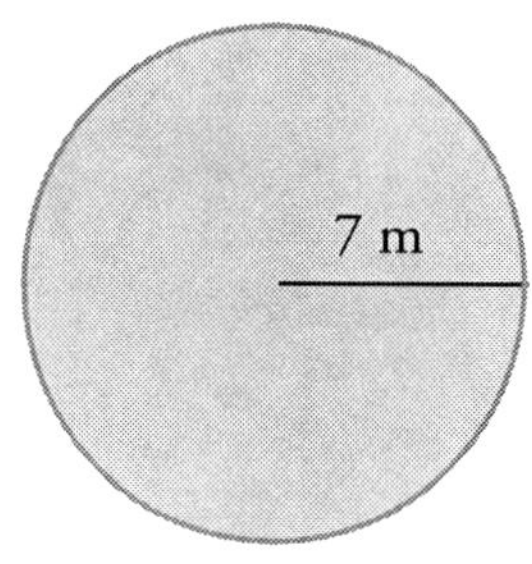

$$\begin{aligned} C &= \pi r \\ &= 2(3.14)(7) \\ &= 43.96 \text{ m} \end{aligned} \qquad \begin{aligned} A &= \pi r^2 \\ &= 3.14(7)(7) \\ &= 153.86 \text{ m}^2 \end{aligned}$$

Volume and Surface Area

We use the following formulas to compute volume and surface area:

FIGURE	VOLUME	TOTAL SURFACE AREA
Right Cylinder	$\pi r^2 h$	$2\pi rh + 2\pi r^2$
Right Cone	$\frac{\pi r^2 h}{3}$	$\pi r\sqrt{r^2 + h^2} + \pi r^2$
Sphere	$\frac{4}{3}\pi r^3$	$4\pi r^2$
Rectangular Solid	LWH	$2LW + 2WH + 2LH$

FIGURE	LATERAL AREA	TOTAL AREA	VOLUME
Regular Pyramid	$\frac{1}{2}Pl$	$\frac{1}{2}Pl + B$	$\frac{1}{3}Bh$

P = Perimeter, h = height, B = Area of Base, l = slant height

Example: What is the volume of a shoe box with a length of 35 cm, a width of 20 cm, and a height of 15 cm?

Volume of a rectangular solid

$= \text{Length} \times \text{Width} \times \text{Height}$

$= 35 \times 20 \times 15$

$= 10500 \text{ cm}^3$

Example: A water company is trying to decide whether to use traditional cylindrical paper cups or to offer conical paper cups, since the cost is the same. The traditional cups are 8 cm wide and 14 cm high. The conical cups are 12 cm wide and 19 cm high. The company will use the cup that holds the most water.

Draw and label a sketch of each.

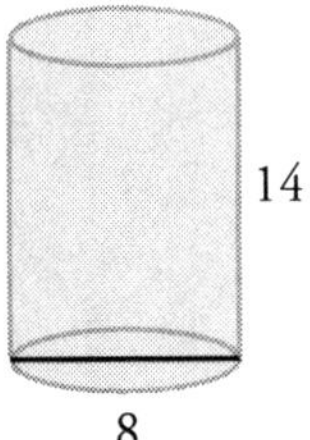

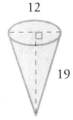

$V = \pi r^2 h$	$V = \frac{\pi r^2 h}{3}$	1. Write a formula.
$V = \pi(4)^2(14)$	$V = \frac{1}{3}\pi(6)^2(19)$	2. Substitute.
$V = 703.717 \text{ cm}^3$	$V = 716.283 \text{ cm}^3$	3. Solve.

The choice should be the conical cup since its volume is greater.

Example: How much material is needed to make a basketball that has a diameter of 15 inches? How much air is needed to fill the basketball?

Draw and label a sketch:

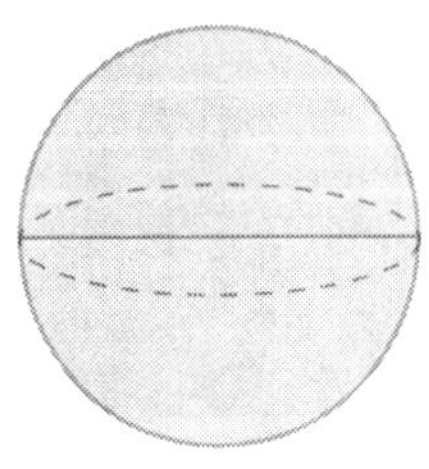

$D = 15$ inches

Total surface area	Volume	
$TSA = 4\pi r^2$	$V = \frac{4}{3}\pi r^3$	1. Write a formula.
$= 4\pi(7.5)^2$	$= \frac{4}{3}\pi(7.5)^3$	2. Substitute.
$= 706.858 \text{ in}^2$	$= 1767.1459 \text{ in}^3$	3. Solve.

SKILL 3.5 **Solve problems using algebraic concepts and formulas** *(e.g., calculating wages based on sales commission)*

Procedure for solving algebraic equations

Example: $3(x + 3) = -2x + 4$

Solve for x.

1. Expand to eliminate all parentheses.
   $3x + 9 = -2x + 4$
2. Multiply each term by the LCD to eliminate all denominators.
3. Combine like terms on each side when possible.
4. Use the properties to put all variables on one side and all constants on the other side.
   $\rightarrow 3x + 9 - 9 = -2x + 4 - 9$ Subtract nine from both sides.
   $\rightarrow 3x = -2x - 5$
   $\rightarrow 3x + 2x = -2x + 2x - 5$ Add $2x$ to both sides.
   $\rightarrow 5x = -5$
   $\rightarrow \frac{5x}{5} = \frac{-5}{5}$ Divide both sides by 5.
   $\rightarrow x = -1$

Example: Mark and Mike are twins. Three times Mark's age plus 4 equals 4 times Mike's age minus 14. How old are the boys?

Because the boys are twins, their ages are the same. "Translate" the English into algebra. Let $x =$ their age.

$3x + 4 = 4x - 14$

$18 = x$

The boys are both 18 years old.

Example: The Simpsons went out for dinner. All 4 of them ordered the aardvark steak dinner. Bert paid for the 4 meals and included a tip of $12 for a total of $84.60. How much was one aardvark steak dinner?

Let $x =$ the price of one aardvark dinner.
So $4x =$ the price of 4 aardvark dinners.

$4x + 12 = 84.60$

$4x = 72.60$

$x = \$18.50$ for each dinner.

Example: Some students want to take a field trip from New York City to Albany to visit the capitol. The trip is approximately 160 miles. If they will be traveling at 50 miles per hour, how long will it take for them to get there (assuming they are traveling at a steady rate)?

Set up the equation as a proportion and solve:

$$\frac{160 \text{ miles}}{x \text{ hours}} = \frac{50 \text{ miles}}{1 \text{ hour}}$$

$$(160 \text{ miles})(1 \text{ hour}) = (50 \text{ miles})(x \text{ hours})$$

$$160 = 50x$$

$$x = 3.2 \text{ hours}$$

Example: A salesman drove 480 miles from Pittsburgh to Hartford. The next day he returned the same distance to Pittsburgh in half an hour less time than his original trip took, because he increased his average speed by 4 mph. Find his original speed.

Since distance = rate × time, then time = $\frac{\text{distance}}{\text{rate}}$

original time $-\ \frac{1}{2}$ hour = shorter return time

$$\frac{480}{x} - \frac{1}{2} = \frac{480}{x+4}$$

Multiplying by the LCD of $2x(x + 4)$, the equation becomes:

$$480[2(x + 4)] - 1[x(x + 4)] = 480(2x)$$

$$960x + 3840 - x^2 - 4x = 960x$$

$$x^2 + 4x - 3840 = 0$$

$$(x + 64)(x - 60) = 0$$

$$x = 60$$

60 mph is the original speed, 64 mph is the faster return speed.

SKILL 3.6 Apply appropriate algebraic equations to the solution of problems *(e.g., determining the original price of a sale item given the rate of discount)*

See Skill 3.2

COMPETENCY 4

UNDERSTAND MAJOR CONCEPTS, PRINCIPLES, AND THEORIES IN SCIENCE AND TECHNOLOGY, AND USE THAT UNDERSTANDING TO ANALYZE PHENOMENA IN THE NATURAL WORLD AND TO INTERPRET INFORMATION PRESENTED IN ILLUSTRATED OR WRITTEN FORM

BRANCHES OF SCIENCE	
LIFE SCIENCE	
Biology	The study of plants and animals
Botany	The branch of biology that deals with plants
Zoology	The branch of biology that deals with animals
Ecology	The study of the relationship of organisms to their environment
Human Health	The branch of Biology that deals with the health and well being of humans
PHYSICAL SCIENCE	
Chemistry	The study of the structure and makeup of matter and the changes matter undergoes
Physics	The branch of physical science that deals with energy and matter and how they interact
EARTH SCIENCE	
Astronomy	The science of the heavenly bodies and of their sizes, motions, and composition
Geology	Deals with the history of the Earth and its life, especially as recorded in rocks
Meteorology	Deals with atmosphere, weather and weather forecasting
Oceanography	The study of oceans

Common scientific concepts and themes

The following are the concepts and processes generally recognized as common to all scientific disciplines:

1. Systems, order, and organization
2. Evidence, models, and explanation

3. Constancy, change, and measurement
4. Evolution and equilibrium
5. Form and function

Because the natural world is so complex, the study of science involves the *organization* of items into smaller groups based on interaction or interdependence. These groups are called *systems*. Examples of organization are the periodic table of elements and the five-kingdom classification scheme for living organisms. Examples of systems are the solar system, cardiovascular system, Newton's laws of force and motion, and the laws of conservation.

ORDER: the behavior and measurability of organisms and events in nature

ORDER is the behavior and measurability of organisms and events in nature The arrangement of planets in the solar system and the life cycle of bacterial cells are examples of order.

Scientists use evidence and models to form explanations of natural events.

Scientists use evidence and models to form explanations of natural events. Models are miniaturized representations of a larger event or system. Evidence is anything that furnishes proof.

Scientists use different systems of measurement to observe change and constancy.

Constancy and change describe the observable properties of natural organisms and events. Scientists use different systems of measurement to observe change and constancy. For examples, the freezing and melting points of given substances and the speed of sound are constant under constant conditions. Growth, decay, and erosion are all examples of natural change.

EVOLUTION: the process of change over a long period of time

EVOLUTION is the process of change over a long period of time. Although biological evolution is the most common example, one can also classify technological advancement, changes in the universe, and changes in the environment as evolution.

EQUILIBRIUM: the state of balance between opposing forces of change

EQUILIBRIUM is the state of balance between opposing forces of change. Homeostasis and ecological balance are examples of equilibrium.

Form and function are properties of organisms and systems that are closely related. The function of an object usually dictates its form, and the form of an object usually facilitates its function. For example, the form of the heart (e.g., muscle, valves) allows it to perform its function of circulating blood through the body.

SKILL 4.1 Use an appropriate illustration, graphic, or physical model to represent a scientific theory, concept, or relationship presented in an excerpt

See also Skill 2.1

Scientific Models

The model is a basic element of the scientific method. Many things in science are studied with models. A model is any simplification of or substitute for what we are actually studying, attempting to understand, or making predictions about. We encounter models at every step of our daily living.

Physicists use Newton's laws to predict how objects such as planets and spaceships will interact. In geology, the continental drift model predicts the past positions of continents. Samples, ideas, and methods are all examples of models. Models are extensively used at every step of scientific study. The primary activity of the hundreds of thousands of U.S. scientists is to produce new models, resulting in tens of thousands of scientific papers published each year.

The Periodic Table of the elements is a model chemists use for predicting the properties of the elements.

Types of models

- Scale models: models that are basically downsized or enlarged copies of their target systems, like the models of protein and DNA
- Idealized models: deliberate simplifications of complicated things with the objective of making them easier to understand. Some examples are frictionless planes, point masses, isolated systems, etc.
- Analogical models: examples of analogical models are the billiard model of a gas, the computer model of the mind, or the liquid-drop model of the nucleus
- Phenomenological models: models that are independent of theories
- Data models: corrected, rectified, regimented, and, in many instances, idealized versions of the data that we gained from immediate observation (raw data)
- Theory models: a structure is a model if it represents an idea (theory). An example of this is a flow chart, which summarizes a set of ideas.

Uses of models

1. Models are crucial for understanding the structures and functions of processes in science.
2. Models help us to visualize the organs/systems they represent, just like putting a face to a person.
3. Models are very useful for predicting and foreseeing future events, like hurricanes.

Limitations of models

1. Though models are very useful to us, they can never replace the real things.
2. Models are not exactly like the real items that they represent.
3. Caution must be exercised before presenting models to the class because they may not be accurate.
4. It is the responsibility of educators to analyze models critically for proportion, content value, and other important data.
5. One must be careful about the representation style. This style differs from person to person.

Graphing

Graphing is an important way to visually display data for analysis. The two types of graphs most commonly used are the **line graph** and the **bar graph** (histogram).

Line graphs

Line graphs are set up to show two variables, represented by one point on the graph. The *x*-axis is the horizontal axis; this is where the independent variable of the experiment is plotted. Independent variables are those that are not affected by any changes in the experimental conditions. A common example of an independent variable is time. Time proceeds regardless of any changes in experimental conditions.

The *y*-axis is the vertical axis; the dependent variable is plotted here. Dependent variables are manipulated by the experimentor. Factors such as the amount of light or the height of a plant are examples of dependent variables. The axes of a graph should be labeled at equal intervals. If one interval represents one day, the next interval should not represent ten days. A "best fit" line is drawn to join the points on a graph. Both axes should always be labeled for a graph to be accurately interpreted. Graphs must always include a descriptive title; a good title will describe both the dependent and the independent variables.

Bar graphs

Bar graphs are set up with category labels along the horizontal axis. An appropriate scale is chosen for the vertical axis that will show the responding variable. A bar is drawn at each category with a height equal to the data along the vertical axis. Each bar represents a separate piece of data and is not joined by a continuous line. Bar graphs should also be given descriptive titles.

Uses for graphs

The type of graph used to represent data depends on the type of data collected. Line graphs are used to compare different sets of related data or to predict data that has not yet been measured. For example, a line graph would be used to compare the rate of activity of different enzymes at varying temperatures. A bar graph or histogram is used to compare different items and make comparisons based on this data. A bar graph would be used to compare the range of ages of children in a classroom. A pie chart is useful when organizing data as part of a whole. A pie chart would be used to display the percent of time students spend on various after-school activities.

The type of graph used to represent data depends on the type of data collected.

SKILL 4.2 Relate a major scientific principle, concept, or theory to a natural phenomenon

Below are several major natural phenomena and the scientific principles that explain them.

Dynamics and Motion

DYNAMICS is the study of the relationship between motion and the forces affecting motion. Force causes motion.

DYNAMICS: the study of the relationship between motion and the forces affecting motion

Mass and weight are not the same qualities. An object's mass gives it a resistance that changes its current state of motion. It is also the measure of an object's resistance to acceleration. The force that the Earth's gravity exerts on an object with a specific mass is the object's weight on Earth. Weight is a force that is measured in Newtons. Weight (W) = mass times acceleration due to gravity (W = mg).

Newton's Laws of Motion

Newton's first law of motion is also called the law of inertia. It states that an object at rest will remain at rest and an object in motion will remain in motion at a constant velocity unless acted upon by an external force.

Newton's second law of motion states that if a net force acts on an object, it will cause the acceleration of the object. The relationship between force and motion is force equals mass times acceleration ($F = ma$).

Newton's third law of motion states that for every action there is an equal and opposite reaction. Therefore, if an object exerts a force on another object, that second object exerts an equal and opposite force on the first.

Work and power

Work is done on an object when an applied force moves across a distance. Power is the work done divided by the amount of time that it took to do it:

$$\text{Power} = \frac{\text{Work}}{\text{Time}}.$$

Motion and Resistance to Motion

Surfaces that touch each other have a certain resistance to motion. This resistance is friction.

1. The materials that make up the surfaces will determine the magnitude of the frictional force
2. The frictional force is independent of the area of contact between the two surfaces
3. The direction of the frictional force is the opposite of the direction of motion
4. The frictional force is proportional to the normal force between the two surfaces in contact

STATIC FRICTION: the force of friction of two surfaces that are in contact but do not have any motion relative to each other

KINETIC FRICTION: the force of friction of two surfaces in contact with each other when there is relative motion between the surfaces

Types of friction and resistance

STATIC FRICTION describes the force of friction of two surfaces that are in contact but do not have any motion relative to each other, such as a block sitting on an inclined plane. **KINETIC FRICTION** describes the force of friction of two surfaces in contact with each other when there is relative motion between the surfaces.

Listed below are some major example of friction and resistance:

- Push and pull: Pushing a vacuum cleaner or pulling a bowstring applies muscular force when the muscles expand and contract. Elastic force occurs when an object returns to its original shape (for example, when a bow string is released).
- Rubbing: Friction opposes the motion of one surface past another. Friction is common when slowing down a car or sledding down a hill.
- Pull of gravity: The force of attraction between two objects is the pull of gravity. Gravity exists not only on Earth but also between planets and in black holes.
- Forces on objects at rest: The formula $F = \frac{m}{a}$ is shorthand for force equals mass over acceleration. An object will not move unless the force is strong enough to move the mass. Also, there can be opposing forces holding the object in place. For instance, a boat can potentially be forced to drift away by underwater currents, but an equal and opposite force, a docking rope, keeps it tied to the dock.
- Forces on a moving object: Inertia is the tendency of any object to resist a change in motion. An object at rest tends to stay at rest. An object that is moving tends to keep moving.
- Inertia and circular motion: Centripetal force is provided by the high banking of a curved road and by friction between the wheels and the road.

Conserving energy

The **LAW OF CONSERVATION OF ENERGY** states that energy may neither be created nor destroyed. Therefore, the sum of all energies in a system remains a constant.

The **LAW OF MOMENTUM CONSERVATION** states that when two objects collide in an isolated system, the total momentum of the two objects before the collision is equal to the total momentum of the two objects after the collision. That is, the momentum lost by Object 1 is equal to the momentum gained by Object 2.

LAW OF CONSERVATION OF ENERGY: states that energy may neither be created nor destroyed

LAW OF MOMENTUM CONSERVATION: states that when two objects collide in an isolated system, the total momentum of the two objects before the collision is equal to the total momentum of the two objects after the collision

Straight-Line, Circular, and Periodic Motion

Matter can move in a straight line, in a circular pattern, and in a periodic fashion. The Greeks were the first recorded people to think about motion. They thought that matter wanted to be stopped and were under the impression that once an object moved, it would not keep moving. They thought that the object would slow down and stop because its nature was to be at rest. These early scientists considered that matter moves. Galileo was the first to realize the error in the early scientists' thought process. Galileo concluded that an object keeps moving, even against the force of gravity.

Straight-line motion

To make an object move, a force must be applied. Friction must also be taken into account; it makes moving objects slow down. This characteristic was also noticed for the first time by Galileo. This is Newton's first law of motion, which states that an object at rest remains at rest unless acted upon by force. Force can have varied effects on moving objects. Force makes objects move, slow down, stop, increase their speed, decrease their speed, and so on.

A moving object has speed, velocity, and acceleration. To summarize, when force is applied to an object it moves in a straight line (Newton's first law), and adding force can make it go faster or slow down.

Circular motion

Circular motion is defined as acceleration along a circle, a circular path or a circular orbit. Circular motion involves acceleration of the moving object by a centripetal force that pulls the moving object towards the center of the circular orbit. Without this acceleration, the object would move in a straight line, according to Newton's first law of motion. Circular motion is accelerated even though the speed is constant, because the object's velocity is constantly changing direction.

Some examples of circular motion are: an artificial satellite orbiting the Earth in a geosynchronous orbit; a stone that is tied to a rope and is being swung in circles; a race car turning through a curve in a racetrack; an electron moving perpendicular to a uniform magnetic field; and a gear turning inside a mechanism.

A special kind of circular motion occurs when an object rotates around its own center of mass. The rotation of a three-dimensional body around a fixed axis involves the circular motion of its parts. This can be called spinning (or rotational) motion. When an object moves in a circular path, a force must be directed toward the center of the circle in order to keep the object moving. This constraining force is called **CENTRIPETAL FORCE**. Gravity is the centripetal force that keeps a satellite orbiting the Earth.

CENTRIPETAL FORCE: the force that must be directed toward the center of the circle in order to keep an object that is moving in a circular path in motion

Periodic motion

Periodic motion occurs when an object moves back and forth in a regular motion. Some examples of periodic motion are a weight on a string swinging back and forth (pendulum), and a ball bouncing up and down. Periodic motion is characterized by three things:

1. Velocity: The objects in motion, i.e., the bouncing ball or weight on a pendulum, all have velocity.

2. Period: The period is the time the object takes to go back and forth. The time the ball takes to bounce back can be measured. Sometimes, the word period is replaced by the word frequency. Frequency is the reciprocal of period.

3. Amplitude: The amplitude is half the distance the object goes from one side of the period to the other (the height of the pendulum or bouncing ball). When an object is rotating, the amplitude is the radius of the circle (half the diameter).

There are many devices that use the characteristics of periodic motion. A clock is the most common example. Periodic motion is always used in the study of wave motion, including light, sound, and music.

Electricity and Magnetism

The electromagnetic spectrum consists of frequency (f), measured in hertz, and wavelength (λ), measured in meters. The frequency times the wavelength of every electromagnetic wave equals the speed of light (3.0×10^9 meters/second).

Roughly, the range of wavelengths in the electromagnetic spectrum is:

	f	λ
Radio waves	10^5 - 10^{-1} hertz	10^3 - 10^9 meters
Microwaves	10^{-1} - 10^{-3} hertz	10^9 - 10^{11} meters
Infrared radiation	10^{-3} - 10^{-6} hertz	$10^{11.2}$ - 10 14.3 meters
Visible light	$10^{-6.2}$ $10^{-6.9}$ hertz	$10^{14.3}$ - 10^{15} meters
Ultraviolet radiation	10^{-7} - 10^{-9} hertz	10^{15} - $10^{17.2}$ meters
X-rays	10^{-9} - 10^{-11} hertz	$10^{17.2}$ - 10^{19} meters
Gamma rays	10^{-11}- 10^{-15} hertz	10^{19} - $10^{23.25}$ meters

Electricity

Electrostatics is the study of stationary electric charges. A plastic rod that is rubbed with fur or a glass rod that is rubbed with silk will become electrically charged and will attract small pieces of paper. The charge on the plastic rod rubbed with fur is negative; the charge on glass rod rubbed with silk is positive.

Electrically charged objects share these characteristics:

1. Like charges repel one another
2. Opposite charges attract one another
3. Charge is conserved

A neutral object has no net charge. If the plastic rod and fur are initially neutral, when the rod becomes charged by the fur a negative charge is transferred from the fur to the rod. The net negative charge on the rod is equal to the net positive charge on the fur.

CONDUCTORS: materials through which electric charges can easily flow

INSULATOR: a material through which electric charges do not move easily, if at all

ELECTROSCOPE: a simple device used to indicate the existence of a positive or negative charge

Materials through which electric charges can easily flow are called **CONDUCTORS**. On the other hand, an **INSULATOR** is a material through which electric charges do not move easily, if at all.

A simple device used to indicate the existence of a positive or negative charge is called an **ELECTROSCOPE**. An electroscope is made up of a conducting knob. Attached to it are very lightweight conducting leaves usually made of foil (gold or aluminum). When a charged object touches the knob, the leaves push away from each other because like charges repel each other. It is not possible to tell whether the charge is positive or negative.

Charging by induction

If you touch a knob with your finger while a charged rod is nearby, the electrons will be repulsed and flow out of the electroscope through the hand. If the hand is removed while the charged rod remains close, the electroscope will retain the charge.

When an object is rubbed with a charged rod, the object will take on the same charge as the rod. However, charging by induction gives the object the opposite charge as that of the charged rod.

Grounding charge

Charge can be removed from an object by connecting it to the Earth through a conductor. The removal of static electricity by conduction is called **GROUNDING**.

GROUNDING: the removal of static electricity by conduction

Circuits

An **ELECTRIC CIRCUIT** is a path along which electrons flow. A simple circuit can be created with a dry cell, wire, and a bell or light bulb. When all are connected, the electrons flow from the negative terminal through the wire to the device, and back to the positive terminal of the dry cell. If there are no breaks in the circuit, the device will work; the circuit is closed. Any break in the flow will create an open circuit and cause the device to shut off.

ELECTRIC CIRCUIT: a path along which electrons flow

Load and switch

The device (bell or bulb) is an example of a load. A load is a device that uses energy. Suppose that you add a buzzer so that the bell rings when you press the buzzer. The buzzer is acting as a switch. A switch is a device that opens or closes a circuit. Pressing the buzzer makes the connection complete and the bell rings. When the buzzer is not engaged, the circuit is open and the bell is silent.

Circuit types

A **SERIES CIRCUIT** is one where the electrons have only one path along which they can move. When one load in a series circuit goes out, the circuit is open. An example of this is a set of Christmas tree lights that is missing a bulb. None of the bulbs will work if one bulb is not working.

SERIES CIRCUIT: a circuit in which the electrons can move along only one path

A **PARALLEL CIRCUIT** is one where the electrons have more than one path to travel along. If a load goes out in a parallel circuit, the other load will continue to work because the electrons can still find a way to continue moving along the path.

PARALLEL CIRCUIT: a circuit in which the electrons can travel along more than one path

Potential difference, voltage, and current

When an electron goes through a load, it does work and therefore loses some of its energy. The measure of how much energy is lost is called the **POTENTIAL DIFFERENCE**. The potential difference between two points is the work needed to move an electron from one point to another.

POTENTIAL DIFFERENCE: the measure of how much energy is lost when an electron goes through a load and does work

Potential difference is measured in a unit called the volt. Voltage is potential difference. The higher the voltage, the more energy the electrons have. This energy is measured by a device called a voltmeter. To use a voltmeter, place it in a circuit parallel with the load you are measuring.

CURRENT is the number of electrons per second that flow past a point in a circuit. Current is measured with a device called an ammeter. To use an ammeter, put it in series with the load you are measuring.

CURRENT: the number of electrons per second that flow past a point in a circuit

As electrons flow through a wire, they lose potential energy. Some of the energy is changed to heat energy because of resistance. **RESISTANCE** is the ability of the material to oppose the flow of electrons through it. All substances have some resistance, even if they are good conductors, such as copper. This resistance is measured in units called ohms. A thin wire will have more resistance than a thick one because it will have less room for electrons to travel. In a thicker wire, there will be more possible paths for the electrons to flow. Resistance also depends upon the length of the wire. The longer the wire, the more resistance it will have.

RESISTANCE: the ability of the material to oppose the flow of electrons through it

Ohm's Law

Potential difference, resistance, and current form a relationship know as **OHM'S LAW**. Current (I) is measured in amperes and is equal to potential difference (V) divided by resistance (R).

$$I = \frac{V}{R}$$

OHM'S LAW: the relationship between potential difference, resistance, and current

If you have a wire with resistance of 5 Ohms and a potential difference of 75 volts, you can calculate the current by:

$$I = \frac{75 \text{ volts}}{5 \text{ ohms}}$$
$$I = 15 \text{ amperes}$$

A current of 10 or more amperes will cause a wire to get hot. The maximum current for a house circuit is about 22 amperes. Current above 25 amperes can start a fire.

Magnetism

Magnetic fields and poles

MAGNETIC FIELD: the space around a magnet where its force affects objects

Magnets have a north pole and a south pole. Like poles repel and opposing poles attract. A **MAGNETIC FIELD** is the space around a magnet where its force affects objects. The closer you are to a magnet, the stronger the force. As you move away, the force becomes weaker.

Some materials act as magnets and some do not. This is because magnetism is a result of electrons in motion. The most important motion in this case is the spinning of the individual electrons. Electrons spin in pairs in opposite directions in most atoms. The magnetic field that each spinning electron creates is canceled by another electron spinning in the opposite direction.

A bar magnet has a north pole and a south pole. If you divide the magnet in half, each half will have a north and south pole.

The Earth has a magnetic field. In a compass, a tiny, lightweight magnet is suspended and will line its south pole up with the north pole magnet of the Earth.

Magnetic domains

In an atom of iron, there are four unpaired electrons. The magnetic fields of these are not canceled out. Their fields add up to make a tiny magnet. Their fields exert forces on each other, setting up small areas in the iron called magnetic domains where atomic magnetic fields line up in the same direction.

You can make a magnet out of an iron nail by stroking the nail in the same direction repeatedly with a magnet. This causes poles in the nail to be attracted to the magnet. The tiny magnetic fields in the nail line up in the direction of the magnet. The magnet causes the domains pointing in its direction to grow in the nail. Eventually, one large domain results and the nail becomes a magnet.

Electromagnets

A magnet can be made out of a coil of wire by connecting the ends of the coil to a battery. When the current goes through the wire, the wire acts in the same way that a magnet does; it is called an electromagnet. The poles of the electromagnet will depend upon which way the electric current runs. An electromagnet can be made more powerful in three ways:

1. Make more coils
2. Put an iron core (nail) inside the coils
3. Use more battery power

Common uses of electromagnets

An electric meter, such as the one found on the side of a house, contains an aluminum disk that sits directly in a magnetic field created by electricity flowing through a conductor. The more the electricity flows (current), the stronger the magnetic field. The stronger the magnetic field, the faster the disk turns. The disk is connected to a series of gears that turn a dial. Meter readers record the number from that dial.

Air conditioners, vacuum cleaners, and washing machines use electric motors. An electric motor uses an electromagnet to change electric energy into mechanical energy.

In a motor, electricity is used to create magnetic fields that oppose each other and cause the rotor to move. The wiring loops attached to the rotating shaft have a magnetic field opposing the magnetic field caused by the wiring in the housing of the motor that cannot move. The repelling action of the opposing magnetic fields turns the rotor.

A generator is a device that turns rotary, mechanical energy into electrical energy. The process is based on the relationship between magnetism and electricity. As a wire, or any other conductor, moves across a magnetic field, an electric current occurs in the wire. The large generators used by electric companies have a stationary conductor; inside, a magnet attached to the end of a rotating shaft is positioned inside a stationary conducting ring that is wrapped with a long, continuous piece of wire. When the magnet rotates, it induces a small electric current in each section of wire as it passes. Each section of wire is a small, separate electric conductor. All the small currents of these individual sections add up to one large current, which is used for electric power.

A transformer is an electrical device that changes electricity of one voltage into another voltage, usually from high to low. You can see transformers at the top of utility poles. It uses two properties of electricity: first, magnetism surrounds an electric circuit, and second, voltage is made when a magnetic field moves or changes strength. **VOLTAGE** is a measure of the strength or amount of electrons flowing through a wire. If another wire is close to an electric current changing

VOLTAGE is a measure of the strength or amount of electrons flowing through a wire

strength, the electric current will also flow into that other wire as the magnetism changes. A transformer takes in electricity at a higher voltage and lets it run through many coils wound around an iron core. An output wire with fewer coils is also around the core. The changing magnetism makes a current in the output wire. Fewer coils means less voltage, so the voltage is reduced.

Common sources of EMFs (electromagnetic fields) include power lines, appliances, medical equipment, cellular phones, and computers.

Sound

Sound waves are produced by a vibrating body that moves forward and compresses the air in front of it. It then reverses direction, so that the pressure on the air is lessened and expansion of the air molecules occurs. One compression and expansion creates one longitudinal wave. Sound can be transmitted through any gas, liquid, or solid. However, it cannot be transmitted through a vacuum, because there are no particles present to vibrate and bump into their adjacent particles to transmit the wave.

The vibrating air molecules move back and forth parallel to the direction of the motion of the wave as they pass the energy from adjacent air molecules (closer to the source) to air molecules farther away from the source.

Levels of sound

The pitch of a sound depends on the frequency that the ear receives. High-pitched sound waves have high frequencies. High notes are produced by an object that is vibrating at a greater rate per second than one that produces a low note.

The intensity of a sound is the amount of energy that crosses a unit of area in a given amount of time. The loudness of the sound is subjective and depends upon the effect on the human ear. Two tones with the same intensity, but different pitches, may appear to have different loudness. The intensity level of sound is measured in decibels. Normal conversation is about 60 decibels, while a power saw is about 110 decibels.

Sound waves

The amplitude of a sound wave determines its loudness, with loud sound waves creating larger amplitudes. The larger the sound wave, the more energy is needed to create the wave.

INTERFERENCE: the interaction of two or more waves that meet

An oscilloscope is useful in studying waves because it gives a picture that shows the crest and trough of the wave. **INTERFERENCE** is the interaction of two or more waves that meet. If the waves interfere constructively, the crest of each one meets the crests of the others. They combine into a crest with greater amplitude, creating a louder sound. If the waves interfere destructively, then the crest of one meets the trough of another. They produce a wave with lower amplitude that produces a softer sound.

If you have two tuning forks that produce different pitches, one will produce sounds of a slightly higher frequency. When you strike the two forks simultaneously, you will hear beats. Beats are a series of loud and soft sounds created when waves meet and the crests combine at some points and produce loud sounds. At other points, they nearly cancel each other out and produce soft sounds.

When a piano tuner tunes a piano, he only uses one tuning fork, even though there are many strings on the piano. He adjusts the first string to be the same pitch as that of the tuning fork. Then he listens to the beats that occur when both the tuned and untuned strings are struck. He adjusts the untuned string until he can hear the correct number of beats per second. This process of striking the untuned and tuned strings together and timing the beats is repeated until all the piano strings are tuned.

Pleasant sounds have a regular wave pattern that is repeated. Sounds that do not happen with regularity are unpleasant and are called **NOISE**.

NOISE: sounds that do not happen with regularity are unpleasant

Doppler Effect

The Doppler Effect is defined as the changes in experienced frequency due to relative motion of the source of the sound. When a siren approaches, the pitch is high. When it passes, the pitch drops. As a moving sound source approaches a listener, the sound waves are closer together, causing an increase in frequency in the sound that is heard. As the source passes the listener, the waves spread out, and the sound experienced by the listener is lower.

Waves

Transverse waves are characterized by particle motion that is perpendicular to the wave motion; longitudinal waves are characterized by particle motion that is parallel to the wave motion.

Interference

Wave interference occurs when two waves meet while traveling along the same medium. The medium takes on a shape resulting from the net effect of the individual waves upon the particles of the medium. There are two types of interference:

1. Constructive
2. Destructive

Constructive interference occurs when two crests or two troughs of the same shape meet. The medium will take on the shape of a crest or a trough with twice the amplitude of the two interfering crests or troughs. If a trough and a crest of the same shape meet, the two pulses will cancel each other out, and the medium will assume the equilibrium position. This is called **destructive interference.**

Destructive interference in sound waves will reduce the loudness of the sound. This is a disadvantage in rooms such as auditoriums, where sound needs to be at its optimum. However, it can be used as an advantage in noise reduction systems. When two sound waves differing slightly in frequency are superimposed, beats are created by the alternation of constructive and destructive interference. The frequency of the beats is equal to the difference between the frequencies of the interfering sound waves.

Wave interference occurs with light waves in much the same manner that it does with sound waves. If two light waves of the same color, frequency, and amplitude are combined, the interference shows up as fringes of alternating light and dark bands. In order for this to happen, the light waves must come from the same source.

Light

When we refer to light, we are usually talking about a type of electromagnetic wave that stimulates the retina of the eye, or visible light. Each individual wavelength within the spectrum of visible light represents a particular color. When a particular wavelength strikes the retina, we perceive that color. The colors of visible light are sometimes referred to as *ROYGBIV* (red, orange, yellow, green, blue, indigo, and violet). The visible light spectrum ranges from red (the longest wavelength) to violet (the shortest wavelength), with a range of wavelengths in between. If all the wavelengths strike your eye at the same time, you will see white. Conversely, when no wavelengths strike your eye, you perceive black.

Shadows illustrate one of the basic properties of light. Light travels in a straight line; if you put your hand between a light source and a wall, you will interrupt the light and produce a shadow.

Reflection, refraction, diffraction

When light hits a surface, it is reflected. The angle of the incoming light (angle of incidence) is the same as the angle of the reflected light (angle of reflection). It is this reflected light that allows you to see objects. This happens when the reflected light reaches your eyes.

Different surfaces reflect light differently. Rough surfaces scatter light in many different directions. A smooth surface reflects the light in one direction. If the surface is smooth and shiny (like a mirror), you can see your image in the surface.

When light enters a different medium, it bends. This bending, or change of speed, is called **REFRACTION**.

REFRACTION: the bending, or change of speed, that occurs when light enters a different medium

Light can be **DIFFRACTED**, or bent around the edges of an object. Diffraction occurs when light goes through a narrow slit. As light passes through it, the light bends slightly around the edges of the slit. You can demonstrate this by pressing your thumb and forefinger together, making a very thin slit between them. Hold them about 8 cm from your eye and look at a distant source of light. The pattern you observe is caused by the diffraction of light.

DIFFRACTION: light that bends around the edges of an object

Light and other electromagnetic radiation can be polarized because the waves are transverse. The distinguishing characteristic of transverse waves is that they are perpendicular to the direction of the motion of the wave. Polarized light has vibrations confined to a single plane that is perpendicular to the direction of motion. Light is able to be polarized by passing it through special filters that block all vibrations except those in a single plane. Polarized sunglasses cut down on glare by blocking out all but one place of vibration.

SKILL 4.3 Use design processes and procedures to pose questions and select solutions to problems and situations

Technological design is the identification of a problem and the application of scientific knowledge to solve the problem. The technological design process has five basic steps:

1. Identify a problem
2. Propose designs and choose between alternative solutions: Scientists often utilize simulations and models in evaluating possible solutions.
3. Implement the proposed solution: Scientists use various tools depending on the problem, solution, and technology. They may use both physical tools and objects and computer software.
4. Evaluate the solution and its consequences against predetermined criteria: Scientists must consider the negative consequences as well as the planned benefits.
5. Report results: Scientists must communicate results in different ways—orally, written, models, diagrams, and demonstrations.

SKILL 4.4 Apply technological knowledge and skills to evaluate the degree to which products and systems meet human and environmental needs

See Skill 6.6

SKILL 4.5 Analyze excerpts describing recent scientific discoveries or technological advances in relation to underlying scientific principles, concepts, or themes

Evaluating Sources of Scientific Information

Because people often attempt to use scientific evidence in support of political or personal agendas, the ability to evaluate the credibility of scientific claims is a necessary skill in today's society. In evaluating scientific claims made in the media, public debates, and advertising, one should follow several guidelines.

First, scientific, peer-reviewed journals are the most accepted source for information on scientific experiments and studies. One should carefully scrutinize any claim that does not reference peer-reviewed literature.

Second, the media and those with an agenda to advance (advertisers and politicians) often overemphasize the certainty and importance of experimental results. One should question any scientific claim that sounds fantastic or overly certain.

Finally, knowledge of experimental design and of the scientific method is important in evaluating the credibility of studies. For example, one should look for the inclusion of control groups and the presence of data to support the given conclusions.

COMPETENCY 5

UNDERSTAND THE HISTORICAL DEVELOPMENT AND CULTURAL CONTEXTS OF MATHEMATICS, SCIENCE, AND TECHNOLOGY, THE RELATIONSHIPS AND COMMON THEMES THAT CONNECT MATHEMATICS, SCIENCE, AND TECHNOLOGY, AND THE IMPACT OF MATHEMATICS, SCIENCE, AND TECHNOLOGY ON HUMAN SOCIETIES

SKILL 5.1 Analyze the historical, societal, or environmental effects of given developments in science and technology *(e.g., computerization)*

With any rapid change, there are always good and bad things associated with it. At the same time, we need technology in our lives, and we cannot afford not to make use of these developments and reap the benefits for the good of humanity.

Environment

The environment is constantly and rapidly undergoing tremendous changes.

The positive effects include the ability to predict hurricanes, measure changes in radioactivity present in our environment, and predict the levels of gases like carbon monoxide, carbon dioxide, and other harmful gases, to name a few. With the help of modern technology, it is possible to know the quantities of harmful gases and to monitor, plan, and implement measures to deal with them.

The negative aspects of the effect of technology on our environment are numerous. The first and foremost is pollution of various kinds—water, air, and noise. Others include the greenhouse effect, the indiscriminate use of fertilizers and pesticides, the use of various additives to our food, deforestation, and the unprecedented exploitation of nonrenewable energy resources.

Human Biology

The strides science and technology have made have lasting effects on human biology. A few examples are organ transplants, in-vitro fertilization, new drugs, new understanding of various diseases, cosmetic surgery, reconstructive surgery, use of computers in operations, lasers in medicine, and forensic science. As always, there are pros and cons to these changes.

Some positive aspects are that people with organ transplants have renewed hope. Quality of life has improved with the use of technology such as pacemakers. Couples who experienced infertility can have babies now. Corrective and cosmetic surgeries are giving new confidence to patients. Glasses to correct vision problems are being replaced slowly by laser surgery.

Some negative aspects are medical blunders, the indiscriminate use of corrective and cosmetic surgery, and overconfidence in the efficacy of these emerging technologies.

Society and Culture

The use of technology has changed our lifestyles, our behavior, our ethical and moral thinking, and our economy and career opportunities.

Some positive aspects are that technology is uniting us to a certain extent (e.g., it is possible to communicate with people of any culture even when we are not seeing them face to face through mediums such as email, live chat, and video conferencing.) It makes business and personal communication much easier over long distances. When we all use the same pieces of technology, we understand each other better, and a common ground is established. Sharing opinions and information has been enhanced.

Despite these positive changes, care must be exercised as to how much of our past culture we are willing to trade for the modern. Positive aspects of any culture must be guarded carefully and passed on to generations to come.

On the whole, we can conclude that science and technology are part of our lives, and we must always exercise caution when adapting to new ideas and new thinking. It is possible that awareness and incorporation of other cultural practices will make us a better nation.

SKILL 5.2 Recognize how mathematical models can be used to understand scientific, social, or environmental phenomena

See also Skills 4.1 and 6.5

Many phenomena in social or physical sciences can be modeled using **probability theory**. The results of an experiment or a set of experiments, whether in the scientific realm, the political realm, or a range of other areas, can be analyzed using statistics and associated methods of data analysis.

Dependent events occur when the probability of the second event depends on the outcome of the first event. For example, consider the two events: A) It is sunny on

Saturday, and B) you go to the beach. If you intend to go to the beach on Saturday, rain or shine, then A and B may be independent. If, however, you plan to go to the beach only if it is sunny, then A and B may be dependent. In this situation, the probability of event B will change depending on the outcome of event A.

Suppose you have a pair of dice, one red and one green. If you roll a three on the red die and then roll a four on the green die, we can see that these events do not depend on each other. The total probability of the two independent events can be found by multiplying the separate probabilities.

$P(\text{A and B}) = P(A) \times P(B)$
$= \frac{1}{6} \times \frac{1}{6}$
$= \frac{1}{36}$

Many times, however, events are not independent. Suppose a jar contains 12 red marbles and 8 blue marbles. If you randomly pick a red marble, replace it, and then randomly pick again, the probability of picking a red marble the second time remains the same. However, if you pick a red marble, and then pick again without replacing the first red marble, the second pick becomes dependent upon the first pick.

$P(\text{red and red})$ with replacement $= P(\text{red}) \times P(\text{red})$
$= \frac{12}{20} \times \frac{12}{20}$
$= \frac{9}{25}$

$P(\text{red and red})$ without replacement $= P(\text{red}) \times P(\text{red})$
$= \frac{12}{20} \times \frac{11}{19}$
$= \frac{33}{95}$

Odds are defined as the ratio of the number of favorable outcomes to the number of unfavorable outcomes. The sum of the favorable outcomes and the unfavorable outcomes should always equal the total number of possible outcomes.

For example, given a bag of 12 red and 7 green marbles, compute the odds of randomly selecting a red marble.

Odds of getting red $= \frac{12}{19} : \frac{7}{19}$ or 12:7
Odds of not getting red $= \frac{7}{19} : \frac{12}{19}$ or 7:12

In the case of flipping a coin, it is equally likely that a head or a tail will be tossed. The odds of tossing a head are 1:1. This is called "even odds."

Sample Spaces

SAMPLE SPACE: a list of all possible outcomes of an experiment

In probability, the **SAMPLE SPACE** is a list of all possible outcomes of an experiment. For example, the sample space of tossing two coins is the set {HH, HT, TT, TH}; the sample space of rolling a six-sided die is the set {1, 2, 3, 4, 5, 6}; and the sample space of measuring the height of students in a class is the set of all real numbers {R}.

When conducting experiments with a large number of possible outcomes, it is important to determine the size of the sample space. The size of the sample space can be determined by using the fundamental counting principle and the rules of combinations and permutations.

The fundamental counting principle states that if there are m possible outcomes for one task and n possible outcomes of another, there are $(m \times n)$ possible outcomes of the two tasks together.

A permutation is the number of possible arrangements of items, without repetition, where order of selection is important.

A combination is the number of possible arrangements, without repetition, where order of selection is not important.

Example: Find the size of the sample space of rolling two six-sided dice and flipping two coins.
List the possible outcomes of each event:
Each die: {1, 2, 3, 4, 5, 6}
Each coin: {Heads, Tails}

Apply the fundamental counting principle:
Size of sample space $= 6 \times 6 \times 2 \times 2 = 144$

MEAN: the sum of the numbers given, divided by the number of items being averaged

MEDIAN: the middle number of a set

MODE: the number that occurs with the greatest frequency in a set of numbers

RANGE: a measure of variability

Mean, Median, and Mode

Descriptive statistics are numbers that describe characteristics of a group of data. Mean, median, and mode are three measures of central tendency. The MEAN is the average of the data items. The MEDIAN is found by putting the data items in order from smallest to largest and selecting the item in the middle (or the average of the two items in the middle). The MODE is the most frequently occurring item.

RANGE is a measure of variability. It is found by subtracting the smallest value from the largest value.

Example: Find the mean, median, mode, and range of these test scores:

85	77	65
92	90	54
88	85	70
75	80	69
85	88	60
72	74	95

Mean = sum of all scores ÷ number of scores = 78

Median = Put the numbers in order from smallest to largest. Pick the middle number.

54 60 65 69 70 72 74 75 | 77 80 | 85 85 85 88 88 90 92 95

both in middle

Therefore, the median is the average of two numbers in the middle, 78.5.

Mode = most frequent number
= 85

Range = the largest number minus the smallest number
= 95 − 54
= 41

Example: Different situations require different information. If we examine the circumstances under which an ice cream store owner may use statistics collected in the store, we find different uses for different information.
Over a seven-day period, the store owner collected data on the ice cream flavors sold. He found that the mean number of scoops sold was 174 per day. The best-selling flavor was vanilla. This information was useful in determining how much ice cream to order in all and how much of each flavor.

In this case, the median and range had little business value for the owner.

Example: Consider the set of test scores from a math class: 0, 16, 19, 65, 65, 65, 68, 69, 70, 72, 73, 73, 75, 78, 80, 85, 88, and 92.
The mean is 64.06 and the median is 71.

Since there are only three scores lower than the mean out of the eighteen scores, the median (71) would be a more descriptive score than the mean.

Using Definitions in Statistical Data

An understanding of the definitions is important in determining the validity and uses of statistical data. All definitions and applications in this section apply to ungrouped data.

Data item: each piece of data, represented by the letter X.

Mean: the average of all data, which is represented by the symbol $\overline{X}$.

Range: the difference between the highest and lowest values of data items.

Sum of the squares: the sum of the squares of the differences between each item and the mean.

$Sx^2 = (X - \overline{X})^2$

Variance: the sum of the squares quantity divided by the number of items. The lowercase Greek letter sigma squared (σ^2) represents variance.

$\frac{Sx^2}{N} = \sigma^2$

The larger the value of the variance, the larger the spread.

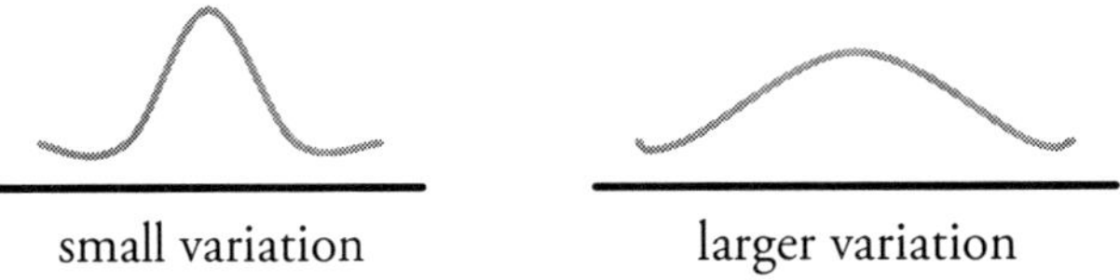

small variation   larger variation

Standard deviation: the square root of the variance. The lowercase Greek letter sigma (σ) is used to represent standard deviation.

$\sigma = \sqrt{\sigma^2}$

Most statistical calculators have standard deviation keys on them; you should use them when asked to calculate statistical functions. It is important to become familiar with the calculator and the location of the keys needed.

Example: Given the ungrouped data below, calculate the mean, range, standard deviation, and variance.

15	22	28	25	34	38
18	25	30	33	19	23

Mean ($\overline{X}$) = 25.8333333
Range: 38 − 15 = 23
Standard deviation (σ) = 6.6936952
Variance (σ^2) = 44.805556

SKILL 5.3 Evaluate how historical and societal factors have promoted or hindered developments in science and technology

The influence of social and cultural factors on science can be profound. Some early societies had trouble accepting science, especially when the science exposed some cultural beliefs as myths. This created a dilemma concerning whether or not to accept the facts provided by scientific investigations or to cling to cultural norms. This struggle went on for centuries. It took a long time for societies to accept scientific facts and to leave some of the cultural beliefs behind or modify them.

It can be extremely difficult for some societies to come to terms with technological advances. Even today, some cultures are not using modern technology, but, at the same time, they are using technology in principle—using simple machines for farming rather than using complex machines like tractors.

Other cultures have so readily adapted to technology that lives are intertwined with it to the extent that individuals utilize the computer, television, microwave, dishwasher, washing machine, cell phone, etc. on a daily basis. It is surprising to realize that we began with no technology and now are surrounded with it.

The religious beliefs and institutions of a culture can greatly influence scientific research and technological innovation. Political factors affect scientific advancement as well, especially in cultures that partially support scientific research with public money. Warfare has traditionally been a strong driver of technological advancement as cultures strive to outpace their neighbors with better weapons and defenses. Technologies developed for military purposes often find their way into the mainstream. Significant advances in flight technology, for example, were made during the two World Wars.

Many cultures have come to value innovation and welcome new products and improvements to older products. This desire to always be advancing and obtaining the latest, newest technology creates economic incentive for innovation.

SKILL 5.4 Analyze how developments in scientific knowledge may affect other areas of life *(e.g., recognizing types of scientific data likely to affect government policymaking regarding pollution control)*

Scientific and technological breakthroughs influence other fields of study and the job market. All academic disciplines utilize computer and information technology to simplify research and information sharing. Advances in science and technology influence the types of jobs available and the desired work skills.

Local, state, national, and global governments and organizations must increasingly consider policy issues related to science and technology. For example, local and state governments must analyze the environmental impact of proposed development and growth. Governments and communities must balance the demands of an expanding human population with the local ecology to ensure sustainable growth.

In addition, advances in science and technology create challenges and ethical dilemmas that national governments and global organizations must attempt to solve. Genetic research and manipulation, antibiotic resistance, stem cell research, and cloning are but a few of the issues facing national governments and global organizations.

In all cases, policy makers must analyze all sides of an issue and attempt to find a solution that protects society while limiting scientific inquiry as little as possible.

COMPETENCY 6

UNDERSTAND AND APPLY SKILLS, PRINCIPLES, AND PROCEDURES ASSOCIATED WITH INQUIRY AND PROBLEM SOLVING IN THE SCIENCES

SKILL 6.1 Apply scientific methods and principles (including nonquantitative methods such as case studies) to investigate a question or problem

See Skills 6.5 and 6.6

SKILL 6.2 Formulate questions to guide research and experimentation toward explanations for phenomena and observations

See Skills 6.5 and 6.6

SKILL 6.3 Infer the scientific principles *(e.g., reliance on experimental data, replication of results)* or skills *(e.g., observation, inductive reasoning, familiarity with statistics and probability)* that contribute to a scientific development as described in an excerpt

See Skills 6.5 and 6.6

SKILL 6.4 Demonstrate familiarity with electronic means for collecting, organizing, and analyzing information *(e.g., databases, spreadsheets)*

See Skills 17.3 and 21.4

SKILL 6.5 Analyze the components of a given experimental design *(e.g., dependent and independent variables, experimental groups, control groups)*

Characteristics of Scientific Investigations

Scientific investigations come in all sizes and forms. One can conduct a simple survey of a population by interviewing a few people with the hope of gaining an understanding of a larger population. This method is often used by medical and pharmaceutical companies and may include a questionnaire that asks about health and lifestyle.

Ecologists use field observation. As with the medical questionnaire, they incorporate small sample sizes to gain a better understanding of a larger group. For example, they may document one animal to determine its migratory patterns, or they may place cameras in one area to capture footage of a roaming animal or pack. Ecologists study an area and all of the organisms within it, but they often limit sampling size and use a representative of the population.

Whenever possible, a scientist would prefer to conduct controlled experiments. This can happen most readily in a laboratory, and it is nearly impossible to achieve in nature. In a controlled experiment, only one variable is manipulated at one time, and a control, or normal, group is always present. This control group gives scientists something to compare the variable against. It tells them what would normally have happened under the experimental conditions had they not introduced the variable.

When evaluating an experiment, it is important to first look at the question it was supposed to answer. How logically did the experiment flow from the question? How many variables existed in the experiment? It is best to test one variable at a time.

An experiment is proposed and performed with the sole objective of testing a hypothesis.

Properly collected data yields information that appropriately answers the original question. For example, one would not try use a graduated cylinder to measure mass or use a ruler to measure a microscopic item. Utilizing appropriate measuring devices, proper units, and careful mathematics will provide strong results. Carefully evaluating and analyzing data creates a reasonable conclusion. The conclusion needs to be backed up by scientific criteria, then, finally, communicated to the audience.

Methods, Measurements, Tools, and Technologies

The procedure used to obtain data is important to the outcome. Experiments consist of controls and variables. A control is the experiment run under normal conditions. The variable is a factor that is changed. In biology, the variable may be light, temperature, pH, time, etc. The differences in tested variables may be used to make a prediction or to form a hypothesis. Only one variable should be tested at a time. One should not alter both the temperature and pH of the experimental subject, for example.

INDEPENDENT VARIABLE: changed or manipulated by the researcher

DEPENDENT VARIABLE: influenced by the independent variable

An **INDEPENDENT VARIABLE** is changed or manipulated by the researcher. This could be the amount of light given to a plant or the temperature at which bacteria is grown.

The **DEPENDENT VARIABLE** is influenced by the independent variable.

Measurements

There is an appropriate measuring device for each aspect of biology. A graduated cylinder is used to measure volume. A balance is used to measure mass. A microscope is used to view microscopic objects. A centrifuge is used to separate two or more parts in a liquid sample. For each variable, there is an appropriate way to measure it.

Tools and technologies

Biologists use a variety of tools and technologies to perform tests, to collect and display data, and to analyze relationships. Examples of commonly used tools include computer-linked probes, spreadsheets, and graphing calculators.

- **Computer-linked probes** measure various environmental factors, including temperature, dissolved oxygen, pH, ionic concentration, and pressure. The advantage of computer-linked probes, as compared to more traditional observational tools, is that the probes automatically gather data and present it in an accessible format. This property of computer-linked probes eliminates the need for constant human observation and manipulation.
- Biologists use **spreadsheets** to organize, analyze, and display data. For example, conservation ecologists use spreadsheets to model population growth and development, to apply sampling techniques, and to create statistical distributions in order to analyze relationships. Spreadsheets simplify data collection and manipulation and allow the presentation of data in a logical and understandable format.
- **Graphing calculators** have many applications in biology. For example, biologists use algebraic functions to analyze growth, development, and other natural processes. Graphing calculators can manipulate algebraic data

and create graphs for analysis and observation. In addition, biologists use the matrix function of graphing calculators to model problems in genetics. Graphing calculators simplify the creation of graphical displays, including histograms, scatter plots, and line graphs. Biologists can also transfer data and displays to computers for further analysis. Finally, biologists connect computer-linked probes used to collect data to graphing calculators to ease the collection, transmission, and analysis of data.

Precision, accuracy, and error

ACCURACY is the degree of conformity of a measurement of some quantity to its actual (true) value. **PRECISION**, also called reproducibility or repeatability, is the degree to which further measurements or calculations will show the same or similar results.

ACCURACY: the degree of conformity of a measurement of some quantity to its actual (true) value

PRECISION: the degree to which further measurements or calculations will show the same or similar results

Accuracy is the degree of veracity; precision is the degree of reproducibility.

The best analogy to explain accuracy and precision is the target comparison. Repeated measurements are compared to arrows that are fired at a target. Accuracy describes the closeness of arrows to the bull's-eye at the target center. Arrows that strike closer to the bull's-eye are considered more accurate.

All experimental uncertainty is due to either random errors or systematic errors.

RANDOM ERRORS are statistical fluctuations in the measured data due to the precision limitations of the measurement device. Random errors usually result from the experimenter's inability to take the same measurement in exactly the same way to get exactly the same number.

RANDOM ERRORS: statistical fluctuations in the measured data due to the precision limitations of the measurement device

SYSTEMATIC ERRORS, by contrast, are reproducible inaccuracies that are consistently made during an experiment at the same point. Systematic errors are often due to a problem that persists throughout the entire experiment.

SYSTEMATIC ERRORS: reproducible inaccuracies that are consistently made during an experiment at the same point

Systematic and random errors refer to problems associated with making measurements. Mistakes made in the calculations or in reading the instrument are not considered in error analysis.

SKILL 6.6 Demonstrate an understanding of the nature of scientific inquiry (including ethical dimensions) and the role of observation and experimentation in science

Scientific Inquiry

Scientific inquiry starts with a simple question. This simple question leads to information gathering and an educated guess, otherwise known as a hypothesis. To prove the hypothesis, an experiment has to be conducted, which yields data and leads to a conclusion. All experiments must be repeated at least twice to get reliable results. Thus, scientific inquiry leads to new knowledge or verifies established theories. Science requires empirical proof or evidence.

The Scientific Method

The scientific method is the basic process behind scientific experimentation. It involves several steps, beginning with formulating a hypothesis and working through the discovery process to make a conclusion based on observation and testing.

Posing a question

Although many discoveries happen by chance, a scientist's standard thought process begins with forming a question to test by conducting research. The more limited the question, the more readily an experiment can be designed to answer that question.

Forming a hypothesis

Once the question is formulated, a scientist makes an educated guess about the answer to the problem or question. This "best guess" is the hypothesis.

Doing the test

Next, a series of steps known as an experiment are outlined to test this hypothesis. To make a test fair, data from an experiment must have a variable or any condition that can be changed; for example, temperature or mass. A good test will try to manipulate as few variables as possible. This allows the researcher to more readily identify the variable or condition that produces a particular result. Experiments also require a second factor known as a control. A control is a factor that remains unchanged throughout the experiment, which allows the researcher to verify that the experiment worked correctly. When using a control, all the conditions are the same except for the variable being tested.

Observing and recording the data

Once the experiment is conducted, data must be gathered based on the results obtained. Data reporting should state specifics of how the measurements were made during the experiment. For example, a graduated cylinder needs to be read properly. For beginning students, technique must be part of the instructional process so as to give validity to the data.

Drawing a conclusion

Careful analysis of the recorded data allows the experimenter to draw a conclusion based on the evidence. After recording data, compare your data with that of other researchers that have conducted similar experiments. A conclusion is the judgment derived from the data results.

Communicating results

Scientific findings are usually documented in the form of a lab report. All lab reports should include a specific title and tell exactly what is being studied. The abstract is a summary of the report that is placed at the beginning of the paper. The purpose should always be defined, clearly stating the question the experiment was designed to answer. The purpose should include the hypothesis (educated guess) of the expected outcome of the experiment. The entire experiment should relate to this purpose. It is important to accurately describe what was done to prove or disprove a hypothesis. A control is needed in every experiment; it is necessary to prove that the results obtained are a result of the manipulated variable. Only one variable should be manipulated at a time. Observations and results of an experiment should be recorded, including all results from data. Drawings, graphs, and illustrations should be included to support information. Observations are objective, whereas analysis and interpretation is subjective. A conclusion should explain why the results of the experiment either prove or disprove the hypothesis.

Scientific theory and experimentation must be repeatable. It is also possible that previously established theories can be disproved and may be changed on the basis of new scientific proof. Science depends on communication, agreement, and disagreement among scientists. It is built on theories, laws, and hypotheses.

- Theory: the formation of principles or relationships that have been verified and accepted; a proven hypothesis
- Law: an explanation of events that occur with uniformity under the same conditions (laws of thermodynamics, law of gravitation)
- Hypothesis: an unproven theory or educated guess followed by research to best explain a phenomena

Scientific Enterprise

Science is a complex activity involving various people and places. A scientist may work alone or in a laboratory, classroom, or, for that matter, anywhere. Science is primarily a group activity requiring cooperation, communication of results or findings, consultations, and discussions.

Bias

Scientific research can be biased in the choice of what data to consider, in the reporting or recording of the data, or in how the data are interpreted. Scientists may be influenced by their nationality, sex, ethnic origin, age, or political convictions. For example, when studying a group of animals, male scientists may focus on the social behavior of the males and typical male characteristics.

Although bias related to the investigator, the sample, the method, or the instrument may not be completely avoidable in every case, it is important to know the possible sources of bias and how bias could affect the evidence. Moreover, scientists need to be attentive to possible bias in their own work and that of other scientists.

Objectivity may not always be attained. However, one precaution that may be taken to guard against undetected bias is to have many different investigators or groups of investigators working on a project. These groups should be made up of people of various nationalities, ethnic origins, ages, and political convictions and composed of both males and females. It is also important to note one's aspirations and to make sure to be truthful to the data even when grants, promotions, and notoriety are at risk.

The importance of verifiable evidence and peer review

Science is a process of checks and balances. It is expected that scientific findings will be challenged and, in many cases, retested. Often, one experiment will be the beginning point for another. Although bias does exist, the use of controlled experiments and awareness on the part of the scientist can go a long way toward ensuring a sound experiment. Even if the science is well done, it may still be questioned. It is through this continual search that hypotheses are made into theories, which sometimes become laws. It is also through this search that new information is discovered.

Differences between ethical and unethical uses of science

To understand scientific ethics, we need to have a clear understanding of ethics itself. Ethics is defined as a system of public, general rules for guiding human conduct (Gert, 1988). The rules are general because they are supposed to apply to all people at all times, and they are public because they are not secret codes or practices.

The following are some of the guiding principles of scientific ethics:

- Scientific Honesty: not to commit fraud or fabricate or misinterpret data for personal gain
- Caution: to avoid errors and sloppiness in all scientific experimentation
- Credit: to give credit where credit is due and not to copy
- Responsibility: only to report reliable information to the public and not to mislead in the name of science
- Freedom: freedom to criticize old ideas, to question new research, and to conduct research

The common ethical code described above could be applied to many areas, including science. When the general code is applied to a particular area of human life, it then becomes an institutional code. Hence, scientific ethics is an institutional code of conduct that reflects the chief concerns and goals of science.

To discuss scientific ethics, we can look at natural phenomena like rain. Rain, in the normal sense, is extremely useful to us, and it is absolutely important that there is a water cycle. When rain gets polluted with acid, it becomes acid rain. Here lies the ethical issue of releasing pollutants into the atmosphere. Should scientists communicate the whole truth about acid rain or withhold some information because it may alarm the public? There are many issues like this. Whatever may be the case, scientists are expected to be honest and forthright with the public.

DOMAIN II
HISTORICAL AND SOCIAL SCIENTIFIC AWARENESS

PERSONALIZED STUDY PLAN

PAGE	COMPETENCY AND SKILL		KNOWN MATERIAL/ SKIP IT
77	**7:**	**Understand the interrelatedness of historical, geographic, cultural, economic, political, and social issues and factors**	☐
	7.1:	Assess the effects of human activities or trends on the environment	☐
	7.2:	Assess how major transformations related to human work, thought, and belief have affected society	☐
	7.3:	Infer aspects of a society's social structure or group interactions	☐
	7.4:	Analyze how social, cultural, geographic, and economic factors influence intergroup relations	☐
	7.5:	Assess the social or economic implications of political views	☐
91	**8:**	**Understand principles and assumptions underlying historical or contemporary arguments, interpretations, explanations,or developments**	☐
	8.1:	Infer the political principles illustrated in situations or arguments	☐
	8.2:	Recognize assumptions that inform the positions taken by political parties	☐
	8.3:	Analyze assumptions on which U.S. policies are based	☐
	8.4:	Recognize concepts underlying alternative interpretations of past events	☐
	8.5:	Infer the economic principle upon which an explanation is based	☐
100	**9:**	**Understand different perspectives and priorities underlying historical or contemporary arguments, interpretations, explanations, or developments**	☐
	9.1:	Identify the values implicit in political, economic, social, or religious points of view	☐
	9.2:	Recognize the motives, beliefs, and interests that inform differing views	☐
	9.3:	Analyze multiple perspectives regarding major historical and contemporary issues	☐
	9.4:	Recognize the values or priorities implicit in public policy positions	☐
	9.5:	Analyze the perceptions of observers or participants from different cultures	☐

PERSONALIZED STUDY PLAN

PAGE	COMPETENCY AND SKILL	KNOWN MATERIAL/ SKIP IT
120	**10: Understanding and applying skills, principles, and procedures associated with inquiry, problem solving, and decision making in history and the social sciences**	☐
	10.1: Analyze research results to identify potential problems	☐
	10.2: Determine the relevance of information for supporting a point of view	☐
	10.3: Assess the reliability of sources	☐
	10.4: Evaluate the appropriateness of specific sources	☐
	10.5: Distinguish between unsupported and informed expressions of opinion	☐
126	**11: Understand and interpret visual representations of historical and social scientific information**	☐
	11.1: Translate written or graphic information from one form to the other	☐
	11.2: Relate information provided in graphic representations to public policy decisions	☐
	11.3: Interpret information provided in graphs, charts, tables, diagrams, or maps	☐
	11.4: Infer information about a historical or contemporary society based on a visual representation	☐

COMPETENCY 7

UNDERSTAND THE INTERRELATEDNESS OF HISTORICAL, GEOGRAPHIC, CULTURAL, ECONOMIC, POLITICAL, AND SOCIAL ISSUES AND FACTORS

SKILL 7.1 Assess the likely effects of human activities or trends (described in written or graphic form) on the local, regional, or global environment

A **POPULATION** is a group of people living within a certain geographic area. Populations are usually measured on a regular basis by census, which also measures age, ethnicity, and other data. Populations change over time due to many factors, and these changes can have significant impact on cultures.

POPULATION: a group of people living within a certain geographic area

When a population grows in size, it becomes necessary for it to either expand its geographic boundaries to make room for new people or to increase its density. Population density is simply the number of people in a population divided by some unit of geographic area in which they live.

Cultures with a high population density are likely to have different ways of interacting with one another than those with a low density.

As a population grows, its economic needs change. More basic needs are required, and more workers are needed to produce them. If a population's production or purchasing power does not keep pace with its growth, its economy can be adversely affected. The age distribution of a population can affect the economy, too, if the number of young and old people who are not working is disproportionate to those who are. Growth in some areas may spur migration to other parts of a population's geographic region that are less densely populated. This redistribution of population also places demands on the economy because infrastructure is needed to connect these new areas to older population centers.

Populations grow when the rate of birth is higher than the rate of death or by adding new people from other populations through immigration. Immigration is often a source of societal change because people from other cultures bring their institutions and language to a new area. Immigration also affects a population's educational and economic institutions because immigrants enter the workforce and place their children in schools.

Populations decline when the death rate exceeds the birth rate or when people migrate to another are. War, famine, disease, and natural disasters can also dramatically reduce a population. The economic problems from population decline can be similar to those from overpopulation because economic demands may be higher than can be met. In extreme cases, a population may decline to the point that it can no longer perpetuate itself, and its members and their culture either disappear or are absorbed into another population.

When human and other population and migration patterns change, climate changes, or natural disasters disrupt the delicate balance of a habitat or an ecosystem, species either adapt or become extinct.

Floods, volcanoes, storms, and earthquakes can alter habitats. These changes can affect the species that exist within the habitats, either by causing extinction or by changing the environment in a way that will no longer support critical ecosystems. Inhabiting species, however, can also alter habitats, particularly through migration. Human civilization, population growth, and efforts to control the environment can have many negative effects on various habitats.

Humans change their environments to suit their particular needs and interests. This can result in changes that result in the extinction of species or changes to the habitat itself. For example, deforestation damages the stability of mountain surfaces.

One particularly devastating example of human environmental change is the removal of the grasses of the Great Plains for agriculture. Tilling the ground and planting crops left the soil unprotected. Sustained drought dried out the soil into dust. Windstorms stripped the topsoil and blew it all the way to the Atlantic Ocean.

Environmental and geographic factors have affected the pattern of **urban development** in the world. In turn, urban infrastructure and development patterns are interrelated factors.

The growth of urban areas is often linked to the advantages provided by geographic location. Before the advent of efficient overland routes of commerce, such as railroads and highways, water provided the primary means for the transportation of commercial goods. Most large American cities are situated along bodies of water. New York's major cities include Buffalo (on Lake Erie), Albany (on the Hudson River), and New York City (on a large harbor where two major rivers meet the Atlantic Ocean). Where water traffic was not provided for naturally, New Yorkers built a series of canals, including the Erie Canal, which sparked the growth of inland cities.

As transportation technology advanced, the supporting infrastructure was built to connect cities with one another and to connect remote areas to larger communities. The railroad, for example, allowed for the quick transport of agricultural products from rural areas to urban centers. This newfound efficiency not only further fueled the growth of urban centers but it also changed the economy of rural America. Whereas once farmers had practiced only subsistence farming (growing enough to support one's own family), the new infrastructure meant that one could convert agricultural products into cash by selling them at market.

Improvements in building technology and advances in transportation allowed for larger cities. Growth brought with it a new set of problems. The bodies of water that had made the development of cities possible in their early days also formed natural barriers to growth. Further infrastructure in the form of bridges, tunnels, and ferry routes were needed to connect central urban areas with outlying communities.

As cities grew in population, living conditions became more crowded. As roads and bridges became better, and transportation technology improved, many people began to look outside the city for living space. Along with the development of these new suburbs came the infrastructure to connect them to the city in the form of commuter railroads and highways. In the case of New York City, a mass-transit system became crucial early on to bring essential workers from outlying areas into the commercial centers.

The growth of suburbs had the effect in many cities of creating a type of economic segregation. Working-class people who could not afford new suburban homes and an automobile to carry them to and from work were relegated to closer, more densely populated areas. Frequently, these areas had to be passed through by those on their way to the suburbs, and rail lines and freeways sometimes bisected these urban communities. In the modern age, advancements in telecommunications infrastructure may have an impact on urban growth patterns as information can pass instantly and freely between almost any two points on the globe, allowing access to some aspects of urban life to those in remote areas.

NATURAL RESOURCES are naturally occurring substances that are considered valuable in their natural form.

NATURAL RESOURCES: naturally occurring substances that are considered valuable in their natural form

Natural resources are often classified into renewable and nonrenewable resources. Renewable resources are generally living resources (fish, coffee, and forests, for example), which can restock (renew) themselves if they are not overharvested. Renewable resources can restock themselves and be used indefinitely if they are properly managed.

A commodity is generally considered a natural resource when the primary activities associated with it are extraction and purification, as opposed to creation. Thus, mining, petroleum extraction, fishing, and forestry are generally considered natural-resource industries, but agriculture is not.

Once renewable resources are consumed at a rate that exceeds their natural rate of replacement, the standing stock will diminish and eventually run out. The rate of sustainable use of a renewable resource is determined by the replacement rate and amount of standing stock of that particular resource. Nonliving renewable natural resources include soil, minerals, and other goods taken more or less as they are from the Earth.

In recent years, the depletion of natural capital and attempts to move to sustainable development have been a major focus of development agencies. Deforestation, or clear cutting, is of particular concern in rainforest regions, which hold most of the Earth's natural biodiversity—irreplaceable, genetic, natural capital. Conservation of natural resources is the major focus of environmentalism, the ecology movement, and Green parties. Some view this depletion as a major source of social unrest and conflicts in developing nations.

ENVIRONMENTAL POLICY: policy concerned with the sustainability of the Earth, of a region under the administration of a governing group, or of a local habitat

ENVIRONMENTAL POLICY is concerned with the sustainability of the Earth, of a region under the administration of a governing group, or of a local habitat. The concern of environmental policy is the preservation of the region, habitat, or ecosystem. Because humans, both individually and in community, rely upon the environment to sustain human life, social and environmental policy must be mutually supportive.

Land use relates to the function of the land. Use and development models are theories that attempt to inform the layout of urban areas.

Two primary land use models are applied to urban regions:

1. Burgess model: (also called the concentric model) Cities are seen to develop in a series of concentric circles with the central business district at the center, ringed by an industrial area, ringed by the low-class residential area, ringed by the middle-class residential area, and, finally, ringed by the upper-class residential area (often suburbs)
2. Hoyt model: (also called the sector model) The central business district occupies a central area of a circle, with factories and industry occupying an elongated area that abuts the city center. The low-class residential area surrounds the industrial area, the middle-class residential area forms a semicircle toward the other side of the city center, and a small upper-class residential sector extends from the city center out through the middle of the middle-class residential area.

SKILL 7.2 Assess ways in which major transformations related to human work, thought, and belief *(e.g., industrialization, the scientific revolution, the development of various religions and belief traditions)* have affected human society

The classical civilization of Greece, based on the foundations already laid by such ancient groups as the Egyptians, Phoenicians, Minoans, and Mycenaeans, reached some of the highest levels of man's achievements. Among the more important contributions of Greece were the Greek alphabet (derived from the Phoenician letters), which formed the basis for the Roman and our present-day alphabets; extensive trading and colonization (resulting in the spread of the Greek civilization); the love of sports with emphasis on a sound body (leading to the tradition of the Olympic games); the rise of independent, strong city-states; the complete contrast between independent, freedom-loving Athens with its practice of pure democracy (direct, personal, active participation in government by qualified citizens) and rigid, totalitarian, militaristic Sparta; important accomplishments in drama, epic and lyric poetry, fables, myths centered around the many gods and goddesses, science, astronomy, medicine, mathematics, philosophy, art, architecture, and history. Above all, classical Greek civilization understood and promoted the value of ideas, wisdom, curiosity, and the desire to learn as much as possible about the world.

Rome was the next and most successful of the ancient empires, building itself from one town that borrowed from its Etruscan neighbors into a worldwide empire stretching from the wilds of Scotland to the shores of the Middle East and Africa. Building on the principles of Hellenization, Rome imported and exported goods and customs, melding the production capabilities and the belief systems of all it conquered into a heterogeneous, yet distinctly Roman, civilization. Like no other empire before it, Rome conquered and absorbed those whom it conquered. Trade, religion, science, political structure—all these things were incorporated into the Roman Empire, benefiting the empire's citizens.

The ancient civilization of Rome lasted approximately 1,000 years, including the periods of republic and empire, although its influence on Europe and its history lasted much longer. The Romans spread and preserved the ideas of ancient Greece and other culture groups. The contributions and accomplishments of the Romans are numerous, but their greatest included language, engineering, building, law, government, roads, trade, and the Pax Romana.

The PAX ROMANA was a long period of peace spanning the first two centuries CE that enabled free travel and trade and spread people, cultures, goods, and ideas over a vast area of the known world. In the end, though, Rome grew too big to manage and its enemies too many to turn back. The sprawling nature of the empire made it too big to protect, and the heterogeneity dissolved into chaos and violence.

PAX ROMANA: a long period of peace enabling free travel and trade, spreading people, cultures, goods, and ideas over a vast area of the known world

The official end of the Roman Empire came when Germanic tribes took over and controlled most of Europe. The five major tribes were the Visigoths, Ostrogoths, Vandals, Saxons, and Franks. In later years, the Franks successfully stopped the invasion of southern Europe by Muslims by defeating them under the leadership of Charles Martel at the Battle of Tours in 732 CE. Thirty-six years later, in 768 CE, the grandson of Charles Martel became King of the Franks and is known throughout history as Charlemagne. Charlemagne was a man of war unique in his respect for and encouragement of learning. He made great efforts to rule fairly and to ensure just treatment for his people.

The nineteenth and twentieth centuries have seen rapid and extensive change on almost every front. Notably, there has been a growing concern for human rights and civil rights. The end of imperialism and the liberation of former colonies and territorial holdings have created new nations and have increased communication and respect among the nations of the world. Democracy has grown; Communism has risen and almost fallen.

Nations are no longer ruled by distant mother countries or their resident governors. But these freedoms have been won at great cost in human lives. Both political and individual freedoms have been won through struggle. Nationalism has risen and created new states, and nations have cultivated national identities. Yet these individual nations have been brought into contact and cooperation in ways never before experienced in human history. Scientific and technological developments, new thinking in religion and philosophy, and new political and economic realities have combined to create a global society that must now learn to define itself and to cooperate and respect diversity in new ways.

INDUSTRIAL REVOLUTION: the development of power-driven machinery (fueled by coal and steam) leading to the accelerated growth of industry

The **INDUSTRIAL REVOLUTION** saw the development of power-driven machinery (fueled by coal and steam) leading to the accelerated growth of industry. It began in Great Britain and spread elsewhere. Large factories replaced homes and small workshops as work centers. The lives of people changed drastically, and a largely agricultural society changed to an industrial one.

NATIONALISM: a belief in one's own nation, country, or people

During the eighteenth and the nineteenth centuries, nationalism emerged as a powerful force in Europe and elsewhere in the world.

NATIONALISM is a belief in one's own nation, country, or people. The people of the European nations began to think in terms of a nation of people who had similar beliefs, concerns, and needs. This was partly a reaction to a growing discontent with the autocratic governments of the day and also just a general realization that there was more to life than the individual. People could feel a part of something like their nation, making themselves more than just an insignificant soul struggling to survive.

In Western Europe, the period of empire and colonialism began. The industrialized nations seized and claimed parts of Africa and Asia in an effort to control and provide the raw materials needed to feed the industries and machines in the mother country.

Nationalism precipitated several changes in government, most notably in France. It also brought large groups of people together, as with the unifications of Germany and Italy. What it did not do, however, was provide sufficient outlets for this sudden rise in national fervor. In the 1700s and 1800s, European powers and peoples began looking to Africa and Asia in order to find colonies for rich sources of goods, trade, and cheap labor. Africa, especially, suffered at the hands of European imperialists bent on expanding their reach outside the borders of Europe. Asia suffered colonial expansion, most notably in India and Southeast Asia.

REFORMATION: the period of religious, political, and economic change in the 16th century

The **REFORMATION** had two phases: the Protestant Revolution and the Catholic Reformation. The Protestant Revolution came about because of religious, political, and economic reasons. The religious reasons stemmed from abuses in the Catholic Church, such as the sale of religious offices, indulgences, and dispensations as well as different theologies within the Church.

FEUDALISM was a system of loyalty and protection. The system of feudalism became a dominant feature of the economic and social system in Europe. The strong protected the weak, who returned the favor with farm labor, military service, and loyalty. Life was lived on a vast estate called a manor, owned by a nobleman and his family. It was a complete village supporting a few hundred people, mostly peasants. Improved tools and farming methods made life more bearable, although most people never left the manor or traveled from their village during their lifetime.

FEUDALISM: a system of loyalty and protection

Feudalism was the organization of people based on the ownership of land by a lord or other noble who allowed individuals known as peasants or serfs to farm the land and to keep a portion of what they grew. The lord or noble, in return for the serfs' loyalty, offered them his protection. In reality, the serf was considered to be owned by his lord, with few or no rights at all. The lord's sole obligation to the serfs was to protect them so that they could continue to work for him. This system lasted for many centuries; in Russia, until the 1860s.

The **BLACK DEATH** was a plague that killed over one-third of the total population of Europe. Those who survived and were skilled in any job or occupation were in demand, and many serfs or peasants found freedom and, for that time, a decidedly improved standard of living. Strong nation-states became powerful, and people developed a renewed interest in life and learning.

BLACK DEATH: a plague that killed over one-third of the total population of Europe

As trade routes developed and travel between cities became easier, trade led to specialization. Trade enabled a people to obtain the goods they desired in exchange for the goods they were able to produce. This, in turn, led to increased refinements of technique and the sharing of ideas. A new discovery or invention provided knowledge and technology that increased the ability to produce goods for trade. As each community learned the value of the goods it produced and improved its ability to produce the goods in greater quantity, industry was born.

The **AGRICULTURAL REVOLUTION** was initiated by the invention of the plow and led to a thorough transformation of human society by making large-scale agricultural production possible and facilitating the development of agrarian societies.

AGRICULTURAL REVOLUTION: initiated by the invention of the plow, it led to a thorough transformation of human society by making large-scale agricultural production possible and facilitating the development of agrarian societies

Numerous changes in lifestyle and thinking accompanied the development of stable agricultural communities. Rather than gathering a wide variety of plants as hunter-gatherers, agricultural communities became dependent on a limited number of plants or crops. Subsistence became vulnerable to the weather and dependent upon planting and harvesting times. Agriculture also required a great deal of physical labor and the development of a sense of discipline. Agricultural communities became sedentary or stable in terms of location. This made the construction of dwellings appropriate. These tended to be built relatively close together, creating villages or towns. Stable communities also freed people from the need to carry everything with them while moving from hunting ground to hunting ground. This facilitated the invention of larger, more complex tools. As new tools were envisioned and developed, it made sense to have some specialization within the society.

The Scientific Revolution and the Enlightenment were two of the most important movements in the history of civilization, resulting in a new sense of self-examination and a wider view of the world than ever before. The **SCIENTIFIC REVOLUTION** was, above all, a shift in focus from belief to evidence. Scientists and philosophers wanted to see proof, not just believe what other people told them.

SCIENTIFIC REVOLUTION: a shift in focus from belief to evidence

The Polish astronomer Nicolaus Copernicus began the Scientific Revolution. He crystallized a lifetime of observations into a book that was published about the time of his death in which he argued that the Sun, not the Earth, was the center of a solar system. This flew in the face of established doctrine. The Church still wielded tremendous power at this time, including the power to banish people or sentence them to prison or even death.

The Danish astronomer Tycho Brahe was the first to catalog his observations of the night sky. Building on Brahe's data, German scientist Johannes Kepler developed his famous Laws of Planetary Movement. Using Brahe's data, Kepler also confirmed Copernicus's observations and argument that the Earth revolved around the Sun.

The most famous defender of this idea was Galileo Galilei, an Italian scientist who conducted many famous experiments in the pursuit of science. He is most well known, however, for his defense of the heliocentric (sun-centered) idea.

Galileo died under house arrest, but his ideas did not die with him. Picking up the baton was an English scientist named Isaac Newton, who became perhaps the most famous scientist of all. He is known as the discoverer of gravity and a pioneering voice in the study of optics (light), calculus, and physics.

More than any other scientist, Newton argued for (and proved) the idea of a mechanistic view of the world: You can see how the world works and prove how the world works through observation; if you can see these things with your own eyes, they must be so. Up to this time, people believed what other people told them.

THE ENLIGHTENMENT: a period of intense self-study that focused on ethics and logic

THE ENLIGHTENMENT was a period of intense self-study that focused on ethics and logic. Scientists and philosophers questioned cherished truths and widely held beliefs in an attempt to discover how the world worked. "I think, therefore I am"

was one of the famous sayings of that day. It was uttered by Rene Descartes, a French scientist-philosopher whose dedication to logic and the rigid rules of observation were a blueprint for the thinkers who came after him.

One of the giants of the era was Scotland's David Hume. A pioneer of the doctrine of empiricism, Hume was also a prime believer in the value of skepticism; in other words, he was naturally suspicious of things that other people told him to be true and constantly set out to discover the truth for himself. The Enlightenment thinker who might be the most famous is Immanuel Kant of Germany. He was both a philosopher and a scientist, and he took a definite scientific view of the world.

Prevalent during the Enlightenment was the idea of the social contract, the belief that government exists because people want it to, and that the people agree to submit to the government as long as it protects them and does not encroach on their basic human rights.

The social contract was first made famous by the Frenchman Jean-Jacques Rousseau, but it was also adopted previously by England's John Locke and concurrently by America's Thomas Jefferson. John Locke was one of the most influential political writers of the seventeenth century and put great emphasis on human rights. He advanced the belief that when governments violate those rights, then people should rebel. He wrote the book *Two Treatises of Government* in 1690, which had tremendous influence on political thought in the American colonies and helped to shape the U.S. Constitution and Declaration of Independence.

The Age of Exploration actually had its beginnings centuries before exploration actually took place. The rise and spread of Islam in the seventh century and its subsequent control over the city of Jerusalem led to the European Crusades to free Jerusalem and the Holy Land from this control. Even though the Crusades were not a success, those who survived and returned to their homes and countries in Western Europe brought back with them new products such as silks, spices, perfumes, and new and different foods. These luxuries gave new meaning to colorless, drab, and dull lives.

New ideas, new inventions, and new methods also went to Western Europe with the returning Crusaders, and from these new influences came the intellectual stimulation that led to the period known as the Renaissance. The revival of interest in classical Greek art, architecture, literature, science, astronomy, and medicine; increased trade between Europe and Asia; and the invention of the printing press helped to push the spread of knowledge.

RENAISSANCE literally means "rebirth" and signaled a rekindling of interest in the glory of classical Greek and Roman civilizations. It was the period in human history marking the start of many ideas and innovations leading to our modern age. The Renaissance began in Italy, with many of its ideas starting in Florence, controlled by the infamous Medici family. Education, especially for some of the merchants, involved reading, writing, math, the study of law, Latin, and Greek.

RENAISSANCE: a period of renewed interest in the glory of ancient classical Greek and Roman civilizations

Most famous are the Renaissance artists, first and foremost, Leonardo da Vinci, Michelangelo, and Raphael, but also Titian, Donatello, and Rembrandt.

Literature was a focus as well during the Renaissance. Humanists Petrarch, Boccaccio, Erasmus, and Sir Thomas More advanced the idea of life here on Earth and the opportunities it could bring, rather than constantly focusing on heaven and its rewards. The monumental works of Shakespeare, Dante, and Cervantes found their origins in these ideas as well.

The Renaissance also changed music. No longer just a religious adjunct, music could be fun and composed for its own sake. Musicians worked for themselves, rather than exclusively for the churches and so could command good money for their work, increasing their prestige.

Science advanced considerably during the Renaissance, especially in the areas of physics and astronomy. Copernicus, Kepler, and Galileo led a Scientific Revolution in proving that Earth was round and certainly not perfect, a shattering revelation to those who clung to medieval ideals of a geocentric, Church-centered existence.

The Industrial Revolution resulted in great changes in human civilization and even greater opportunities for trade, increased production, and the exchange of ideas and knowledge in the eighteenth and nineteenth centuries.

The first phase of the Industrial Revolution (1750–1830) saw the mechanization of the textile industry; vast improvements in mining with the invention of the steam engine; and numerous improvements in transportation with the development and improvement of turnpikes, canals, and the railroad.

The second phase (1830–1910) resulted in vast improvements in a number of industries that had already been mechanized through such inventions as the Bessemer steel process and the invention of steamships. New industries arose as a result of the new technological advances such as photography, electricity, and chemical processes. New sources of power were harnessed and applied, including petroleum and hydroelectric power. Precision instruments were developed and engineering was launched. It was during this second phase that the Industrial Revolution spread to other European countries, Japan, and the United States.

The direct results of the Industrial Revolution, particularly as they affected industry, commerce, and agriculture, included:

- Enormous increase in productivity
- Huge increase in world trade
- Specialization and division of labor
- Standardization of parts and mass production

- Growth of giant business conglomerates and monopolies
- A new revolution in agriculture facilitated by the steam engine, machinery, chemical fertilizers, processing, canning, and refrigeration

The political results included:

- Growth of complex government
- Centralization of government, including regulatory administrative agencies
- Advantages to democratic development, including extension of franchise to the middle class and, later, to all elements of the population; mass education to meet the needs of an industrial society; and the development of media of public communication, including radio, television, and cheap newspapers
- Dangers to democracy including the risk of manipulation of the media of mass communication; facilitation of dictatorial centralization and totalitarian control; subordination of the legislative function to administrative directives; efforts to achieve uniformity and conformity; and social impersonalization

The economic results included:

- The conflict between free trade and low tariffs and protectionism
- The issue of free enterprise versus government regulation
- Struggles between labor and capital, including the trade union movement
- The rise of socialism
- The rise of Marxism

The social results included:

- Increase in population, especially in industrial centers
- Advances in science applied to agriculture, sanitation, and medicine
- Growth of great cities
- Disappearance of the difference between city dwellers and farmers
- Faster tempo of life and increased stress from the monotony of the work routine
- The emancipation of women
- The decline of religion
- Rise of scientific materialism

ROMANTICISM: the main literary and artistic development in the nineteenth century, which focused on emotion and the imagination

ROMANTICISM emphasized emotion and the imagination and was a direct reaction to the logic and reason stressed in the preceding Enlightenment. It was the main literary and artistic development in the nineteenth century. Famous Romantic authors include John Keats, William Wordsworth, Victor Hugo, and Johann Wolfgang von Goethe. The Industrial Revolution gave rise to the very famous realists Charles Dickens, Fyodor Dostoevsky, Leo Tolstoy, and Mark Twain who described life as they saw it. In Europe, Italy and Germany both united their peoples into their respective nations from many smaller states. There were revolutions in Austria and Hungary, the Franco-Prussian War, the dividing of Africa among the strong European nations, interference and intervention of Western nations in Asia, and the breakup of Turkish dominance in the Balkans.

In Africa, France, Great Britain, Italy, Portugal, Spain, Germany, and Belgium controlled the entire continent except for Liberia and Ethiopia. In Asia and the Pacific Islands, only China, Japan, and present-day Thailand kept their independence. The others were controlled by the strong European nations.

An additional reason for European imperialism was the harsh, urgent demand for the raw materials needed to fuel and feed the great Industrial Revolution. These resources were not available in the huge quantities so desperately needed, which necessitated (and rationalized) the partitioning of the continent of Africa and parts of Asia. In turn, these colonial areas purchased the finished manufactured goods.

Europe in the nineteenth century was a crowded place. Populations were growing, but resources were not. The peoples of many European countries were also agitating for rights as never before. To address these concerns, European powers began to look elsewhere for relief.

SKILL 7.3 Infer aspects of a society's social structure or group interactions based on information presented in an excerpt

Language is a primary way in which culture is passed between people of a society and from generation to generation. By examining the language used in an excerpt of dialogue or literature, one can make some general observations about a society and how its members interact.

Most languages have formal and informal ways of speaking and writing, for instance, in response to the relative social positions of the participants in a conversation. Examining how these forms are used in an excerpt can indicate the social standing of the speaker and the intended audience. Many languages use certain words to refer to other groups in a derogatory way. The use of these words can indicate cultural opinions and the social standing of various groups in relation to one another.

SKILL 7.4 Analyze ways in which social, cultural, geographic, and economic factors influence intergroup relations and the formation of values, beliefs, and attitudes

Socialization takes place among adults who change their environment and are expected to adopt new behaviors. Joining the military, for example, requires a different type of dress and behavior than civilian culture. Taking a new job or going to a new school are other examples of situations where adults must resocialize.

Two primary ways that socialization takes place are through **positive and negative sanctions**. Positive sanctions are rewards for appropriate or desirable behavior, and negative sanctions are punishments for inappropriate behavior. Recognition from peers and praise from a parent are examples of positive sanctions that reinforce expected social behaviors. Negative sanctions might include teasing by peers or punishment by a parent.

Sanctions can be either formal or informal. Public awards and prizes are ways a society formally reinforces positive behaviors. Laws that provide for punishment of specific infractions are formal negative sanctions.

The family is the primary social unit in most societies. It is through the family that children learn the most essential skills for functioning in their society, such as language and appropriate forms of interaction. The family is connected to ethnicity, which is partly defined by a person's heritage.

Sociologists have identified five different types of institutions around which societies are structured: family, education, government, religion, and economy.

Education is an important institution in a society because it allows for the formal passing on of a culture's collected knowledge. The institution of education is connected to the family because that is where a child's earliest education takes place. The United States has a public school system administered by the states that ensures a basic education and provides a common experience for most children.

A society's governmental institutions often embody its beliefs and values. Laws, for instance, reflect a society's values by enforcing its ideas of right and wrong. The structure of a society's government can reflect a society's ideals about the role of an individual. The form of democracy in the United State emphasizes the rights of the individual, but, in return, expects individuals to respect the rights of others, including those of ethnic and political minorities.

Religion frequently provides a society's primary beliefs and values and can be closely related to other social institutions. Many religions have definite teachings on the structure and importance of the family, for instance. The U.S. Constitution guarantees the free practice of religion.

A society's economic institutions define how an individual can contribute and receive economic reward. The United States has a capitalist economy driven by free enterprise. Although this system allows for economic advancement for many individuals, it can also produce areas of poverty and economic depression.

SKILL 7.5 Assess the social or economic implications of political views presented in an excerpt

A synthesis of information from multiple sources requires an understanding of the content chosen for the synthesis. Writers of syntheses will, no doubt, wish to incorporate their own ideas, particularly in any conclusions that are drawn, and show relationships to those of the chosen sources. That can only happen if writers have a firm grip on what others have said or written. The focus is not so much on documentary methods, but on techniques of critically examining and evaluating the ideas of others. Even so, careful documentation is extremely important in this type of presentation, particularly with regard to which particular edition is being read, in the case of written sources, or date and location of online sources. The phrase "downloaded from this Web site on that date" is useful. If the conversation, interview, or speech is live, the date, circumstances, and location must be indicated.

The purpose of a synthesis is to understand the work of others and to use that work in shaping a conclusion. Writers or speakers must clearly differentiate between the ideas that come from a source and their own ideas.

COMPETENCY 8

UNDERSTAND PRINCIPLES AND ASSUMPTIONS UNDERLYING HISTORICAL OR CONTEMPORARY ARGUMENTS, INTERPRETATIONS, EXPLANATIONS, OR DEVELOPMENTS

SKILL 8.1 Infer the political principles *(e.g., popular sovereignty, separation of powers, due process of the law)* illustrated in given situations or arguments

The **CONSTITUTION OF THE UNITED STATES** is the fundamental law of the republic. It is a precise, formal, written document of the extraordinary, or supreme, type of constitution. *The Constitution is the fundamental law and is distinguished from, and superior to, statutory law.*

CONSTITUTION OF THE UNITED STATES: the fundamental law of the republic

The Constitution binds the states in a governmental unity in everything that affects the welfare of all. At the same time, it recognizes the right of the people of each state to independence of action in matters that relate only to them. Since the U.S. Constitution is the law of the land, all other laws must conform to it.

The debates conducted during the Constitutional Convention of 1787 represent the issues and the arguments that led to the compromises in the final document. The debates also reflect the concerns of the Founding Fathers that the rights of the people be protected from abrogation by the government itself and the determination that no branch of government should have enough power to dominate the others. There is, therefore, a system of checks and balances.

The United States was founded with the idea that the people would have a large degree of autonomy and liberty. The famous maxim "no taxation without representation" was a rallying cry for the American Revolution, not only because the people did not want to suffer the increasingly oppressive series of taxes imposed on them by the British Parliament but also because the people could not in any way influence the lawmakers in Parliament in regard to those taxes. No American colonist had a seat in Parliament, and no American colonist could vote for members of Parliament.

One of the most famous words in the Declaration of Independence is liberty, the pursuit of which all people should be free to attempt. That idea, that people should be free to pursue their own courses, even to the extent of making their own mistakes, has dominated political thought in the 200-plus years of the United States.

Representation, the idea that people elect their lawmakers, was not a new idea. However, residents of other British colonies did not have these rights, and America was only a colony. What the Sons of Liberty and other revolutionaries were asking for was to stand on an equal footing with the mother country. Along with representation comes the idea that public matters can be deliberated and discussed, with, theoretically, everyone having a chance to voice their views.

Another key concept in the American ideal is equality. The consequence of this idea is that people can be governed only with their consent. The Great Britain that the American colonists knew was one of a stratified society, with social classes and privileges firmly in place. Not everyone was equal under the law or in the coffers. It was clear that the more money and power a person had, the easier it was for that person to avoid things like serving in the army and being charged with a crime. The goal of the Declaration of Independence and of the Constitution was to provide equality for all.

BILL OF RIGHTS: the first ten amendments to the U.S. Constitution

THE BILL OF RIGHTS consists of the first ten amendments to the U.S. Constitution. It deals with the following civil liberties and civil rights:

1. Freedom of religion
2. Right to bear arms
3. Security from the quartering of troops in homes
4. Right against unreasonable search and seizures
5. Right against self-incrimination
6. Right to trial by jury and right to legal counsel
7. Right to jury trial for civil actions
8. No cruel or unusual punishment
9. These rights shall not deny other rights the people enjoy
10. Powers not mentioned in the Constitution shall be retained by the states or the people

An amendment is a change or addition to the United States Constitution. To date, there are only twenty-seven amendments to the Constitution. An amendment may be used to cancel out a previous one, such as when the Eighteenth Amendment (1919), known as Prohibition, was canceled by the Twenty-First Amendment (1933). Amending the Constitution is not easy.

The Eleventh and Twelfth Amendments were ratified around the turn of the nineteenth century and, respectively, voided foreign suits against states and revised the method of presidential election. The Thirteenth, Fourteenth, and Fifteenth Amendments were passed in succession after the end of the Civil War. Slavery was outlawed by the Thirteenth Amendment. The Fourteenth and Fifteenth Amendments provided for equal protection and for voting rights, respectively, without consideration of skin color.

The first twentieth-century amendment was the Sixteenth, which provided for a federal income tax. The Seventeenth Amendment provided for direct election to the Senate. Until then, senators were elected by state legislatures, not directly elected by the people.

The Eighteenth Amendment prohibited the use or sale of alcohol across the country.

The long battle for voting rights for women ended in success with the passage of the Nineteenth Amendment.

The date for the beginning of terms for the president and the Congress was changed from March to January by the Twentieth Amendment.

The Twenty-First Amendment was the only instance in which an amendment was repealed—the Eighteenth Amendment.

The Twenty-Second Amendment limited the number of terms that a president could serve to two. Presidents since George Washington had followed the practice of not running for a third term. This changed in 1940 when Franklin D. Roosevelt ran for a third term. He was reelected again for a fourth term four years later. He did not live out his fourth term, but he did convince Congress and most of the state legislatures that some sort of term limit should be put in place.

The little-known Twenty-Third Amendment provided for representation of Washington, D.C., in the Electoral College. The Twenty-Fourth Amendment prohibited poll taxes, which people had to pay in order to vote.

The Twenty-Fifth Amendment established the order of presidential succession.

The Twenty-Sixth Amendment lowered the legal voting age from twenty-one to eighteen.

The Twenty-Seventh Amendment prohibited members of Congress from substantially raising their own salaries. This amendment was one of twelve originally proposed in the late eighteenth century. Ten of those twelve became the Bill of Rights, and one has yet to become law.

SKILL 8.2 Recognize assumptions *(e.g., regarding the nature of power relationships)* that inform the positions taken by political parties

Government ultimately began as a form of protection. A strong person, usually one of the best warriors or someone who had the support of many strong men, assumed command of a people, city, or land. The power to rule those people rested in his hands. Laws existed insofar as the pronouncements and decisions of the ruler and were not, in practice, written down, which led to inconsistency. Religious leaders had a strong hand in governing the lives of people, and, in many instances, the political leader was also the primary religious figure.

First in Greece, and then in Rome and other places throughout the world, the idea of government by more than one person emerged. Even though more people were involved, the purpose of government had not changed. These governments still existed to keep the peace and to protect their people from encroachments by both foreign and domestic forces.

Today, people are subject to laws made by many levels of government. Local governments, such as city and county, are allowed to pass ordinances covering certain local matters, such as property taxation, school districting, civil infractions, and business licensing. These local bodies have perhaps the least political power in the governmental hierarchy, but, being small and relatively accessible, they are often the level at which many citizens become directly involved with government. Funding for local governments often comes from property and sales taxes.

State governments in the United States are mainly patterned after the federal government, with an elected legislative body, a judicial system, and a governor who oversees the executive branch. Like the federal government, state governments derive their authority from **constitutions**. State legislation applies to all residents of that state, and local laws must conform. State government funding is frequently from state income tax and sales taxes.

The national, or federal, government of the United States derives its power from the U.S. Constitution and has three branches, the legislative, executive, and judicial. The federal government exists to make national policy, to legislate matters that affect the residents of all states, and to settle matters between states. The federal income tax is the primary source of federal funding. The U.S. Constitution also provides the federal government with the authority to make treaties and enter agreements with foreign countries. Although there is no authoritative international government, organizations such as the United Nations, the European Union, and other smaller groups exist to promote economic and political cooperation between nations.

POPULISM is the philosophy concerned with the common-sense needs of average people. Populism often finds expression as a reaction against perceived oppression of the average people by the wealthy elite in society. The prevalent claim of populist movements is that they will put the people first. Populist movements claim to represent the majority of the people and call them to stand up to institutions or practices that seem detrimental to their well-being.

POPULISM: the philosophy concerned with the common-sense needs of average people

Populism flourished in the late nineteenth and early twentieth centuries. Several political parties were formed out of this philosophy, including the Greenback Party, the Populist Party, the Farmer-Labor Party, the Single Tax movement of Henry George, the Share Our Wealth movement of Huey Long, the Progressive Party, and the Union Party.

The tremendous change that resulted from the industrial revolution led to a demand for reform that would control the power wielded by big corporations. The gap between the industrial moguls and the working people was growing. This disparity between rich and poor resulted in a public outcry for reform at the same time that there was an outcry for governmental reform that would end the political corruption and elitism of the day.

The reforms initiated by these leaders and the spirit of Progressivism were far-reaching. Many states enacted the initiative and the referendum. The adoption of the recall occurred in many states. Several states enacted legislation intended to undermine the power of political machines. On a national level, the two most significant political changes were the ratification of the Seventeenth Amendment, which required that all U.S. senators be chosen by popular election, and the ratification of the Nineteenth Amendment, which granted women the right to vote.

SKILL 8.3 **Analyze assumptions on which given U.S. policies** *(e.g., national health insurance, foreign relations)* **are based**

The purposes and aims of social policy are to improve human welfare and to meet basic human needs within the society. Social policy addresses basic human needs for the sustainability of the individual and the society. The concerns of social policy, then, include food, clean water, shelter, clothing, education, health, and social security. Social policy is part of public policy, determined by the city, the state, the nation, or the multinational organization responsible for human welfare in a particular region.

Because humans, both individually and in community, rely upon the environment to sustain human life, social and environmental policy must be mutually supportive.

Competition for control of areas of the Earth's surface is a common trait of human interaction throughout history. This competition has resulted in both destructive conflict and peaceful and productive cooperation. Societies and groups have sought control of regions of the Earth's surface for a wide variety of reasons, including religion, economics, politics, and administration. Numerous wars have been fought through the centuries for the control of territory for each of these reasons. At the same time, groups of people, even whole societies, have peacefully worked together to establish boundaries around regions or territories that served specific purposes in order to sustain the activities that support life and social organization.

Individuals and societies have divided the Earth's surface through conflict for a number of reasons:

1. The domination of peoples or societies, e.g., colonialism
2. The control of valuable resources, e.g., oil
3. The control of strategic routes, e.g., the Panama Canal

Conflicts can be spurred by religion, political ideology, national origin, language, or race. Conflicts can result from disagreement over how land, ocean, or natural resources will be developed, shared, and used. Conflicts have resulted from trade, migration, and settlement rights. Conflicts can occur between small groups of people, between cities, between nations, between religious groups, and between multinational alliances.

Today, the world is primarily divided by political and administrative interests into state sovereignties. The only area of the Earth's surface not defined by state or national sovereignty is Antarctica.

Alliances are developed among nations on the basis of political philosophy, economic concerns, cultural similarities, religious interests, or for military defense. Some of the most notable alliances today are:

- The United Nations
- The North Atlantic Treaty Organization
- The Caribbean Community
- The Common Market
- The Council of Arab Economic Unity
- The European Union

Large companies and multinational corporations also compete for control of natural resources for manufacturing, development, and distribution.

SKILL 8.4 Recognize concepts and ideas underlying alternative interpretations of past events

The world of social science research has never been so open to new possibilities. Where our predecessors worried about exceeding the limits of the available data, data access and data transfer, analytic routines, or computing power, today's social scientists can advance with confidence. Political science examines the theory of politics and how it behaves in countries and in international situations. Political science has certain varied aspects, including political history, political philosophy, economics, and international relations. All of these aspects can be used to examine both general and specific political issues today.

Political science examines the theory of politics and how it behaves in countries and in international situations. Political science has certain varied aspects, including political history, political philosophy, economics, and international relations. All of these aspects can be used to examine both general and specific political issues today.

For example, a general issue in the United States is the preponderance of the two-party system. American politics is full of political parties, but only the Democrats and Republicans get major funding and large slates of candidates for elections across the country. This is due in large part to the political history of the country, which has tended to discourage any other participation.

The ideologies of the Democratic and Republican parties could be considered wide enough to cover the views of most Americans. Other left- or right-wing parties have their adherents, but they rarely receive national attention.

Economics speaks to this in that it is very difficult for parties other than the two major ones to afford any kind of parity. The two big parties are so much a dichotomous part of American political thinking that any outside forces face an inherently uphill battle just to get dollars and cents to conduct campaigns.

In international relations, as well, the Democratic and Republican parties are familiar to leaders of and observers from other countries. The ideologies of these parties do encompass a wide range of political beliefs, many of which are common to the leaders of other countries as well.

A specific issue that can be examined in these terms is capital punishment.

The political history of the United States includes a long history of capital punishment presided over by both federal and state governments. The U.S. Supreme Court has, from time to time, found elements of capital punishment unconstitutional because of the Eighth Amendment prohibition of cruel and unusual punishment, but execution by lethal injection is used in many states.

In general, conservatives and liberals are on opposite sides of issues. A prime example of this is abortion. Generally speaking, liberals support a woman's right to choose to have an abortion, and conservatives oppose this, seeing abortion as the killing of an unborn child. Liberals see that right as a personal issue, one protected by the constitutional right to privacy. This right is guaranteed under a famous Supreme Court case *Roe v. Wade* (1973). Conservatives, on the other hand, see the case as bad law and dangerous precedent.

SKILL 8.5 Infer the economic principle *(e.g., supply and demand, redistribution of wealth)* upon which a given explanation is based

TRADITIONAL ECONOMY: an economy based on custom and usually present in less developed countries

LAISSEZ-FAIRE CAPITALISM: an economy based on the premise of no governmental intervention in the economy

MARKET ECONOMY: a free market system in which decisions regarding resource allocation, production, and consumption, as well as price levels and competition, are made by the collective actions of individuals or organizations seeking their own advantage

COMMAND ECONOMY: one based on government ownership of the means of production

MIXED ECONOMY: a combination of markets and planning, with the degree of each varying according to country

A **TRADITIONAL ECONOMY** is based on custom and usually exists in less developed countries. The people do things the way their ancestors did, and do not necessarily value technological advances. There is very little upward mobility in this type of economy. The model of capitalism is based on private ownership of the means of production and operates on the basis of free markets on both the input and output side. The free markets function to coordinate market activity and to achieve an efficient allocation of resources.

LAISSEZ-FAIRE CAPITALISM is based on the premise of no governmental intervention in the economy. The market will eliminate any unemployment or inflation that occurs. Government needs only to provide the framework for the functioning of the economy and to protect private property.

A **MARKET ECONOMY** is a free market system in which decisions regarding resource allocation, production, and consumption, as well as price levels and competition, are made by the collective actions of individuals or organizations seeking their own advantage. In all market economies, however, freedom of the markets is limited and governments intervene occasionally to encourage or dampen demand or to promote competition to thwart the emergence of monopolies.

A **COMMAND ECONOMY** is based on government ownership of the means of production and the use of planning to take the place of the market. Instead of the market determining the output mix and the allocation of resources, the bureaucracy fulfills this role by determining the output mix and establishing production target for the enterprises, which are publicly owned.

A **MIXED ECONOMY** uses a combination of markets and planning, with the degree of each varying according to country. Most countries today have mixed economies

The scarcity of resources is the basis for the existence of economics. **ECONOMICS** is defined as a study of how scarce resources are allocated to satisfy unlimited wants. Resources refer to the four factors of production: labor, capital, land, and entrepreneurs. Labor refers to anyone who sells his ability to produce goods and services. Capital is anything that is manufactured to be used in the production process. **Land** refers to the land itself and everything occurring naturally on it, like oil, minerals, and lumber. **Entrepreneurship** is the ability of an individual to combine the three inputs with his own talents to produce a viable good or service. The entrepreneur takes the risk and experiences the losses or profits.

ECONOMICS: a study of how scarce resources are allocated to satisfy unlimited wants

The fact that the supply of these resources is finite means that society cannot have as much of everything as it wants. There is a constraint on production and consumption and on the kinds of goods and services that can be produced and consumed.

SCARCITY means that choices have to be made. If society decides to produce more of one good, this means that there are fewer resources available for the production of other goods. Assume a society can produce two goods, good X and good Y. The society uses resources in the production of each good. If producing one unit of good X uses an amount of resources needed to produce three units of good Y, then producing one more unit of good X results of a decrease of three units of good Y. In effect, one unit of good X costs three units of good Y. This cost is referred to as **OPPORTUNITY COST**—the value of the sacrificed alternative.

SCARCITY: fewer resources available for the production of goods

OPPORTUNITY COST: the value of the sacrificed alternative

Opportunity cost does not refer just to production. Your opportunity cost of studying with this guide is the value of what you are not doing because you are studying, whether it is watching TV, spending time with family or working. Every choice has an opportunity cost.

If wants were limited or if resources were unlimited, then the concepts of choice and opportunity cost would not exist and neither would the field of economics. There would be enough resources to satisfy the wants of consumers, businesses, and governments. The allocation of resources wouldn't be a problem. Society could have more of both good X and good Y without having to give up anything. There would be no opportunity cost. But this is not the situation that societies are faced with.

Economic systems refer to the arrangements a society has devised to answer what are known as the Three Questions:

1. *What goods to produce?*
2. *How to produce the goods?*
3. *For whom are the goods being produced or how is the allocation of the output determined?*

How do producers know which goods consumers want? Consumers buy the goods they want and vote with their spending. A desirable good, one that consumers want, earns profits. A good that incurs losses is a good that society does not want and therefore does not purchase.

The opposite of the market economy is called the **centrally planned economy**. This used to be called Communism, even though the term is not correct in a strict Marxist sense. In a planned economy, the means of production are publicly owned with little, if any, private ownership. Instead of the Three Questions being solved by markets, these economies have a planning authority that makes the decisions in place of markets. The planning authority decides what will be produced and how. Since most planned economies direct resources into the production of capital and military goods, little remains for consumer goods and the result is chronic shortage. Price functions as an accounting measure and does not reflect scarcity. The former Soviet Union and most of the former Eastern Bloc countries were planned economies of this sort.

Between the two extremes is market socialism. This is a mixed economic system that uses markets and planning. Planning is usually used to direct resources at the upper levels of the economy, with markets being used to determine prices of consumer goods and wages. This kind of economic system answers the three questions with planning and markets. Today, Vietnam and Laos have market socialist economies.

COMPETENCY 9

UNDERSTAND DIFFERENT PERSPECTIVES AND PRIORITIES UNDERLYING HISTORICAL OR CONTEMPORARY ARGUMENTS, INTERPRETATIONS, EXPLANATIONS, OR DEVELOPMENTS

SKILL 9.1 Identify the values *(e.g., a commitment to democratic institutions)* implicit in given political, economic, social, or religious points of view

Social and political movements are group actions in which large informal groups, persons, and organizations focus on specific social or political issues and work to either implement or undo something. Social movements originated in England and North America during the first decades of the nineteenth century. Several types of social and political movements are often identified and distinguished by key factors:

- Scope
  - Reform movements aim to change some norms
  - Radical movements seek to change some value systems
- Type of change
  - Innovation movements attempt to introduce new norms or values
  - Conservative movements want to preserve existing norms or values

- Target group
  - Group-focused movements attempt to affect either society in general or specific groups
  - Individual-focused movements seek to transform individuals
- Method of action
  - Peaceful movements
  - Violent movements
- Time
  - Old movements – prior to the 20th century
  - New movements – since the second half of the 20th century
- Range
  - Global movements
  - Local movements

The role of religion in political movements or as a basis for political action can be quite varied, depending upon the religion and the exigencies of the time. In general, one's interpretation of how people should act within the political sphere will take one of three approaches:

1. Withdrawal from politics (and sometimes from the world)
2. Quietism
3. Activism

Religion has always been a factor in life in the United States Many early settlers came to America in search of religious freedom. Religion, particularly Christianity, was an essential element of the value and belief structure shared by the Founding Fathers. However, the Constitution encourages a separation of church and state. Religion is a basis for the actions of believers, no matter which religion is practiced or embraced. Because religion determines values and ethics, it influences individuals and groups to work to change conditions that are perceived to be wrong.

The **FIRST GREAT AWAKENING** was a religious movement within American Protestantism in the 1730s and 1740s. This was primarily a movement among Puritans seeking a return to strict interpretation of morality and values and emphasizing the importance and power of personal religious or spiritual experience. Many historians believe the First Great Awakening unified the people of the original colonies and supported the independence of the colonists.

FIRST GREAT AWAKENING: a religious movement within American Protestantism in the 1730s and 1740s

SECOND GREAT AWAKENING (THE GREAT REVIVAL): a broad movement within American Protestantism that led to several kinds of activities that were distinguished by region and denomination

The **SECOND GREAT AWAKENING (THE GREAT REVIVAL)** was a broad movement within American Protestantism that led to several kinds of activities that were distinguished by region and denomination. In general terms, the Second Great Awakening, which began in the 1820s, was a time of recognition that "awakened religion" must weed out sin on both a personal and a social level. It inspired a wave of social activism. In New England, the Congregationalists established missionary societies to evangelize the West. Publication and education societies arose, most notably, the American Bible Society. This social activism gave rise to the temperance movement, prison reform efforts, and help for the handicapped and mentally ill. This period was particularly notable for the abolition movement.

THIRD GREAT AWAKENING (THE MISSIONARY AWAKENING): gave rise to the Social Gospel Movement; this period (1858 to 1908) resulted in a massive growth in membership of all major Protestant denominations through their missionary activities

The **THIRD GREAT AWAKENING (THE MISSIONARY AWAKENING)** gave rise to the Social Gospel Movement. This period (1858 to 1908) resulted in a massive growth in membership of all major Protestant denominations through their missionary activities. This movement was partly a response to claims that the Bible was fallible. Many churches attempted to reconcile or change biblical teaching to fit scientific theories and discoveries. Colleges associated with Protestant churches began to appear rapidly throughout the nation.

In terms of social and political movements, the Third Great Awakening was the most expansive and profound. Coinciding with many changes in production and labor, it won battles against child labor and stopped the exploitation of women in factories. Compulsory elementary education for children came from this movement, as did the establishment of a set workday. Much was also done to protect and rescue children from abandonment and abuse, to improve the care of the sick, to prohibit the use of alcohol and tobacco, and to address numerous other social ills.

SKILL 9.2 Recognize the motives, beliefs, and interests that inform differing political, economic, social, or religious points of view

(e.g., arguments related to equity, equality, and comparisons between groups or nations)

Americans had good reason to fear the emergence of political parties. They had witnessed how parties worked in Great Britain. Parties, called "factions" in Britain, were made up of a few people who schemed to win favors from the government. They were more interested in their own personal profit and advantage than in the public good. Thus, the new American leaders were very interested in keeping factions from forming. It was, ironically, disagreements between Thomas Jefferson and Alexander Hamilton, two of George Washington's chief advisors, that spurred the formation of the first political parties in the early United States.

By the time Washington retired from office in 1797, the new political parties had come to play an important role in choosing his successor. Each party put up its own candidates for office. The election of 1796 was the first one in which political parties played a role; a role that, for better or worse, continues to this day. By the beginning of the 1800s, the Federalist Party, led by Alexander Hamilton, torn by internal divisions, began suffering a decline. The election in 1800 of Thomas Jefferson, Hamilton's bitter rival, as president, and Hamilton's subsequent death in an 1804 duel with Aaron Burr, marked the beginning of the collapse of the Federalist Party.

By 1816, after losing a string of important elections (Jefferson was reelected in 1804, and James Madison, a Democratic Republican, was elected in 1808), the Federalist Party ceased to be an effective political force and soon passed off the national stage.

By the late 1820s, new political parties had grown up. The **Democratic-Republican Party**, or simply the **Republican Party**, had been the major party for many years, but differences within it about the direction the country was headed in caused a split after 1824. Those who favored strong national growth took the name **Whigs** after a similar party in Great Britain and united around President John Quincy Adams. Many business people in the Northeast as well as some wealthy planters in the South supported it.

By the time of the Civil War (1861–1865), the present form of the major political parties had been formed.

Those who favored slower growth and were more oriented toward the common worker and small farmer went on to form the new Democratic Party led by Andrew Jackson, who won the presidency in 1828. It is the forerunner of today's party of the same name.

In the mid-1850s, the slavery issue was beginning to heat up, and, in 1854, those opposed to slavery, the Whigs, and some Northern Democrats opposed to slavery united to form the Republican Party. Before the Civil War, the Democratic Party was more heavily represented in the South and was thus largely pro-slavery.

INDIAN REMOVAL ACT OF 1830: authorized the government to negotiate treaties with Native Americans to provide land west of the Mississippi River in exchange for lands east of the river

The **INDIAN REMOVAL ACT OF 1830** authorized the government to negotiate treaties with Native Americans to provide land west of the Mississippi River in exchange for lands east of the river. This policy resulted in the relocation of more than 100,000 Native Americans. Theoretically, the treaties were expected to result in voluntary relocation of the native people. In fact, however, many of the native chiefs were forced to sign the treaties.

EMANCIPATION PROCLAMATION: written by Abraham Lincoln and put into effect January 1,1863; this proclamation ended slavery *only* in areas controlled by the Confederacy

The **EMANCIPATION PROCLAMATION** was written by Abraham Lincoln and took effect January 1,1863. It ended slavery *only* in areas controlled by the Confederacy. The Thirteenth Amendment in 1865 finally ended all slavery in the United States, but these measures did not erase the centuries of racial prejudices among whites that held blacks to be inferior in intelligence and morality. These prejudices, along with fear of economic competition from newly freed slaves, led to a series of state laws that permitted or required businesses, landlords, school boards, and others to physically segregate blacks and whites in their everyday lives.

BLACK CODES: strict laws proposed by some southern states during the Reconstruction period that sought to recreate the conditions of prewar servitude

The **BLACK CODES** were strict laws proposed by some southern states during the Reconstruction period that sought, essentially, to recreate the conditions of prewar servitude. Under these codes, blacks were to remain subservient to their white employers and were subject to fines and beatings if they failed to work. Freedmen, newly freed slaves, were afforded some civil rights protection during the Reconstruction period; however, beginning around 1876, so called **Redeemer governments** began to take office in southern states after the removal of federal troops that had supported Reconstruction goals. The Redeemer state legislatures began passing segregation laws that came to be known as Jim Crow laws.

JIM CROW LAWS: segregation laws passed by southern Redeemer state legislatures

The **JIM CROW LAWS** varied from state to state, but the most significant of them required separate school systems and libraries for blacks and whites and separate ticket windows, waiting rooms, and seating areas on trains and, later, other public transportation. Restaurant owners were permitted (or, sometimes, required) to provide separate entrances and tables and counters for blacks and whites in order that the two races would not see one another while dining. Public parks and playgrounds were constructed for each race. Landlords were not allowed to mix black and white tenants in apartment houses in some states.

The Jim Crow laws were given credibility in 1896 when the Supreme Court handed down its decision in the case *Plessy v. Ferguson*. In 1890, Louisiana passed a law requiring separate train cars for blacks and whites. To challenge this law, in 1892, Homer Plessy, a man who had a black great-grandparent and so was considered legally "black" in that state, purchased a ticket in the white section and took his seat. Upon informing the conductor that he was black, he was told to move to the black car. He refused and was arrested. His case was eventually elevated to the Supreme Court. The Court ruled against Plessy, thereby ensuring that the Jim Crow laws would continue to proliferate and be enforced. The Court held that segregating races was not unconstitutional as long as the facilities for each were identical. This became known as the **"separate but equal"** principle.

Legal segregation was a part of life for generations of Americans until the separate but equal fallacy was finally challenged in 1954 in another Supreme Court case, *Brown v. Board of Education*. This case arose when a Topeka, Kansas, man attempted to enroll his third-grade daughter in a segregated, white elementary school and was refused. In the Court decision, the policy of maintaining separate schools was found to be inherently unequal and unconstitutional.

Even with the new legal interpretation, some states refused to integrate their schools. In Virginia, the state closed some schools rather than integrate them. In

Arkansas, Governor Orville Faubus mobilized the National Guard to prevent the integration of Little Rock High School. President Eisenhower sent federal troops to enforce the integration.

Opposition to Jim Crow laws became an important part of the civil rights movement led by Martin Luther King, Jr., and others. Congress finally acted in 1964.

The **CIVIL RIGHTS ACT OF 1964** ended legal segregation in the United States; however, some forms of *de facto* segregation continued to exist, particularly in the area of housing.

CIVIL RIGHTS ACT OF 1964: ended legal segregation in the United States; however, some forms of de facto segregation continued to exist, particularly in the area of housing

Paralleling the development of segregation legislation in the mid-nineteenth century was the appearance of organized groups opposed to any integration of blacks into white society. The most notable of these was the Ku Klux Klan.

First organized in the Reconstruction South, the **KU KLUX KLAN** was a loosely formed group made up mainly of former Confederate soldiers who opposed the Reconstruction government and espoused a doctrine of white supremacy. KKK members intimidated and sometimes killed their proclaimed enemies. The first KKK was never completely organized, despite having nominal leadership. In 1871, President Ulysses S. Grant took action to use federal troops to halt the activities of the KKK and actively prosecuted them in federal court. Klan activity waned, and the organization disappeared.

KU KLUX KLAN: a group made up mainly of former Confederate soldiers who opposed the Reconstruction government and espoused a doctrine of white supremacy

Foreign Policy

In the early years of the American nation, three primary ideas determined U.S. foreign policy:

1. Isolationism: The Founding Fathers and the earliest Americans (after the Revolution) tended to believe that the United States had been created and destined for a unique role as what was called the "City on the Hill." They understood personal and religious freedom as a unique blessing given by God to the people of the nation. Although many believed that the nation would grow, this expectation did not extend to efforts to plant colonies in other parts of the world.
2. "No Entangling Alliances": George Washington's farewell address had initially espoused the intention of avoiding permanent alliances in any part of the world. This was echoed in Jefferson's inaugural address. In fact, when James Madison led the nation into the War of 1812, he refrained from entering into an alliance with France, which was also at war with England at the time.

3. **Nationalism:** The American experience had created a profound wariness of any encroachment into the Western Hemisphere by European countries. The Monroe Doctrine was a clear warning: no new colonies in the Americas.

Until the middle of the nineteenth century, U.S. foreign policy and expansionism were essentially restricted to the North American continent. America had shown no interest in establishing colonies in other lands. Specifically, the United States had stayed out of the rush to claim African territories. The variety of imperialism that found expression under the administrations of William McKinley and Theodore Roosevelt was not precisely comparable to the imperialistic goals of European nations.

There was a type of idealism in American foreign policy that sought to use military power in territories and other lands only in the interest of human rights and of spreading democratic principles. Much of the concern and involvement in Central and South America and the Caribbean was to link the two coasts of the nation and to protect the American economy from European encroachment.

Other foreign policy landmarks include the political, economic, and geographic significance of the Panama Canal; the **OPEN DOOR POLICY** with China; Theodore Roosevelt's "Big Stick" Diplomacy; William Howard Taft's "Dollar" Diplomacy; and Woodrow Wilson's Moral Diplomacy.

OPEN DOOR POLICY: refers to maintaining equal commercial and industrial rights for the people of all countries in a particular territory

The **OPEN DOOR POLICY** refers to maintaining equal commercial and industrial rights for the people of all countries in a particular territory. The Open Door policy generally refers to China, but it has also been used in application to the Congo basin. The policy was first suggested by the United States, but its basis is a clause of the treaties made with China after the Opium War (1829–1842). The essential purpose of the policy was to permit equal access to trade for all nations having treaties with China, while protecting the integrity of the Chinese empire. This policy was in effect from about 1900 until the end of the 1945. After the Second World War, China was recognized as a sovereign state.

BIG STICK DIPLOMACY: describes President Theodore Roosevelt's policy of the United States assuming international police power in the Western Hemisphere

BIG STICK DIPLOMACY is a term adopted from an African proverb, "speak softly and carry a big stick," used to describe President Theodore Roosevelt's policy of the United States assuming international police power in the Western Hemisphere. The phrase implied the power to retaliate if necessary. The intention was to safeguard American economic interests in Latin America. The policy led to the expansion of the U.S. Navy and to greater involvement in world affairs. Should any nation in the Western Hemisphere become vulnerable to European control because of political or economic instability, the United States had the right and obligation to intervene.

DOLLAR DIPLOMACY: describes U.S. efforts under President Howard Taft to extend its foreign policy goals in Latin America and East Asia via economic power

DOLLAR DIPLOMACY describes U.S. efforts under President Howard Taft to extend its foreign policy goals in Latin America and East Asia via economic power. The

designation derives from Taft's claim that U.S. interests in Latin America had changed from "warlike and political" to "peaceful and economic." Taft justified this policy in terms of protecting the Panama Canal. The practice of Dollar Diplomacy was from time to time anything but peaceful, particularly in Nicaragua. When revolts or revolutions occurred, the United States sent troops to resolve the situation. Immediately upon resolution, bankers were sent in to loan money to the new regimes.

Wilson repudiated the Dollar Diplomacy approach to foreign policy within weeks of his inauguration. Wilson's **MORAL DIPLOMACY** became the model for American foreign policy to this day. Wilson envisioned a federation of democratic nations, believing that democracy and representative government were the foundation stones of world stability. Specifically, he saw Great Britain and the United States as the champions of self-government and the promoters of world peace. Wilson's beliefs and actions set in motion an American foreign policy that was dedicated to the interests of all humanity rather than merely American national interests. Wilson promoted the power of free trade and international commerce as the keys to enlarging the national economy into world markets as a means of acquiring a voice in world events.

MORAL DIPLOMACY: American foreign policy dedicated to the interests of all humanity, not just U.S. interests

President Wilson's foreign policy was based on three elements:

1. Maintaining a combat-ready military to meet the needs of the nation
2. Promoting democracy abroad
3. Improving the U.S. economy through international trade

Wilson believed that democratic states would be less inclined to threaten U.S. interests.

Domestic Affairs

REGIONALISM can be defined as the political division of an area into partially autonomous regions or as loyalty to the interests of a particular region.

REGIONALISM: the political division of an area into partially autonomous regions or as loyalty to the interests of a particular region

SECTIONALISM is generally defined as excessive devotion to local interests and customs.

SECTIONALISM: excessive devotion to local interests and customs

Closely allied to the Second Great Awakening was the temperance movement. This movement to end the sale and consumption of alcohol arose from religious beliefs, from the violence many women and children experienced from heavy drinkers, and from the effect of alcohol consumption on the workforce. The Society for the Promotion of Temperance was organized in Boston in 1826.

Other social issues were also addressed. It was during this period that efforts were made to transform the prison system and its emphasis on punishment into a penitentiary system that attempted rehabilitation. It was also during this period that Dorothea Dix led a struggle in the North and the South to establish hospitals for the insane. A group of women emerged in the 1840s that was the beginning of the first women's rights movement in the nation's history.

UTOPIANISM: the dream or the desire to create the perfect society

UTOPIANISM is the dream or the desire to create the perfect society. However, by the nineteenth century few believed this was possible. One of the major "causes" of utopianism is the desire for moral clarity. Against the backdrop of the efforts of a young nation to define itself and to ensure the rights and freedoms of its citizens, and within the context of the Second Great Awakening, it becomes quite easy to see how the reform movements, the religious sentiment, and the gathering national storm would lead to the desire to create the perfect society.

The industrial boom produced several very wealthy and powerful captains of industry (Andrew Carnegie, John D. Rockefeller, Jay Gould, J. P. Morgan, and Philip Armour). Although they were envied and respected for their business acumen and success, they were also condemned for their exploitation of workers and questionable business practices and were feared because of their power. Critics labeled these men Robber Barons.

While these captains of industry were becoming wealthy, the average worker enjoyed some increase in the standard of living. Most workers were required to put in long hours in dangerous conditions doing monotonous work for low wages. Most were not able to afford to participate in the new comforts and forms of entertainment that were becoming available. Farmers believed they were also being exploited by the bankers, suppliers, and the railroads. This produced enough instability to fuel several recessions and two severe depressions.

One result of industrialization was the growth of the Labor Movement. There were numerous boycotts and strikes, which often became violent when the police or the militia was called in to stop them. Labor and farmer organizations became a political force. Industrialization also brought an influx of immigrants from Asia (particularly Chinese and Japanese) and from Europe (particularly European Jews, the Irish, and Russians).

High rates of immigration led to the creation of communities in various cities like "Little Russia" or "Little Italy." Industrialization also led to an overwhelming growth of cities as workers moved closer to their places of work. The economy was booming, but that economy was based on basic needs and luxury goods for which there was to be only limited demand, especially during times of economic recession or depression.

The reforms initiated by these leaders and the spirit of Progressivism were far-reaching. Politically, many states enacted the initiative and the referendum. The adoption of the recall occurred in many states. Several states enacted legislation that would undermine the power of political machines. On a national level, the two most significant political changes were the ratification of the Seventeenth Amendment, which required that all U.S. senators be chosen by popular election, and the ratification of the Nineteenth Amendment, which granted women the right to vote.

Within the context of fear of radicalism, rampant racism, and efforts to repress various groups within the population, it is not surprising that several groups were formed to protect the civil rights and liberties guaranteed to all citizens by the U.S. Constitution.

The American Civil Liberties Union was formed in 1920. It was originally an outgrowth of the American Union against Militarism, which had opposed American involvement in the First World War and provided legal advice and assistance for conscientious objectors and for those who were being prosecuted under the Espionage Act of 1917 and the Sedition Act of 1918. With the name change, there was attention to additional concerns and activities. The agency began to try to protect immigrants threatened with deportation and citizens threatened with prosecution for communist activities and agendas. They also opposed efforts to repress the Industrial Workers of the World and other labor unions.

The **NATIONAL ASSOCIATION FOR THE ADVANCEMENT OF COLORED PEOPLE (NAACP)** was founded in 1909 to assist African Americans. In the early years, the work of the organization focused on working through the courts to overturn Jim Crow statutes that legalized racial discrimination. The group organized voters to oppose Woodrow Wilson's efforts to weave racial segregation into federal government policy. Between the world wars, much energy was devoted to stopping the lynching of blacks throughout the country.

NATIONAL ASSOCIATION FOR THE ADVANCEMENT OF COLORED PEOPLE (NAACP): an organization founded in 1909 to assist African Americans

The **ANTI-DEFAMATION LEAGUE** was created in 1913 to stop discrimination against Jewish people. Its charter states, "Its ultimate purpose is to secure justice and fair treatment to all citizens alike and to put an end forever to unjust and unfair discrimination against and ridicule of any sect or body of citizens." The organization has historically opposed all groups considered anti-Semitic and/or racist. This has included the Ku Klux Klan, the Nazis, and a variety of others.

THE ANTI-DEFAMATION LEAGUE: created in 1913 to stop discrimination against Jewish people

The end of the First World War and the decade of the 1920s saw tremendous changes in the United States, signifying the beginning of its development into its modern form. The shift from farm to city life was occurring at a rapid pace. Social changes and problems were occurring so quickly that it was extremely difficult and perplexing for many Americans to adjust to them. Politically, the Eighteenth Amendment to the Constitution, the so-called Prohibition amendment, prohibited selling alcoholic beverages throughout the United States, resulting in problems affecting all aspects of society.

The passage of the Nineteenth Amendment gave to women the right to vote in all elections. The decade of the 1920s also showed a marked change in roles and opportunities for women, with more and more of them seeking and finding careers outside the home. Women began to think of themselves as the equals of men instead of as simply housewives and mothers.

The influence of the automobile, the entertainment industry, and the rejection of prewar morals and values resulted in the fast-paced Roaring Twenties. There were significant effects on events leading to the Depression-era 1930s and another world war. Many Americans greatly desired the prewar life and supported political policies and candidates that would end government's strong role and adopt a policy of isolating the country from world affairs.

Changes in American Immigration Policy in the 1920s

Immigration has played a crucial role in the growth and settlement of the United States from the start. With a large interior territory to fill and ample opportunity, the United States encouraged immigration throughout most of the nineteenth century, maintaining an almost completely open policy. Famines in Ireland and Germany in the 1840s resulted in over 3.5 million immigrants from these two countries alone between the years of 1830 and 1860.

Following the Civil War, rapid expansion in rail transportation brought the interior states within easy reach of new immigrants who still came primarily from Western Europe and entered the United States on the East Coast. As immigration increased, several states adopted individual immigration laws, and, in 1875, the U.S. Supreme Court declared immigration a federal matter.

Following a huge surge in European immigration in 1880, the United States began to regulate immigration, first by passing a tax on new immigrants, then by instituting literacy requirements and barring those with mental or physical illness. Even with these new limits in place, immigration remained relatively open in the United States for those from European countries and increased steadily until the First World War.

With much of Europe left in ruins after the First World War, immigration to the United States exploded. In 1920 and 1921, some 800,000 new immigrants arrived. The United States responded to this sudden shift in the makeup of new immigrants with a quota system, first enacted by Congress in 1921. This system limited immigration in proportion to the ethnic groups that were already settled in the United States according to previous census records. This national origins policy was extended and further defined by Congress in 1924.

This policy remained the official policy of the United States for the next forty years. Occasional challenges to the law from nonwhite immigrants reaffirmed that the intention of the policy was to limit immigration primarily to white, Western Europeans, who the government felt were most likely to assimilate into American culture. Strict limitations on Chinese immigration were extended throughout the period and was not relaxed until 1940.

In 1965, Congress overhauled immigration policy, removing the quotas and replacing them with a preference-based system. Now, immigrants reuniting with family members and those with special skills or education were given preference. As a result, immigration from Asian and African countries began to increase. The forty-year legacy of the 1920s immigration restrictions had a direct and dramatic impact on the makeup of modern American society.

The Great Depression and the New Deal

The 1929 Stock Market Crash was the powerful event that is generally interpreted as the beginning of the Great Depression in America. Although the crash of the stock market was unexpected, it was not without identifiable causes. The 1920s had been a decade of social and economic growth and hope. The other factor contributing to the Great Depression was the economic condition of Europe. The United States was lending money to European nations to rebuild following the war. Many of these countries used this money to purchase U.S. food and manufactured goods, but they were not able to pay off their debts. And while the United States was providing money, food, and goods to Europe, it was not willing to buy European goods. Trade barriers were enacted to maintain a favorable trade balance.

Several other factors are cited by some scholars as contributing to the Great Depression. First, in 1929, the Federal Reserve increased interest rates. Second, some believe that as interest rates rose and the stock market began to decline, people began to hoard money.

In September 1929, stock prices began to slip somewhat, yet people remained optimistic. On Monday, October 21, prices began to fall quickly. The volume of stocks traded was so high that the tickers were unable to keep up. Investors were frightened and they started selling very quickly. This caused further collapse. For the next two days prices stabilized somewhat. On Black Thursday, October 24, prices plummeted again. By this time investors had lost confidence. On Friday and Saturday an attempt to stop the crash was made by some leading bankers. But on Monday, October 28, prices began to fall again, declining by 13 percent in one day. The next day, Black Tuesday, October 29, saw 16.4 million shares traded. Stock prices fell so far that stocks could not sell at any price.

Unemployment quickly reached 25 percent nationwide. People who were thrown out of their homes moved into makeshift homes of cardboard, and tents.

NEW DEAL: a massive program of innovation and experimentation to try to bring the Depression to an end

SECURITIES AND EXCHANGE COMMISSION: created to regulate dangerous speculative practices on Wall Street

SOCIAL SECURITY ACT OF 1935: established pensions for the aged and infirm and a system of unemployment insurance

Many of the steps taken by the Roosevelt administration have had far-reaching effects. They alleviated the economic disaster of the Great Depression, they enacted controls that would mitigate the risk of another stock market crash, and they provided greater security for workers. The nation's economy, however, did not fully recover until the United States entered the Second World War.

DUST BOWL: severe and prolonged drought in the Great Plains and a series of devastating dust storms that occurred in the 1930s and resulted in economic ruin and dramatic ecological change

With unabashed reference to President Hoover, these communities were called "Hoovervilles." Families stood in bread lines, rural workers left the dust bowl of the plains to search for work in California, and banks failed. More than 100,000 businesses failed between 1929 and 1932. The despair that swept the nation left an indelible scar on all who endured the Depression.

Hoover's bid for reelection in 1932 failed. Franklin D. Roosevelt won the White House with his promise to the American people of a **NEW DEAL**, a series of economic programs passed by Congress during FDR's first term. Upon assuming the office, Roosevelt and his advisers immediately launched a massive program of innovation and experimentation to try to bring the Depression to an end and to get the nation back on track. Congress gave the president unprecedented power to act to save the nation. During the next eight years, the most extensive and broadly based legislation in the nation's history was enacted. The legislation was intended to accomplish three goals: relief, recovery, and reform.

The first step in the New Deal was to relieve suffering. This was accomplished through a number of job-creation projects. The second step, the recovery aspect, was to stimulate the economy. The third step was to create social and economic change through innovative legislation.

To provide economic stability and prevent another crash, Congress passed the Glass-Steagall Act, which separated banking and investing.

The **SECURITIES AND EXCHANGE COMMISSION** was created to regulate dangerous speculative practices on Wall Street.

The **SOCIAL SECURITY ACT OF 1935** established pensions for the aged and infirm and a system of unemployment insurance.

The was caused by severe and prolonged drought in the Great Plains in the 1930s and previous reliance on inappropriate farming techniques. It resulted in destruction, economic ruin for many, and dramatic ecological change.

Fifteen percent of Oklahoma's population left. Because so many of the migrants were from Oklahoma, all migrants came to be called Okies no matter where they came from. Estimates of the number of people displaced by this disaster range from 300,000 or 400,000 to 2.5 million.

Several important major events or actions in the history of organized labor occured during this decade:

- The Davis-Bacon Act provided that employees of contractors and subcontractors on public construction should be paid the prevailing wages (1931).
- The Anti-Injunction Act prohibited federal injunctions in most labor disputes (1932).

- Wisconsin created the first unemployment insurance act in the country (1932).
- The Wagner-Peyser Act created the United States Employment Service within the Department of Labor (1933).
- The Wagner Act (National Labor Relations Act) established a legal basis for unions, set collective bargaining as a matter of national policy required by the law, provided for secret-ballot elections for choosing unions, and protected union members from employer intimidation and coercion. This law was later amended by the Taft-Hartley Act (1947) and by the Landrum Griffin Act (1959).
- The Social Security Act was approved (1935).
- The Committee for Industrial Organization (CIO) was formed within the American Federation of Labor (AFL) to carry unionism to the industrial sector (1935).
- The United Rubber Workers staged the first sit-down strike (1936).
- The United Auto Workers used the sit-down strike against General Motors (1936).
- The Public Contracts Act (Walsh-Healey Act) of 1936 established labor standards, including minimum wages, overtime pay, child and convict labor provisions, and safety standards on federal contracts.
- The Fair Labor Standards Act created a $0.25 minimum wage and stipulated time-and-a-half pay for hours over 40 per week.
- The CIO became the Congress of Industrial Organizations.

After the Second World War

Because of unstable economic conditions and political unrest, harsh dictatorships arose in several countries, especially where there was no history of experience in democratic government. Countries such as Germany, Japan, and Italy began to aggressively expand their borders and acquire additional territory.

In all, fifty-nine nations became embroiled in the Second World War, which began September 1, 1939, and ended September 2, 1945. These dates include both the European and Pacific theaters of war. The horrible and tragic result of this second global conflagration was more deaths and more destruction than in any other armed conflict. It completely uprooted and displaced millions of people. The end of the war brought renewed power struggles, especially in Europe and China, with many Eastern European nations as well as China coming under complete control and domination of the Communists, supported and backed by the Soviet Union. With the development and two-time deployment of an atomic bomb against two Japanese cities, the world found itself in the nuclear age. The peace settlement established the United Nations.

Upon the death of FDR in April 1945, Harry S. Truman became president. He is credited with some of the most important decisions in history. When Japan refused to surrender, Truman authorized the dropping of atomic bombs on Japanese cities dedicated to war support: Hiroshima and Nagasaki. He took to the Congress a twenty-point plan that came to be known as the **Fair Deal**. It included expansion of Social Security, a full-employment program, public housing and slum clearance, and a permanent Fair Employment Practices Act. Respected now, Truman left office very unpopular and was forced to quit the 1952 presidential race.

The Truman Doctrine provided support for Greece and Turkey when they were threatened by the Soviet Union. The Marshall Plan (named after Secretary of State George Marshall) stimulated amazing economic recovery for Western Europe. Truman participated in the negotiations that resulted in the formation of the North Atlantic Treaty Organization (NATO).

He and his administration believed it necessary to support South Korea when it was threatened by the Communist government of North Korea. But he contained American involvement in Korea so as not to risk conflict with China or Russia.

Dwight David Eisenhower succeeded Truman. Eisenhower obtained a truce in Korea in 1953 and worked during his two terms to mitigate the tension of the cold war. When Stalin died, he was able to negotiate a peace treaty with Russia that neutralized Austria. His domestic policy was a middle road. He continued most of the programs introduced under both the New Deal and the Fair Deal. When desegregation of schools began, he sent troops to Little Rock, Arkansas, to enforce desegregation of the schools. He ordered the complete desegregation of the military. During his administration, the Department of Health, Education, and Welfare was established, and the National Aeronautics and Space Administration (**NASA**) was formed. He started the massive project of building our nation's highways.

John F. Kennedy is widely remembered for his inaugural address in which he said, "Ask not what your country can do for you, ask what you can do for your country." His campaign pledge was to get America moving again. During his brief presidency, his tax cuts helped to create the longest period of continuous expansion in the country since the Second World War. He wanted the United States to again take up the mission as the first country committed to the revolution of human rights. Through the **Alliance for Progress** and the **Peace Corps**, with hope and idealism, the nation reached out to assist developing nations. After some reluctance, Kennedy became involved in the cause of equal rights for all Americans, and he drafted new civil rights legislation. He also drafted plans for a broad attack on the systemic problems of privation and poverty. In foreign policy, he presided over the debacle of the **Bay of Pigs** and the successful brinksmanship of the **Cuban Missile Crisis**.

Lyndon B. Johnson assumed the presidency after the assassination of Kennedy in November 1963. His vision for America was called the **GREAT SOCIETY**. He won support in Congress for the largest group of legislative programs in the history of the nation. He defined the Great Society as "a place where the meaning of man's life matches the marvels of man's labor." The legislation enacted during his administration included: an attack on disease, urban renewal, Medicare, aid to education, conservation and beautification, development of economically depressed areas, a war on poverty, voting rights for all, and control of crime and delinquency. Johnson managed an unpopular military action in Vietnam, which led him to drop out of the 1968 presidential race.

GREAT SOCIETY: Lyndon B. Johnson's vision for America

Richard Nixon inherited racial unrest and the Vietnam War, from which he extracted the U.S. military. His administration is probably best known for improved relations with both China and the USSR. His major domestic achievements were the appointment of conservative justices to the Supreme Court, new anticrime legislation, a broad environmental program, revenue-sharing legislation, and ending the draft. Probably the highlight of the foreign policy of President Nixon, after the end of the Vietnam War and withdrawal of troops, was his 1972 trip to China. When the Communists gained control of China in 1949, the policy of the U.S. government was refusal to recognize the Communist government. It regarded as the legitimate government of China to be that of Chiang Kai-shek, exiled on the island of Taiwan. Nixon resigned in disgrace in August 1974 because of the Watergate scandal.

Gerald Ford was the first vice president selected under the Twenty-Fifth Amendment. The challenges that faced his administration were a depressed economy, inflation, energy shortages, and the need to champion world peace. Once inflation slowed and recession was the major economic problem, he instituted measures that would stimulate the economy. He tried to reduce the role of the federal government. He reduced business taxes and lessened the controls on business. His international focus was on preventing a major war in the Middle East. He negotiated with Russia limitations on nuclear weapons.

Jimmy Carter's presidency was defined by the Iranian hostage crisis. Iran's Ayatollah Khomeini's extreme hatred for the United States was the result of the 1953 overthrow of Iran's Mossadegh government, sponsored by the CIA. To make matters worse, the CIA proceeded to train the Shah's ruthless secret police force. So, when the terminally ill, exiled Shah was allowed into the United States for medical treatment, a fanatical mob, supported and encouraged by Khomeini, stormed into the U.S. embassy, taking fifty-three Americans prisoners

Jimmy Carter, elected in 1976, strove to make the government "competent and compassionate" in response to the American people and their expectations. The economic situation of the nation was intensely difficult when he took office. Although significant progress was made by his administration in creating jobs and decreasing the budget deficit, inflation and interest rates were nearly at record highs. There were several notable achievements during his administration: establishment of a national energy policy to deal with the energy shortage, decontrolling petroleum prices to stimulate production, civil service reform that improved governmental efficiency, deregulation of the trucking and airline industries, the creation of the Department of Education, the framework for peace in the Middle East, the establishment of diplomatic relations with China, and a Strategic Arms

Limitation Agreement with the Soviet Union. He expanded the national park system, supported the Social Security system, and appointed a record number of women and minorities to government jobs.

Ronald Reagan introduced an innovative program that came to be known as the Reagan Revolution. The goal of this program was to reduce the reliance of the American people upon government. The Reagan administration restored the hope and enthusiasm of the nation. His legislative accomplishments include economic growth stimulation, curbing inflation, increasing employment, and strengthening the national defense. He won congressional support for a complete overhaul of the income tax code in 1986. By the time he left office, there was prosperity in peacetime. His foreign policy was "peace through strength." Reagan nominated Sandra Day O'Connor as the first female justice on the Supreme Court.

George H. W. Bush, the next president, was committed to "traditional American values" and to making America a "kinder and gentler nation." During the Reagan administration, Bush held responsibility for antidrug programs and federal deregulation. When the cold war ended and the Soviet Union broke apart, he supported the rise of democracy, but he took a position of restraint toward the new nations. Bush also dealt with defense of the Panama Canal and Iraq's invasion of Kuwait, which led to the first Gulf War, known as Desert Storm. He failed to win reelection in 1992, partly because of a strong third-party challenge by businessman Ross Perot and partly because he reneged on his oft-repeated promise of "no new taxes."

William Jefferson Clinton led the country during one of its more peaceful and economically sound times. His two-term presidency included the lowest unemployment and inflation rates in decades, decreased crime rates, and increased home ownership. While Clinton was unable to establish health care reform, he attained a budget surplus, sought an end to "big government," and was involved in issues such as education improvement legislation, handgun sales restrictions, and increased environmental protection. Due to implications of personal misconduct, Clinton was the second U.S. president to be impeached by the House of Representatives. Apologizing to the nation for his indiscretions, he was tried in the Senate and found not guilty. Despite the incident, Clinton's popular approval ratings as president remained high through the rest of his presidency.

Since 1941 a number of antidiscrimination laws have been passed by the Congress. These acts have protected the civil rights of several groups of Americans. These laws include

- Fair Employment Act of 1941
- Civil Rights Act of 1964

- Immigration and Nationality Services Act of 1965
- Voting Rights Act of 1965
- Civil Rights Act of 1968
- Age Discrimination in Employment Act of 1967
- Age Discrimination Act of 1975
- Pregnancy Discrimination Act of 1978
- Americans with Disabilities Act of 1990
- Civil Rights Act of 1991
- Employment Nondiscrimination Act

Minority rights encompasses two ideas: the first is the normal individual rights of members of ethnic, racial, class, religious, or sexual minorities; the second is collective rights of minority groups. Various civil rights movements have sought to guarantee that the individual's rights are not denied on the basis of being part of a minority group. The effects of these movements may be seen in guarantees of minority representation and affirmative action quotas.

Immigrant rights movements have provided for employment and housing rights and have discouraged abuse of immigrants through hate crimes. In some states, immigrant rights movements have led to bilingual education and public information access.

Another group movement to obtain equal rights is the lesbian, gay, bisexual, and transgender social movement. This movement seeks equal housing, freedom from social and employment discrimination, and equal recognition of relationships under the law.

The women's rights movement is concerned with the freedoms of women as differentiated from broader ideas of human rights. These issues are generally different from those that affect men and boys because of biological conditions or social constructs.

SKILL 9.3 Analyze multiple perspectives within U.S. society regarding major historical and contemporary issues

Analyzing an event or issue from multiple perspectives involves seeking out sources that advocate or express those perspectives and comparing them. Listening to the speeches of Martin Luther King, Jr., provides insight to the perspective of one group of people concerning the issue of civil rights in the United States in the 1950s and 1960s. Public statements of George Wallace, governor of Alabama, who was opposed to desegregation, provide another perspective from the same time period. Looking at the legislation that was proposed at the time and how it came into effect offers a window into the political thinking of the day.

Comparing these perspectives on the matter of civil rights provides information on the key issues that each group was concerned about and gives a fuller picture of the societal changes that were occurring at that time. Analysis of any social event, issue, problem, or phenomenon requires that various perspectives be taken into account in this way.

ETHNOCENTRISM: the belief that one's own culture is the central and usually superior culture

Humans are social animals who naturally form groups based on familial, cultural, and national lines. Conflicts and differences of opinion are natural between these groups. One source of differing views among groups is ethnocentrism. **ETHNOCENTRISM**, as the word suggests, is the belief that one's own culture is the central and usually superior culture. An ethnocentric view usually considers different practices in other cultures as inferior or even "savage."

Psychologists have suggested that ethnocentrism is a naturally occurring attitude. People are generally most comfortable among other people who share their same upbringing, language, and cultural background and are likely to judge other cultural behaviors as alien or foreign.

Historical developments are likely to affect different groups in different ways, some positively and some negatively. These effects can strengthen the ties that individuals feel to the group to which they belong and solidify differences between groups.

SKILL 9.4 Recognize the values or priorities implicit in given public policy positions

PUBLIC POLICY: the official stance of a government on an issue and a primary source for studying a society's dominant political beliefs

PUBLIC POLICY is the official stance of a government on an issue and is a primary source for studying a society's dominant political beliefs. It can also give insight into a society's cultural values.

The Social Security system of the United States is a program where current workers are required to give a portion of their earnings to the system, which is then paid out to eligible recipients who have reached a certain age and have stopped working. The underlying value behind the system is that society should continue to care for those who can no longer work and that people should be able to retire from working at a certain age.

SKILL 9.5 Analyze the perceptions or opinions of observers or participants from different cultures regarding a given world event or development

Two of the most notable conversions to democracy in the twentieth century were India and Japan. India, one of the most ancient of societies, was most recently a colony of Great Britain. Thanks largely to the efforts of Mohandas Gandhi and other activists, India achieved its independence by the mid-twentieth century. The country became a democracy, with a president at the head of a representative government. The change in political theory, however, did not mean an end to the internal strife that India has seemingly always felt. At the heart of the country's political identity is a religious dichotomy—a struggle between Muslims and Hindus. This religious conflict has continued for many hundreds of years and has certainly not been diminished by the fact that the Indian people can elect their own leaders.

Another huge conflict in the Indian part of the world is with Pakistan over the Kashmir region. The entire area was known as India at various times under various masters, including Great Britain. But the country was partitioned when it was freed, and the result has been a dangerous dispute over political borders that has resulted in much loss of life and the procurement of atomic weapons by both sides. Another main source of internal strife in India is an economic one. India is the world's second most populous country, and a huge number of these people have few or no resources of their own. A half-century of representative government has not made much of a difference in the economic prosperity of these people.

Japan, by contrast, has suffered much less religious and political strife since becoming a democracy after its defeat in the Second World War. The occupying American army instituted a new constitution, which provided for a representative government and also led efforts to rebuild the country. The result has been, for the most part, an economic powerhouse that is now one of the world's strongest economies. Japan has had its periods of economic weakness, of course, but has bounced back each time stronger than ever.

Political divisions on the Korean Peninsula and in Southeast Asia have created intense internal strife of a mostly economic and political nature. North Korea, an authoritarian state, has lived in relative isolation from the rest of the world and has suffered economically from that isolation. South Korea became a democracy after the end of Japanese occupation after the Second World War and has prospered economically, although the specter of war with North Korea has loomed large for more than fifty years. The two countries did, in fact, go to war in 1950.

The resulting three-year conflict involved forces from a handful of other countries, most noticeably China and the United States, and resulted in a stalemate. The most notable facet of life in either Korean country is the idea that another war could begin tomorrow. Indeed, an intensely patrolled area known as the Demilitarized Zone (DMZ) serves as the border between the countries. North Korea has become more and more public in its militancy in recent years.

Southeast Asia has also seen its share of strife since the 1950s, most notably in Vietnam, which was once two countries, a mirror image of Korea—a Communist North and democratic South. Those two countries began fighting not long after the end of the Second World War, and Communist China and the United States again became involved. The war consumed the two countries and most of their neighbors for many years, resulting in horrible economic and social conditions throughout the region for many years afterward. North Vietnam ended up winning the war, absorbing all of South Vietnam into one country, which continues under an authoritarian government, but it is a bit of an economic powerhouse these days.

COMPETENCY 10

UNDERSTANDING AND APPLYING SKILLS, PRINCIPLES, AND PROCEDURES ASSOCIATED WITH INQUIRY, PROBLEM SOLVING, AND DECISION MAKING IN HISTORY AND THE SOCIAL SCIENCES

SKILL 10.1 Analyze a description of research results to identify additional unanswered questions or to determine potential problems in research methodology

A clearly presented description of research results will spell out what question the researchers hoped to answer. Analyzing research results includes comparing the information given as it relates to this initial question. One must also consider the methods used to gather the data and whether they truly measure what the researchers claim they do.

A research project that sets out to measure the effect of a change in average temperature on the feeding habits of birds, for instance, should use appropriate measurements, such as weather observations and observations of the birds in question. Measuring rainfall would not be an appropriate method for this research because it is not related to the primary area of research. If, during the experiment, it appeared that rainfall may be affecting the research, a researcher should design another experiment to investigate this additional question.

SKILL 10.2 Determine the relevance or sufficiency of given information for supporting or refuting a point of view

Making a decision based on a set of given information requires a careful interpretation of the information to decide the strength of the evidence supplied and what it means.

Making a decision based on a set of given information requires a careful interpretation of the information to decide the strength of the evidence supplied and what it means.

A chart showing that the number of people of foreign birth living in the United States has increased annually over the last ten years might allow one to make conclusions about population growth and changes in the relative sizes of ethnic groups in the United States. The chart would not give information about the reason the number of foreign-born citizens increased or address matters of immigration status. Conclusions in these areas would be invalid based on this information.

In the court of public opinion, the newspaper or radio offers politicians a fairly easy way to give information for supporting or refuting a point of view. Television changed all that with its visual record of events. The proliferation of cable and satellite television channels has made a variety of venues available to lawmakers and others who wish to share their opinions. The Internet offers a vast, heterogeneous world of opportunities. Internet opportunities include not just news Web sites, but personal Web sites and blogs, public opinion pieces that may or may not be true.

The key thing to remember about information on Web pages is that they might not have undergone the sort of scrutiny as comparable efforts released by major media outlets (newspapers, radio, and television) are subjected to. Those media formats have built-in safety officers called editors who will verify information before it is released to the world. In contrast, to blog all you need is access to a Web-enabled computer and time to write a column. Bloggers routinely do not use editors or run their copy by anyone else before publishing it—they have lower standards of professionalism overall and need to be regarded as somewhat suspect.

Public officials will hire one or more people, a whole department, or an entire business to conduct public relations. A public relations person or firm will have an overreaching goal of satisfying the lawmaker, who provides compensation, and will gladly write press releases, arrange media events (like tours of schools or soup kitchens), and, basically, do everything else to keep promote that person. This includes making the lawmaker's position on important issues known to the public. Gauging what constituents think about the issues of the day is an important consideration for political candidates at reelection time.

SKILL 10.3 Assess the reliability of sources of information cited in historical or contemporary accounts or arguments, and determine whether specific conclusions or generalizations are supported by verifiable evidence

Primary Sources

- Documents that reflect the immediate, everyday concerns of people: memoranda, bills, deeds, charters, newspaper reports, pamphlets, graffiti, popular writings, journals or diaries, records of decision-making bodies, letters, receipts, snapshots, etc.
- Theoretical writings reflecting care and consideration in composition and an attempt to convince or persuade. The topic will generally be deeper and have more pervasive values than is the case with "immediate" documents. These may include newspaper or magazine editorials, sermons, political speeches, philosophical writings, etc.
- Narrative accounts of events, ideas, trends, etc., written with intention by a contemporary of the events described.
- Statistical data, although statistics may be misleading.
- Literature and nonverbal materials, novels, stories, poetry, and essays from the period; and coins, archaeological artifacts, and art produced during the period.

Guidelines for the use of primary resources

- Be certain that you understand how language was used at the time of writing and that you understand the context in which the item was produced
- Do not read history blindly; but be certain that you understand both explicit and implicit references in the material
- Read the entire text you are reviewing; do not simply extract a few sentences to read
- Although anthologies of materials may help you to identify primary source materials, the full, original text should be consulted

Secondary Sources

- Books written on the basis of primary materials about the period of time
- Books written on the basis of primary materials about people who played a major role in the events under consideration
- Books and articles written on the basis of primary materials about the culture, the social norms, the language, and the values of the period
- Quotations from primary sources
- Statistical data on the period
- The conclusions and inferences of other historians
- Multiple interpretations of the ethos of the time

Guidelines for the use of secondary sources

- Do not rely upon only a single secondary source
- Check facts and interpretations against primary sources whenever possible
- Do not accept the conclusions of other historians uncritically
- Place greatest reliance on secondary sources created by the best and most respected scholars
- Do not use the inferences of other scholars as if they were facts
- Ensure that you recognize any bias that writers bring to their interpretation of history
- Understand the primary point of the book as a basis for evaluating the relevance of the material presented in it to your topic

SKILL 10.4 **Evaluate the appropriateness of specific sources** *(e.g., atlas, periodical guide, economic database)* **to meet given information needs** *(e.g., the distribution of natural resources in a given region, the political philosophy of a presidential candidate)*

See Skills 11.2 and 11.3

Libraries of all sorts are valuable when conducting research, and almost all have digitalized search systems to assist in finding information on almost any subject. Even so, the Internet, with powerful search engines like Google readily available, can retrieve information that does not exist in libraries or, if it does exist, is much more difficult to retrieve.

Encyclopedias are reference materials that appear in book or electronic form. Encyclopedias can be considered general or specific. They are good first sources of information.

Almanacs provide statistical information on various topics. Typically, these references are rather specific. They often cover a specific period of time. One famous example is the *Farmer's Almanac*. This annual publication summarizes, among many other things, weather conditions for the previous year.

Bibliographies contain references for further research. Bibliographies are usually organized topically. They help point people to the in-depth resources they will need for a complete view of a topic.

Conducting a research project once involved the use of punch cards, microfiche, and other manual means of storing the data in a retrievable fashion. No more. With high-powered computers available to anyone who chooses to conduct research, the organizing of the data in a retrievable fashion has been revolutionized. Creating multilevel folders, copying and pasting into the folders, making ongoing additions to the bibliography at the very time that a source is consulted, and using search-and-find functions make this stage of the research process go much faster with less frustration and a decrease in the likelihood that important data might be overlooked.

Serious research requires high-level analytical skills when it comes to processing and interpreting data. A degree in statistics or at least a graduate-level concentration is very useful. However, a team approach to a research project will include a statistician in addition to those members who are knowledgeable in the social sciences.

The world of social science research has never been so open to new possibilities. Where our predecessors were unable to tread for fear of exceeding the limits of the available data, data access and transfer, analytic routines, or computing power; today's social scientists can advance with confidence. Advances in technology can free social scientists from the tyranny of simplification that has often hampered attempts to grasp the complexity of the world.

SKILL 10.5 Distinguish between unsupported and informed expressions of opinion

Consider the statements, "The sky is blue," or "the sky looks like rain." One is a fact, and the other is an opinion. This is because one is readily provable by objective empirical data, but the other is a subjective evaluation based upon personal bias. This means that facts are things that can be proved by the usual means of study and experimentation. We can look and see the color of the sky. Since the shade we are observing is expressed as the color blue and is an accepted norm, the observation that the sky is blue is therefore a fact. (Of course, this depends on other external factors such as time and weather conditions).

This brings us to our next idea: that it looks like rain. This is a subjective observation in that one individual's perception will differ from another. What looks like rain to one person will not necessarily look like that to another.

This is an important concept to understand since much of what actually is studied in political science is, in reality, simply the opinions of various political theorists and philosophers. The truth of their individual philosophies is demonstrated by how well they (if and when they have been tried) work in the so-called real world.

The question thus remains as to how to differentiate fact from opinion. The best and only way is to ask if what is being stated can be proved from other sources, by other methods, or by the simple process of reasoning.

Primary sources are the basic materials that provide the raw data and information for the historian. Secondary sources are the works that contain the explications of, and judgments on, this primary material.

—Norman F. Cantor and Richard I. Schneider, How to Study History *(Harlan Davidson, Inc., 1967), 23–24.*

Historians use primary sources from the actual time they are studying whenever possible. Ancient Greek records of interaction with Egypt, letters from an Egyptian ruler to regional governors, and inscriptions from the Fourteenth Egyptian Dynasty are all primary sources created at or near the actual time being studied. Letters from a nineteenth-century Egyptologist would not be considered as primary sources because they were created thousands of years after the fact and may not actually be about the subject being studied.

The resources used in the study of history can be divided into two major groups: primary sources and secondary sources. Primary sources are works and records that were created during the period being studied or immediately after it. Secondary sources are works written significantly after the period being studied and based upon primary sources.

COMPETENCY 11

UNDERSTAND AND INTERPRET VISUAL REPRESENTATIONS OF HISTORICAL AND SOCIAL SCIENTIFIC INFORMATION

SKILL 11.1 Translate written or graphic information from one form to the other *(e.g., selecting an appropriate graphic representation of information from an article on historical changes in global population)*

See Skill 11.3

To apply information obtained from graphs, one must understand the two major reasons why graphs are used:

1. To present a model or theory visually in order to show how two or more variables interrelate.
2. To present real world data visually in order to show how two or more variables interrelate.

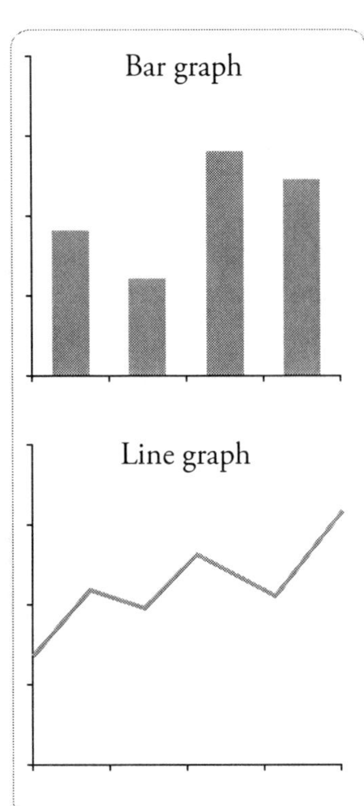

Most often used are those known as bar graphs and line graphs. Graphs themselves are most useful when one wishes to demonstrate the sequential increase or decrease of a variable or to show specific correlations between two or more variables in a given circumstance.

Most common is the bar graph because it is easy to see and understand a visual showing the difference in a given set of variables. However, it is limited in that it cannot really show the actual proportional increase or decrease of each given variable to each other. In order to show a decrease, a bar graph must show the "bar" under the starting line, thus removing the ability to really show how the various different variables would relate to each other.

Thus, in order to accomplish this, one must use a line graph. Line graphs can be of two types, linear or nonlinear. A linear line graph uses a series of straight lines; a nonlinear line graph uses a curved line. Though the lines can be either straight or curved, all of the lines are called curves.

A line graph uses a number line or axis. The numbers are generally placed in order, equal distances from one another, and the number line is used to represent a number, degree, or some such other variable at an appropriate point on the line. Two lines are used and intersect at a specific point. They are referred to as the

X-axis and the Y-axis. The Y-axis is a vertical line, and the X-axis is a horizontal line. Together they form a **coordinate system**. The difference between a point on the line of the X-axis and the Y-axis is called the **slope** of the line, or the change in the value on the vertical axis divided by the change in the value on the horizontal axis. The Y-axis number is called the rise and the X-axis number is called the **run**, thus the equation for slope is:

$$\text{SLOPE} = \frac{\text{RISE (Change in value on the vertical axis)}}{\text{RUN (Change in value on the horizontal axis)}}$$

The slope tells the amount of increase or decrease of a given specific variable. When using two or more variables, one can plot the amount of difference between them in any given situation. This makes presenting information on a line graph more involved. It also makes it more informative and accurate than a simple bar graph. Knowledge of the term slope and what it is and how it is measured helps us to describe verbally the pictures we are seeing visually. For example, if a curve is said to have a slope of "zero," you should picture a flat line. If a curve has a slope of "one," you should picture a rising line that makes a 45-degree angle with the horizontal and vertical axis lines.

The preceding examples are of *linear* (straight line) curves. With *nonlinear* curves (the ones that really do curve), the slope of the curve is constantly changing, so we must then understand that the slope of the nonlinear curved line will be at a specific point. How is this done? The slope of a nonlinear curve is determined by the slope of a straight line that intersects the curve at that specific point.

In all graphs, an upward sloping line represents a direct relationship between the two variables. A downward slope represents an inverse relationship between the two variables. In reading any graph, one must always be very careful to understand what is being measured, what can be deduced, and what cannot be deduced from the given graph.

To use charts correctly, one should remember the reasons one uses graphs. The general ideas are similar. It is usually a question as to which, a graph or chart, is more capable of adequately portraying the information one wants to illustrate. One can see the difference between them and realize that in many ways graphs and charts are interrelated. One of the most common types, because it is easiest to read and understand, even for the layperson, is the **piechart**.

You see piecharts used often, especially when one is trying to illustrate the differences in percentages among various items or when one is demonstrating the divisions of a whole.

SKILL 11.2 Relate information provided in graphic representations *(e.g., regarding population or economic trends)* to public policy decisions

Suppose you are preparing for a presentation on the Civil War, and you intend to focus on causes, an issue that has often been debated. If you were examining the matter of slavery as a cause, a graph of the increase in the number of slaves by area of the country for the previous one hundred years would be very useful in the discussion. If you were focusing on the economic conditions that were driving the politics of the age, graphs of GDP, distribution of wealth geographically and individually, and relationship of wealth to ownership of slaves would be useful.

If you were discussing the war in Iraq, detailed maps with geopolitical elements would help clarify not only the day-to-day happenings, but also the historical features that led up to it. A map showing the number of oil fields and where they are situated with regard to the various political factions and charts and showing the output of those fields historically would be useful.

If you are teaching the history of space travel, photos of the most famous astronauts will add interest to the discussion. Graphs showing the growth of the industry and charts showing discoveries and their relationship to the lives of everyday Americans would be helpful.

DEMOGRAPHY: the branch of statistics most concerned with the social well-being of people

DEMOGRAPHY is the branch of statistics most concerned with the social well-being of people. Demographic tables may include:

- Analysis of the population on the basis of age, parentage, physical condition, race, occupation, and civil position; giving the actual size and the density of each separate area
- Changes in the population as a result of birth, marriage, and death
- Statistics on population movements and their effects and their relations to given economic, social, and political conditions
- Statistics of crime, illegitimacy, and suicide
- Levels of education and economic and social statistics

Such information is also similar to vital statistics and, as such, is indispensable in studying social trends and making important legislative, economic, and social decisions. Such demographic information is gathered from census, registrar reports, and the like; and, by state laws, such information, especially the vital kind, is kept by physicians, attorneys, funeral directors, member of the clergy, and similar professional people. In the United States, such demographic information is compiled, kept, and published by the Public Health Service of the United States Department of Health, Education, and Welfare.

The most important element of this information is the so-called rate, which customarily represents the average of births and deaths for a unit of 1,000 population over a given calendar year. These general rates are called crude rates, which are then subdivided into sex, color, age, occupation, locality, etc. They are then known as refined rates.

In examining statistics and the sources of statistical data, one must also be aware of the methods of statistical information gathering. For instance, there are many good sources of raw statistical data. Books such as *The Statistical Abstract of the United States*, published by the United States Chamber of Commerce; *The World Fact Book*, published by the Central Intelligence Agency; or *The Monthly Labor Review*, published by the United States Department of Labor, are excellent examples that contain much raw data.

Many such yearbooks and the like on various topics are readily available from any library or from the government itself. However, knowing how that data and information was gathered is at least as important as the figures themselves.

In collecting any such statistical information and data, care and adequate precautions must always be taken in order to ensure that the knowledge obtained is complete and accurate. It is also important to be aware of just how much data is necessary to collect in order to establish the idea that is attempting to be formulated.

One important idea to understand is that statistics usually deal with a specific model, hypothesis, or theory that someone is attempting to support. One should be aware that a theory can never actually be proved correct; it can only really be corroborated. (Corroboration meaning that the data presented is more consistent with this theory than with any other theory, so it makes sense to use this theory.) One should also be aware that what is known as correlation (the joint movement of various data points) does not infer causation (the change in one of those data points caused the other data points to change). It is important that one take these aspects into account in order that one can be in a better position to appreciate what the collected data is really saying

Once collected, data must then be arranged, tabulated, and presented to permit ready and meaningful analysis and interpretation. Often, tables, charts, or graphs will be used to present the information in a concise, easy-to-see manner with the information sometimes presented in raw numerical order as well. Tests of reliability are performed by researchers who bear in mind the manner in which the data has been collected and the inherent biases of any artificially created model to be used to explain real world events. Indeed the methods used and the inherent biases and reasons actually for doing the study by the individual(s) involved, must never be discounted.

SKILL 11.3 Interpret historical or social scientific information provided in one or more graphs, charts, tables, diagrams, or maps

We use *illustrations* of various sorts because it is often easier to demonstrate a given idea visually instead of verbally—written or spoken. This is especially true in the areas of education and research because humans are visually stimulated. It is a fact that any idea presented visually in some manner is usually easier to understand and to comprehend than simply getting it verbally by hearing it or reading it. Among the more common illustrations used are various types of maps, graphs, and charts.

Photographs and globes are useful as well, but they are limited in what kind of information that they can show and are rarely used unless, as in the case of a photograph, the photograph is of a particular political figure or depicts a time that one wishes to visualize.

Maps

Although maps have advantages over globes and photographs, they do have a major disadvantage. The major problem of all maps comes about because most maps are flat and Earth is a sphere. It is impossible to reproduce exactly on a flat surface an object shaped like a sphere. In order to put Earth's features onto a map, they must be stretched in some way. This stretching is called **distortion.**

Distortion does not mean that maps are wrong; it simply means that they are not perfect representations of Earth or its parts. Cartographers, or mapmakers, understand the problems of distortion. They try to design them so that there is as little distortion as possible in the maps.

The process of putting the features of Earth onto a flat surface is called **projection**. All maps are really map projections. There are many different types. Each one deals in a different way with the problem of distortion. Map projections are made in a number of ways. Some are done using complicated mathematics. However, the basic ideas behind map projections can be understood by looking at the three most common types:

1. **Cylindrical projections:** These are created by taking a cylinder of paper and wrapping it around a globe. A light is used to project the globe's features onto the paper. Distortion is least where the paper touches the globe. For example, suppose that the paper was wrapped so that it touched the globe at the equator, the map from this projection would have just a little distortion near the equator. However, in moving north or south of the equator, the distortion would increase as you moved further away from the equator.

The best known and most widely used cylindrical projection is the Mercator projection. It was first developed in 1569 by Gerardus Mercator, a Flemish mapmaker.

2. Conical projections: These take their name from the fact that the projection is made onto a cone of paper. The cone is made so that it touches a globe at the base of the cone only. It can also be made so that it cuts through part of the globe in two different places. Again, there is the least distortion where the paper touches the globe. If the cone touches at two different points, there is some distortion at both of them. Conical projections are most often used to map areas in the middle latitudes. Maps of the United States are most often conical projections. This is because most of the country lies within these latitudes.

3. Flat-plane projections: These are made with a flat piece of paper. It touches the globe at one point only. Areas near this point show little distortion. Flat-plane projections are often used to show the areas of the North and South Poles. One such flat projection is called a Gnomonic Projection. On this kind of map, all meridians appear as straight lines, Gnomonic projections are useful because any straight line drawn between points on them form a Great-Circle Route. Great-Circle Routes can best be described by thinking of a globe and understanding that, when using the globe, the shortest route between two points on it can be found by simply stretching a string from one point to the other.

To properly analyze a given map, one must be familiar with the various parts and symbols that most modern maps use. For the most part, this is standardized, with different maps using similar parts and symbols. These can include:

- Title: All maps should have a title, just like all books should. The title tells you what information is to be found on the map.
- Legend: Most maps have a legend. A legend explains the various symbols that are used on that particular map and what the symbols represent, (also called a *map key*).
- Grid: A grid is a series of lines that are used to find exact places and locations on the map. There are several different kinds of grid systems in use; however, most maps do use the longitude and latitude system, known as the Geographic Grid System.
- Directions: Most maps have some directional system to show which way the map is being presented. Often on a map, a small compass will be present, with arrows showing the four basic directions—north, south, east, and west.

- Scale: This is used to show the relationship between a unit of measurement on the map versus the real world measure on Earth. Maps are drawn to many different scales. Some maps show a lot of detail for a small area. Others show a greater span of distance. Whichever is being used, one should always be aware of just what scale is being used. For instance, the scale might be something like 1 inch = 10 miles for a small area, or, for a map showing the whole world, it might have a scale in which 1 inch = 1,000 miles. The point is that one must look at the map key in order to see what units of measurements the map is using.

Maps have four main properties: the size of the areas shown on the map, the shapes of the areas, consistent scales, and straight-line directions. A map can be drawn so that it is correct in one or more of these properties. No map can be correct in all of them.

- Equal areas: One property that maps can have is that of equal areas. In an equal-area map, the meridians and parallels are drawn so that the areas shown have the same proportions as they do on Earth. For example, Greenland is about one-eighteenth the size of South America, thus it will be show as one-eighteenth the size on an equal area map. The Mercator projection is an example of a map that does not have equal areas. In it, Greenland appears to be about the same size as South America. This is because the distortion is very bad at the poles and Greenland lies near the North Pole.
- Conformal: A second map property is conformal, or correct, shapes. There are no maps that can show very large areas of Earth in their exact shapes. Only globes can really do that, but Conformal maps are as close as possible to true shapes. The United States is often shown by a Lambert Conformal Conic Projection Map.
- Consistent scales: Many maps attempt to use the same scale on all parts of the map. Generally, this is easier when maps show a relatively small part of Earth's surface. For example, a map of Florida might be a Consistent Scale map. Generally, maps showing large areas are not consistent scale maps. This is so because of distortion. Often, such maps will have two scales noted in the key. One scale, for example, might be accurate to measure distances between points along the Equator. Another might be then used to measure distances between the North Pole and the South Pole.

ELEVATION: the distance above or below sea level

Maps showing physical features often try to show information about the elevation or relief of the land. **ELEVATION** is the distance above or below the sea level. The elevation is usually shown with colors. For instance, all areas on a map at a certain level will be shown in the same color.

- Relief maps: Show the shape of the land surface as flat, rugged, or steep. Relief maps usually give more detail than simply showing the overall elevation of the land's surface. Relief is also sometimes shown with colors, but another way to show relief is by using contour lines. These lines connect all points of a land surface that are the same height surrounding the particular area of land.
- Thematic maps: These are used to show more specific information, often on a single theme, or topic. Thematic maps show the distribution or amount of something over a given area, such as population density, climate, economic information, cultural and political information, etc.

Information can be gained by looking at a map that might take hundreds of words to explain otherwise. Maps reflect the great variety of knowledge covered by political science. To show such a variety of information, maps are made in many different ways. Because of this variety, maps must be studied carefully.

Spatial organization is a description of how things are grouped in a given space. In geographical terms, this can describe people, places, and environments anywhere and everywhere on Earth.

The most basic form of spatial organization for people is where they live. The vast majority of people live near other people in villages, towns, cities, and settlements. These people live near others in order to take advantage of the goods and services that naturally arise from cooperation. These villages, towns, cities, and settlements are, to varying degrees, near bodies of water. Water is a staple of survival for every person on the planet, a good source of energy for factories and other industries, and a form of transportation for people and goods.

Another way to describe where people live is by the geography and topography around them. The vast majority of people on the planet live in areas that are very hospitable. Yes, people live in the Himalayas and in the Sahara, but the populations in those areas are small indeed when compared to the plains of China, India, Europe, and the United States. People naturally want to live where they will not have to work really hard just to survive, and world population patterns reflect this.

We can examine the spatial organization of the places where people live. For example, in a city, where are the factories and heavy industry buildings? Are they near airports or train stations? Are they on the edge of town, near major roads? What about housing developments? Are they near these industries, or are they far away? Where are the other industry buildings? Where are the schools, hospitals, and parks? What about the police and fire stations? How close are homes to each of these things? Towns, and especially cities, are routinely organized into neighborhoods in order that each house or home is near to most things that its residents might need on a regular basis. This means that large cities have multiple schools, hospitals, grocery stores, fire stations, etc.

Related to this is the distance between cities, towns, villages, or settlements. In certain parts of the United States, and definitely in many countries in Europe, the population settlement patterns achieve megalopolis standards, with no clear boundaries from one town to the next. Other more sparsely populated areas have towns that are few and far between and have relatively few people in them. Some exceptions to this exist, of course, like oases in the deserts; for the most part, however, population centers tend to be relatively near one another or, at least, near smaller towns.

Most places in the world are in some manner close to agricultural land as well. Food makes the world go round, and some cities are more agriculturally inclined than others. Rare is the city, however, that grows absolutely no crops. The kind of food grown is almost entirely dependent on the kind of land available and the climate surrounding that land. Rice does not grow well in the desert, for instance, nor do bananas grow well in snowy lands. Certain crops are easier to transport than others, and the ones that are not are usually grown near ports or other areas of export.

Settlements begin in areas that offer the natural resources to support life—food and water. With the ability to manage the environment, one finds a concentration of populations. With the ability to transport raw materials and finished products comes mobility. With increasing technology and the rise of industrial centers comes a migration of the workforce.

Cities are the major hubs of human settlement. Almost half of the population of the world now lives in cities.

These percentages are much higher in developed regions. Established cities continue to grow. The fastest growth, however, is occurring in developing areas. In some regions, there are "metropolitan areas" made up of urban and suburban areas. In some places, cities and urban areas have become interconnected into "megalopoli" (e.g., Tokyo-Kawasaki-Yokohama).

The concentrations of populations and the divisions of these areas among various groups that constitute the cities can differ significantly. North American cities are different from European cities in terms of shape, size, population density, and modes of transportation. In North America the wealthiest economic groups tend to live outside the cities, the opposite is true in Latin American cities.

There are significant differences among the cities of the world in terms of connectedness to other cities. European and North American cities tend to be linked both by transportation and communication connections, but there are other places in the world in which communication between the cities of the country may be inferior to communication with the rest of the world.

SKILL 11.4 Infer significant information *(e.g., geographic, economic, sociological)* about a historical or contemporary society based on examination of a photograph, painting, drawing, cartoon, or other visual representation

- Posters: The power of the political poster in the twenty-first century seems trivial considering the barrage of electronic campaigning, mudslinging, and reporting that seems to have taken over the video and audio media in election season. Even so, the political poster has been a powerful propaganda tool, and it has been around for a long time. For example, in the first century CE a poster that calls for the election of a man named Satrius has survived to this day. Nowhere have political posters been used more powerfully or effectively than in Russia in the 1920s in the campaign to promote Communism. Many of the greatest Russian writers of that era were the poster writers. Those posters would not be understood at all except in the light of what was going on in the country at the time.

  However, today we see them primarily at rallies and protests, where they are usually hand-lettered and hand-drawn. The message is rarely subtle. Understanding the messages of posters requires little thought as a rule. However, they are usually meaningless unless the context is clearly understood. For example, a poster reading "Camp Democracy" can only be understood in the context of the protests of the Iraq War near President George W. Bush's home near Crawford, Texas. "Impeach" posters are understood in 2006 to be directed at President Bush, not at Bill Clinton.

- Cartoons: The political cartoon (or editorial cartoon) presents a message or point of view concerning people, events, or situations using caricature and symbolism to convey the cartoonist's ideas, sometimes subtly, sometimes brashly, but always quickly. A good political cartoon will have wit and humor, which is usually obtained by exaggeration that is slick and not used merely for comic effect. It will also have a foundation in truth; that is, the characters must be recognizable to the viewer, and the point of the drawing must have some basis in fact even if it has a philosophical bias. The third requirement is a moral purpose.

  Using political cartoons as a teaching tool enlivens lectures, prompts classroom discussion, promotes critical thinking, develops multiple talents and learning styles, and helps prepare students for standardized tests. It also provides humor. However, it may be the most difficult form of literature to teach. Many teachers who choose to include them in their social studies curricula caution that, although students may enjoy them, it is doubtful whether they are actually getting the cartoonists' messages.

The best strategy for teaching such units is through a subskills approach that leads students step-by-step to higher orders of critical thinking. For example, the teacher can introduce caricature and use cartoons to illustrate the principles. Students are able to identify and interpret symbols if they are given the principles for doing so and get plenty of practice, and cartoons are excellent for this. It can cut down the time it takes for students to develop these skills, and many of the students who might lose the struggle to learn to identify symbols may overcome the roadblocks through the analysis of political cartoons. Many political cartoons exist for the teacher to use in the classroom and they are more readily available than ever before.

DOMAIN III
ARTISTIC EXPRESSION AND THE HUMANITIES

PERSONALIZED STUDY PLAN

PAGE	COMPETENCY AND SKILL		KNOWN MATERIAL/ SKIP IT
141	**12:**	**Understand and analyze elements of form and content in works from the visual and performing arts from different periods and cultures**	☐
	12.1:	Recognize important elements in the visual or performing arts	☐
	12.2:	Determine how unity or balance is achieved in the visual or performing arts	☐
	12.3:	Characterizing theme, mood, or tone	☐
	12.4:	Determine how elements of the arts affect audience perceptions	☐
148	**13:**	**Analyze and interpret works from the visual and performing arts representing different periods and cultures and understand the relationship of works of art to their social and historical contexts**	☐
	13.1:	Identify similarities and differences in forms and styles of art	☐
	13.2:	Compare and contrast works in terms of mood, theme, or technique	☐
	13.3:	Demonstrate an understanding of art as a form of communication	☐
	13.4:	Analyze how the visual or performing arts reflect a specific cultural or historical contex	☐
156	**14:**	**Understand forms and themes used in literature from different periods and cultures**	☐
	14.1:	Identify characteristic features of various genres of fiction and nonfiction	☐
	14.2:	Distinguish the dominant theme in a literary passage	☐
	14.3:	Recognize common literary elements and techniques	☐
	14.4:	Determine the meaning of figurative language	☐
	14.5:	Recognize how a text conveys multiple meaning	☐

PERSONALIZED STUDY PLAN

PAGE	COMPETENCY AND SKILL	KNOWN MATERIAL/ SKIP IT
162	**15: Analyze and interpret literature from different periods and cultures, and understand the relationship of works of literature to their social and historical contexts**	☐
	15.1: Analyze how the parts of a literary passage contribute to the whole	☐
	15.2: Compare and contrast the tone or mood of literary passages	☐
	15.3: Analyze aspects of cultural or historical context implied in a literary passage	☐
	15.4: Distinguish characteristic features of different literary genres, periods, and traditions	☐
	15.5: Make inferences about character, setting, author's point of view	☐
171	**16: Analyze and interpret examples of religious or philosophical ideas from various periods of time, and understand their significance in shaping societies and cultures**	☐
	16.1: Distinguish the religious and philosophical traditions associated with cultures and world regions	☐
	16.2: Recognize assumptions and beliefs underlying ideas presented in religious or philosophical writing	☐
	16.3: Analyze societal implications of philosophical or religious ideas	☐
	16.4: Compare and contrast key concepts presented in different philosophical or religious traditions	☐

COMPETENCY 12

UNDERSTAND AND ANALYZE ELEMENTS OF FORM AND CONTENT IN WORKS FROM THE VISUAL AND PERFORMING ARTS FROM DIFFERENT PERIODS AND CULTURES

SKILL 12.1 Recognize important elements in a given work of the visual or performing arts *(e.g., focal point, symmetry, repetition of shapes, perspective, motif, rhythm)*

Visual Art

Students should have an early introduction to the principles of visual art and should become familiar with these terms:

Abstract	An image that reduces a subject to its essential visual elements, such as lines, shapes, and colors
Background	Those portions or areas of composition that are behind the primary or dominant subject matter or design areas
Balance	A principle of art and design concerned with the arrangement of one or more elements in a work of art so that they appear symmetrical or asymmetrical in design and proportion
Contrast	A principle of art and design concerned with juxtaposing one or more elements in opposition, in order to show their differences
Emphasis	A principle of art and design concerned with making one or more elements in a work of art stand out in such a way that they appear more important or significant
Sketch	An image-development strategy; a preliminary drawing
Texture	An element of art and design that pertains to the way something feels by representation of the tactile character of surfaces
Unity	A principle of art and design concerned with the arrangement of one or more of the elements used to create a coherence of parts and a feeling of completeness or wholeness

Basic Music Techniques

Melody, harmony, rhythm, timbre, dynamics and texture are some of the basic components of music.

MELODY: the tune, a specific arrangement of sounds in a pleasing pattern

MELODY is the tune, a specific arrangement of sounds in a pleasing pattern. Melody is often seen as the horizontal aspect of music, because melodic notes on a page travel along horizontally.

HARMONY: the vertical aspect of music, or the musical chords related to a melody

HARMONY refers to the vertical aspect of music, or the musical chords related to a melody. So, when looking at a piece of music, the harmony notes are the ones lined up below each note of the melody, providing a more complex, fuller sound to a piece of music.

RHYTHM: the duration of musical notes

RHYTHM refers to the duration of musical notes. Rhythms are patterns of long and short music note durations. A clear way to describe rhythm to young students is through percussion instruments. A teacher creates a rhythmic pattern of long and short drum beats and asks the students to repeat the rhythm.

TIMBRE: the quality of a sound

TIMBRE is the quality of a sound. If a clarinet and a trumpet play the same exact note, they will still have a different timbre, or unique quality of sound. You can also describe different timbres using the same instrument. You may have two singers, but one has a harsh timbre and the other has a warm or soothing timbre to their voice. Timbre is subjective and lends itself to a number of creative exercises for early childhood students to describe what they hear in terms of the timbre of the sound.

DYNAMICS: the loudness or softness of music

DYNAMICS refer to the loudness or softness of music. Early Childhood students should develop a basic understanding of music vocabulary for dynamics. Piano describes soft music. Forte describes loud music. Pianissimo is very soft music. Double Forte refers to very loud music. Mezzo piano is kind of soft, while mezzo forte is kind of loud. These definitions can be organized on a continuum of soft to loud, with music examples for each.

TEXTURE: in music, this usually refers to the number of separate components making up the whole of a piece

TEXTURE in music usually refers to the number of separate components making up the whole of a piece. A monophonic texture is a single melody line, such as a voice singing a tune. Polyphonic texture denotes two or more music lines playing at the same time. A single melodic line with harmonic accompaniment is called homophonic texture.

SKILL 12.2 Determine how a sense of unity or balance is achieved in a given work from the visual or performing arts

In the mid-eighteenth century, the neoclassical style that came to dominate the visual arts was inspired by the rational ideas of the European Enlightenment as well as the revival of Greco-Roman culture and the widespread interest in art, architecture, and ideas from antiquity. Enlightenment ideals of reason and liberty were manifested in the unified, balanced composition of neoclassical works of art.

In 1784, Jacques-Louis David, one of the pioneers of the emerging style, completed *The Oath of the Horatii*—one of the most stylistically exemplary, and influential, paintings of the eighteenth century. David's *The Oath of the Horatii* illustrates a historical Roman event that was a rather popular subject in eighteenth-century France. David captures the dramatic moment when three brothers of the Horatii family face their father and pledge their lives to defend their city, Rome, against the threat of the opposing Curiatii family.

The three brothers' sense of solidarity and loyalty to their cause is emphasized by the picture's composition, or the way figures and areas of color are arranged on the picture plane. The statuesque Horatii brothers stand on the left side of the painting. They raise their arms in salute to their father, who stands at the center of the painting, while, on the right side, the Horatii mother and sisters gather together in despair over the imminent events. David has positioned all three groups of figures along the same horizontal line the runs from left to right across the picture plane. The background, a Roman colonnade of three even archways frames each of the figure groups: the brothers, the father, and the women. Further unity and balance is achieved by the repetition of triangular forms, one of the most geometrically stable forms, which can be seen in the wide stances of the brothers and the father and in the pyramidal shape of the cluster of women.

David's painterly technique employs austere, somber colors, clearly delineated, hard-edged figural forms. This combine with the composition's overall controlled, rational formal elements contribute to the scene's clarity of narrative and emotional weight—such a unified, balanced composition serves to echo the ideas behind the period's return to Europe's classical heritage.

SKILL 12.3 Characterizing the theme, mood, or tone of a given work from the visual or performing arts

The field of the humanities is overflowing with examples of works of art that hold in common various themes, motifs, and symbols. Themes, motifs, and symbols effortlessly cross the lines between the visual arts, literature, music, theater, and dance. Listed below are a few examples culled from the immense heritage of the arts.

Works that Share Thematic and Symbolic Motifs

A popular symbol or motif of the fifteenth, sixteenth, and seventeenth centuries was David, the heroic second king of the Hebrews. The richness of the stories pertaining to David and the opportunities for visual interpretation made him a favorite among artists.

Donatello's bronze statue of *David* is a classically proportioned nude portrayed with Goliath's head between his feet. This David is not gloating over his kill, but instead seems to be viewing his own, sensuous body with a Renaissance air of self-awareness.

Verrocchio's bronze sculpture of *David*, also with the severed head of Goliath, represents a confident young man proud of his accomplishment and seemingly basking in praise.

Michelangelo, always original, gives us a universal interpretation of the David theme. Weapon in hand, Michelangelo's marble *David* tenses muscles as he summons up the power to deal with his colossal enemy, symbolizing as he does every person or community having had to battle against overwhelming odds.

Bernini's marble *David*, created as it was during the Baroque era, explodes with energy as it captures forever the most dramatic moment of David's action, the throwing of the stone that kills Goliath.

Caravaggio's painting titled *David and Goliath* treats the theme in yet another way. Here, David is shown as if in the glare of a spotlight, looking with revulsion at the bloodied, grotesque head of Goliath, leaving the viewer to speculate about the reason for disgust. Is David revolted at the ungodliness of Goliath, or is he sickened at his own murderous action?

Symbols related to the David theme include David, Goliath's head, and the stone and slingshot.

Another popular religious motif, especially during the medieval and Renaissance periods, was the Annunciation. This event was the announcement by the archangel Gabriel to the Virgin Mary that she would bear a son and name him Jesus. It is also believed that this signified the moment of Incarnation. Anonymous medieval artists treated this theme in altarpieces, murals, and illuminated manuscripts. During the thirteenth century, both Nicola Pisano and his son, Giovanni, carved reliefs of the Annunciation theme. Both men included the Annunciation and the Nativity theme into a single panel. Martini's painted rendition of the *Annunciation* owes something to the court etiquette of the day in the use of the heraldic devises of the symbolic colorings and stilted manner of the Virgin.

Della Francesca's fresco of the *Annunciation* borders on the abstract with its simplified gestures and lack of emotion and the ionic column providing a barrier between Gabriel and Mary.

Fra Angelico's *Annunciation* is a lyrical painting combining soft, harmonious coloring with simplicity of form and gesture.

Symbols related to the Annunciation theme are Gabriel, Mary, the dove of the Holy Spirit, the lily, an olive branch, a garden, a basket of wool, a closed book, and various inscriptions.

During the 1800s, a new viewpoint surfaced in Europe. Intellectuals from several countries became painfully aware of the consequences of social conditions and abuses of the day and set out to expose them. The English social satirist William Hogarth created a series of paintings titled *Marriage a-la-Mode*, which honed in on the absurdity of arranged marriages. Other works by Hogarth explored conditions that led to prostitution and the poorhouse.

In France, Voltaire was working on the play *Candide*, which recounted the misfortunes of a young man while providing biting commentary on the social abuses of the period.

In the field of music, Mozart's *Marriage of Figaro*, based on a play by Beaumarchais, explores the emotion of love as experienced by people from all ages and walks of life. At the same time, it portrays the follies of convention in society.

Universal themes are themes that reflect the human experience regardless of time period, location, social standing, economic considerations, or religious or cultural beliefs. However, individuals or societies may condone or object to the particular manner in which a theme is approached.

Attitudes toward universal themes reflected in the humanities

Each artist and author brings to his/her work a personal view of the world. Those of us who view the works and read the books also bring our own biases to the experience. Therefore, the universal themes that are reflected in artistic works are colored both by the hands that create the works and the eyes that perceive them. Is it any wonder, then, that every work in the arts and humanities is open to so many varied interpretations?

For example, during the Renaissance, Michelangelo painted the ceiling of the Sistine Chapel with glowing frescoes depicting the creation of the universe and man. Although the frescoes are based on stories from the Old Testament, the theme is universal in that mankind has always sought to understand his origins. During Michelangelo's own time, controversy surrounded the ceiling frescoes, in large measure because of the nudity they depicted.

Church scholars were divided over whether Michelangelo had departed too far from the classical notions of beauty advocated by the ancient Greeks or whether he had followed the Greek conventions (including nudity) too closely! Michelangelo contended that his style was a personal one, derived in part from observation of classical sculpture and in part from his observations from life. He expressed a desire to paint differently from the Greeks because the society he was painting for was dramatically different from the Greek society.

The most obvious way in which attitudes toward universal themes are reflected in the humanities is the ability of the artist to express his opinions through his work.

The most obvious way in which attitudes toward universal themes are reflected in the humanities is the ability of the artist to express his opinions through his work.

For example, Hogarth addressed the universal themes of social cruelty through his paintings. Because of his dramatic portrayals and biting satire, Hogarth's works reflect his own humanitarian viewpoints regarding his eighteenth-century English society. The fact that his paintings aroused similar emotions among the general public is evidenced by the fact that his paintings were made into engravings in order to provide low-cost prints. The wide distribution of these prints indicates the extent to which the public sought social change.

SKILL 12.4 Determine how specific elements in a given work of the visual or performing arts *(e.g., color, composition, scale, instrumentation, set design, choreography)* affect audience perceptions of the content of the work

The advent and use of photography as both a documentary and artistic medium dramatically changed the way people perceived images. The birth of the photograph was also an obvious challenge to the authority of the artist, who, in many cultures was seen as an imitator of nature; however, the dissemination of their images to a broader audience through photographic reproduction helped to spread an artists' fame. As a result, the mid- to late-nineteenth century proved to be a highly creative time for artists working in the more historic medium of painting. Artists' responses to photography, and spread of information that went along with the medium, varied. Some artists were able to realize the camera's potential to free them from the role of imitator. They felt empowered to explore more impressionistic or expressionistic representational modes. While others, like Edgar Degas, embraced the technical capabilities that were unique to photography—like the ability to capture a series of images of a galloping horse and observe the pattern of its motion frame by frame or, more simply, the ability to crop a photographic composition. Degas employed such representative advances in his paintings of racehorses and ballerinas.

Edouard Manet artfully combined the conventional subject of the reclining nude female figure, which celebrates a long history dating back to ancient Greece, with the realism and immediacy of photographic representation. His *Olympia* from 1863 is perhaps the best example of how his unique style evoked strong reaction from his audience.

The reclining female nude was traditionally a subtly erotic subject. Often, the highly idealized figure represented a sleeping woman who was oblivious to or unaware of the gaze of the viewer. Giorgione's *Sleeping Venus* (c. 1510) best illustrates a typical female nude subject from the Renaissance; as evidence by the painting's title, the subject is the goddess of love herself. She does not address the viewer with her eyes, and her highly idealized body and her divine nature keep her distanced from the audience—she is unattainable.

Manet's *Olympia* (1863), on the other hand, "debases" the tradition by presenting the viewer with an in-your-face female nude. The subject, Olympia, directly addresses the viewer with her gaze. Viewers during Manet's time would have identified her immediately as a high-class prostitute based on her adornments—the black ribbon around her throat and her silk slippers. The influence of current photographic techniques shows up in the way the figure of Olympia is brightly lit. Her stocky body is sharply delineated by thick, dark outlines, and Manet uses minimal shading or modeling of the figures contours—he renders her pasty white flesh in an unflattering flat style.

The model herself, Victorine Meurent, was highly recognizable as well. She was a popular model in Paris at the time, and a friend of Manet's family. The fact that a person so widely recognizable was painted in the nude was very controversial. Reaction to *Olympia*, largely owing to Manet's dramatic, unconventional representational style, was overwhelmingly negative. Although female nudity had been accepted in Europe for centuries, Manet's unique formal elements turned the subject into something much more uncomfortable for his contemporaries. His audience was shocked, and the picture was declared scandalous.

COMPETENCY 13

ANALYZE AND INTERPRET WORKS FROM THE VISUAL AND PERFORMING ARTS REPRESENTING DIFFERENT PERIODS AND CULTURES AND UNDERSTAND THE RELATIONSHIP OF WORKS OF ART TO THEIR SOCIAL AND HISTORICAL CONTEXTS

SKILL 13.1 Identify similarities and differences in forms and styles of art from different movements or periods of time

Theatre

Greece

The history of theatre can be dated back to early sixth century BCE in Greece. The Greek theatre was the earliest known theater experience. Drama was expressed in many Greek spiritual ceremonies. There are two main forms of drama; both evolved in their own time.

TRAGEDY: a work portraying conflict between characters and a fatal flaw in the main character resulting in his or her destruction

COMEDY: a work portraying a paradoxical relationship between humans and the gods

- TRAGEDY: Typically involving conflict between characters and a fatal flaw in the main character resulting in his or her destruction. Sophocles, Euripides, and Aeschylus are the most notable Greek authors in this genre.
- COMEDY: Typically involving paradoxical relationships between humans and the gods. Aristophanes is the most notable Greek author in this genre.

Rome

The history of theatre in Rome began with theater shows in the third century BCE, based on religious aspects of the lives of Roman gods and goddesses. Drama was not able to withstand the fall of the Roman Empire in 476 A.D. By the end of the sixth century, drama was nearly dead in Rome. Plautus and Terence, however, were famous early Roman authors of comedy.

Medieval drama

Medieval theatre was a new revelation of drama that appeared around the tenth century. New phases of religion were introduced in many holiday services such as Christmas and Easter. In the Church itself, many troupes that toured churches presented religious narratives and life stories meant to encourage morality. Over time, these presentations of small traveling groups evolved into full-sized plays, presentations, and elaborate passions. Performances became spectacles at outdoor theaters, marketplaces, and any place large audiences could gather. The main focus of these presentations of drama was to glorify God and humanity and to celebrate local artisan trades.

Puritan Commonwealth and the Restoration

The Puritan Commonwealth, ruled by Oliver Cromwell, outlawed dramatic performances, and that ban lasted for nearly twenty years. Following the Puritan era was the restoration of the English monarchy, and new, more well-rounded plays became the focus of art. For the first time in history, women were allowed to participate.

Melodrama

Melodrama, in which good always triumphed over evil, eventually took over the stage. This form of drama was usually pleasing to the audience, though it was-sometimes unrealistic.

Realism and serious drama

Serious Drama emerged late in the nineteenth and twentieth centuries, following the movement of realism. Realism attempted to combine the dealings of nature with realistic and ordinary situations on stage.

Today, realism is the most common form of stage presentation. The techniques used today to stage drama combine many of the past histories and cultures of drama.

Visual Art

UNIVERSAL THEMES THROUGHOUT HISTORY	
Prehistoric Arts (circa 1,000,000–circa 8,000 BCE)	Major themes of this vast period appear to center around religious fertility rites and sympathetic magic, consisting of imagery of pregnant animals and faceless, pregnant women.
Mesopotamian Arts (circa 8,000–400 BCE)	The prayer statues and cult deities of the period point to the theme of polytheism in religious worship.
Egyptian Arts (circa 3,000–100 BCE)	The predominance of funerary art from ancient Egypt illustrates the theme of preparation for the afterlife and polytheistic worship. Another dominant theme, reflected by artistic convention, is the divinity of the pharaohs. In architecture, the themes were monumentality and adherence to ritual.

Continued on next page

Greek Arts (800–100 BCE)	The sculpture of ancient Greece is replete with human figures, most nude and some draped. Most of these sculptures represent athletes and various gods and goddesses. The predominant theme is that of the ideal human, in both mind and body. In architecture, the theme was scale based on the ideal human proportions.
Roman Arts (circa 480 BCE–476 CE)	Judging from Roman arts, the predominant themes of the period deal with the realistic depiction of human beings and how they relate to Greek classical ideals. The emphasis is on practical realism. Another major theme is the glory in serving the Roman state. In architecture, the theme was rugged practicality mixed with Greek proportions and elements.
Middle Ages Arts (300–1400 CE)	Although the time span is expansive, the major themes remain relatively constant throughout. Since the Roman Catholic Church was the primary patron of the arts, most work was religious in nature. The purpose of much of the art was to educate. Specific themes varied from the illustration of Bible stories to interpretations of theological allegory, to lives of the saints, to consequences of good and evil. Depictions of the Holy Family were popular. Themes found in secular art and literature centered around chivalric love and warfare. In architecture, the theme was glorification of God and education of congregation to religious principles.
Renaissance Arts (circa 1400–1630 CE)	Renaissance themes include Christian religious depiction *(see also Middle Ages)*, but tend to reflect a renewed interest in all things classical. Specific themes include Greek and Roman mythological and philosophic figures, ancient battles, and legends. Dominant themes mirror the philosophic beliefs of Humanism, emphasizing individuality and human reason, such as those of the High Renaissance, which center around the psychological attributes of individuals. In architecture, the theme was scale based on human proportions.
Baroque Arts (1630–1700 CE)	The predominant themes found in the arts of the Baroque period include the dramatic climaxes of well-known stories, legends, and battles and the grand spectacle of mythology. Religious themes are found frequently, but it is drama and insight that are emphasized and not the medieval "salvation factor." Baroque artists and authors incorporated various types of characters into their works, careful to include minute details. Portraiture focused on the psychology of the sitters. In architecture, the theme was large-scale grandeur and splendor.
Eighteenth Century Arts (1700–1800 CE)	Rococo themes of this century focused on religion, light mythology, portraiture of aristocrats, pleasure and escapism, and, occasionally, satire. In architecture, the theme was artifice and gaiety, combined with an organic quality of form. Neoclassic themes centered around examples of virtue and heroism, usually in classical settings, and historical stories. In architecture, classical simplicity and utility of design was regained.

Continued on next page

Nineteenth Century Arts (1800–1900 CE)	Romantic themes include human freedom, equality, and civil rights, a love for nature, and a tendency toward the melancholic and mystic. The underlying theme is that the most important discoveries are made within the self, and not in the exterior world. In architecture, the theme was fantasy and whimsy, known as picturesque. Realistic themes included social awareness and a focus on society victimizing individuals. The themes behind Impressionism were the constant flux of the universe and the immediacy of the moment. In architecture, the themes were strength, simplicity, and upward thrust as skyscrapers entered the scene.
Twentieth Century Arts (1900–2000 CE)	Diverse artistic themes of the century reflect a parting with traditional religious values and a painful awareness of man's inhumanity to man. Themes also illustrate a growing reliance on science, while simultaneously expressing disillusionment with man's failure to adequately control science. A constant theme is the quest for originality and self-expression, while seeking to express the universal in human experience. In architecture, "form follows function."

SKILL 13.2 Compare and contrast two or more works from the visual or performing arts in terms of mood, theme, or technique

Greek attitudes toward their enemies evolved over time. Those attitudes are directly reflected in how they portrayed their warrior opponents in the tone and techniques used to create their works of art.

In the Classical period in Greek art, Athenians represented their opponents as sub-human, savage beasts. Take the Battle of the *Lapiths and Centaurs* (c. 450 BCE) from the southern metope facade of the acropolis's Parthenon. Greek artists of the period created mammoth marble reliefs; positioned high up on the facade of the Parthenon, such works were not for a human audience, but for the pantheon of gods that figure so centrally to the ancient Greek tradition. The subject matter, too, comes from Greek mythology: the legendary battle between the Lapiths, the ancient heroic ancestors of the Greeks, and the Centaurs, which were mythological wild half man/half horse creatures. The battle between the Centaurs and the Lapiths broke out during the wedding feast of the king of the Lapiths. During the feast, the mercurial, drunken, and uninvited Centaurs arrived and reacted violently under the influence of wine, attempting to abduct the Lapith women. The result was a fight between the Centaurs and the Lapiths.

The Centaurs have human faces with animal features, which reflect their mixed temperament. Although the subject is mythological, the tone alludes to the Greek's attitudes toward any real enemy in battle—that is, that the Greeks, who are more refined in behavior and physicality, perceive themselves as superior to their barbaric enemies. The Centaurs are shown wearing animal skins and they are armed with tree-branches. On the other hand, the Lapiths fight nude, several of them hold a sword or a spear, showing that the Lapiths/Greeks are technologically superior as well.

Created about two centuries later, the Greek Hellenistic period's *Dying Gaul* (c. 150 BCE) depicts another Greek enemy; however, this subject does not come from mythology, but is directly related to Greek history. The artist has depicted this particular Gaul as nude, and therefore just as heroic and traditional as the Lapith warriors in the classical relief. Such a depiction is a great departure from the Classical period's attempt to dehumanize the opposition. The realistically rendered, unique facial features and expressive pathos of the statue arouse great admiration. The *Dying Gaul* is therefore lent the dignity of heroic nudity or pathetic (eliciting pathos) nudity. The message conveyed by the sculpture is that despite a vicious conflict, the Greeks developed a representational style that even elevates the heroics of the enemy, and that in turn duly supports the notion that the Greeks are the great warriors—for they can beat even the most worthy and fierce opponents.

For more details about characterizing theme, mood, and tone see Skill 12.3

SKILL 13.3 Demonstrate an understanding of art as a form of communication *(e.g., conveying political or moral concepts, serving as a means of individual expression)*

Artistic styles in the visual arts, music, and performing arts can refer to a more general style that is defined by the period and place in which a work of art is created—the broader historical and cultural context.

Artistic styles in the visual arts, music, and performing arts can refer to a more general style that is defined by the period and place in which a work of art is created—the broader historical and cultural context. Style may also describe an individual artist's unique artistic fingerprint. For example, the quick, modulating, and playful manner of a piece of music by Chopin is recognizable as unique to that composer, but the broader themes or individuality and artistic expression also relate to the more general Romantic style which prevailed in Europe during the mid-eighteenth century. Likewise, someone even only vaguely familiar with Michelangelo's style can see in the muscular, twisted historical figures painted on the ceiling of the Sistine Chapel clues that hint at the work's artistic attribution, but such details also link, more broadly, to the increased interest in anatomy in Renaissance Italy.

Works of art, therefore, can be expressive on different levels: Art expresses the artist's unique point of view, but images, music, and literature are inextricably linked also to the greater social, historical, regional, and political context in which they were created.

Artists have long used their means of expression to communicate political or moral concepts. Artists' responses to war are often particularly resonant, given how combat affects civilian populations. On one April afternoon in 1937, during the Spanish Civil War (1936-1939) that pitted republican forces against General Franco's Fascist dictatorship, the German air force (in cooperation with the Spanish Fascist forces) dropped bombs on the town of Guernica in northeast Spain. News of the event, which was the first aerial bombardment of a civilian target, spread quickly across Europe. When Picasso read illustrated newspaper accounts of the attack and as the death toll mounted, he was horrified. Earlier that year, Picasso had been invited to contribute a painting to the Paris World's Fair's Spanish pavilion. Guernica's bombing would provide Picasso with ample inspiration for his submission—a huge mural that would become the twentieth century's most unforgettable antiwar image.

Artists have long used their means of expression to communicate political or moral concepts.

Picasso's *Guernica* (1937) captures the senseless brutality and suffering of wartime. He used the ashen grays of incineration to create a chaotic, bleak picture of the aftermath of the Guernica bombing. His abstract treatment of the picture plane pushes the distorted figures, disjointed limbs to the foreground, where they are presented to the viewer with his typical Cubist style—which, given this subject matter, is decidedly aggressive. Picasso often used the symbols of the bull and horse in his work, which for Spain are patriotic symbols of the Spanish bullfight, and, for Picasso, move beyond nationalistic pride and express savage discord. These symbols share the composition with a broken statue of a warrior and four women—one holds her dead baby. This figure, mouth agape, issues a voiceless scream. Guernica, however, because of Picasso's aggressive expression and direct, evocative style, is in itself a protest against militant idealism and war. It illustrates his insistent argument for art as a "weapon against the enemy."

See also Skill 13.4

SKILL 13.4 Analyze ways in which the content of a given work from the visual or performing arts reflects a specific cultural or historical context

Although the elements of design have remained consistent throughout history, the emphasis on specific aesthetic principles has periodically shifted. Aesthetic standards or principles vary from time period to time period and from society to society.

In attempts to convey the illusion of depth or visual space in a work of art, Eastern and Western artists use different techniques. Eastern artists prefer a diagonal projection of eye movement into the picture plane and often leave large areas of the surface untouched by detail. The result is the illusion of vast space, an infinite view that coincides with the spiritual philosophies of the Orient. Western artists rely on techniques such as overlapping planes, variation of object size, object position on the picture plane, linear and aerial perspective, color change, and various points of perspective to convey the illusion of depth. The result is space that is limited and closed.

In the application of color, Eastern artists use arbitrary choices of color. Western artists generally rely on literal color usage or emotional choices of color. The result is that Eastern art tends to be more universal in nature, while Western art is more individualized.

An interesting change in aesthetic principles occurred between the Renaissance period and the Baroque period in Europe. The shift is easy to understand when viewed in the light of Wölfflin's categories of stylistic development.

The Renaissance period was concerned with the rediscovery of the works of classical Greece and Rome. The art, literature, and architecture was inspired by classical orders, which tended to be formal, simple, and concerned with the ideal human proportions. This means that the painting, sculpture, and architecture was of a Teutonic, or closed nature, composed of forms that were restrained and compact. For example, consider the visual masterpieces of the period: Raphael's painting *The School of Athens*, with its highly precise use of space; Michelangelo's sculpture *David*, with its compact mass; and the facade of the *Palazzo Strozzi*, with its defined use of the rectangle, arches, and rustication of the masonry.

Compare the Renaissance characteristics to those of the Baroque period. One connotation of the word "baroque" is "grotesque," which was the contemporary criticism of the new style. In comparison to the styles of the Renaissance, the Baroque was concerned with the imaginative flights of human fancy. The painting, sculpture, and architecture were of an a-Teutonic, or open nature, composed of forms that were whimsical and free flowing. Consider again the masterpieces of the period: Ruben's painting *The Elevation of the Cross*, with its turbulent forms of light and dark tumbling diagonally through space; Puget's sculpture *Milo of Crotona*, with its use of open space and twisted forms; and Borromini's *Chapel of St. Ivo*, with a facade that plays convex forms against concave ones.

In the 1920s and 30s, the German art historian Heinrich Wölfflin outlined these shifts in aesthetic principles in his influential book *Principles of Art History*. He arranged these changes into five categories of "visual analysis," sometimes referred to as the "categories of stylistic development." Wölfflin was careful to point out that no style is inherently superior to any other. They are simply indicators of the phase of development of that particular time or society.

However, Wölfflin goes on to state, correctly or not, that once the evolution occurs, it is impossible to regress. These modes of perception apply to drawing, painting, sculpture, and architecture. They are as follows:

1. From a linear mode to a painterly mode: This shift refers to stylistic changes that occur when perception or expression evolves from a linear form that is concerned with the contours and boundaries of objects to perception or expression that stresses the masses and volumes of objects. From viewing objects in isolation to seeing the relationships between objects is an important change in perception. Linear mode implies that objects are stationary and unchanging, while the painterly mode implies that objects and their relationships to other objects are always in a state of flux.

2. From plane to recession: This shift refers to perception or expression that evolves from a planar style, when the artist views movement in the work in an "up and down" and "side to side" manner to a recessional style, when the artist views the balance of a work in an "in and out" manner. The illusion of depth may be achieved through either style, but only the recessional style uses an angular movement forward and backward through the visual plane.

3. From closed to open form: This shift refers to perception or expression that evolves from a sense of enclosure or limited space, "closed form," to a sense of freedom in "open form." The concept is obvious in architecture, as it is easy to differentiate between the buildings with obvious "outside" and "inside" space and those that open up the space to allow the outside to interact with the inside.

4. From multiplicity to unity: This shift refers to an evolution from expressing unity through the use of balancing many individual parts to expressing unity by subordinating some individual parts to others. Multiplicity stresses the balance between existing elements; whereas unity stresses emphasis, domination, and accent of some elements over other elements.

5. From absolute to relative clarity: This shift refers to an evolution from works which clearly and thoroughly express everything there is to know about the object to works that express only part of what there is to know and leave the viewer to fill in the rest from his own experiences. Relative clarity, then, is a sophisticated mode because it requires the viewer to actively participate in the "artistic dialogue." Each of the previous four categories is reflected in this, as linearity is considered to be concise while painterliness is more subject to interpretation. Planarity is more factual, while recessional movement is an illusion, and so on.

COMPETENCY 14

UNDERSTAND FORMS AND THEMES USED IN LITERATURE FROM DIFFERENT PERIODS AND CULTURES

SKILL 14.1 Identify characteristic features of various genres of fiction and nonfiction *(e.g., novels, plays, essays, autobiographies)*

MAJOR LITERARY GENRES	
Allegory	A story in verse or prose with characters representing virtues and vices. There are two meanings, symbolic and literal. John Bunyan's *The Pilgrim's Progress* is the most renowned of this genre.
Ballad	An *in medias res* story, told or sung, usually in verse and accompanied by music. Literary devices found in ballads include the refrain, or repeated section, and incremental repetition, or anaphora, for effect. Earliest forms were anonymous folk ballads. Later forms include Coleridge's Romantic masterpiece, *The Rime of the Ancient Mariner.*
Children's Literature	A genre of its own and emerged as a distinct and independent form in the second half of the eighteenth century. *The Visible World in Pictures* by John Amos Comenius, a Czech educator, was one of the first printed works and the first picture book. For the first time, educators acknowledged that children are different from adults in many respects. Modern educators acknowledge that introducing elementary students to a wide range of reading experiences plays an important role in their mental/social/psychological development.
Drama	Plays—comedy, modern, or tragedy—typically in five acts. Traditionalists and neoclassicists adhere to Aristotle's unities of time, place, and action. Plot development is advanced via dialogue. Literary devices include asides, soliloquies, and the chorus representing public opinion. Greatest of all dramatists/playwrights is William Shakespeare. Other dramaturges include Ibsen, Williams, Miller, Shaw, Stoppard, Racine, Moliére, Sophocles, Aeschylus, Euripides, and Aristophanes.
Epic	Long poem usually of book length reflecting values inherent in the generative society. Epic devices include an invocation to a Muse for inspiration, purpose for writing, universal setting, protagonist and antagonist who possess supernatural strength and acumen, and interventions of a God or the gods. Understandably, there are very few epics: Homer's *Iliad* and *Odyssey*, Virgil's *Aeneid*, Milton's *Paradise Lost*, Spenser's *The Fairie Queene*, Barrett Browning's *Aurora Leigh*, and Pope's mock-epic, *The Rape of the Lock*.
Epistle	A letter that is not always originally intended for public distribution, but due to the fame of the sender and/or recipient, becomes public domain. Paul wrote epistles that were later placed in the Bible.

Continued on next page

Essay	Typically a limited length prose work focusing on a topic and propounding a definite point of view and authoritative tone. Great essayists include Carlyle, Lamb, DeQuincy, Emerson, and Montaigne, who is credited with defining this genre.
Fable	Terse tale offering up a moral or exemplum. Chaucer's "The Nun's Priest's Tale" is a fine example of a *bête fabliau* or beast fable in which animals speak and act characteristically human, illustrating human foibles.
Legend	A traditional narrative or collection of related narratives, popularly regarded as historically factual but actually a mixture of fact and fiction.
Myth	Stories that are more or less universally shared within a culture to explain its history and traditions.
Novel	The longest form of fictional prose containing a variety of characterizations, settings, local color, and regionalism. Most have complex plots, expanded description, and attention to detail. Some of the great novelists include Austin, the Brontes, Twain, Tolstoy, Hugo, Hardy, Dickens, Hawthorne, Forster, and Flaubert.
Poem	The only requirement is rhythm. Subgenres include fixed types of literature such as the sonnet, elegy, ode, pastoral, and villanelle. Unfixed types of literature include blank verse and dramatic monologue.
Romance	A highly imaginative tale set in a fantastical realm dealing with the conflicts between heroes, villains and/or monsters. "The Knight's Tale" from Chaucer's *Canterbury Tales*, *Sir Gawain and the Green Knight* and Keats's "The Eve of St. Agnes" are prime examples.
Short Story	Typically a terse narrative, with less developmental background about characters. Short stories may include description, author's point of view, and tone. Poe emphasized that a successful short story should create one focused impact. Considered to be great short story writers are Hemingway, Faulkner, Twain, Joyce, Shirley Jackson, Flannery O'Connor, de Maupassant, Saki, Edgar Allen Poe, and Pushkin.

SKILL 14.2 Distinguish the dominant theme in a literary passage

Theme in a work of fiction is similar to a thesis in an essay. It is the *point* the story makes. In a story, it may possibly be spoken by one of the characters, but, more often, it is left to the writer to determine. This requires careful reading and should take into account the other aspects of the story before a firm decision is made. Different analysts will come to different conclusions about what a story means. Very often, the thesis of an analytical essay will be expressed as a well-reasoned opinion.

SKILL 14.3 Recognize common literary elements and techniques *(e.g., imagery, metaphor, symbolism, allegory, foreshadowing, irony)*, and use those elements to interpret a literary passage

Simile

A direct comparison of two things, often using the term *like* or *as* to foster the comparison. A common example is, "My love is like a red, red rose."

Metaphor

An indirect comparison of two things. Metaphor is the use of a word or phrase denoting one kind of object or action in place of another. Poets use metaphors extensively, but they are also essential to understanding everyday speech. For example, chairs are said to have "legs" and "arms," even though they are typically unique to humans and other animals.

Parallelism

The arrangement of ideas into phrases, sentences, and paragraphs that balance one element with another of equal importance and similar wording. An example from Francis Bacon's *Of Studies* is, "Reading maketh a full man, conference a ready man, and writing an exact man."

Personification

The attribution of human characteristics to an inanimate object, an abstract quality, or an animal. For example, John Bunyan wrote characters named Death, Knowledge, Giant Despair, Sloth, and Piety in *Pilgrim's Progress*. The metaphor of the "arm" of a chair is also a form of personification.

Euphemism

The substitution of an agreeable or inoffensive term for one that might offend or suggest something unpleasant. Many euphemisms are used to refer to death, including "passed away," "crossed over," or even simply "passed."

Hyperbole

A deliberate exaggeration for effect. This passage from Shakespeare's *The Merchant of Venice* is an example:

> *Why, if two gods should play some heavenly match*
> *And on the wager lay two earthly women,*
> *And Portia one, there must be something else*
> *Pawned with the other, for the poor rude world*
> *Hath not her fellow.*

Climax

A number of phrases or sentences arranged in ascending order of rhetorical forcefulness. This passage from Melville's *Moby Dick* is an example:

> *All that most maddens and torments; all that stirs up the lees of things; all truth with malice in it; all that cracks the sinews and cakes the brain; all the subtle demonisms of life and thought; all evil, to crazy Ahab, were visibly personified and made practically assailable in Moby Dick.*

Bathos

A ludicrous attempt to portray pathos—that is, to evoke pity, sympathy, or sorrow. It may result from inappropriately dignifying the commonplace, using elevated language to describe something trivial, or greatly exaggerating pathos.

Oxymoron

A contradiction in terms deliberately employed for effect. It is usually seen in a qualifying adjective whose meaning is contrary to that of the noun it modifies, such as "wise folly." For example, a fairly common oxymoron is "jumbo shrimp."

Irony

The expression of something other than, and particularly the opposite of, the literal meaning, such as words of praise when blame is intended. In poetry, irony is often used as a sophisticated or resigned awareness of contrast between what is and what ought to be; it expresses a controlled pathos without sentimentality. It is a form of indirectness that avoids overt praise or censure. An early example is the Greek comic character Eiron, a clever underdog who, by his wit, repeatedly triumphs over the boastful character Alazon.

Alliteration

The repetition of consonant sounds in two or more neighboring words or syllables. In its simplest form, alliteration reinforces one or two consonant sounds. For example, notice the repetition in Shakespeare's Sonnet 12:

> *When I do **c**ount the **c**lock that **t**ells the **t**ime.*

Some poets have used more complex patterns of alliteration by creating similar consonant sounds both at the beginning of words and at the beginning of stressed syllables within words. For example, hear the sounds in Shelley's "Stanzas Written in Dejection Near Naples":

> *The **C**ity's voi**c**e it**s**elf is **s**oft like **S**olitude's*

Onomatopoeia

The naming of a thing or action by a vocal imitation of the sound associated with it, such as *buzz* or *hiss*. It is marked by the use of words whose sound suggests the sense. One good example is from "The Brook" by Tennyson:

> *I chatter over stony ways,*
> *In little sharps and trebles,*
> *I bubble into eddying bays,*
> *I babble on the pebbles.*

Malapropism

A verbal blunder in which one word is replaced by another that is similar in sound but different in meaning. The term itself comes from Sheridan's Mrs. Malaprop in *The Rivals* (1775). Thinking of the geography of contiguous countries, she spoke of the "geometry" of "contagious countries."

SKILL 14.4 Determine the meaning of figurative language used in a literary passage

IMAGERY: a word or sequence of words that refers to any sensory experience—anything that can be seen, tasted, smelled, heard, or felt

IMAGERY is a word or sequence of words that refers to any sensory experience—that is, anything that can be seen, tasted, smelled, heard, or felt on the skin or fingers. Writers of prose may also use these devices, but it is most distinctive of poetry. Poets intend to make an experience available to readers. In order to do that, they must appeal to one of the senses. One, of course, is the visual imagery. Poets will deliberately paint a scene in such a way that readers can see it. However, the purpose is not simply to elicit the vision but also to stir the emotions. A good example is "The Piercing Chill" by Taniguchi Buson (1715–1783):

> *The piercing chill I feel:*
> *My dead wife's comb, in our bedroom,*
> *Under my heel.*

In only a few short words, the reader can feel many things: the shock that might come from touching the comb, a literal sense of death, the contrast between her death and the memories he has of her when she was alive. Imagery might be defined as speaking of the abstract in concrete terms—a powerful device in the hands of a skillful poet.

A **SYMBOL** is an object or action that can be observed with the senses in addition to its suggesting many other things. The lion is a symbol of courage; the cross a symbol of Christianity; the color green a symbol of envy. These can almost be defined as metaphors because society pretty much agrees on the one-to-one meaning of them. Symbols used in literature are usually of a different sort. They tend to be private and personal; their significance is only evident in the context of the work where they are used. A good example is the huge pair of spectacles on a billboard in Fitzgerald's *The Great Gatsby*. They are interesting as a part of the landscape, but they also symbolize divine myopia.

SYMBOL: an object or action that can be observed with the senses in addition to its suggesting many other things

A symbol can certainly have more than one meaning, and the meaning may be as personal as the memories and experiences of the particular reader. In analyzing a poem or a story, it's important to identify the symbols and their possible meanings.

Some things a symbol is not—an abstraction such as truth, death, and love; in narrative, a well-developed character who is not at all mysterious.

An **ALLUSION** is very much like a symbol, and the two sometimes tend to run together. An allusion is defined by Merriam Webster's *Encyclopedia of Literature* as "an implied reference to a person, event, thing, or a part of another text." Allusions are based on the assumption that there is a common body of knowledge shared by poets and readers and that a reference to that body of knowledge will be immediately understood. Allusions to the Bible and to classical mythology are common in Western literature on the assumption that they will be immediately understood. This is not always the case, of course. T. S. Eliot's *The Wasteland* requires research and annotation for understanding. He assumed more background on the part of average readers than actually exists.

ALLUSION: very much like a symbol, and the two sometimes tend to run together; an allusion is defined by Merriam Webster's *Encyclopedia of Literature* as "an implied reference to a person, event, thing, or a part of another text"

COMPETENCY 15

ANALYZE AND INTERPRET LITERATURE FROM DIFFERENT PERIODS AND CULTURES, AND UNDERSTAND THE RELATIONSHIP OF WORKS OF LITERATURE TO THEIR SOCIAL AND HISTORICAL CONTEXTS

SKILL 15.1 Analyze how the parts of a literary passage contribute to the whole

See Skill 15.2

SKILL 15.2 Compare and contrast the tone or mood of two or more literary passages

A piece of writing is an integrated whole. It is not enough to just look at the various parts—the total entity must be examined. It should be read as an emotional expression of the author and as an artistic embodiment of a meaning or set of meanings. This is what is sometimes called **tone** in literary criticism.

Writers are telling readers about the world as they see it and will give voice to certain phases of their own personalities. By reading their works, we can know something of their personal qualities and emotions. However, it is important to remember that not all their characteristics will be revealed in a single work. People change and may have very different attitudes at different times in their lives. Sometimes, they will be influenced by a desire to have a piece of work accepted, to appear to be current, or simply to satisfy the interests and desires of potential readers. It can destroy a work or make it less than it might be. Sometimes the best works are not commercial successes in the generation when they were written but are discovered at a later time and by another generation. There are four places to look for tone:

- **Choice of form:** Tragedy or comedy; melodrama or farce; parody or sober lyric.
- **Choice of materials:** Characters who have attractive human qualities; others who are repugnant. What authors show in a setting will often indicate what their interests are.

- Writers' interpretations: They may be explicit—telling us how they feel.
- Writers' implicit interpretations: Their feelings for a character come through in the description. For example, the use of "smirked" instead of "laughed"; "minced," "stalked," "marched," instead of "walked."

Readers are asked to join writers in the feelings expressed about the world and the things that happen in it. The tone of a piece of writing is important in a critical review of it.

Style, in literature, means a distinctive manner of expression and applies to all levels of language, beginning at the phonemic level—word choices, alliteration, assonance, etc.; the syntactic level—length of sentences, choice of structure and phraseology, patterns, etc.; and extends even beyond the sentence to paragraphs and chapters. In Steinbeck's *Grapes of Wrath*, for instance, the style is quite simple in the narrative sections, and the dialogue employs dialect. Because the emphasis is on the story—the narrative—his style is straightforward, for the most part. He just tells the story.

However, there are chapters where he varies his style. He uses symbols and combines them with description that is realistic. He sometimes shifts to a crisp, repetitive pattern to underscore the beeping and speeding of cars. By contrast, some of those inner chapters are lyrical, almost poetic.

These shifts in style reflect the attitude of authors toward their subject matter. They intend to make statements, and they use a variety of styles to strengthen their points.

SKILL 15.3 Analyze aspects of cultural or historical context implied in a literary passage

Prior to twentieth-century research on child development and child/adolescent literature's relationship to that development, books for adolescents were primarily didactic. They were designed to be instructive concerning history, manners, and morals.

Middle Ages

As early as the eleventh century, Anselm, the Archbishop of Canterbury, wrote an encyclopedia designed to instill in children the beliefs and principles of conduct acceptable to adults in medieval society. Early monastic translations of the Bible and other religious writings were written in Latin for the edification of the upper classes.

Fifteenth-century hornbooks were designed to teach reading and religious lessons. William Claxton printed English versions of Aesop's *Fables*, Malory's *Le Morte d'Arthur,* and stories from Greek and Roman mythology. Though printed for adults, tales of the adventures of Odysseus and the Arthurian knights were also popular with literate adolescents.

Renaissance

Chapbooks were condensed versions of myths and fairy tales. They were small in size and length and designed to be read by the common people.

The Renaissance saw the introduction of inexpensive chapbooks, small in size and sixteen to sixty-four pages in length. Chapbooks were condensed versions of myths and fairy tales. Designed for the common people, chapbooks were grammatically imperfect but immensely popular because of their adventurous contents. Though most serious, educated adults frowned on the sometimes vulgar little books, they received praise from Richard Steele of *Tattler* fame for inspiring his grandson's interest in reading and in pursuing his other studies.

The Puritans' three most popular reads were the Bible, John Foe's Book of Martyrs, *and John Bunyan's* Pilgrim's Progress.

Meanwhile, the Puritans' three most popular reads were the Bible, John Foe's *Book of Martyrs*, and John Bunyan's *Pilgrim's Progress*. Though venerating religious martyrs and preaching the moral propriety that would lead to eternal happiness, the stories of the *Book of Martyrs* were often lurid in their descriptions of the fate of the damned. In contrast, *Pilgrim's Progress*, not written for children and difficult reading even for adults, was as attractive to adolescents for its adventurous plot as for its moral outcome. In Puritan America, the *New England Primer* set forth the prayers, catechisms, Bible verses, and illustrations meant to instruct children in the Puritan ethic. The seventeenth-century French used fables and fairy tales to entertain adults, but children found them enjoyable as well.

Seventeenth century

The late seventeenth century brought the first literature that specifically targeted the young. Pierre Peril's *Fairy Tales*, Jean de la Fontaine's retellings of famous fables, Mme. d'Aulnoy's novels based on old folktales, and Mme. de Beaumont's *Beauty and the Beast* were written to delight as well as instruct young people. In England, publisher John Newbury was the first to publish a literary line for children. This line included a translation of Perrault's *Tales of Mother Goose*; *A Little Pretty Pocket-Book*, "intended for instruction and amusement" but decidedly moralistic and bland in comparison to the previous century's chapbooks; and *The Renowned History of Little Goody Two Shoes*, allegedly written by Oliver Goldsmith for a juvenile audience.

Eighteenth century

Largely, eighteenth-century adolescents found their reading pleasure in adult books: Daniel Defoe's *Robinson Crusoe*, Jonathan Swift's *Gulliver's Travels*, and Johann Wyss's *Swiss Family Robinson*. More books were being written for children, and moral didacticism, though less religious, was nevertheless everpresent.

The short stories of Maria Edgeworth, the four-volume *The History of Sandford and Merton* by Thomas Day, and Martha Farquharson's 26-volume *Elsie Dinsmore* series dealt with pious protagonists who learned restraint, repentance, and rehabilitation through sin and redemption.

Two bright spots in this period of didacticism were Jean Jacques Rousseau's *Emile* and *The Tales of Shakespeare*, Charles and Mary Lamb's simplified versions of Shakespeare's plays. Rousseau believed that a child's abilities were enhanced by a free, happy life, and the Lambs subscribed to the notion that children were entitled to entertaining literature written in language that was comprehensible to them.

Nineteenth century

Child and adolescent literature truly began its modern rise in nineteenth-century Europe. Hans Christian Andersen's *Fairy Tales* were fanciful adaptations of the somber tales of the Grimm brothers in the previous century. Andrew Lang's series of colorful fairy books contained the folklores of many nations and are still parts of the collections of many modern libraries. Clement Moore's "A Visit from St. Nicholas" is a cheery, nonthreatening child's view of the night before Christmas. Lewis Carroll's books about Alice's adventures, Edward Lear's poems with caricatures, and Lucretia Nole's stories of the Philadelphia Peterkin family are full of fancy and contain not a smidgen of morality.

Other popular Victorian novels introduced the modern fantasy and science fiction genres; William Makepeace Thackeray's *The Rose and the Ring*, Charles Dickens' *The Magic Fishbone*, and Jules Verne's *Twenty Thousand Leagues Under the Sea* are examples. Adventures to exotic places became a popular topic; Rudyard Kipling's *Jungle Books*, Verne's *Around the World in Eighty Days*, and Robert Louis Stevenson's *Treasure Island* and *Kidnapped* were popular reads. In 1884, the first English translation of Johanna Spyri's *Heidi* appeared on the scene.

North America was also finding its voice for adolescent readers. American Louisa May Alcott's *Little Women* and Canadian L.M. Montgomery's *Anne of Green Gables* ushered in the modern age of realistic fiction. American youth were enjoying *The Adventures of Tom Sawyer* and *Huckleberry Finn*. For the first time, children were able to read books about real people just like themselves.

Twentieth century

For more information, read Introductory Lecture on Children's & Adolescent Literature:

http://homepages.wmich.edu/~tarboxg/Introductory_Lecture_on_Children's_&_Adol_Lit.html

Childhood and adolescent literature of the twentieth century is extensive, diverse and, as in previous centuries, influenced by the adults who write, edit, and select books for youth consumption. In the first third of the twentieth century, suitable adolescent literature dealt with children from large families and good homes. These books projected an image of a peaceful, rural existence.

Though the characters and plots were more realistic, the stories maintained focus on topics that were considered emotionally and intellectually proper. Popular at this time were Laura Ingalls Wilder's *Little House on the Prairie* series and Carl Sandburg's biography *Abe Lincoln Grows Up*. English author J.R.R. Tolkein's fantasy *The Hobbit* prefaced modern adolescent readers' fascination with the works of Piers Antony, Madelaine L'Engle, and Anne McCaffery.

Fiction and Nonfiction

Fiction is the opposite of fact, and, simple as that may seem, it's the major distinction between fiction works and nonfiction works. The earliest nonfiction came in the form of cave paintings, the record of what prehistoric man procured on hunting trips. On the other hand, we do not know that some of it might be fiction—that is, what they would like to catch on future hunting trips. Cuneiform inscriptions, which hold the earliest writings, are probably nonfiction about conveying goods such as oxen and barley and dealing with the buying and selling of these items.

Some types of nonfiction

- Almanac
- Autobiography
- Biography
- Blueprin
- Book report
- Diary
- Dictionary
- Documentary film
- Encyclopedia
- Essay
- History
- Journal
- Letter
- Philosophy
- Science book
- Textbook
- User manual

These can also be called genres of nonfiction—divisions of a particular art according to criteria particular to that form. How these divisions are formed is vague.

There are actually no fixed boundaries for either fiction or nonfiction. They are formed by sets of conventions, and many works cross into multiple genres by way of borrowing and recombining these conventions.

Some genres of fiction

- Action-adventure
- Crime
- Detective
- Erotica
- Fantasy
- Horror
- Mystery
- Romance
- Science fiction
- Thriller
- Western

BILDUNGSROMAN (from the German) means "novel of education" or "novel of formation" and is a novel that traces the spiritual, moral, psychological, or social development and growth of the main character from childhood to maturity. Dickens's *David Copperfield* (1850) represents this genre, as does Thomas Wolfe's *Look Homeward Angel* (1929).

BILDUNGSROMAN: a novel that traces the spiritual, moral, psychological, or social development and growth of the main character from childhood to maturity

A work of fiction typically has a central character, called the protagonist, and a character that stands in opposition, called the antagonist. The antagonist might be something other than a person. In Stephen Crane's short story "The Open Boat," for example, the antagonist is a hostile environment, a stormy sea. Conflicts between protagonist and antagonist are typical of a work of fiction, and climax is the point at which those conflicts are resolved. The plot has to do with the form or shape that the conflicts take as they move toward resolution. A fiction writer artistically uses devices labeled characterization to reveal character. Characterization can depend on dialogue, description, and/or the attitude or attitudes of one or more characters toward one another.

Enjoying fiction depends upon the ability of readers to suspend disbelief, to some extent. Readers make a deal with writers that for the time it takes to read the story, their own belief will be put aside and be replaced by the convictions and reality that the writer has presented in the story. This is not true in nonfiction. Writers of nonfiction declare in the choice of that genre that their work is reliably based upon reality.

SKILL 15.4 Distinguish characteristic features of different literary genres, periods, and traditions reflected in one or more literary passages

For details about characteristics of difference literary genres, see Skill 14.1. See skill 15.3 for characteristics of different literary periods.

SKILL 15.5 Make inferences about character, setting, author's point of view, etc., based on the content of a literary passage

It is no accident that plot is sometimes called action. If the plot does not move, the story quickly dies. Therefore, successful writers of stories use a wide variety of active verbs in creative and unusual ways. If readers are kept on their toes by the movement of the story, then the experience of reading it will be pleasurable. Those readers will probably want to read more of the writers' work. Careful, unique, and unusual choices of active verbs will bring about that effect.

William Faulkner is a good example of a successful writer whose stories are lively and memorable because of his use of unusual active verbs. In analyzing the development of plot, it is wise to look at the verbs. However, the development of believable conflicts is also vital. If there is no conflict, there is no story. What devices do writers use to develop the conflicts, and are those conflicts real and believable?

Character is portrayed in many ways: description of physical characteristics, dialogue, interior monologue, the thoughts of the character, the attitudes of other characters toward this one, etc. Descriptive language depends on the ability to recreate a sensory experience for readers. If the description of the character's appearance is a visual one, then readers must be able to see the character. What's the shape of the nose? What color are the eyes? How tall or how short is this character? Thin or chubby? How does the character move? How does the character walk?

Terms must be chosen that will create a picture for readers. It's not enough to say the eyes are blue, for example. What blue? Often the color of eyes is compared to something else to enhance readers' ability to visualize the character. A good test of characterization is the level of emotional involvement of readers in the character. If readers are to become involved, the description must provide an actual experience—seeing, smelling, hearing, tasting, or feeling.

Dialogue will reflect characteristics. Is it clipped? Does it employ significant dialect? Does a character use a lot of colloquialisms? The ability to portray the speech of a character can make or break a story. The kind of person the character is in the mind of readers is dependent on impressions created by description and dialogue. How do other characters feel about a particular character as revealed by their interactions with that character, their discussions with each other about that character, or their overt descriptions of that character? For example, "John, of course, can't be trusted with another person's possessions." In analyzing a story, it's useful to discuss the devices used to produce character.

Setting may be visual, temporal, psychological, or social. Descriptive words are often used here, also. In Edgar Allan Poe's description of the house in "The Fall of the House of Usher," as the protagonist/narrator approaches it, the air of dread and gloom that pervades the story is caught in the setting and sets the stage. A setting may also be symbolic (it is in Poe's story): the house is a symbol of the family that lives in it. As the house disintegrates, so does the family.

The language used in all of these aspects of a story—plot, character, and setting—work together to create the mood of a story. Poe's first sentence establishes the mood of the story:

During the whole of a dull, dark, and soundless day in the autumn of the year, when the clouds hung oppressively low in the heavens, I had been passing alone, on horseback, through a singularly dreary tract of country; and at length found myself, as the shades of the evening drew on, within view of the melancholy House of Usher.

SKILL 15.6 Recognize how a text conveys multiple levels of meaning

Understanding the cultural context of a poem can often help our understanding of some aspect of the poem itself. The social, political, and economic currents surrounding a writer can, and usually do, impact the writer's literary creation. Sometimes this influence is **allegorical**. The simple analogy of life as a journey serves as perhaps the most important key to understanding many of Robert Frost's early-twentieth century poems.

Understanding the cultural context of a poem can often help our understanding of some aspect of the poem itself.

The Road Not Taken

Two roads diverged in a yellow wood
And sorry I could not travel both
And be one traveler, long I stood
And looked down one as far as I could
To where it bent in the undergrowth;

Then took the other, as just as fair
And having perhaps the better claim,
Because it was grassy and wanted wear;
Though as for that, the passing there
Had worn them really about the same,

And both that morning equally lay
In leaves no step had trodden black.
Oh, I kept the first for another day!
Yet knowing how way leads on to way,
I doubted if I should ever come back.

I shall be telling this with a sigh
Somewhere ages and ages hence:
Two roads diverged in a wood and I—
I took the one less traveled by,
And that has made all the difference.

—Robert Frost

Robert Frost's well-loved poem "The Road Not Taken" (1915) interests readers because it is at once so simple and so resonant. The speaker recalls his walk in the woods. He describes arriving at a fork in the road and the need to make a choice by taking one path and leaving another for some other day, "sorry" that he "could not travel both." The activity seems simple initially, but the action has a level of symbolic significance, which, upon a closer reading, is revealed in the speaker's reflections about his choice. In this poem, the speaker's thoughts following the choice of which path to take are just as important as the action of choosing.

The final stanza indicates that the choice concerns more than simply following a road. The speaker says that choosing the road "less traveled" has "made all the difference." In other words, that choice has affected his whole life. The metaphor of life being a journey is quite familiar, but having to select one road—one path—alludes to the basic truth that we can't have it all. Although we can imagine what would have happened had we made different choice—pursued alternative paths—these ruminations of a parallel life are just fantasies. Making one choice precludes another.

Frost's choosing "the one less traveled by" leads the reader to wonder if this is a statement about individuality, but the matter is complicated when we revisit the second and third stanza in which he describes one path as "just as fair" as the other; each was "worn … really about the same." Often situations requiring decision are ambiguous—there are not clear positive or negative foreseeable outcomes. In the speaker's case, "all the difference" seems to affirm his self-reliance—he did take "the path "less traveled" after all. However, when the speaker recalls what happened in "the yellow wood," an image that evokes a nostalgic glow, he appears more concerned with the path he did not take—the unrealized possibilities in his life.

Poetry often asks the reader to look closely, reread, and examine the text—often a poet will say one thing in terms of another, and the discovery of additional layers of meaning.

Further investigation of layers of meaning in literature often involves taking a critical approach. Critical approaches to literature reveal how or why a particular work is constructed and what its social and cultural implications are. Understanding critical perspectives will help you to see and appreciate a literary work as a multilayered construct of meaning. Reading literary criticism will inspire you to reread, rethink, and respond. Soon you will be a full participant in an endless and enriching conversation about literature.

COMPETENCY 16

ANALYZE AND INTERPRET EXAMPLES OF RELIGIOUS OR PHILOSOPHICAL IDEAS FROM VARIOUS PERIODS OF TIME, AND UNDERSTAND THEIR SIGNIFICANCE IN SHAPING SOCIETIES AND CULTURES

SKILL 16.1 Distinguish the religious and philosophical traditions associated with given cultures and world regions

There are the eight main religions practiced today. They have divisions or smaller sects within them; not one of them is completely unified.

Judaism	The oldest of the eight religions and the first to teach and practice the belief in one God, Yahweh.
Christianity	The name "Christian" means one who is a follower of Jesus Christ. Christians follow his teachings and examples, living by the laws and principles of the New Testament. It grew and spread in the first century throughout the Roman Empire, despite persecution. A later schism resulted in the Western (Roman Catholic) and Eastern (Orthodox) churches. Protestant sects developed after the Protestant Reformation.
Islam	This religion was founded in Arabia by Mohammed, who preached about God, Allah. Islam spread through trade, travel, and conquest; followers of it fought in the Crusades. In addition, Islam figures in other wars against Christians and, today, against the Jewish nation of Israel. Followers of Islam, called Muslims, live by the teachings of the Koran, their holy book, and of their prophets.
Hinduism	A complex religion, Hinduism centers around the belief that, through many reincarnations of the soul, man will eventually be united with the universal soul, which assumes the three forms of Brahma (the creator), Vishnu (the preserver), and Siva (the destroyer). Hinduism was begun by people called Aryans around 1500 BCE and spread into India. The Aryans blended their culture with the culture of the Dravidians, the natives that they conquered. Today it has many sects and promotes the worship of hundreds of gods and goddesses and the belief in reincarnation. Though forbidden today by law, a prominent feature of Hinduism in the past was a rigid adherence to, and practice of, the infamous caste system.

Continued on next page

Buddhism	Similar to Hinduism, Buddhism rejects the caste system in favor of all men following the "eightfold path" toward spiritual living. Nirvana (spiritual peace) may be reached even in one lifetime by righteous living. Buddhism was developed in India from the teachings of Prince Gautama and spread to most of Asia. Its beliefs opposed the worship of numerous deities, the Hindu caste system, and preoccupation with the supernatural. Worshippers must be free of attachment to all things worldly and devote themselves to finding release from life's suffering.
Confucianism	This is a Chinese religion based on the teachings of the fifth century BCE Chinese philosopher Confucius. Noted for his teachings that reflect faith in mankind, Confucius advocated living an active life of learning, participating in government, and devotion to family. There is no clergy, no organization, and no belief in a deity or in life after death. It emphasizes political and moral ideas with respect for authority and ancestors. Rulers were expected to govern according to high moral standards.
Taoism	Begun by sixth-century BCE philosopher Lao-tse, Taoism teaches that laws cannot improve man's lot, so government should be a minimal force in man's life. Man should live passively in harmony with Tao (nature). Lao-tse wrote a book known as *Te-Tao Ching*.
Shinto	Shinto was strongly influenced by Buddhism and Confucianism, but never had strong doctrines on salvation or life after death. It consists of ancient religious beliefs, known as the "Way of the Gods," and incorporates nature and ancestor worship with shamanistic practices, such as belief in magic to control nature, heal sickness, and predict the future. The native religion of Japan developed from native folk beliefs worshipping spirits and demons in animals, trees, and mountains. According to its mythology, deities created Japan and its people, which resulted in worshipping the emperor as a god.

SKILL 16.2 Recognize assumptions and beliefs underlying ideas presented in religious or philosophical writing

Preliterate societies probably passed religious and historical information on from one generation to the next by using mnemonic exercises as part of initiation rites and religious rituals. Group memories of important tribal events were the domain of the community storytellers and were transmitted from one generation to the next through the use of long poems and chants set to music. It is likely that dance was also enlisted to communicate tribal history and to ensure its continuity in the tribe's traditions. Ancient cultures relied on oral epic poems and mythologies from the past on which to base their traditions. Often the historical information was couched in religious terms, as in the Sumerian mythologies in which warring gods and goddesses actually portrayed feuding city-states. Eventually, these orally transmitted stories were written down, forming the basis for the mythologies and legends we know today.

"To the victors go the spoils," and so, apparently, do the publishing rights. The winners in any war gain the privilege of having history viewed through their eyes, and, usually, through their eyes alone. The Romans were masters at propaganda and enlisted the aid of many historians and other writers to create history books favorable to the Roman perspective. They also wrote Roman mythologies that "altered" the past in order to help the new Roman conquerors gain respectability with their new subjects.

During the Medieval period, the Roman Catholic Church served as both religious institution and government. Because there was no real separation of church and state, portrayals of religious events and historical events tended to mesh together, as evidenced by the many church paintings depicting both historical characters and contemporary people in religious settings. Religious law became state law, and religious truths were assumed to be the truths that all people, regardless of personal beliefs, must adhere to. Because the Church collected taxes, it had money to construct buildings that served both church and municipal functions. The churches were filled with religious art, depicting stories that were accepted as historically accurate fact.

Social, Political, and Religious Forces and the Humanities

It is often said that the arts are a mirror of society, reflecting the morals, attitudes, and concerns of people in any given culture. Because the humanities deal with the expression of the human experience, it stands to reason that society's views of what is appropriate to reveal about that experience plays a major role in what artists express. At any time in history, political, social, and religious powers have influenced what artists feel comfortable expressing.

In contrast to this is the view of "art for art's sake," a slogan touted by Oscar Wilde and Samuel Coleridge, among others. This opinion holds that the arts, out of necessity, are outside the realm of these forces, and that art can and should exist solely for its own benefit and because of its intrinsic beauty.

Political influence can be seen in the monumental sculpture of the Roman Empire, constructed to glorify the state. An example is the 6'8'' sculpture *Augustus in Armor*, depicting the emperor as a consul confidently striding forward to deliver an inspiring speech to his legions. His bare feet denote courage, and his staff symbolizes the power of the emperor over the Roman Senate. The bronze *Equestrian Statue of Marcus Aurelius* serves as another example, illustrating the "philosopher-king" concept of the emperor as a man of learning ruling over Rome with wisdom and justice instead of brute force.

A recent example of how governmental powers affect the humanities can be seen in the context of the early twentieth century in the Soviet Union. The Communist regime feared that artists might encourage the onset of capitalism and democracy and, accordingly, took actions to repress freedom of expression in favor of rhetoric favorable to the cause of Communism, including persecution of artists and authors. The result was an outpouring of state-produced, stilted graphic art and literature, so meaningful expressions in the arts had to be smuggled out of the country to receive acclaim. Aleksandr Solzhenitsyn, author of *One Day in the Life of Ivan Denisovich* and *The Gulag Archipelago*, was forced to live in exile for several years.

The influence of religion on art can most clearly be viewed in the works of the medieval European period. During this era, the Roman Catholic Church ruled as a state government and, as such, was the major patron of the arts. As a result, much of the art from this period was religious in nature. Examples are Duccio's *Christ Entering Jerusalem* and Master Honore's *David and Goliath*.

SKILL 16.3 Analyze societal implications of philosophical or religious ideas

One of the most ancient of the world's religions practiced today is Hinduism, which has its roots in India's earliest known civilizations.

CASTE SYSTEM: a highly rigid hierarchal order based on class and race stratifications

KARMA: the cosmic principle according to which each person is rewarded or punished in one incarnation according to that person's deeds in the previous incarnation

One of the most ancient of the world's religions practiced today is Hinduism, which has its roots in India's earliest known civilizations. Differing from many of today's religions, Hinduism identifies the sacred not as a superhuman personality, but as an objective, all-pervading spirit called Brahma. Hinduism holds that, through many reincarnations of the soul, a human will eventually be united with the universal soul.

Hinduism is also a pantheistic religion, that is, having to do with the belief that divinity is inherent in all things. Therefore, all nature is an expression of Brahma. Ancient Hindus viewed the life of the individual as one with, rather than subject to, an impersonal divine force; Hindus embrace a multitude of deities who are perceived as emanations or embodiments of Brahma. They sought the sublimation of the self by means of meditation and a stilling of the senses. Achieving nirvana, a final release for the cycle of life and death and rebirth, is the ultimate goal.

Part of the social and religious makeup of early Hindu society in India was the **CASTE SYSTEM**, a highly rigid hierarchal order based on class and race stratifications. The rigidity may well be due to the influence of the idea of karma, that poor birth is morally deserved. **KARMA** is the cosmic principle according to which each person is rewarded or punished in one incarnation according to that person's deeds in the previous incarnation. Therefore, some Hindus believe, if someone is born into a lower caste, or even outside of the caste system, it may be a manifestation of cosmic justice for bad deeds in a past life. The caste system, which is incredibly complicated and nuanced, prevailed as the social system of India until modern times. By 1000 BCE, four principal castes existed: priests and scholars, rulers and warriors, artisans and merchants, and unskilled workers. Slowly, these casts began to subdivide according to occupation. At the very bottom of the social order, or, arguably, outside of it—lay those who held the most menial occupations. They became known as the untouchables. The caste system worked to enforce a distance between rulers and the ruled in the medieval period in India, between the end of the Gupta dynasty (c. 500 BCE) and the Mongol invasion.

SKILL 16.4 Compare and contrast key concepts presented in two excerpts reflecting different philosophical or religious traditions

Confucianism and Legalism

Parallel to, and contemporaneously with, the rise of classical philosophy in ancient Greece, ancient China also reached an intellectual pinnacle. For the ancient Chinese, the natural order of the world was central to all aspects of material and spiritual existence. This holistic outlook contributed to the evolution of leadership and the formation of the social order. The ancient Chinese regarded the natural order as the basis for spiritual life and the social order. Ideally, one would know one's place within this order and act accordingly, effectively contributing to the overall harmony of the community.

For the ancient Chinese, the natural order of the world was central to all aspects of material and spiritual existence.

In the fifth century BCE, Confucius emerged as China's most important philosopher. He was a proponent of ancient Chinese ethics, which emphasized ethical and moral harmony in relation to the health of a community—and a government. Confucius earned renown through his teaching, which his students transcribed. His *Analects*, as his teachings are called, are diverse in origin, but they embody his thoughts on matters such as the arts, relationships, and death.

In the fifth century BCE, Confucius emerged as China's most important philosopher. He believed that human character, not birth or social status, determined the worth of the individual.

Confucius believed that human character, not birth or social status, determined the worth of the individual.

The following excerpts come from Confucius's *Analects*:

2.1 The Master said: "He who rules by virtue is like the polestar, which remains unmoving in its mansion while all the other stars revolve respectfully around it."

2.3 The Master said: "Lead them by political maneuvers, restrain them with punishment: the people will become cunning and shameless. Lead them by virtue, restrain them with ritual: they will develop a sense of shame and a sense of participation."

4.24 The Master said: "A gentleman brings out the good that is in people, he does not bring out the bad. A vulgar man does the opposite."

Confucian thinking also generally perceives humankind as good. An opposing point of view challenged these Confucian beliefs about human nature. This other philosophical contingent, known as the Legalists, described the nature of humankind as inherently evil. The leading Legalist, Han Fei Zi, emerged in the third century BCE and asserted that the innate selfishness of humankind necessitated a strong central authority and harsh punishment.

The leading Legalist, Han Fei Zi, emerged in the third century BCE and asserted that the innate selfishness of humankind necessitated a strong central authority and harsh punishment.

Legalist opinion is best exemplified by the following excerpt:

"Now take a young fellow who is a bad character," writes Han Fei Zi. "His parents may get angry at him, but he never makes any change. The villages may reprove him, but he is not moved. His teachers and elders may admonish him, but he never reforms. The love of his parent, the efforts of the villages, and the wisdom of his teachers and elders ... are applied to him, and yet not even a hair on his chin is altered. It is only after the district magistrate sends out his soldiers and in the name of the law searches for wicked individuals that the young man becomes afraid and changes his ways and alters his deeds. So while the love of parents is not sufficient to discipline the children, the severe penalties of the district magistrate are. This is because men become naturally spoiled by love, but are submissive to authority.

These two opposing philosophical traditions coexisted in ancient China; it is the Legalist view that would later be adopted by China's first dynasty at the beginning of the third century BCE.

DOMAIN IV

COMMUNICATION AND RESEARCH SKILLS

PERSONALIZED STUDY PLAN

PAGE	COMPETENCY AND SKILL		KNOWN MATERIAL/ SKIP IT
181	**17:**	**Derive information from a variety of sources (e.g., magazines, articles, essays, web sites)**	☐
	17.1:	Identify the stated or implied main idea of a paragraph or passage	☐
	17.2:	Select an accurate summary or outline of a passage	☐
	17.3:	Organize information presented electronically	☐
	17.4:	Comprehend stated or implied relationships in an excerpt	☐
	17.5:	Recognize information that supports, illustrates, or elaborates the main idea of a passage	☐
187	**18:**	**Analyze and interpret written materials from a variety of sources**	☐
	18.1:	Recognize a writer's purpose for writing	☐
	18.2:	Draw conclusions based on information presented in an excerpt	☐
	18.3:	Interpret figurative language in an excerpt	☐
	18.4:	Compare and contrast views presented in two or more excerpts	☐
193	**19:**	**Use critical reasoning skills to assess an author's treatment of content in written material from a variety of sources**	☐
	19.1:	Analyze the logical structure or faulty reasoning	☐
	19.2:	Distinguish between fact and opinion	☐
	19.3:	Determine the relevance of specific facts, examples, or data to a writer's argument	☐
	19.4:	Interpret the content of a passage to determine a writer's opinions, point of view, or position	☐
	19.5:	Evaluate credibility, objectivity, or bias	☐
198	**20:**	**Analyze and evaluate the effectiveness of expression in a written paragraph or passage according to the conventions of edited American English**	☐
	20.1:	Revise text to correct problems relating to grammar	☐
	20.2:	Revise text to correct problems relating to sentence construction	☐
	20.3:	Revise text to improve unity and coherence	☐
	20.4:	Analyze problems related to the organization of a given text	☐

PERSONALIZED STUDY PLAN

PAGE	COMPETENCY AND SKILL	KNOWN MATERIAL/ SKIP IT
230	**21: Demonstrate the ability to locate, retrieve, organize, and interpret information from a variety of traditional and electronic sources**	☐
	21.1: Demonstrate familiarity with basic reference tools	☐
	21.2: Recognize the difference between primary and secondary sources	☐
	21.3: Formulate research questions and hypotheses	☐
	21.4: Apply procedures for retrieving information from traditional and technological sources	☐
	21.5: Interpret data presented in visual, graphic, tabular, and quantitative forms	☐
	21.6: Organize information into logical and coherent outlines	☐
	21.7: Evaluate the reliability of different sources of information	☐

COMPETENCY 17

DERIVE INFORMATION FROM A VARIETY OF SOURCES

(e.g., MAGAZINES, ARTICLES, ESSAYS, WEB SITES)

SKILL 17.1 Identify the stated or implied main idea of a paragraph or passage

Main Idea

The MAIN IDEA of a passage or paragraph is the basic message, idea, point concept, or meaning that the author wants to convey to you, the reader. Understanding the main idea of a passage or paragraph is the key to understanding the more subtle components of the author's message. The main idea is what is being said about a topic or subject. Once you have identified the basic message, you will have an easier time answering other questions that test critical skills.

MAIN IDEA: the basic message, idea, point concept, or meaning that the author wants to convey to you

Main ideas are either stated or implied. A stated main idea is explicit: it is directly expressed in a sentence or two in the paragraph or passage. An implied main idea is suggested by the overall reading selection. In the first case, you need not pull information from various points in the paragraph or passage in order to form the main idea because it is already stated by the author. If a main idea is implied, however, you must formulate, in your own words, a main idea statement by condensing the overall message contained in the material itself.

SKILL 17.2 Select an accurate summary or outline of a passage

SAMPLE PASSAGE

Sometimes too much of a good thing can become a very bad thing indeed. In an earnest attempt to consume a healthy diet, dietary supplement enthusiasts have been known to overdose. Vitamin C, for example, long thought to help people ward off cold viruses, is currently being studied for its possible role in warding off cancer and other diseases that cause tissue degeneration. Unfortunately, an overdose of vitamin C—more than 10,000 mg—on a daily basis can cause nausea and diarrhea. Calcium supplements, commonly taken by women, are helpful in warding off osteoporosis. More than just a few grams a day, however, can lead to stomach upset and even to kidney and bladder stones. Niacin, proven useful in reducing cholesterol levels, can be dangerous in large doses for those who suffer from heart problems, asthma, or ulcers.

The main idea expressed in this paragraph is that

A. Supplements taken in excess can be a bad thing indeed

B. Dietary supplement enthusiasts have been known to overdose

C. Vitamins can cause nausea, diarrhea, and kidney or bladder stones

D. People who take supplements are preoccupied with their health

Answer A is a paraphrase of the first sentence and provides a general framework for the rest of the paragraph: excess supplement intake is bad. The rest of the paragraph discusses the consequences of taking too many vitamins. Answers B and C refer to major details, and Answer D introduces the idea of preoccupation, which is not included in this paragraph.

SKILL 17.3 Organize information presented on a Web site or other electronic means of communication

When information has been obtained from a Web site or other electronic means, it must be organized as carefully as information obtained from a traditional source. Operate as though another user will need to locate the information at a later time. In addition to recording information such as title, author, and source, it is also necessary to include the Web address and the date the Web site was accessed. The date stamp is particularly necessary in the dynamic online environment where updates can result in information being very different from one day to the next. Upon deciding on the appropriate categories to record, it is then necessary to record and organize the information in a systematic manner. To achieve this goal, there are several techniques available, from the simple to the complex.

The simplest strategy is to organize the material in word processing software such as OpenOffice.org Writer, Microsoft Word, or Word Perfect. Under this method, the information can be presented in a table or as bulleted or numbered text. Word processors are also useful when presenting information in narrative form. For instance, this is the tool of choice when writing lesson plans or creating student assignments.

A more advanced method is organizing the information in a spreadsheet application such as OpenOffice.org Calc, Microsoft Excel, or Lotus 1-2-3. This strategy allows categories to be created in columns (e.g., author, date, type of source, key words). Each source is then recorded in its own row. This method is preferable when large numbers of categories must be created or many sources will be recorded.

The most advanced system of information organization is using an electronic database such as OpenOffice.org Base, Microsoft Access, or Lotus Approach. These software programs allow the creation of relationships between the various categories of information. For instance, if a great deal of information will be researched, it may be good to create tables for each category. This facilitates recording repetitive information such as type of source or location where information was accessed. A main table would link to the category tables and each source would then be recorded in its own row.

SKILL 17.4 Comprehend stated or implied relationships in an excerpt *(e.g., cause and effect, sequence of events)*

The **organization** of a written work includes two factors:

1. The order in which writers have chosen to present the different parts of the discussion or argument
2. The relationships they construct between these parts

Written ideas need to be presented in a logical order so that readers can follow the information easily and quickly. There are many different ways in which to order a series of ideas, but they all share two related foundations: to lead readers along a desired path to the main idea, and to avoid backtracking and skipping around.

WAYS TO ORGANIZE A WRITTEN WORK	
ORGANIZATION	**EXPLANATION**
Sequence of Events	In this type of organization, the details are presented in the order in which they have occurred. Paragraphs that describe a process or procedure, give directions, or outline a given time period (such as a day or a month) are often arranged chronologically.
Statement Support	In this type of organization, the main idea is stated and the rest of the paragraph explains or proves it. This type of organization is also referred to as *relative* or *order of importance*. This type of order is organized in four ways: most to least, least to most, most-least-most, and least-most-least.
Comparison-Contrast	The compare-contrast pattern is used when a paragraph describes the differences or similarities between two or more ideas, actions, events, or things. Usually, the topic sentence describes the basic relationship between the ideas or items, and the rest of the paragraph explains this relationship.

Continued on next page

ORGANIZATION	EXPLANATION
Classification	In this type of organization, the paragraph presents grouped information about a topic. The topic sentence usually states the general category, and the rest of the sentences show how various elements of the category have a common base and how they differ from the common base.
Cause and Effect	This pattern describes how two or more events are connected. The main sentence usually states the primary cause(s) and the primary effect(s) and how they are connected. The rest of the sentences explain the connection—how one event caused the next.
Spatial/Place	In this type of organization, certain descriptions are organized according to the location of items in relation to each other and to a larger context. The orderly arrangement guides the reader's eye as he or she mentally envisions the scene or place being described.
Example, Clarification, and Definition	These types of organization show, explain, or elaborate on the main idea. This can be done by showing specific cases, examining meaning multiple times, or describing one term extensively. Many times, all of these organizations follow the basic P.I.E. sequence: P—the point, or main idea, of the paragraph I—the information (data, details, facts) that supports the main idea E—the explanation or analysis of the information and how it proves, is related to, or connects to the main idea

TRANSITIONS: words that signal relationships between ideas

Even if the sentences that make up a given paragraph or passage are arranged in logical order, the document as a whole can still seem choppy, and the various ideas disconnected. **TRANSITIONS**—words that signal relationships between ideas—can help improve the flow of a document. Transitions can help achieve clear and effective presentation of information by establishing connections between sentences, paragraphs, and sections of a document. With transitions, each sentence builds on the ideas in the last, and each paragraph has clear links to the preceding one. As a result, the reader receives clear directions on how to piece together the writer's ideas in a logically coherent argument. By signaling how to organize, interpret, and react to information, transitions enable writers to explain their ideas effectively and elegantly. Below is a list of common transitional expressions.

COMMON TRANSITIONS	
LOGICAL RELATIONSHIP	**TRANSITIONAL EXPRESSION**
Similarity	also, in the same way, just as ... so too, likewise, similarly
Exception/Contrast	but, however, in spite of, on the one hand ... on the other hand, nevertheless, nonetheless, notwithstanding, in contrast, on the contrary, still, yet, although
Sequence/Order	first, second, third, ... next, then, finally, until
Time	after, afterward, at last, before, currently, during, earlier, immediately, later, meanwhile, now, presently, recently, simultaneously, since, subsequently, then
Example	for example, for instance, namely, specifically, to illustrate
Emphasis	even, indeed, in fact, of course, truly
Place/Position	above, adjacent, below, beyond, here, in front, in back, nearby, there
Cause and Effect	accordingly, consequently, hence, so, therefore, thus, as a result, because, consequently, hence, if...then, in short
Additional Support or Evidence	additionally, again, also, and, as well, besides, equally important, further, furthermore, in addition, moreover, then
Conclusion/ Summary	finally, in a word, in brief, in conclusion, in the end, in the final analysis, on the whole, thus, to conclude, to summarize, in sum, in summary
Statement Support	most important, more significant, primarily, most essential
Addition	again, also, and, besides, equally important, finally, furthermore, in addition, last, likewise, moreover, too
Clarification	actually, clearly, evidently, in fact, in other words, obviously, of course, indeed

The following example shows good logical order and transitions. The transition words are highlighted in **bold**.

> *No one really knows how Valentine's Day started. There are several legends, **however**, which are often told. The **first** attributes Valentine's Day to a Christian priest who lived in Rome during the third century under the rule of Emperor Claudius. Rome was at war and, **apparently,** Claudius felt that married men did not fight as well as bachelors. **Consequently**, Claudius banned marriage for the duration of the war. **But** Valentinus, the priest, risked his life to marry couples secretly in violation of Claudius' law. The **second** legend is **even more** romantic. In this story, Valentinus is a prisoner, having been condemned to death for refusing to worship pagan deities. **While** in jail, he fell in love with his jailer's daughter, who happened to be blind. Daily, he prayed for her sight to return and miraculously, it did. On February 14, the day that he was condemned to die, he was allowed to write the young woman a note. **In this farewell letter**, he promised eternal love and signed at the bottom of the page the now famous words, "Your Valentine."*

SKILL 17.5 Recognize information that supports, illustrates, or elaborates the main idea of a passage

Supporting Details

Paragraphs should contain concrete, interesting information, and supporting details to support the main idea or point of view. Fact statements add weight to opinions, especially when writers are trying to convince readers of their viewpoints Because every good thesis has an assertion, a well-written passage offers specifics, facts, data, anecdotes, expert opinions, and other details to show or prove that assertion. Although the authors know what they want to convey, the readers do not.

In the following paragraph, the sentences in **bold** print provide a skeleton of a paragraph on the benefits of recycling. The sentences in bold are generalizations that by themselves do not explain the need to recycle. The sentences in italics add details to SHOW the general points in bold. Notice how the supporting details help you to understand the necessity for recycling.

Although, one day, recycling may become mandatory in all states, right now it is voluntary in many communities. Those of us who participate in recycling are amazed by how much material is recycled. **For many communities, the blue-box recycling program has had an immediate effect.** By just recycling glass, aluminum cans, and plastic bottles, we have reduced the volume of disposable trash by one third, thus extending the useful life of local landfills by over a decade. Imagine the difference if those dramatic results were achieved nationwide. **The number of reusable items we thoughtlessly dispose of is staggering.** For example, Americans dispose of enough steel every day to supply Detroit car manufacturers for three months. Additionally, we dispose of enough aluminum annually to rebuild the nation's air fleet. These statistics, available from the Environmental Protection Agency (EPA), should encourage all of us to watch what we throw away. **Clearly, recycling in our homes and in our communities directly improves the environment.**

COMPETENCY 18

ANALYZE AND INTERPRET WRITTEN MATERIALS FROM A VARIETY OF SOURCES

SKILL 18.1 Recognize a writer's purpose for writing *(e.g., to persuade, to describe)*

An essay is an extended discussion of a writer's point of view about a particular topic. This point of view may be supported by using such writing modes as examples, argument and persuasion, analysis, or comparison/contrast. In any case, a good essay is clear, coherent, well organized, and fully developed.

An essay is an extended discussion of a writer's point of view about a particular topic. This point of view may be supported by using such writing modes as examples, argument and persuasion, analysis, or comparison/contrast.

The author's purpose may be to simply give information that might be interesting or useful to some readers or other; it may be to persuade the reader to a point of view or to move the reader to act in a particular way; it may be to tell a story; or it may be to describe something in such a way that an experience becomes available to the reader.

The following are the primary devices for expressing a particular purpose in a piece of writing:

- **Basic expository writing** gives information not previously known about a topic or is used to explain or define one. Facts, examples, statistics, cause and effect, direct tone, objective rather than subjective delivery, and non-emotional information are presented in a formal manner.
- **Descriptive writing** centers on a person, place, or object. Descriptive writing uses concrete and sensory words to create a mood or impression, arranging details in a chronological or spatial sequence.
- **Narrative writing** is developed using an incident, an anecdote, or a related series of events. Chronology, the five Ws, a topic sentence, and a conclusion are essential ingredients.
- **Persuasive writing** implies the writer's ability to select vocabulary and arrange facts and opinions in such a way as to direct the beliefs or actions of the listener/reader. Persuasive writing may incorporate exposition and narration to illustrate the main idea.
- **Journalistic writing** is theoretically free of author bias. It is essential, when relaying information about an event, a person, or a thing, that the information be factual and objective. Provide students with an opportunity to examine newspapers and create their own newspaper. Many newspapers have educational programs that are offered free to schools.

Tailoring language for a particular **audience** is an important skill. Writing to be read by a business associate will surely sound different from writing to be read by a younger sibling. Not only are the vocabularies different, but the formality/informality of the discourse will need to be adjusted.

The things to be aware of in determining what the language should be for a particular audience, then, hinges on two things: word choice and formality/informality. The most formal language does not use contractions or slang. The most informal language will probably feature a more casual use of common sayings and anecdotes. Formal language will use longer sentences and will not sound like a conversation. The most informal language will use shorter sentences (not necessarily simple sentences) and may sound like a conversation.

TONE: conveys a writer's attitude toward the material and/or the reader

In both formal and informal writing, there exists a **TONE** conveying writers' attitudes toward the material and/or the readers. Tone may be playful, formal, intimate, angry, serious, ironic, outraged, baffled, tender, serene, or depressed. The overall tone of a piece of writing is dictated by both the subject matter and the audience. Tone is also related to the actual words that make up the document because we attach affective meanings to words; these are called **connotations**. Gaining this conscious control over language makes it possible to use language appropriately in various situations and to evaluate its uses in literature and other forms of communication. By evoking the proper responses from readers/listeners, we can prompt them to take action.

The following questions are an excellent way to assess the audience and tone of a given piece of writing.

- Who is your audience? (friend, teacher, business person, someone else)
- How much does this person know about you and/or your topic?
- What is your purpose? (to prove an argument, to persuade, to amuse, to register a complaint, to ask for a raise)
- What emotions do you have about the topic? (nervous, happy, confident, angry, sad, no feelings at all)
- What emotions do you want to register with your audience? (anger, nervousness, happiness, boredom, interest)
- What persona do you need to create in order to achieve your purpose?
- What choice of language is best suited to achieving your purpose with your particular subject? (slang, friendly but respectful, formal)
- What emotional quality do you want to transmit to achieve your purpose (matter of fact, informative, authoritative, inquisitive, sympathetic, angry), and to what degree do you want to express this tone?

If a writer's attitude toward snakes involves active dislike and fear, then the tone would also reflect that attitude by being negative:

> *Countless species of snakes, some more dangerous than others, still lurk on the urban fringes of Florida's towns and cities. They will often invade domestic spaces, terrorizing people and their pets.*

Here, obviously, the snakes are the villains. They lurk, they invade, and they terrorize. The tone of this paragraph might be said to be distressed.

In the same manner, a writer can use language to portray characters as good or bad. A writer uses positive and negative adjectives, as seen above, to convey an impression of a character.

SKILL 18.2 Draw conclusions, or make generalizations, based on information presented in an excerpt

INFERENCE: an educated guess based on given facts and premises

An **INFERENCE** is sometimes called an "educated guess" because it requires going beyond the strictly obvious to create additional meaning by taking the text one logical step further. Inferences and conclusions are based on the content of the passage—that is, on what the passage says or how the writer says it—and are derived by reasoning.

Inference is an essential and automatic component of most reading. Examples include making educated guesses about the meaning of unknown words, the author's main idea, or the existence of bias. Such is the essence of inference. You use your own ability to reason in order to figure out what the writer is implying.

Consider the following example. Assume you are an employer, and you are reading over the letters of reference submitted by a prospective employee for the position of clerk/typist in your real estate office. The position requires the applicant to be neat, careful, trustworthy, and punctual. You come across this letter of reference submitted by an applicant:

> *To Whom It May Concern:*
>
> *Todd Finley has asked me to write a letter of reference for him. I am well qualified to do so because he worked for me for three months last year. His duties included answering the phone, greeting the public, and producing some simple memos and notices on the computer. Although Todd initially had few computer skills and little knowledge of telephone etiquette, he did acquire some during his stay with us. Todd's manner of speaking, both on the telephone and with the clients who came to my establishment, could be described as casual. He was particularly effective when communicating with peers. Please contact me by telephone if you wish to have further information about my experience with Todd.*

Here the writer implies, rather than openly states, the main idea. This letter calls attention to itself because there is a problem with its tone. A truly positive letter would say something such as, "I have the distinct honor of recommending Todd Finley." Here, however, the letter simply verifies that Todd worked in the office. Second, the praise is obviously lukewarm. For example, the writer says that Todd "was particularly effective when communicating with peers." An educated guess translates that statement into a nice way of saying Todd was not serious about his communication with clients.

In order to draw inferences and make conclusions, a reader must use prior knowledge and apply it to the current situation. A conclusion or inference is never stated. The reader must rely on common sense.

Practice Questions: Inference

Read the following passages and select an answer.

1. Tim Sullivan had just turned fifteen. As a birthday present, his parents had given him a guitar and a certificate for ten guitar lessons. He had always shown a love of music and a desire to learn an instrument. Tim began his lessons, and before long, he was making up his own songs. At the music studio, Tim met Josh, who played the piano, and Roger, whose instrument was the saxophone. They all shared the same dream—to start a band—and each was praised by his teacher as having real talent.

   From this passage, one can infer that:

   A. Tim, Roger, and Josh are going to start their own band

   B. Tim is going to give up his guitar lessons

   C. Tim, Josh, and Roger will no longer be friends

   D. Josh and Roger are going to start their own band

2. The Smith family waited patiently around carousel number 7 for their luggage to arrive. They were exhausted after their five-hour trip and were anxious to get to their hotel. After about an hour, they realized that they no longer recognized any of the other passengers' faces. Mrs. Smith asked the person who appeared to be in charge if they were at the right carousel. The man replied, "Yes, this is it, but we finished unloading that baggage almost half an hour ago."

   From the man's response, we can infer that:

   A. The Smiths were ready to go to their hotel

   B. The Smiths' luggage was lost

   C. The man had the Smiths' luggage

   D. The Smiths were at the wrong carousel

Answer Key: Inference

1. A

   Given the facts that Tim wanted to be a musician and start his own band, after he met others who shared the same dreams, we can infer that the friends joined in an attempt to make their dreams become a reality.

2. B

   Because the Smiths were still waiting for their luggage, we know that they were not yet ready to go to their hotel. From the man's response, we know that they were not at the wrong carousel and that he did not have their luggage. Therefore, though not directly stated, it appears that their luggage was lost.

SKILL 18.3 Interpret figurative language in an excerpt

See Skill 14.3

SKILL 18.4 Compare and contrast views or arguments presented in two or more excerpts

Comparison and contrast, two skills that seem quite complementary, require different sets of skills. Simply put, when we compare two or more views or arguments, we find the similarities between them. When we contrast, we find the differences.

Teachers who are not careful in their selections of materials for which students will compare and contrast will find great difficulty. While there are differences and similarities in just about everything conceivable, the best compare/contrast exercise is one in which there is a good balance between similarities and differences. When looking at arguments, this is fairly easy. We can simply compare and contrast two views on the same subject.

Often, when considering arguments, we are drawn toward arguments that are completely opposite each other. The similarity is the topic; the difference is the attitude or opinion about the topic. In younger grades, this is a very easy way to teach the concepts of compare and contrast. But note that in terms of balance, distinctly opposite perspectives yield similarities only in topic and differences only in viewpoint.

A more important skill involves teaching students how to compare and contrast arguments or viewpoints that share common ground, but differ more subtly. Generally, in the real world, most people can find some agreement on most topics. For example, consider arguments about environmental regulation. Two completely opposite viewpoints might look like this: One side believes that all regulation hurts the economy; the other side believes that no considerations for the economy should be given when developing regulations.

Most of us can quickly see that very few people fall into either of these camps. Instead, most people compromise a bit. This is the type of compare and contrast that is most important for students. They need to be able to understand the similarities in belief (or the areas of compromise), as well as the areas that each side will not compromise on.

So, to make this more specific to extracting viewpoints from excerpts, students can first identify the topic that is up for discussion and argument. Immediately, that is known to be a similarity. Next, students can identify differences. It is better to start with the distinct differences than the specific similarities, as it will help students to put an identity on each argument. Finally, students can look for similarities or areas of compromise.

In an excerpt, students should not only look at the message but they should also look for tone. Often, in argumentation, irony and exaggeration are used. When students pick up on these traits, the task of comparison and contrast is much easier.

COMPETENCY 19

USE CRITICAL REASONING SKILLS TO ASSESS AN AUTHOR'S TREATMENT OF CONTENT IN WRITTEN MATERIAL FROM A VARIETY OF SOURCES

SKILL 19.1 Analyze the logical structure of an argument in an excerpt, and identify possible instances of faulty reasoning

On the certification test, the terms valid and invalid have special meaning. If an argument is valid, it is reasonable. It is objective (not biased) and can be supported by evidence. If an argument is invalid, it is not reasonable and it is not objective. In other words, one can find evidence of bias.

Read the following passage:

Most dentists agree that Bright Smile Toothpaste is the best for fighting cavities. It tastes good and leaves your mouth minty fresh.

Is this a valid or an invalid argument?

It is invalid. It mentions that most dentists agree. What about those who do not agree? The author is clearly exhibiting bias in leaving those who disagree out.

Read the following passage:

It is difficult to decide who will make the best presidential candidate, Senator Johnson or Senator Keeley. They have both been involved in scandals and have both gone through messy divorces while in office.

Is this argument valid or invalid?

The argument is valid. The author appears to be listing facts. He does not seem to favor one candidate over the other.

SKILL 19.2 Distinguish between fact and opinion in written material

FACTS: verifiable statements that report what has happened or what exists

OPINIONS: statements that must be supported in order to be accepted

JUDGMENTS: opinions, decisions, or declarations based on observation or reasoning that express approval or disapproval

FACTS are verifiable statements. **OPINIONS** are statements that must be supported in order to be accepted, such as beliefs, values, judgments, or feelings. Facts are objective statements used to support subjective opinions. For example, "Jane is a bad girl" is an opinion. However, "Jane hit her sister with a baseball bat" is a fact upon which the opinion is based. **JUDGMENTS** are opinions, decisions, or declarations based on observation or reasoning that express approval or disapproval. Facts report what has happened or what exists and come from observation, measurement, or calculation. Facts can be tested and verified, whereas opinions and judgments cannot. They can only be supported with facts.

Most statements cannot be so clearly distinguished. "I believe that Jane is a bad girl" is a fact. The speaker knows what he or she believes. However, it obviously includes a judgment that could be disputed by another person who might believe otherwise. Judgments are not usually so firm. They are, rather, plausible opinions that provoke thought or lead to factual development.

Mickey Mantle replaced Joe DiMaggio, a Yankees centerfielder, in 1952.

This is a fact. If necessary, evidence can be produced to support this statement.

First-year players are more ambitious than seasoned players.

This is an opinion. There is no proof to support that everyone feels this way.

Practice Questions: Fact and Opinion

1. **The Inca were a group of Indians who ruled an empire in South America.**

   A. Fact

   B. Opinion

2. **The Inca were clever.**

   A. Fact

   B. Opinion

3. **The Inca built very complex systems of bridges.**

   A. Fact

   B. Opinion

Answer Key: Fact and Opinion

1. A

   Research can prove this statement true.

2. B

   It is doubtful that all people who have studied the Inca agree with this statement. Therefore, no proof is available.

3. A

   As with question number one, research can prove this statement true.

SKILL 19.3 Determine the relevance of specific facts, examples, or data to a writer's argument

The main idea of a passage may contain a wide variety of supporting information, but it is important that each sentence be related to the main idea. When a sentence contains information that bears little or no connection to the main idea, it is said to be **IRRELEVANT**. It is important to continually assess whether or not a sentence contributes to the overall task of supporting the main idea. When a sentence is deemed irrelevant, it is best either to omit it from the passage or to make it relevant by one of the following strategies:

IRRELEVANT: bears little or no connection to the main idea

1. Adding detail: Sometimes a sentence can seem out of place if it does not contain enough information to link it to the topic. Adding specific information can show how the sentence relates to the main idea.
2. Adding an example: This is especially important in passages in which information is being argued or compared and contrasted. Examples can support the main idea and give the document credibility.
3. Using diction effectively: It is important to understand connotation, avoid ambiguity, and avoid too much repetition when selecting words.
4. Adding transitions: Transitions are extremely helpful for making sentences relevant because they are specifically designed to connect one idea to another. They can also reduce a paragraph's choppiness.

The following passage has several irrelevant sentences that are highlighted in **bold**:

The New City Planning Committee is proposing a new capitol building to represent the multicultural face of New City. ***The current mayor is a Democrat.*** *The new capitol building will be on 10th Street across from the grocery store and next to the recreational center. It will be within walking distance to the subway and bus depot, as the designers want to emphasize the importance of public transportation. Aesthetically, the building will have a contemporary design, featuring a brushed-steel exterior and large, floor-to-ceiling windows.* ***It is important for employees to have a connection with the outside world even when they are in their offices.*** *Inside the building, the walls will be moveable. This will not only facilitate a multitude of creative floor plans, but it will also create a focus on open communication and flow of information.* ***It sounds a bit gimmicky to me.*** *Finally, the capitol will feature a large outdoor courtyard full of lush greenery and serene fountains.* ***Work will now seem like Club Med to those who work at the New City capitol building!***

SKILL 19.4 Interpret the content, word choice, and phrasing of a passage to determine a writer's opinions, point of view, or position on an issue

Tone is the author's attitude as reflected in the statement or passage. The choice of words will help readers to determine the overall tone of a statement or passage.

Read the following paragraph.

I was shocked by your article, which said that sitting down to breakfast was a thing of the past. Many families consider breakfast time, family time. Children need to realize the importance of having a good breakfast. It is imperative that they be taught this at a young age. I cannot believe that a writer with your reputation has difficulty comprehending this.

The author's tone in this passage is one of

A. Concern

B. Anger

C. Excitement

D. Disbelief

Because the author directly states that he "cannot believe" that the writer feels this way, the answer is D, Disbelief.

Read the following paragraph.

> *I remember when I first started teaching, twenty years ago. I was apprehensive at first, but, within a short time, I felt like an old pro. If I had my life to live over again, I would still choose to be a teacher.*

The author's tone can be best described as:

A. Joyous

B. Nostalgic

C. Bitter

D. Optimistic

B is the correct answer. The author appears to be "taking a trip down memory lane."

See also Skill 18.1

SKILL 19.5 Evaluate the credibility, objectivity, or bias of an author's argument or sources

Bias is defined as an opinion, feeling, or influence that strongly favors one side in an argument. A statement or passage is biased if an author attempts to convince a reader of something.

Read the following statement.

> *Using a calculator cannot help a student understand the process of graphing, so its use is a waste of time.*

Is there evidence of bias in the above statement?

A. Yes

B. No

Because the author makes it perfectly clear that he does not favor the use of the calculator, the answer is A. He has included his opinion in this statement.

Read the following paragraph.

> *There are teachers who feel that computer programs are quite helpful in helping students grasp certain math concepts. There are also those who disagree with this feeling. It is up to individual math teachers to decide if computer programs benefit their particular group of students*

Is there evidence of bias in this paragraph?

A. Yes

B. No

B is the correct answer. The author seems to state both sides of the argument without favoring a particular side.

See also Skill 21.7

COMPETENCY 20
ANALYZE AND EVALUATE THE EFFECTIVENESS OF EXPRESSION IN A WRITTEN PARAGRAPH OR PASSAGE ACCORDING TO THE CONVENTIONS OF EDITED AMERICAN ENGLISH

SKILL 20.1 Revise text to correct problems relating to grammar *(e.g., syntax, pronoun-antecedent agreement)*

Identify Inappropriate Shifts in Verb Tense

Verb tenses must refer to the same time consistently, unless a change in time is required.

Error: *Despite the increased number of students attending school this year, overall attendance is higher last year at the sporting events.*

Problem: The verb *is* represents an inconsistent shift to the present tense when the action refers to a past occurrence.

Correction: *Despite the increased number of students attending school this year, overall attendance was higher last year at sporting events.*

Error: *My friend Lou, who just competed in the marathon, ran since he was twelve years old.*

Problem: Because Lou continues to run, the present perfect tense is needed.

Correction: *My friend Lou, who just competed in the marathon, has run since he was twelve years old.*

Error: *The mayor congratulated Wallace Mangham, who renovates the city hall last year.*

Problem: Although the speaker is talking in the present, the action of renovating the city hall was in the past.

Correction: *The mayor congratulated Wallace Mangham, who renovated the city hall last year.*

Practice Exercise: Shifts in Tense

Choose the option that corrects an error in the underlined portion(s). If no error exists, choose "No change is necessary."

1. **After we washed the fruit that had growing in the garden, we knew there was a store that would buy the fruit.**
   - A. washing
   - B. grown
   - C. is
   - D. No change is necessary

2. **The tourists used to visit the Atlantic City boardwalk whenever they vacationed during the summer. Unfortunately, their numbers have diminished every year.**
   - A. use
   - B. vacation
   - C. diminish
   - D. No change is necessary

3. **When the temperature drops to below thirty-two degrees Fahrenheit, the water on the lake freezes, which allowed children to skate across it.**
   - A. dropped
   - B. froze
   - C. allows
   - D. No change is necessary

4. **The artists were hired to create a monument that would pay tribute to the men who were killed in World War II.**
   - A. hiring
   - B. created
   - C. killing
   - D. No change is necessary

5. **Emergency medical personnel rushed to the scene of the shooting, where many injured people waiting for treatment.**
   - A. wait
   - B. waited
   - C. waits
   - D. No change is necessary

Answer Key: Shifts in Tense

1. B

The past participle *grown* is needed instead of *growing*, which is the progressive tense. Option A is incorrect because the past participle *washed* takes the *-ed*. Option C incorrectly replaces the past participle was with the present tense *is*.

2. D

Option A is incorrect because *use* is the present tense. Option B incorrectly uses the present tense of the verb *vacation.* Option C incorrectly uses the present tense *diminish* instead of the past tense *diminished.*

3. C

The present tense *allows* is necessary in the context of the sentence. Option A is incorrect because *dropped* is a past participle. Option B is incorrect because *froze* is also a past participle.

4. D

Option A is incorrect because *hiring* is the present tense. Option B is incorrect because *created* is a past participle. In Option C, *killing* does not fit into the context of the sentence.

5. B

In Option B, *waited* corresponds with the past tense *rushed.* In Option A, *wait* is incorrect because it is present tense. In Option C, *waits* is incorrect because the noun *people* is plural and requires the singular form of the verb.

Note: *A simple subject is never found in a prepositional phrase (that is, a phrase beginning with a word such as of, by, over, through, until).*

A verb must correspond in the singular or plural form with the simple subject; interfering elements do not affect it.

PRESENT TENSE VERB FORM		
	Singular	**Plural**
1st person (talking about oneself)	I do	We do
2nd person (talking to another)	You do	You do
3rd person (talking about someone or something)	He does She does It does	They do

Error: *Sally, as well as her sister, plan to go into nursing.*

Problem: The subject of the sentence is *Sally* and does not include the word *sister*. Therefore, the verb must be singular.

Correction: *Sally, as well as her sister, plans to go into nursing.*

Error: *There has been many car accidents lately on that street.*

Problem: The subject *accidents* in this sentence is plural; the verb must be plural also, even though it comes before the subject.

Correction: *There have been many car accidents lately on that street.*

Error: *Every one of us have a reason to attend the school musical.*

Problem: The simple subject is the phrase *every one*, not the *us* in the prepositional phrase. Therefore, the verb must be singular also.

Correction: *Every one of us has a reason to attend the school musical.*

Error: *Either the police captain or his officers is going to the convention.*

Problem: In either/or and neither/nor constructions, the verb agrees with the subject closer to it.

Correction: *Either the police captain or his officers are going to the convention.*

Practice Exercise: Subject-Verb Agreement

Choose the option that corrects an error in the underlined portion(s). If no error exists, choose "No change is necessary."

1. **Every year, the store <u>stays</u> open late while shoppers desperately <u>try</u> to purchase Christmas presents as they <u>prepare</u> for the holiday.**

   A. stay

   B. tries

   C. prepared

   D. No change is necessary

2. **Paul McCartney, together with George Harrison and Ringo Starr, <u>sing</u> classic Beatles songs on a special greatest-hits CD.**

   A. singing

   B. sings

   C. sung

   D. No change is necessary

Practice Exercise: Subject-Verb Agreement (cont.)

3. **My friend's cocker spaniel, while chasing cats across the street, always manages to knock over the trash cans.**
   A. chased
   B. manage
   C. knocks
   D. No change is necessary

4. **Some of the ice on the driveway have melted.**
   A. having melted
   B. has melted
   C. has melt
   D. No change is necessary

5. **Neither the criminal forensics expert nor the DNA blood evidence provide enough support for that verdict.**
   A. provides
   B. were providing
   C. are providing
   D. No change is necessary

Answer Key: Subject-Verb Agreement

1. D

   Option D is correct because *store* is third person singular and requires the third person singular verb *stays.* Option B is incorrect because the plural noun *shoppers* requires a plural verb *try.* In Option C, there is no reason to shift to the past tense *prepared.*

2. B

   Option B is correct because the subject, Paul McCartney, is singular and requires the singular verb *sings.* Option A is incorrect because the present participle *singing* does not stand alone as a verb. Option C is incorrect because the past participle *sung* cannot function as the verb in this sentence.

3. D

   Option D is the correct answer because the subject *cocker spaniel* is singular and requires the singular verb *manages.* Options A, B, and C do not work structurally with the sentence.

4. B

   The subject of the sentence is *some,* which requires a third-person, singular verb: *has melted.* Option A incorrectly uses the present participle *having,* which does not act as a helping verb. Option C does not work structurally with the sentence.

5. A

   In Option A, the singular subject *evidence* is closer to the verb and thus requires the singular in the neither/nor construction. Both Options B and C are plural forms with the helping verb and the present participle.

Identify Agreements between Pronoun and Antecedent

A pronoun must correspond to its antecedent in number (singular or plural), person (first, second, or third person), and gender (male, female, or neutral). A pronoun must refer clearly to a single word, not to a complete idea.

A pronoun shift is a grammatical error in which the author starts a sentence, paragraph, or section using one particular type of pronoun and then suddenly shifts to another. This often confuses the reader.

Error: *A teacher should treat all their students fairly.*

Problem: Since *teacher* is singular, the pronoun referring to it must also be singular. Otherwise, the noun has to be made plural.

Correction: *Teachers should treat all their students fairly.*

Error: *When an actor is rehearsing for a play, it often helps if you can memorize the lines in advance.*

Problem: *Actor* is a third-person word; that is, the writer is talking about the subject. The pronoun *you* is in the second person, which means the writer is talking to the subject.

Correction: *When actors are rehearsing for plays, it helps if they can memorize the lines in advance.*

Error: *The workers in the factory were upset when his or her paychecks didn't arrive on time.*

Problem: *Workers* is a plural form, while *his or her* refers to one person.

Correction: *The workers in the factory were upset when their paychecks didn't arrive on time.*

Error: *The charity auction was highly successful, which pleased everyone.*

Problem: In this sentence, the pronoun *which* refers to the idea of the auction's success. In fact, *which* has no antecedent in the sentence; the word *success* is not stated.

Correction: *Everyone was pleased at the success of the auction.*

Error: *Lana told Melanie that she would like aerobics.*

Problem: The person that *she* refers to is unclear; *she* could be either Lana or Melanie.

Correction: *Lana said that Melanie would like aerobics.*

-OR-

Lana told Melanie that she, Melanie, would like aerobics.

Error: *I dislike accounting even though my brother is one.*

Problem: A person's occupation is not the same as a field, and the pronoun *one* is thus incorrect. Note that the word *accountant* is not used in the sentence, so *one* has no antecedent.

Correction: *I dislike accounting even though my brother is an accountant.*

Practice Exercise: Pronoun/Antecedent Agreement

Choose the option that corrects an error in the underlined portion(s). If no error exists, choose "No change is necessary."

1. **You can get to Martha's Vineyard by driving from Boston to Woods Hole. Once there, you can travel on a ship, but you may find traveling by airplane to be an exciting experience.**

   A. They

   B. visitors

   C. it

   D. No change is necessary

2. **Both the city leader and the journalist are worried about the new interstate; she fears the new roadway will destroy precious farmland.**

   A. journalist herself

   B. they fear

   C. it

   D. No change is necessary

3. **When hunters are looking for deer in the woods, you must remain quiet for long periods of time.**

   A. you

   B. it

   C. they

   D. No change is necessary

4. **The strong economy is based on the importance of the citrus industry. Producing orange juice for most of the country.**

   A. They produce

   B. Who produce

   C. Farmers there produce

   D. No change is necessary

5. **Dr. Kennedy told Paul Elliot, his assistant, that he would have to finish grading the tests before going home, no matter how long it took.**

   A. their

   B. he, Paul,

   C. they

   D. No change is necessary

Answer Key: Pronoun/Antecedent Agreement

1. D

   Pronouns must be consistent. As *you* is used throughout the sentence, the shift to *visitors* is incorrect. Option A, *They*, is vague and unclear. Option C, *it*, is also unclear.

2. B

   The plural pronoun *they* is necessary to agree with the two nouns *leader* and *journalist*. There is no need for the reflexive pronoun *herself* in Option A. In Option C, *it* is vague.

3. C

   The shift to *you* is unnecessary. The plural pronoun *they* is necessary to agree with the noun *hunters*. The word *it* in Option B is vague; the reader does not know to what the word *it* refers. *It* has no antecedent.

4. C

   The noun *farmers* is needed for clarification because *producing* alone creates a fragment. Option A is incorrect because *they produce* is vague. Option B is incorrect because *who* has no antecedent and creates a fragment.

5. B

   The repetition of the name *Paul* is necessary to clarify who the pronoun *he* refers to. (*He* could be Dr. Kennedy.) Option A is incorrect because the singular pronoun *his* is needed, not the plural pronoun *their*. Option C is incorrect because the pronoun *it* refers to the grading of the tests, not the tests themselves.

Rules for Clearly Identifying Pronoun Reference

Make sure that the antecedent reference is clear and cannot refer to something else

A "distant relative" is a relative pronoun or a relative clause that has been placed too far away from the antecedent to which it refers. It is a common error to place a verb between the relative pronoun and its antecedent.

Error: *Return the books to the library that are overdue.*

Problem: The relative clause that are overdue refers to the books and should be placed immediately after the antecedent.

Correction: *Return the books that are overdue to the library.*
-OR-
Return the overdue books to the library.

A pronoun should not refer to adjectives or possessive nouns

Adjectives, nouns, or possessive pronouns should not be used as antecedents. This will create ambiguity in sentences.

Error: *In Todd's letter, he told his mom he'd broken the priceless vase.*

Problem: In this sentence, the pronoun *he* seems to refer to the noun phrase *Todd's letter*, though it is probably meant to refer to the possessive noun *Todd's*.

Correction: *In his letter, Todd told his mom that he had broken the priceless vase.*

A pronoun should not refer to an implied idea

A pronoun must refer to a specific antecedent rather than an implied antecedent. When an antecedent is not stated specifically, the reader has to guess or assume the meaning of a sentence. Pronouns that do not have antecedents are called **EXPLETIVES**. "It" and "there" are the most common expletives, though other pronouns can become expletives as well. In informal conversation, expletives allow for casual presentation of ideas without supporting evidence. However, in more formal writing, it is best to be more precise.

EXPLETIVE: a pronoun that does not have an antecedent

Error: *She said that it is important to floss every day.*

Problem: The pronoun *it* refers to an implied idea.

Correction: *She said that flossing every day is important.*

Error: *Milt and Bette returned the books because they had missing pages.*

Problem: The pronoun *they* does not refer to the antecedent.

Correction: *The customers returned the books with missing pages.*

Using Who, That, and Which

Who, whom, and *whose* refer to human beings and can introduce either essential or nonessential clauses. *That* refers to things other than humans and is used to introduce essential clauses. *Which* refers to things other than humans and is used to introduce nonessential clauses.

Error: *The doctor that performed the surgery said the patient would recover fully.*

Problem: Since the relative pronoun is referring to a human, *who* should be used.

Correction: *The doctor who performed the surgery said the patient would recover fully.*

Error: *That ice cream cone that you just ate looked delicious.*

Problem: *That* has already been used, so you must use *which* to introduce the next clause, whether it is essential or nonessential.

Correction: *That ice cream cone, which you just ate, looked delicious.*

Identify Proper Case Forms

Pronouns, unlike nouns, change case forms. Pronouns must be in the subjective, objective, or possessive form, according to their function in the sentence.

PERSONAL PRONOUNS						
SUBJECTIVE (NOMINATIVE)			POSSESSIVE		OBJECTIVE	
	Singular	Plural	Singular	Plural	Singular	Plural
1st person	I	We	My	Our Ours	Me	Us
2nd person	You	You	Your Yours	Your Yours	You	You
3rd person	He She It	They	His Her/ Hers Its	Their Theirs	Him Her It	Them

RELATIVE PRONOUNS	
Who	Subjective/Nominative
Whom	Objective
Whose	Possessive

Error: *Tom and me have reserved seats for next week's baseball game.*

Problem: The pronoun *me* is the subject of the verb *have reserved* and should be in the subjective form.

Correction: *Tom and I have reserved seats for next week's baseball game.*

Error: *Mr. Green showed all of we students how to make paper hats.*

Problem: The pronoun *we* is the object of the preposition *of.* It should be in the objective form, us.

Correction: *Mr. Green showed all of us students how to make paper hats.*

Error: *Who's coat is this?*

Problem: The interrogative possessive pronoun is *whose*; *who's* is the contraction for *who is.*

Correction: *Whose coat is this?*

Practice Exercise: Pronoun Case

Choose the option that corrects an error in the underlined portion(s). If no error exists, choose "No change is necessary."

1. **Even though Sheila and he had planned to be alone at the diner, they were joined by three friends of their's instead.**
   A. him
   B. him and her
   C. theirs
   D. No change is necessary

2. **Uncle Walter promised to give his car to whomever would guarantee to drive it safely.**
   A. whom
   B. whoever
   C. them
   D. No change is necessary

3. **Eddie and him gently laid the body on the ground next to the sign.**
   A. he
   B. them
   C. it
   D. No change is necessary

4. **Mary, who is competing in the chess tournament, is a better player than me.**
   A. whose
   B. whom
   C. I
   D. No change is necessary

5. **We ourselves have decided not to buy property in that development; however, our friends have already bought themselves some land.**
   A. We, ourself,
   B. their selves
   C. their self
   D. No change is necessary

Answer Key: Pronoun Case

1. C

   The possessive pronoun *theirs* does not need an apostrophe. Option A is incorrect because the subjective pronoun *he* is needed in this sentence. Option B is incorrect because the subjective pronoun *they*, not the objective pronouns *him* and *her*, is needed.

2. B

   The subjective case *whoever*—not the objective case *whomever*—is the subject of the relative clause *whoever would guarantee to drive it safely*. Option A is incorrect because *whom* is an objective pronoun. Option C is incorrect because *car* is singular and takes the pronoun *it*.

3. A

   The subjective pronoun *he* is needed as the subject of the verb *laid*. Option B is incorrect because *them* is vague; the noun *body* is needed to clarify *it*. Option C is incorrect because *it* is vague, and the noun *sign* is necessary for clarification.

4. C

   The subjective pronoun *I* is needed because the comparison is understood. Option A incorrectly uses the possessive *whose*. Option B is incorrect because the subjective pronoun *who*, and not the objective *whom*, is needed.

5. D

   The reflexive pronoun *themselves* refers to the plural *friends*. Option A is incorrect because the plural we requires the reflexive *ourselves*. Option C is incorrect because the possessive pronoun *their* is never joined with either *self* or *selves*.

ADJECTIVES are words that modify or describe nouns or pronouns. Adjectives usually precede the words they modify but not always; for example, an adjective may occur after a linking verb.

ADVERBS are words that modify verbs, adjectives, or other adverbs. They cannot modify nouns. Adverbs answer such questions as how, why, when, where, how much, or how often. Many adverbs are formed by adding *-ly*.

ADJECTIVES: words that modify or describe nouns or pronouns

ADVERBS: words that modify verbs, adjectives, or other adverbs

Error: *The birthday cake tasted sweetly.*

Problem: *Tasted* is a linking verb; the modifier that follows should be an adjective, not an adverb.

Correction: *The birthday cake tasted sweet.*

Error: *You have done good with this project.*

Problem: *Good* is an adjective and cannot be used to modify a verb phrase such as *have done.*

Correction: *You have done well with this project.*

Error: *The coach was positive happy about the team's chance of winning.*

Problem: The adjective positive cannot be used to modify another adjective, *happy*. An adverb is needed instead.

Correction: *The coach was positively happy about the team's chance of winning.*

Error: *The fireman acted quick and brave to save the child from the burning building.*

Problem: *Quick* and *brave* are adjectives and cannot be used to describe a verb. Adverbs are needed instead.

Correction: *The fireman acted quickly and bravely to save the child from the burning building.*

Practice Exercise: Adjectives and Adverbs

Choose the option that corrects an error in the underlined portion(s). If no error exists, choose "No change is necessary."

1. **Moving <u>quick</u> throughout the house, the burglar <u>removed</u> several priceless antiques before <u>carelessly</u> dropping his wallet.**
   A. quickly
   B. remove
   C. careless
   D. No change is necessary

2. **The car <u>crashed</u> <u>loudly</u> into the retaining wall before spinning <u>wildly</u> on the sidewalk.**
   A. crashes
   B. loudly
   C. wild
   D. No change is necessary

Practice Exercise: Adjectives and Adverbs (cont.)

3. **The airplane <u>landed</u> <u>safe</u> on the runway after <u>nearly</u> colliding with a helicopter.**

    A. land

    B. safely

    C. near

    D. No change is necessary

4. **The <u>horribly</u> <u>bad</u> special effects in the movie disappointed us <u>great</u>.**

    A. horrible

    B. badly

    C. greatly

    D. No change is necessary

5. **The man promised to obey <u>faithfully</u> the rules of the social club.**

    A. faithful

    B. faithfulness

    C. faith

    D. No change is necessary

Answer Key: Adjectives and Adverbs

1. A

    The adverb *quickly* is needed to modify *moving*. Option B is incorrect because it uses the wrong form of the verb. Option C is incorrect because the adverb *carelessly*, not the adjective *careless*, is needed before the verb *dropping*.

2. D

    The sentence is correct as it is written. The adverbs *loudly* and *wildly* are needed to modify *crashed* and *spinning*. Option A incorrectly uses the verb *crashes* instead of the participle *crashing*, which acts as an adjective.

3. B

    The adverb *safely* is needed to modify the verb *landed*. Option A is incorrect because *land* is a noun. Option C is incorrect because *near* is an adjective, not an adverb.

4. C

    The adverb *greatly* is needed to modify the verb *disappointed*. Option A is incorrect because *horrible* is an adjective, not an adverb. Option B is incorrect because the adverb *horribly* needs to modify the adjective *bad*.

5. D

    The adverb *faithfully* is the correct modifier of the verb *promised*. Option A is an adjective used to modify nouns. Neither Option B nor Option C, both of which are nouns, is a modifier.

COMPARATIVE FORM: used to compare two items

SUPERLATIVE FORM: used to compare more than two items

When comparisons are made, the correct form of the adjective or adverb must be used. The **COMPARATIVE FORM** is used for two items. The **SUPERLATIVE FORM** is used for more than two items.

	Comparative	Superlative
slow	slower	slowest
young	younger	youngest
tall	taller	tallest

With some words, *more* and *most* are used to make comparisons instead of *-er* and *-est*.

	Comparative	Superlative
energetic	more energetic	most energetic
quick	more quickly	most quickly

Comparisons must be made between similar structures or items. In the sentence "My house is similar in color to Steve's," one house is being compared to another house, as understood by the use of the possessive *Steve's*.

On the other hand, if the sentence reads "My house is similar in color to Steve," the comparison would be faulty because it would be comparing the house to Steve, not to Steve's house.

Error: *Last year's rides at the carnival were bigger than this year.*

Problem: In the sentence as it is worded, the rides at the carnival are being compared to this year, not to this year's rides.

Correction: *Last year's rides at the carnival were bigger than this year's.*

Practice Exercise: Logical Comparisons

Choose the sentence that logically and correctly expresses the comparison.

1. A. This year's standards are higher than last year.
   B. This year's standards are more high than last year.
   C. This year's standards are higher than last year's.

2. A. Tom's attitudes are very different from his father's.
   B. Toms attitudes are very different from his father.
   C. Tom's attitudes are very different from his father.

3. A. John is the stronger member of the gymnastics team.
   B. John is the strongest member of the gymnastics team.
   C. John is the most strong member of the gymnastics team.

4. A. Tracy's book report was longer than Tony's.
   B. Tracy's book report was more long than Tony's.
   C. Tracy's book report was longer than Tony.

5. A. Becoming a lawyer is as difficult as, if not more difficult than, becoming a doctor.
   B. Becoming a lawyer is as difficult, if not more difficult, than becoming a doctor.
   C. Becoming a lawyer is difficult, if not more difficult, than becoming a doctor.

6. A. Better than any movie of the modern era, *Schindler's List* portrays the destructiveness of hate.
   B. More better than any movie of the modern era, *Schindler's List* portrays the destructiveness of hate.
   C. Better than any other movie of the modern era, *Schindler's List* portrays the destructiveness of hate.

Answer Key: Logical Comparisons

1. C

   Option C is correct because the comparison is between this year's standards and last year's (*standards* is understood). Option A compares the standards to last year. In Option B, the faulty comparative *more high* should be *higher*.

2. A

   Option A is correct because Tom's attitudes are compared to his father's (*attitudes* is understood). Option B deletes the apostrophe that is necessary to show possession (*Tom's*), and the comparison is faulty because *attitudes* is compared to *father*. While Option C uses the correct possessive, it retains the faulty comparison shown in Option B.

3. B

   In Option B, John is correctly the strongest member of a team that consists of more than two people. Option A uses the comparative *stronger* (comparison of two items) rather than the superlative *strongest* (comparison of more than two items). Option C uses a faulty superlative, *most strong*.

4. A

   Option A is correct because the comparison is between Tracy's book report and Tony's (book report). Option B uses the faulty comparative *more long* instead of *longer*. Option C wrongly compares Tracy's book report to Tony.

5. A

   In Option A, the dual comparison is correctly stated: *as difficult as, if not more difficult than*. Remember to test the dual comparison by taking out the intervening comparison. Option B deletes the necessary *as* after the first *difficult*. Option C deletes the *as* before and after the first *difficult*.

6. C

   Option C includes the necessary word *other* in the comparison *better than any other movie*. The comparison in Option A is not complete, and Option B uses the faulty comparative *more better*.

SKILL 20.2 Revise text to correct problems relating to sentence construction *(e.g., those involving parallel structure, misplaced modifiers, run-on sentences)*

Fundamentals of Sentence Structure

TYPES OF SENTENCES	
Simple	Consists of one independent clause. *Joyce wrote a letter.*
Compound	Consists of two or more independent clauses. The two clauses are usually connected by a coordinating conjunction (and, but, or, nor, for, so, yet). Semicolons sometimes connect compound sentences. *Joyce wrote a letter, and Dot drew a picture.*
Complex	Consists of an independent clause plus one or more dependent clauses. The dependent clause may precede the independent clause or follow it. *While Joyce wrote a letter, Dot drew a picture.*
Compound-Complex	Consists of one or more dependent clauses plus two or more independent clauses. *When Mother asked the girls to demonstrate their newfound skills, Joyce wrote a letter, and Dot drew a picture.*

Note: Do not confuse compound sentence elements with compound sentences.

Simple sentence with compound subject:

Joyce and Dot wrote letters.
The girl in row three and the boy next to her were passing notes across the aisle.

Simple sentence with compound predicate:

Joyce wrote letters and drew pictures.
The captain of the high school debate team graduated with honors and studied broadcast journalism in college.

Simple sentence with compound object of preposition:

Coleen graded the students' essays for style and mechanical accuracy.

Types of Clauses

CLAUSES: connected word groups that are composed of at least one subject and one verb

SUBJECT: the doer of an action or the element that is being joined

VERB: a word that conveys either the action or the link

INDEPENDENT CLAUSES: word groups that can stand alone or that can be joined to other clauses

DEPENDENT CLAUSES: word groups that have a subject and a verb but cannot stand alone as a complete sentence

CLAUSES are connected word groups that are composed of at least one subject and one verb. (A SUBJECT is the doer of an action or the element that is being joined. A VERB conveys either the action or the link.)

Students are waiting for the start of the assembly.
(subject) (verb)

At the end of the play, students wait for the curtain to come down.
(subject) (verb)

Clauses can be *independent* or *dependent*.

INDEPENDENT CLAUSES can stand alone or they can be joined to other clauses.

LINKING CLAUSES		
Independent clause	for and nor	Independent clause
Independent clause	but or yet so	Independent clause
Independent clause	;	Independent clause
Dependent clause	,	Independent clause
Independent clause	,	Dependent clause

DEPENDENT CLAUSES, by definition, contain at least one subject and one verb. However, they cannot stand alone as a complete sentence. They are structurally dependent on the main clause.

There are two types of dependent clauses:

1. Those with a subordinating conjunction
2. Those with a relative pronoun

Unless a cure is discovered, many more people will die of the disease.
Dependent clause + Independent clause

The White House has an official website, which contains press releases, news updates, and biographies of the president and vice president.
(independent clause + relative pronoun + relative dependent clause)

Recognize correct placement of modifiers

Participial phrases that are not placed near the word they modify often result in misplaced modifiers. Participial phrases that do not relate to the subject being modified result in dangling modifiers.

Error: *Weighing the options carefully, a decision was made regarding the punishment of the convicted murderer.*

Problem: Who is weighing the options? No one capable of weighing is named in the sentence; thus, the participle phrase weighing the options carefully dangles. This problem can be corrected by adding a subject capable of doing the action.

Correction: *Weighing the options carefully, the judge made a decision regarding the punishment of the convicted murderer.*

Error: *Returning to my favorite watering hole, brought back many fond memories.*

Problem: The person who returned is never indicated, and the participial phrase dangles. This problem can be corrected by creating a dependent clause from the modifying phrase.

Correction: *When I returned to my favorite watering hole, many fond memories came back to me.*

Error: *One damaged house stood only to remind townspeople of the hurricane.*

Problem: The placement of the modifier *only* suggests that the sole reason the house remained was to serve as a reminder. The faulty modifier creates ambiguity.

Correction: *Only one damaged house stood, reminding townspeople of the hurricane.*

Error: *Recovered from the five-mile hike, the obstacle course was a piece of cake for the Boy Scout troop.*

Problem: The obstacle course is not recovered from the five-mile hike, so the modifying phrase must be placed closer to the word, troop, that it modifies.

Correction: *The obstacle course was a piece of cake for the Boy Scout troop, which had just recovered from a five-mile hike.*

Practice Exercise: Misplaced and Dangling Modifiers

Choose the sentence that expresses the thought most clearly and effectively and that has no error in structure.

1. A. Attempting to remove the dog from the well, the paramedic tripped and fell in, also.
   B. As the paramedic attempted to remove the dog from the well, he tripped and fell in, also.
   C. The paramedic tripped and fell in also attempting to remove the dog from the well.

2. A. To save the wounded child, a powerful explosion ripped through the operating room as the doctors worked.
   B. In the operating room, as the wounded child was being saved, a powerful explosion ripped through.
   C. To save the wounded child, the doctors worked as an explosion ripped through the operating room.

3. A. One hot July morning, a herd of giraffes screamed wildly in the jungle next to the wildlife habitat.
   B. One hot July morning, a herd of giraffes screamed in the jungle wildly next to the wildlife habitat.
   C. One hot July morning, a herd of giraffes screamed in the jungle next to the wildlife habitat, wildly.

4. A. Looking through the file cabinets in the office, the photographs of the crime scene revealed a new suspect in the investigation.
   B. Looking through the file cabinets in the office, the detective discovered photographs of the crime scene which revealed a new suspect in the investigation.
   C. A new suspect in the investigation was revealed in photographs of the crime scene that were discovered while looking through the file cabinets in the office.

Answer Key: Misplaced and Dangling Modifiers

1. B

B corrects the dangling participle attempting to remove the dog from the well by creating a dependent clause introducing the main clause. In A, the introductory participle phrase *Attempting . . . well* does not refer to a paramedic, the subject of the main clause. The word *also* in C incorrectly implies that the paramedic was doing something besides trying to remove the dog.

2. C

C corrects the dangling modifier to save the wounded child by adding the concrete subject *doctors*. A infers that an explosion was working to save the wounded child. B never tells who was trying to save the wounded child.

3. A

A places the adverb *wildly* closest to the verb *screamed*, which it modifies. B and C incorrectly place the modifier away from the verb.

4. B

B corrects the modifier *looking through the file cabinets in the office* by placing it next to the detective who is doing the looking. A sounds as though the photographs were looking; C has no one doing the looking.

Faulty Parallelism

Two or more elements stated in a single clause should be expressed with the same (or parallel) structure (e.g., all adjectives, all verb forms, or all nouns).

Error: *She needed to be beautiful, successful, and have fame.*

Problem: The phrase *to be* is followed by two different structures: beautiful and successful are adjectives, and have fame is a verb phrase.

Correction: *She needed to be beautiful, successful, and famous.*
(adjective) (adjective) (adjective)

-OR-
She needed <u>beauty</u>, <u>success</u>, and <u>fame</u>.
(noun) (noun) (noun)

Error: *I plan either to sell my car during the spring or during the summer.*

Problem: Paired conjunctions (also called *correlative conjunctions*, such as *either-or, both-and, neither-nor,* and *not only-but also*) need to be followed with similar structures. In the sentence above, *either* is followed by *to sell my car during the spring*, while *or* is followed only by the phrase *during the summer*.

Correction: *I plan to sell my car during either the spring or the summer.*

Error: *The president pledged to lower taxes and that he would cut spending to lower the national debt.*

Problem: Since the phrase *to lower taxes* follows the verb *pledged*, a similar structure of *to* is needed with the phrase *cut spending*.

Correction: *The president pledged to lower taxes and to cut spending to lower the national debt.*
-OR-
The president pledged that he would lower taxes and cut spending to lower the national debt.

Practice Exercise: Parallelism

Choose the sentence that expresses the thought most clearly and effectively and that has no error in structure.

1. A. Andy found the family tree, researches the Irish descendents, and he was compiling a book for everyone to read.

   B. Andy found the family tree, researched the Irish descendents, and compiled a book for everyone to read.

   C. Andy finds the family tree, researched the Irish descendents, and compiled a book for everyone to read.

2. A. In the last ten years, computer technology has advanced so quickly that workers have had difficulty keeping up with the new equipment and the increased number of functions.

   B. Computer technology has advanced so quickly in the last ten years that workers have had difficulty to keep up with the new equipment and by increasing number of functions.

   C. In the last ten years, computer technology has advanced so quickly that workers have had difficulty keeping up with the new equipment, and the number of functions are increasing.

3. A. The History Museum contains exhibits honoring famous residents, a video presentation about the state's history, an art gallery featuring paintings and sculptures, and they even display a replica of the State House.

   B. The State History Museum contains exhibits honoring famous residents, a video presentation about the state's history, an art gallery featuring paintings and sculptures, and even a replica of the State House.

   C. The State History Museum contains exhibits honoring famous residents, a video presentation about the state's history, an art gallery featuring paintings and sculptures, and there is even a replica of the State House.

4. A. Either the criminal justice students had too much practical experience and limited academic preparation or too much academic preparation and little practical experience.

   B. The criminal justice students either had too much practical experience and limited academic preparation or too much academic preparation and little practical experience.

   C. The criminal justice students either had too much practical experience and limited academic preparation or had too much academic preparation and limited practical experience.

5. A. Filmmaking is an arduous process in which the producer hires the cast and crew, chooses locations for filming, supervises the actual production, and guides the editing.

   B. Because it is an arduous process, filmmaking requires the producer to hire a cast and crew and choose locations, supervise the actual production, and guides the editing.

   C. Filmmaking is an arduous process in which the producer hires the cast and crew, chooses locations for filming, supervises the actual production, and guided the editing.

Answer Key: Parallelism

1. B

   Option B uses parallelism by presenting a series of past tense Verbs: *found, researched, and compiled.* Option A interrupts the parallel structure of past tense verbs: found, researches, and *he was compiling*. Option C uses present tense verbs and then shifts to past tense: *finds, researched, and compiled.*

2. A

   Option A uses parallel structure at the end of the sentence: *the new equipment and the increased number of functions*. Option B creates a faulty structure with *to keep up with the new equipment and by increasing number of functions*. Option C creates faulty parallelism with *the number of functions are increasing* (and uses a plural verb for a singular noun).

3. B

   Option B uses parallelism by presenting a series of noun phrases acting as objects of the verb *contains*. Option A interrupts that parallelism by inserting *they even display*, and Option C interrupts the parallelism with the addition of *there is*.

4. C

   In the either-or parallel construction, look for a balance on both sides. Option C creates that balanced parallel structure: *either had ... or had.* Options A and B do not create the balance. In Option A, the structure is *Either the criminal justice students ... or too much*. In Option B, the structure is *either had ... or too much.*

5. A

   Option A uses parallelism by presenting a series of verbs with objects: *hires the cast and crew, chooses locations for filming, supervises the actual production, and guides the editing*. The structure of Option B incorrectly suggests that filmmaking chooses locations, supervises the actual production, and guides the editing. Option C interrupts the series of present tense verbs by inserting the participle *guided* instead of the present tense *guides*.

Fragments

Fragments occur when word groups standing alone are missing either a subject or a verb, or when word groups containing a subject and verb and standing alone are made dependent through the use of subordinating conjunctions or relative pronouns.

Error: *The teacher waiting for the class to complete the assignment.*

Problem: This sentence is not complete because an *-ing* word alone does not function as a verb. When a helping verb is added (for example, *was waiting*), the fragment becomes a sentence.

Correction: *The teacher was waiting for the class to complete the assignment.*

Error: *Until the last toy was removed from the floor.*

Problem: Words such as *until, because, although, when*, and *if* make a clause dependent and thus incapable of standing alone. An independent clause must be added to make the sentence complete.

Correction: *Until the last toy was removed from the floor, the kids could not go outside to play.*

Error: *The city will close the public library. Because of a shortage of funds.*

Problem: The problem is the same as above. The dependent clause must be joined to the independent clause.

Correction: *The city will close the public library because of a shortage of funds.*

Error: *Anyone planning to go on the trip should bring the necessary items. Such as a backpack, boots, a canteen, and bug spray.*

Problem: The second word group is a phrase and cannot stand alone because there is neither a subject nor a verb. The fragment can be corrected by adding the phrase to the sentence.

Correction: *Anyone planning to go on the trip should bring the necessary items, such as a backpack, boots, a canteen, and bug spray.*

Practice Exercise: Fragments

Choose the option that corrects an error in the underlined portion(s). If no error exists, choose "No change is necessary."

1. **Despite the lack of funds in the budget it was necessary to rebuild the roads that were damaged from the recent floods.**
   A. budget: it
   B. budget, it
   C. budget; it
   D. No change is necessary

2. **After determining that the fire was caused by faulty wiring, the building inspector said the construction company should be fined.**
   A. wiring. The
   B. wiring the
   C. wiring; the
   D. No change is necessary

3. **Many years after buying a grand piano Henry decided he'd rather play the violin instead.**
   A. piano: Henry
   B. piano, Henry
   C. piano; Henry
   D. No change is necessary

4. **Computers are being used more and more frequently. because of their capacity to store information.**
   A. frequently because
   B. frequently, because
   C. frequently; because
   D. No change is necessary

5. **Doug washed the floors every day. to keep them clean for the guests.**
   A. every day to
   B. every day, to
   C. every day; to
   D. No change is necessary

Answer Key: Fragments

1. B

   The clause that begins with *despite* is introductory and must be separated from the clause that follows by a comma. Option A is incorrect because a colon is used to set off a list or to emphasize what follows. In Option B, a comma incorrectly suggests that the two clauses are dependent.

2. D

   A comma correctly separates the dependent clause *After...wiring* at the beginning of the sentence from the independent clause that follows. Option A incorrectly breaks the two clauses into separate sentences, Option B omits the comma, and Option C incorrectly suggests that the phrase is an independent clause.

3. B

   The phrase *Henry decided... instead* must be joined to the independent clause. Option A incorrectly puts a colon before *Henry decided*, and Option C incorrectly separates the phrase as if it were an independent clause.

4. A

   The second clause *because... information* is dependent and must be joined to the first independent clause. Option B is incorrect because, as the dependent clause comes at the end of the sentence rather than at the beginning, a comma is not necessary. In Option C, a semicolon incorrectly suggests that the two clauses are independent.

5. A

   The second clause to *keep...guests* is dependent and must be joined to the first independent clause. Option B is incorrect because, as the dependent clause comes at the end of the sentence rather than at the beginning, a comma is not necessary. In Option C, a semicolon incorrectly suggests that the two clauses are independent.

Run-on Sentences and Comma Splices

Comma splices appear when a comma joins two sentences. Fused sentences appear when two sentences are run together with no punctuation at all.

Error: *Dr. Sanders is a brilliant scientist, his research on genetic disorders won him a Nobel Prize.*

Problem: A comma alone cannot join two independent clauses (complete sentences). The two clauses can be joined by a semicolon, joined by a conjunction and a comma, or separated into two sentences by a period.

Correction: *Dr. Sanders is a brilliant scientist; his research on genetic disorders won him a Nobel Prize.*
-OR-
Dr. Sanders is a brilliant scientist. His research on genetic disorders won him a Nobel Prize.
-OR-
Dr. Sanders is a brilliant scientist, and his research on genetic disorders won him a Nobel Prize.

Error: *Paradise Island is noted for its beaches they are long, sandy, and beautiful.*

Problem: The first independent clause ends with the word *beaches*, and the second independent clause is fused to the first. The fused sentence error can be corrected in several ways:

1. One clause may be made dependent on another by inserting a subordinating conjunction or a relative pronoun
2. A semicolon may be used to combine two equally important ideas
3. The two independent clauses may be separated by a period
4. The independent clauses may be joined by a conjunction and a comma

Correction: *Paradise Island is noted for its beaches, which are long, sandy, and beautiful.*
-OR-
Paradise Island is noted for its beaches; they are long, sandy, and beautiful.
-OR -
Paradise Island is noted for its beaches. They are long, sandy, and beautiful.

-OR-
Paradise Island is noted for its beaches, for they are long, sandy, and beautiful.

Error: *The number of hotels has increased, however, the number of visitors has grown also.*

Problem: The first sentence ends with the word increased, and a comma is not strong enough to connect it to the second sentence. The adverbial transition however does not function in the same way as a coordinating conjunction and cannot be used with commas to link two sentences. Several different corrections are available.

Correction: *The number of hotels has increased; however, the number of visitors has grown also.*
[Two separate but closely related sentences are created with the use of the semicolon.]
-OR-
The number of hotels has increased. However, the number of visitors has grown also.
[Two separate sentences are created.]
-OR-
Although the number of hotels has increased, the number of visitors has grown also.
[One idea is made subordinate to the other and separated with a comma.]
-OR-
The number of hotels has increased, but the number of visitors has grown also.
[The comma before the coordinating conjunction *but* is appropriate. The adverbial transition *however* does not function in the same way as the coordinating conjunction *but*.]

Practice Exercise: Fused Sentences and Comma Splices

Choose the option that corrects an error in the underlined portion(s). If no error exists, choose "No change is necessary."

1. **Scientists are excited at the ability to clone a sheep: however, it is not yet known if the same can be done to humans.**

   A. sheep, however,

   B. sheep. However,

   C. sheep, however;

   D. No change is necessary

2. **Because of the rising cost of college tuition the federal government now offers special financial assistance, such as loans, to students.**

   A. tuition, the

   B. tuition; the

   C. such as loans

   D. No change is necessary

3. **As the number of homeless people continues to rise, the major cities such as New York and Chicago, are now investing millions of dollars in low-income housing.**

   A. rise. The major cities

   B. rise; the major cities

   C. New York and Chicago

   D. No change is necessary

4. **Unlike in the 1950s, in most households the husband and wife work full-time to make ends meet in many different career fields.**

   A. the 1950s; in most

   B. the 1950s in most

   C. ends meet, in many

   D. No change is necessary

Answer Key: Fused Sentences and Comma Splices

1. B

   Option B correctly separates two independent clauses. The comma in Option A after the word *sheep* creates a run-on sentence. The semicolon in Option C does not separate the two clauses because it occurs at an inappropriate point.

2. A

   The comma in Option A correctly separates the independent clause and the dependent clause. The semicolon in Option B is incorrect because one of the clauses is independent. Option C requires a comma to prevent a run-on sentence.

3. C

   Option C is correct because a comma creates a run-on sentence. Option A is incorrect because the first clause is dependent. The semicolon in Option B incorrectly separates the dependent clause from the independent clause.

4. D

   Option D correctly separates the two clauses with a comma. Option A incorrectly uses a semicolon to separate the clauses. The lack of a comma in Option B creates a run-on sentence. Option C puts a comma in an inappropriate place.

SKILL 20.3 **Revise text to improve unity and coherence** *(e.g., eliminating unnecessary sentences or paragraphs, adding a topic sentence or introductory paragraph, clarifying transitions between, and relationships among, ideas presented)*

See Competency 17

SKILL 20.4 Analyze problems related to the organization of a given text *(e.g., logical flow of ideas, grouping of related ideas, development of main points)*

See Competency 17

COMPETENCY 21

DEMONSTRATE THE ABILITY TO LOCATE, RETRIEVE, ORGANIZE, AND INTERPRET INFORMATION FROM A VARIETY OF TRADITIONAL AND ELECTRONIC SOURCES

SKILL 21.1 Demonstrate familiarity with basic reference tools *(e.g.,encyclopedias, almanacs, bibliographies, databases, atlases, periodical guides)*

In our increasingly knowledge-based world, educators have found that it is not good enough to simply teach students factual information. The information teachers pass on to students is inherently going to be limited and soon outdated. It is said that the body of knowledge in most academic fields doubles within a matter of years. So, we can assume that the factual information students do get in the classroom will not necessarily represent the most current, accurate information available.

Therefore, educators cannot shirk the responsibility of teaching students how to access sources of information. References sources can be of great value, and, by teaching students how to access these first, students will later have skills that will help them access more in-depth databases and sources of information.

Encyclopedias are reference materials that appear in book or electronic form. Encyclopedias can be considered general or specific. General encyclopedias cover most fields of knowledge; specific encyclopedias include a smaller number of entries treated in greater depth. Encyclopedias are good first sources of information for students. Their total scope is limited, but they can provide a quick introduction to topics so that students can get familiar with the topics before exploring topics in greater depth.

Almanacs provide statistical information on various topics. Typically, these references are rather specific. They often cover a specific period of time. One famous example is the *Farmer's Almanac*. This annual publication summarizes, among many other things, weather conditions for the previous year.

Bibliographies contain references for further research. Bibliographies are usually organized topically. They help point people to the in-depth resources they will need for a complete view of a topic.

Databases, typically all electronic now, are collections of material on specific topics. For example, teachers can go online and find many databases for science articles for students in a variety of topics.

Atlases are visual representations of geographic areas. Often, they cover specific attributes. Some atlases demonstrate geologic attributes, while others emphasize populations of various areas.

Finally, **periodical guides** categorize articles and special editions of journals and magazines to help archive and organize the vast amount of material that is put in periodicals each year.

In all, reference tools are highly valuable for students. Surprisingly, it takes a very long time for students to become competent with most reference tools, but the effort and time are definitely worth it.

SKILL 21.2 Recognize the difference between primary and secondary sources

See Skill 10.3

SKILL 21.3 Formulate research questions and hypotheses

Once a topic is decided on, a **research question** must be formulated. A research question is a relevant, researchable, feasible statement that identifies the information to be studied. Once this initial question is formulated, it is a good idea to think of specific issues related to the topic. This will help to create a hypothesis. A research **HYPOTHESIS** is a statement of the researcher's expectations

HYPOTHESIS: a statement of the researcher's expectations for the outcome of the research problem

for the outcome of the research problem. It is a summary statement of the problem to be addressed in any research document. A good hypothesis states, clearly and concisely, the researchers' expected outcomes regarding the variables under investigation.

Once a hypothesis is decided, the rest of the research paper should focus on analyzing a set of information or arguing a specific point. Thus, there are two types of research papers: analytical and argumentative.

Analytical papers focus on examining and understanding the various parts of a research topic and reformulating them in a new way to support an initial statement. In this type of research paper, the research question is used as both a basis for investigation and as a topic for the paper. Once a variety of information is collected on the given topic, it is coalesced into a clear discussion

Argumentative papers focus on supporting a claim with evidence or reasoning. Instead of presenting research to provide information, an argumentative paper presents research in order to prove a debatable statement and interpretation.

SKILL 21.4 Apply procedures for retrieving information from traditional and technological sources *(e.g., newspapers, CD-ROMS, the Internet)*

Information retrieval is an important skill to develop, whether using traditional sources such as newspapers or technological resources such as CD-ROMS and the Internet. In this age of budget deficits and spending freezes, educators must be particularly savvy about how to use free or very low-cost methods to do five things: search, find, organize, store, and distribute information. For example, while there may be slight differences between conducting these five steps on a computer versus at the library, both options are less costly than purchasing books at a retailer. Nevertheless, some skills are universal.

***Tip:** It may be helpful to create questions and then work to find the answers.*

Step One: Searching for information

- Clearly identify what you want to find out
- Create key terms and phrases to search using:
  - Search engines such as Yahoo, Google, Google Scholar, and Bing
  - Books or periodicals, in the index or table of contents
  - The library, in the card catalog or to ask a librarian

Step Two: Finding information

- When a potentially good source is identified, record vital information such as where it was found (Web address, name of library, etc.) title, author, publication date, type of publication (Web site, book, or magazine), and which of your questions/areas it covers.
- Verify, verify, verify. Though print sources are typically edited and fact-checked, it is still good to verify information obtained from hard-copy sources. Doing so on electronic sources is a must. Users can make this easier by selecting Web sites that are reputable (this typically includes using Web sites connected to reputable entities as distinguished by domain extensions .edu, .org, .gov, etc.). Use .com addresses only if the site is owned by a company known for verifying its information prior to publishing on the Web.

Step Three: Organizing information

- While each person may have his/her own preference, it is generally best to organize the information using key terms or topics. This method helps the information to be located at a later time even when it is needed for another project or purpose. For instance, if you usually prefer to file books by author, in addition to filing under "Dr. Seuss," it may be good to also record *The Foot Book* under "parts of the body" so that you can pull this resource when planning an anatomy lesson.
- Whether using traditional or technological resources, it is good to use an electronic method to organize the information. This can be as simple as using a word processing table and as complex as creating a relational database. *For more information on using productivity software, see skill 17.3.*

Step Four: Storing information

- Store information electronically on an easily accessible device such as a desktop computer or laptop. Also, back up this information by emailing it to yourself and/or saving it on an external/portable storage device such as a USB drive or CD.
- In an effort to be environmentally conscious, it is tempting to avoid printing; however, this is disastrous when computers crash and external devices cannot be found. Though this seems far-fetched, it is quite common and some believe it occurs exactly when the information is most needed. Therefore, print a hard-copy of vital information and file it neatly in a memorable place. This is particularly advisable with intensely researched topics that took a long time to compile.

Step Five: Distributing information

- When it comes to distributing information, once again electronic methods trump traditional ones. This can be done via email, blogs, personal and school Web pages, networking groups, and LCD or overhead projectors.
- In the classroom, the traditional method of providing hard copies is still the most common and most useful.

Together these five steps allow users to retrieve and access information in a consistent and useful manner.

SKILL 21.5 Interpret data presented in visual, graphic, tabular, and quantitative forms *(e.g., recognizing level of statistical significance)*

Tables

To interpret data in tables, we read across rows and down columns. Each item of interest has different data points listed under different column headings.

SAMPLE PURCHASE ORDER				
Item	**Unit**	**$/Unit**	**Qty.**	**Tot. $**
Coffee	lb.	2.79	45	125.55
Milk	gal.	1.05	72	75.60
Sugar	lb.	0.23	150	34.50

In the table, the first column on the left contains the items in a purchase order. The other columns contain data about each item, labeled with column headings. The second column from the left gives the unit of measurement for each item, the third column gives the price per unit, the fourth column gives the quantity of each item ordered, and the fifth column gives the total cost of each item.

Examples: Use the table to answer the following questions.

1. What does the 1.05 value in the table represent?

   Answer: Price in dollars per gallon of milk.

2. What is the total cost of the purchase order?

   Answer: $235.65

3. How many combined pounds of coffee and sugar does this purchase order include?

   Answer: 195 lbs.

Quantitative data is often easily presented in graphs and charts in many content areas. However, if students are unable to decipher the graph, its use is limited. Since information can clearly be displayed in a graph or chart form, accurate interpretation of the information is an important skill for students.

For graphs, students should be taught to evaluate all the features of the graph, including main title, what the horizontal axis represents, and what the vertical axis represents. Also, students should locate and evaluate the graph's key (if there is one) in the event that there is more than one variable on the graph.

For example, line graphs are often used to plot data from a scientific experiment. If more than one variable was used, a key or legend would indicate what each line on the line graph represented. Then, once students have evaluated the axes and titles, they can begin to assess the results of the experiment.

For charts (such as a pie chart), the process is similar to interpreting bar or line graphs. The key, which depicts what each section of the pie chart represents, is very important in interpreting the pie chart. Be sure to provide students with lots of assistance and practice with reading and interpreting graphs and charts.

Many educational disciplines require the ability to recognize representations of written information in graphic or tabular form. Tables help condense and organize written data, and graphs help reveal and emphasize comparisons and trends.

Construct a data table and line graph that represents the survey information for the following information:

> *A survey asked five elementary school students to list the number and type of pets that they had at home. The first student had three dogs and three fish. The second student had two cats and one dog. The third student had three fish and two dogs. The fourth student had one rabbit, two cats, and one dog. The fifth student had no pets.*

This table appropriately represents the data.

Student #	# of Dogs	# of Cats	# of Fish	# of Rabbits	Total # of Pets
1	3	0	3	0	6
2	1	2	0	0	3
3	2	0	3	0	5
4	1	2	0	1	4
5	0	0	0	0	0

This line graph a appropriately represents the total number of pets each student has.

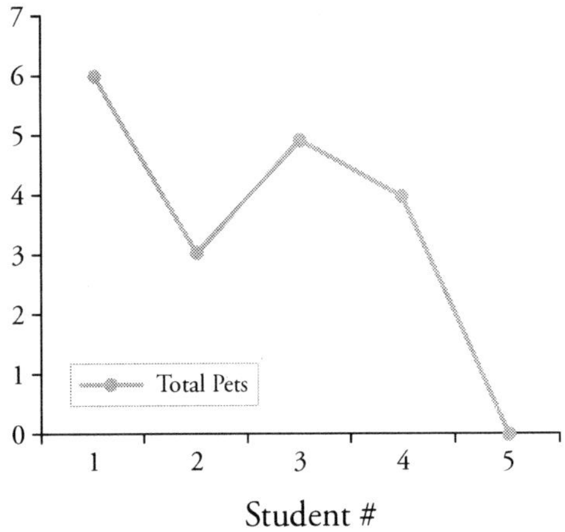

SKILL 21.6 Organize information into logical and coherent outlines

A good thesis gives structure to your essay and helps focus your thoughts. When forming your thesis, look at your prewriting strategy—clustering, questioning, or brainstorming. Then, decide quickly which two or three major areas you will discuss. Remember, you must limit the scope of the paper because of the time factor.

OUTLINE: lists the main points of a thesis that will be used as topics for each paragraph

The **OUTLINE** lists the main points as topics for each paragraph. Looking at a prewriting cluster on computers, you might choose several areas in which computers help us; for example, in science and medicine, business, and education. You might also consider people's reliance on this "wonder" and include at least one paragraph about this reliance. A formal outline for this essay might look like the one below:

I. Introduction and thesis
II. Computers used in science and medicine
III. Computers used in business
IV. Computers used in education
V. People's reliance on computers
VI. Conclusion

Under time pressure, however, you may use a shorter organizational plan, such as abbreviated key words in a list. For example:

1. intro: wonders of the computer *-OR-* *a. intro: wonders of computers—science*
2. science *b. in the space industry*
3. med *c. in medical technology*
4. schools *d. conclusion*
5. business
6. conclusion

Developing the Essay

With a working thesis and an outline, you can begin writing the essay. The essay should be divided into three main sections:

1. The introduction sets up the essay and leads to the thesis statement
2. The body paragraphs are developed with concrete information leading from the topic sentences
3. The conclusion ties the essay together

Introduction

Put your thesis statement into a clear, coherent opening paragraph. One effective device is to use a funnel approach, in which you begin with a brief description of the broader issue and then move to a clearly focused, specific thesis statement.

Consider the following possible introductions to the essay on computers. The length of each is obviously different. Read each, and consider the other differences.

Does each introduce the subject generally?
Does each lead to a stated thesis?
Does each relate to the topic prompt?

Introduction 1: *Computers are used every day. They have many uses. Some people who use them are workers, teachers, and doctors.*

Analysis: This introduction does give the general topic—computers are used every day—but it does not explain what those uses are. This introduction does not offer a point of view in a clearly stated thesis, nor does it convey the idea that computers are a modern wonder.

Introduction 2: *Computers are used just about everywhere these days. I don't think there's an office around that doesn't use computers, and we use them a lot in all kinds of jobs. Computers are great for making life easier and work better. I don't think we'd get along without the computer.*

Analysis: This introduction gives the general topic as computers and mentions one area that uses computers. The thesis states that people could not get along without computers, but it does not state the specific areas the essay will discuss. Note, too, that the meaning is not helped by vague diction, such as *a lot* and *great.*

Introduction 3: *Each day, we either use computers or see them being used around us. We wake to the sound of a digital alarm operated by a microchip. Our cars run by computerized machinery. We use computers to help us learn. We receive phone calls and letters transferred from computers across continents. Our astronauts walked on the moon and returned safely, all because of computer technology. The computer is a wonderful electronic brain that we have come to rely on, and it has changed our world through advances in science, business, and education.*

Analysis: This introduction is the most thorough and fluent because it provides interest in the general topic and offers specific information about computers as a modern wonder. It also leads to a thesis that directs the reader to the scope of the discussion—advances in science, business, and education.

Topic sentences

Just as the essay must have an overall focus reflected in the thesis statement, each paragraph must have a central idea reflected in the topic sentence. A good topic sentence provides transition from the previous paragraph and relates to the essay's thesis. Good topic sentences, therefore, provide unity throughout the essay.

Consider the following potential topic sentences. Determine whether each provides transition and clearly states the subject of the paragraph.

Topic Sentence 1: *Computers are used in science.*

Analysis: This sentence simply states the topic: Computers are used in science. It does not relate to the thesis nor provide transition from the introduction. The reader still does not know how computers are used in science.

Topic Sentence 2: *Now I will talk about computers used in science.*

Analysis: Like the faulty "announcer" thesis statement, this "announcer" topic sentence is vague and merely names the topic.

Topic Sentence 3: *First, computers used in science have improved our lives.*

Analysis: The transition word *First* helps link the introduction and this paragraph. It adds unity to the essay. It does not, however, give specifics about the improvements computers have made in our lives.

Topic Sentence 4: *First used in scientific research and spaceflights, computers are now used extensively in the diagnosis and treatment of disease.*

Analysis: This sentence is the most thorough and fluent. It provides specific areas that will be discussed in the paragraph and it offers more than an announcement of the topic. The writer gives concrete information about the content of the paragraph that will follow.

SUMMARY GUIDELINES FOR WRITING TOPIC SENTENCES
Specifically relate the topic to the thesis statement.
State clearly and concretely the subject of the paragraph.
Provide some transition from the previous paragraph.
Avoid topic sentences that are facts, questions, or announcements.

SKILL 21.7 Evaluate the reliability of different sources of information

See Skill 10.5

DOMAIN V

WRITTEN ANALYSIS AND EXPRESSION

PERSONALIZED STUDY PLAN

PAGE	COMPETENCY AND SKILL	KNOWN MATERIAL/ SKIP IT
243	**22: Prepare an organized, developed composition in edited American English in response to instructions regarding audience, purpose, and content**	☐
	22.1: Take a position on an issue and defend it with reasoned arguments and supporting examples	☐
	22.2: Analyze and respond to an opinion presented in an excerpt	☐
	22.3: Compare and contrast conflicting viewpoints on a social, political, or educational topic explored in one or more excerpts	☐
	22.4: Evaluate information and propose a solution to a stated problem	☐
	22.5: Synthesize information presented in two or more excerpts	☐

COMPETENCY 22

PREPARE AN ORGANIZED, DEVELOPED COMPOSITION IN EDITED AMERICAN ENGLISH IN RESPONSE TO INSTRUCTIONS REGARDING AUDIENCE, PURPOSE, AND CONTENT

This section of the test consists of a written assignment. You are to prepare a written response of about 300–600 words on the assigned topic. Your response to the written assignment will be evaluated on the basis of the following criteria:

- Focus and unity: Comprehend and focus on a unified, controlling topic
- Appropriateness: Select and use a strategy of expression that is appropriate for the intended audience and purpose
- Reason and organization: Present a reasoned, organized argument or exposition
- Support and development: Use support and evidence to develop and bolster ideas, and account for the views of others
- Structure and conventions: Ensure that sentence and paragraph structure, choice and use of words, and mechanics (i.e., spelling, punctuation, capitalization) reflect careful revision and editing

Your response will be evaluated based on your demonstrated ability to express and support opinions, not on the nature or content of the opinions expressed. The final version of your response should conform to the conventions of edited American English. This should be your original work, written in your own words, and not copied or paraphrased from some other work.

Topics will vary, and you will be asked to respond in a specific manner. For example, you may:

- Skill 22.1: Take a position on an issue of contemporary concern and defend that position with reasoned arguments and supporting examples
- Skill 22.2: Analyze and respond to an opinion presented in an excerpt
- Skill 22.3: Compare and contrast conflicting viewpoints on a social, political, or educational topic explored in one or more excerpts
- Skill 22.4: Evaluate information and propose a solution to a stated problem
- Skill 22.5: Synthesize information presented in two or more excerpts

Writing Assignment

In the field of education, the concept of homework has been hotly debated. Presented below are brief summaries of arguments for and against homework:

- For Homework: Homework is an important part of the cognitive, social, and personal development of students. It encourages students to develop discipline and responsibility, and it furthers students' learning beyond the short school day.
- Against Homework: Homework often consists of busy-work. It rarely encourages deeper or better learning, and it often deprives students of time to pursue personal interests. It is a tradition that adds little to students' learning or development.

Write an essay in which you offer your opinion about this topic. Provide a well-reasoned argument with supporting evidence to back up your claims.

SAMPLE STRONG ESSAY

Homework has been a mainstay in American education for decades. It has served as a time for practicing academic skills and as an opportunity to instill, personal responsibility and time-management skills. Expertise takes great time to develop, and homework time simply extends the limited time students get in the classroom to learn complex subjects. However, homework also has been seen by many as a vehicle for useless, repetitive practice that contributes little to students' learning. Considering that more and more of the school day is taken up by academics (and less time is reserved for social time, play, or electives), homework simply adds more of the basic subjects to students' daily lives and reduces their chances of doing things to develop personal interests. It also reduces chances that students will engage in physical activities, and, therefore, contributes more to sedentary behaviors. Overall, both sides have strong arguments. The problem is not with homework itself. The problem is with the ways in which homework is used. Homework would be a positive element in students' academic lives if it fostered true intellectual growth and if it were limited only to truly prioritized topics.

First, homework should increase intellectual stimulation. Students should be able to truly learn things from their work. For example, teachers can ask students to conduct mini-experiments at home. In units on argumentative writing, for example, teachers can ask students to go home and conduct a short survey with neighbors and family members. Additionally, long-term, extensive projects that require a great deal of initiative, time-management, and conceptualization—all done at home—can provide students with a good experience in working on a project of interest to them while still honing necessary academic skills.

Continued on next page

Second, there are many learning experiences students should have that cannot reasonably be completed in the classroom or during the school day. For example, as mentioned above, assignments that ask students to do surveys or mini-research activities should be done in natural places, rather than in schools. Conducting such activities as experiments or surveys gives students the opportunity to practice real-world academic activities that they cannot get in the classroom. Additionally, extensive reading assignments, which are necessary for good reading development, should be done on students' own time so that valuable class time can be reserved for discussion and analysis.

In general, homework is a valuable tool when it is used right. When homework is used as a vehicle for mindless, repetitive activity, it fails to provide students with valuable opportunities to grow intellectually and socially. Homework really can be used as a stimulant to productive growth, and, therefore, if homework is assigned, the value of the work should be extensive and highly apparent

SAMPLE TEST

SAMPLE TEST

Scientific, Mathematical, and Technological Processes

(Easy) (Skill 1.4)

1. **When is a hypothesis formed?**

   A. Before the data is taken

   B. After the data is taken

   C. After the data is analyzed

   D. Concurrent with graphing the data

(Average) (Skill 2.1)

2. **In an experiment measuring the growth of bacteria at different temperatures, what is the independent variable?**

   A. Number of bacteria

   B. Growth rate of bacteria

   C. Temperature

   D. Size of bacteria

(Rigorous) (Skill 2.1)

3. **A scientist exposes mice to cigarette smoke and notes that their lungs develop tumors. Mice that were not exposed to the smoke do not develop as many tumors. Which of the following conclusions may be drawn from these results?**

   I. Cigarette smoke causes lung tumors

   II. Cigarette smoke exposure has a positive correlation with lung tumors in mice

   III. Some mice are predisposed to develop lung tumors

   IV. Mice are often a good model for humans in scientific research.

   A. I and II only

   B. II only

   C. I , II, and III only

   D. II and IV only

(Easy) (Skill 2.1)

4. **The following chart shows the yearly average number of international tourists visiting Palm Beach for 1990-1994. How many more international tourists visited Palm Beach in 1994 than in 1991?**

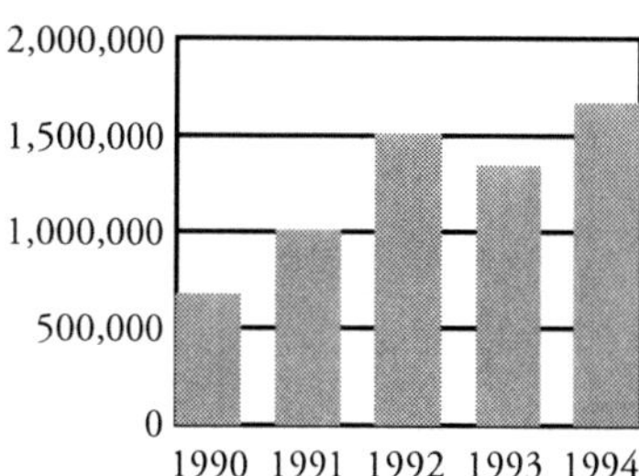

   A. 100,000

   B. 600,000

   C. 1,600,000

   D. 8,000,000

(Average) (Skill 2.1)

5. **What is the mode of the data in the following sample?**

   9, 10, 11, 9, 10, 11, 9, 13

   A. 9

   B. 9.5

   C. 10

   D. 11

(Average) (Skill 2.1)

6. **Consider the graph of the distribution of the length of time it took individuals to complete an employment form.**

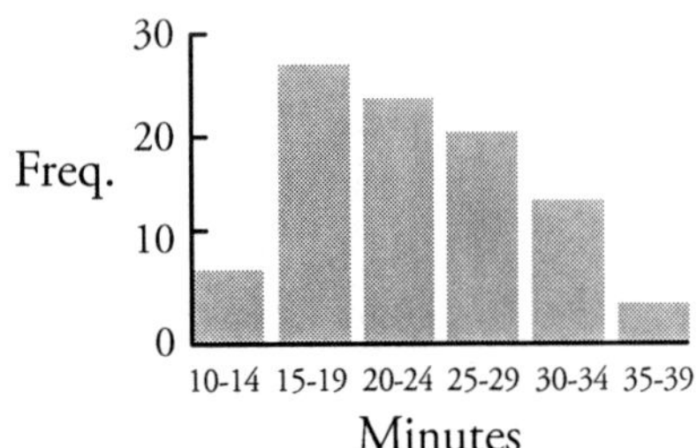

Approximately how many individuals took less than 15 minutes to complete the employment form?

A. 35

B. 28

C. 7

D. 4

(Easy) (Skill 3.1)

7. **0.74 =**

A. $\frac{74}{100}$

B. 7.4%

C. $\frac{33}{50}$

D. $\frac{74}{10}$

(Average) (Skill 3.1)

8. **303 is what percent of 600?**

A. 0.505%

B. 5.05%

C. 505%

D. 50.5%

(Average) (Skill 3.1)

9. **Select the rule of logical equivalence that directly (in one step) transforms the statement (I) into statement (II),**

I. Not all the students have books.

II. Some students do not have books.

A. "If p, then q" is equivalent to "if not q, then b"

B. "Not all are p" is equivalent to "some are not p"

C. "Not q" is equivalent to "p"

D. "All are not p" is equivalent to "none are p"

(Rigorous) (Skill 3.1)

10. **Given that:**

I. No athletes are weak

II. All football players are athletes

determine which conclusion can be logically deduced.

A. Some football players are weak

B. All football players are weak

C. No football player is weak

D. None of the above is true

(Rigorous) (Skill 3.2)

11. $(\frac{-4}{9}) + (\frac{-7}{10}) =$

A. $\frac{23}{90}$

B. $\frac{-23}{90}$

C. $\frac{103}{90}$

D. $\frac{-103}{90}$

(Average) (Skill 3.2)

12. $(5.6) \times (-0.11) =$

    A. -0.616

    B. 0.616

    C. -6.110

    D. 6.110

(Average) (Skill 3.2)

13. $\frac{7}{9} + \frac{1}{3} \div \frac{2}{3} =$

    A. $\frac{5}{3}$

    B. $\frac{3}{2}$

    C. 2

    D. $\frac{23}{18}$

(Rigorous) (Skill 3.2)

14. **Choose the statement that is true for all real numbers.**

    A. $a = 0, b \neq 0$, then $\frac{b}{a}$ = undefined

    B. $-(a + (-a)) = 2a$

    C. $2(ab) = -(2a)b$

    D. $-a(b + 1) = ab - a$

(Rigorous) (Skill 3.4)

15. **The owner of a rectangular piece of land 40 yards in length and 30 yards in width wants to divide it into two parts. She plans to join two opposite corners with a fence as shown in the diagram below. The cost of the fence will be approximately $25 per linear foot. What is the estimated cost for the fence needed by the owner?**

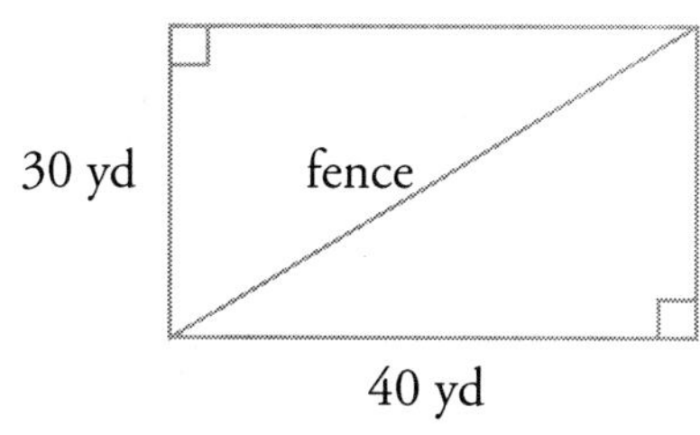

    A. $1,250

    B. $62,500

    C. $5,250

    D. $3,750

(Easy) (Skill 3.4)

16. **What is the area of a square whose side is 13 feet?**

    A. 169 feet

    B. 169 square feet

    C. 52 feet

    D. 52 square feet

(Easy) (Skill 3.4)

17. **The trunk of a tree has a 2.1 meter radius. What is its circumference?**

    A. 2.1π square meters

    B. 4.2π meters

    C. 2.1π meters

    D. 4.2π square meters

(Easy) (Skill 3.4)

18. **What is the area of this triangle?**

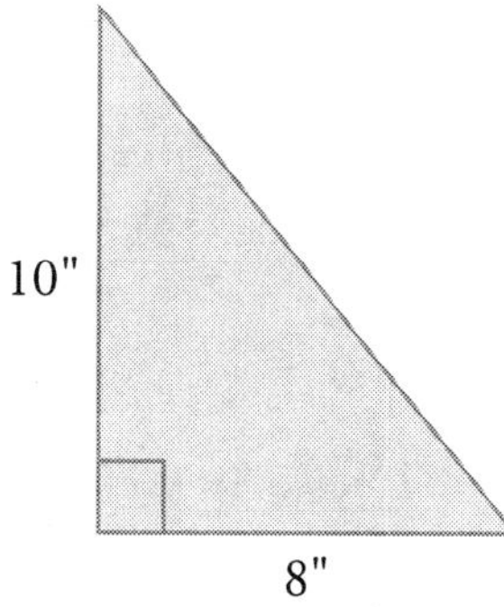

    A. 80 square inches

    B. 20 square inches

    C. 40 square inches

    D. 30 square inches

(Average) (Skill 3.5)

19. **A car gets 25.36 miles per gallon. The car has been driven 83,310 miles. What is a reasonable estimate for the number of gallons of gas used?**

A. 2,087 gallons

B. 3,000 gallons

C. 1,800 gallons

D. 164 gallons

(Rigorous) (Skill 3.5)

20. **If $4x - (3 - x) = 7(x - 3) + 10$, then:**

A. $x = 8$

B. $x = -8$

C. $x = 4$

D. $x = -4$

(Average) (Skill 3.5)

21. **Given the formula $d = rt$, (where d = distance, r = rate, and t = time), calculate the time required for a vehicle to travel 585 miles at a rate of 65 miles per hour.**

A. 8.5 hours

B. 6.5 hours

C. 9.5 hours

D. 9 hours

(Rigorous) (Skill 3.5)

22. **$3x - \frac{2}{3} = \frac{5x}{2} + 2$ Solve for x.**

A. $5\frac{1}{3}$

B. $\frac{17}{3}$

C. 2

D. $\frac{16}{2}$

(Average) (Skill 3.6)

23. **An item that sells for \$375 is put on sale at \$120. What is the percent of decrease?**

A. 25%

B. 28%

C. 68%

D. 34%

(Rigorous) (Skill 3.6)

24. **It takes five equally skilled people 9 hours to shingle Mr. Joe's roof. Let t be the time required for only 3 of these men to do the same job. Select the correct statement of the given condition.**

A. $\frac{3}{5} = \frac{9}{t}$

B. $\frac{9}{5} = \frac{3}{t}$

C. $\frac{5}{9} = \frac{3}{t}$

D. $\frac{14}{9} = \frac{t}{5}$

(Rigorous) (Skill 3.6)

25. **In a sample of 40 full-time employees at a particular company, 35 were also holding down a part-time job requiring at least 10 hours/week. If this proportion holds for the entire company of 25,000 employees, how many full-time employees at this company are actually holding down a part-time job of at least 10 hours per week.**

A. 714

B. 625

C. 21,875

D. 28,571

Answer Key

1. A	11. D	21. D
2. C	12. A	22. A
3. B	13. D	23. C
4. B	14. A	24. B
5. A	15. D	25. C
6. C	16. B	
7. A	17. B	
8. D	18. C	
9. B	19. B	
10. C	20. C	

Rigor Table

RIGOR TABLE	
Rigor level	**Questions**
Easy 20%	1, 4, 7, 16, 17, 18
Average 40%	2, 5, 6, 8, 9, 12, 13, 19, 21, 23
Rigorous 40%	3, 10, 11, 14, 15, 20, 22, 24, 25

Sample Test Questions and Rationale: Scientific, Mathematical, and Technological Processes

(Easy) (Skill 1.4)

1. **When is a hypothesis formed?**

   A. Before the data is taken

   B. After the data is taken

   C. After the data is analyzed

   D. Concurrent with graphing the data

   Answer: A.

   A hypothesis is an educated guess made before undertaking an experiment. The hypothesis is then evaluated based on the observed data. Therefore, the hypothesis must be formed before the data is taken, not during or after the experiment.

(Average) (Skill 2.1)

2. **In an experiment measuring the growth of bacteria at different temperatures, what is the independent variable?**

   A. Number of bacteria

   B. Growth rate of bacteria

   C. Temperature

   D. Size of bacteria

   Answer: C.

   To answer this question, recall that the independent variable in an experiment is the entity that is changed by the scientist in order to observe the effects (the dependent variable(s)). In this experiment, temperature is changed in order to measure growth of bacteria.

(Rigorous) (Skill 2.1)

3. **A scientist exposes mice to cigarette smoke and notes that their lungs develop tumors. Mice that were not exposed to the smoke do not develop as many tumors. Which of the following conclusions may be drawn from these results?**

   I. Cigarette smoke causes lung tumors

   II. Cigarette smoke exposure has a positive correlation with lung tumors in mice

   III. Some mice are predisposed to develop lung tumors

   IV. Mice are often a good model for humans in scientific research

   A. I and II only

   B. II only

   C. I , II, and III only

   D. II and IV only

   Answer: B.

   Although cigarette smoke has been found to cause lung tumors (and many other problems), this particular experiment shows only that there is a positive correlation between smoke exposure and tumor development in these mice. It may be true that some mice are more likely to develop tumors than others, which is why a control group of identical mice should have been used for comparison. Mice are often used to model human reactions, but this is as much due to their low financial and emotional cost as it is due to their being a "good model" for humans.

(Easy) (Skill 2.1)

4. **The following chart shows the yearly average number of international tourists visiting Palm Beach for 1990-1994. How many more international tourists visited Palm Beach in 1994 than in 1991?**

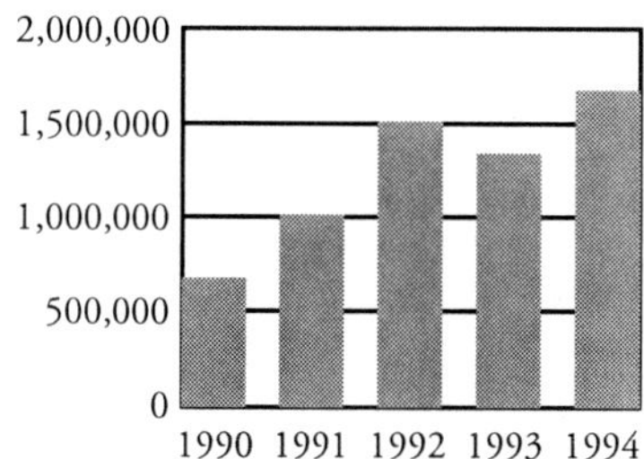

A. 100,000

B. 600,000

C. 1,600,000

D. 8,000,000

Answer: B.

The number of tourists in 1991 was 1,000,000 and the number in 1994 was 1,600,000. Subtract to get a difference of 600,000.

(Average) (Skill 2.1)

5. **What is the mode of the data in the following sample?**

9, 10, 11, 9, 10, 11, 9, 13

A. 9

B. 9.5

C. 10

D. 11

Answer: A.

The mode is the number that appears most frequently. 9 appears 3 times, which is more than the other numbers.

(Average) (Skill 2.1)

6. **Consider the graph of the distribution of the length of time it took individuals to complete an employment form.**

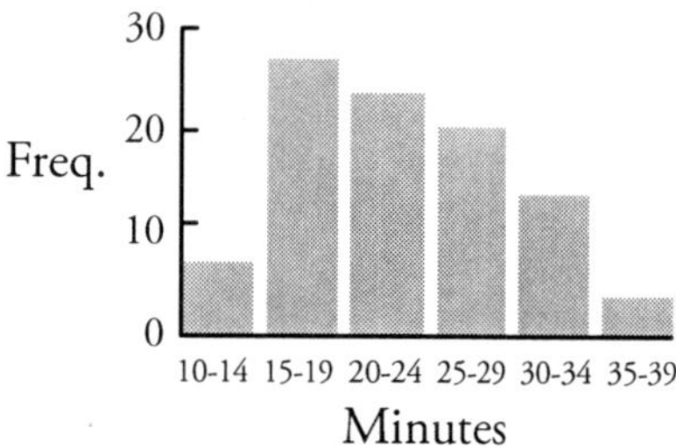

Approximately how many individuals took less than 15 minutes to complete the employment form?

A. 35

B. 28

C. 7

D. 4

Answer: C.

According to the chart, the number of people who took under 15 minutes is 7.

(Easy) (Skill 3.1)

7. **0.74 =**

A. $\frac{74}{100}$

B. 7.4%

C. $\frac{33}{50}$

D. $\frac{74}{10}$

Answer: A.

$0.74 \rightarrow 4$ is in the hundredths place, so the answer is $\frac{74}{100}$.

(Average) (Skill 3.1)

8. **303 is what percent of 600?**

A. 0.505%

B. 5.05%

C. 505%

D. 50.5%

Answer: D.

Use x for the percent. $600x = 303$. $\frac{600x}{600} = \frac{303}{600} \rightarrow x = 0.505 = 50.5\%$.

(Average) (Skill 3.1)

9. **Select the rule of logical equivalence that directly (in one step) transforms the statement (I) into statement (II),**

I. Not all the students have books.

II. Some students do not have books.

A. "If p, then q" is equivalent to "if not q, then b"

B. "Not all are p" is equivalent to "some are not p"

C. "Not q" is equivalent to "p"

D. "All are not p" is equivalent to "none are p"

Answer: B.

If we assume that the statement p is "students have books," then "not p" is "students do not have books." It is clear that statements (I) and (II) are equivalent to choice B.

(Rigorous) (Skill 3.1)

10. **Given that:**

I. No athletes are weak

II. All football players are athletes

determine which conclusion can be logically deduced.

A. Some football players are weak

B. All football players are weak

C. No football player is weak

D. None of the above is true

Answer: C.

According to the law of syllogism, "if p then q and if q then r" implies "if p then r." We can rephrase the statements above to read:

I. If a person is a football player, he or she is an athlete

II. If a person is an athlete, he or she is not weak

Then, using the law of syllogism, we can conclude: If a person is a football player, he or she is not weak. This statement is equivalent to the one in choice C.

(Rigorous) (Skill 3.2)

11. $(\frac{-4}{9}) + (\frac{-7}{10}) =$

A. $\frac{23}{90}$

B. $\frac{-23}{90}$

C. $\frac{103}{90}$

D. $\frac{-103}{90}$

Answer: D.

Find the LCD of $\frac{-4}{9}$ and $\frac{-7}{10}$. The LCD is 90, so you get $\frac{-40}{90} + \frac{-63}{90} = \frac{-103}{90}$.

(Average) (Skill 3.2)

12. **(5.6) × (-0.11) =**

A. -0.616

B. 0.616

C. -6.110

D. 6.110

Answer: A. -0.616

This problem involves simple multiplication. The answer will be negative because a positive number times a negative number is a negative number. 5.6 × -0.11 = -0.616.

(Average) (Skill 3.2)

13. $\frac{7}{9} + \frac{1}{3} \div \frac{2}{3} =$

A. $\frac{5}{3}$

B. $\frac{3}{2}$

C. 2

D. $\frac{23}{18}$

Answer: D.

First, do the division.
$\frac{1}{3} \div \frac{2}{3} = \frac{1}{3} \times \frac{3}{2} = \frac{1}{2}$

Then add.
$\frac{7}{9} + \frac{1}{2} = \frac{14}{18} + \frac{9}{18} = \frac{23}{18}$.

(Rigorous) (Skill 3.2)

14. **Choose the statement that is true for all real numbers.**

A. $a = 0, b \neq 0$, then $\frac{b}{a} =$ undefined

B. $-(a + (-a)) = 2a$

C. $2(ab) = -(2a)b$

D. $-a(\mathrm{b} + 1) = ab - a$

Answer: A.

A is the correct answer because any number divided by 0 is undefined.

(Rigorous) (Skill 3.4)

15. **The owner of a rectangular piece of land 40 yards in length and 30 yards in width wants to divide it into two parts. She plans to join two opposite corners with a fence as shown in the diagram below. The cost of the fence will be approximately $25 per linear foot. What is the estimated cost for the fence needed by the owner?**

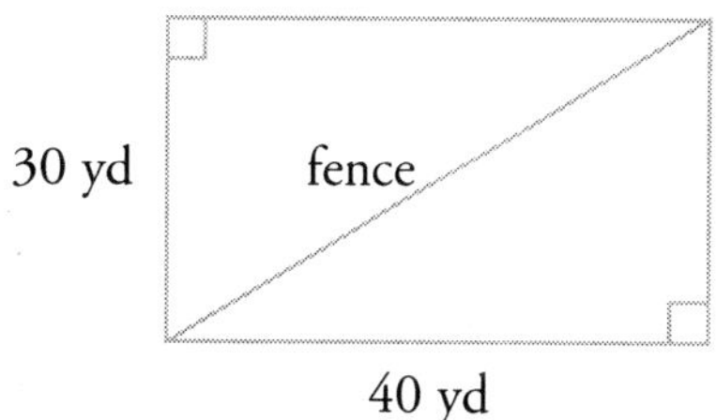

A. $1,250

B. $62,500

C. $5,250

D. $3,750

Answer: D.

Find the length of the diagonal by using the Pythagorean theorem. Let x be the length of the diagonal.

$30^2 + 40^2 = x^2 \rightarrow 900 + 1600 = x^2$
$2500 = x^2 \rightarrow \sqrt{2500} = \sqrt{x^2}$
$x = 50$ yards

Convert to feet:

$\frac{\text{50 yards}}{x\text{ feet}} = \frac{\text{1 yard}}{\text{3 feet}} \rightarrow 1500$ feet

It cost $25 per linear foot, so the cost is (1500 ft)($25) = $3,750.

(Easy) (Skill 3.4)

16. **What is the area of a square whose side is 13 feet?**

A. 169 feet

B. 169 square feet

C. 52 feet

D. 52 square feet

Answer: B.

Area = length times width (lw).
Length = 13 feet.
Width = 13 feet (in square, length and width are the same)
Area = $13 \times 13 = 169$ square feet.
Area is measured in square feet.

(Easy) (Skill 3.4)

17. **The trunk of a tree has a 2.1 meter radius. What is its circumference?**

A. 2.1π square meters

B. 4.2π meters

C. 2.1π meters

D. 4.2π square meters

Answer: B.

Circumference is $2\pi r$, where r is the radius. The circumference is $2\pi 2.1 = 4.2\pi$ meters (not square meters because we are not measuring area).

(Easy) (Skill 3.4)

18. **What is the area of this triangle?**

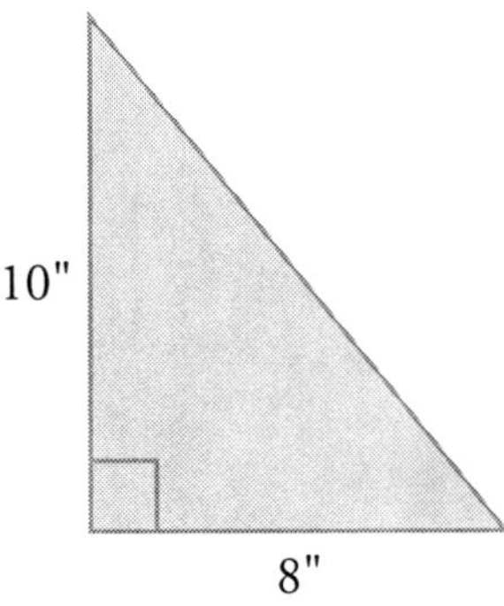

A. 80 square inches

B. 20 square inches

C. 40 square inches

D. 30 square inches

Answer: C.

The area of a triangle is $\frac{1}{2}bh$.
$\frac{1}{2} \times 8 \times 10 = 40$ square inches.

(Average) (Skill 3.5)

19. **A car gets 25.36 miles per gallon. The car has been driven 83,310 miles. What is a reasonable estimate for the number of gallons of gas used?**

A. 2,087 gallons

B. 3,000 gallons

C. 1,800 gallons

D. 164 gallons

Answer: B.

Divide the number of miles by the miles per gallon to determine the approximate number of gallons of gas used. $\frac{\text{83310 miles}}{\text{25.36 miles per gallon}} = 3285$ gallons. This is approximately 3,000 gallons.

(Rigorous) (Skill 3.5)

20. **If $4x - (3 - x) = 7(x - 3) + 10$, then:**

A. $x = 8$

B. $x = -8$

C. $x = 4$

D. $x = -4$

Answer: C.

Solve for x.
$4x - (3 - x) = 7(x - 3) + 10$
$4x - 3 + x = 7x - 21 + 10$
$5x - 3 = 7x - 11$
$5x = 7x - 11 + 3$
$5x - 7x = -8$
$-2x = -8$
$x = 4$

(Average) (Skill 3.5)

21. **Given the formula $d = rt$, (where d = distance, r = rate, and t = time), calculate the time required for a vehicle to travel 585 miles at a rate of 65 miles per hour.**

A. 8.5 hours

B. 6.5 hours

C. 9.5 hours

D. 9 hours

Answer: D.

We are given $d = 585$ miles and $r = 65$ miles per hour and $d = rt$. Solve for t.
$585 = 65t \rightarrow t = 9$ hours.

(Rigorous) (Skill 3.5)

22. **$3x - \frac{2}{3} = \frac{5x}{2} + 2$ Solve for x.**

A. $5\frac{1}{3}$

B. $\frac{17}{3}$

C. 2

D. $\frac{16}{2}$

Answer: A.

$3x(6) - \frac{2}{3}(6) = \frac{5x}{2}(6) + 2(6)$
6 is the LCD of 2 and 3
$18x - 4 = 15x + 12$
$18x = 15x + 16$
$3x = 16$
$x = \frac{16}{3} = 5\frac{1}{3}$

(Average) (Skill 3.6)

23. **An item that sells for \$375 is put on sale at \$120. What is the percent of decrease?**

A. 25%

B. 28%

C. 68%

D. 34%

Answer: C.

Use $(1 - x)$ as the discount. $375x = 120$.
$375(1 - x) = 120 \rightarrow 375 - 375x = 120 \rightarrow 375x = 255 \rightarrow x = 0.68 = 68\%$

(Rigorous) (Skill 3.6)

24. **It takes five equally skilled people 9 hours to shingle Mr. Joe's roof. Let t be the time required for only 3 of these men to do the same job. Select the correct statement of the given condition.**

A. $\frac{3}{5} = \frac{9}{t}$

B. $\frac{9}{5} = \frac{3}{t}$

C. $\frac{5}{9} = \frac{3}{t}$

D. $\frac{14}{9} = \frac{t}{5}$

Answer: B.

$$\frac{9 \text{ hours}}{5 \text{ people}} = \frac{3 \text{ people}}{t \text{ hours}}$$

(Rigorous) (Skill 3.6)

25. **In a sample of 40 full-time employees at a particular company, 35 were also holding down a part-time job requiring at least 10 hours/week. If this proportion holds for the entire company of 25,000 employees, how many full-time employees at this company are actually holding down a part-time job of at least 10 hours per week.**

A. 714

B. 625

C. 21,875

D. 28,571

Answer: C.

$\frac{35}{40}$ full time employees have a part time job also. Out of 25,000 full time employees, the number that also have a part time job is $\frac{35}{40} = \frac{x}{25000} \rightarrow 40x = 875000 \rightarrow x = 21875$, so 21,875 full time employees also have a part time job.

SAMPLE TEST

Historical and Social Scientific Awareness

(Average) (Skill 7.2)

1. **The major force in eighteenth- and nineteenth-century politics was:**

   A. Nationalism

   B. Revolution

   C. War

   D. Diplomacy

(Average) (Skill 7.2)

2. **The end to hunting, gathering, and fishing of prehistoric people was due to:**

   A. Domestication of animals

   B. Building crude huts and houses

   C. Development of agriculture

   D. Organized government in villages

(Rigorous) (Skill 7.2)

3. **Which of these is NOT a true statement about Roman civilization?**

   A. Its period of *Pax Romana* provided long periods of peace during which travel and trade increased, enabling the spread of culture, goods, and ideas over the known world

   B. It borrowed the concept of democracy from the Greeks and developed it into a complex representative government

   C. It flourished in the arts with realistic approach to art and a dramatic use of architecture

   D. It developed agricultural innovations such as crop rotation and terrace farming

(Rigorous) (Skill 7.2)

4. **How did the ideology of John Locke influence Thomas Jefferson in writing the Declaration of Independence?**

   A. Locke emphasized human rights and believed that people should rebel against governments who violated those rights

   B. Locke emphasized the rights of government to protect its people and to levy taxes

   C. Locke believed in the British system of monarchy and the rights of Parliament to make laws

   D. Locke advocated individual rights over the collective whole

(Rigorous) (Skill 7.4)

5. **As a sociologist, you would be most likely to observe:**

   A. The effects of an earthquake on farmland

   B. The behavior of rats in sensory-deprivation experiments

   C. The change over time in Babylonian obelisk styles

   D. The behavior of human beings in television focus groups

(Easy) (Skill 8.1)

6. **The U.S. Constitution:**

   A. Is an unwritten constitution

   B. Is a precise, formal, written document

   C. Does not allow states to be sovereign in their own affairs

   D. Can be amended on the vote of two-thirds of the states

(Rigorous) (Skill 8.1)

7. **In 2002, then-president George W. Bush briefly transferred his presidential power to Vice President Dick Cheney for about an hour while undergoing a colonoscopy. Under what amendment was this covered?**

   A. The Nineteenth Amendment

   B. The Twentieth Amendment

   C. The Twenty-second Amendment

   D. The Twenty-fifth Amendment

(Easy) (Skill 8.2)

8. **Populism arises out of a feeling:**

   A. Of intense happiness

   B. Of satisfaction with the activities of large corporations

   C. That women should not be allowed to vote

   D. Perceived oppression

(Easy) (Skill 8.5)

9. **Economics is best described as:**

   A. The study of how money is used in different societies

   B. The study of how different political systems produce goods and services

   C. The study of how human beings use limited resources to supply their necessities and wants

   D. The study of how human beings have developed trading practices through the years

(Average) (Skill 8.5)

10. **Capitalism and Communism are alike in that they are both:**

    A. Organic systems

    B. Political systems

    C. Centrally planned systems

    D. Economic systems

(Rigorous) (Skill 8.5)

11. **Which of the following countries has historically operated in a market economy?**

    A. Great Britain

    B. Cuba

    C. Yugoslavia

    D. India

(Rigorous) (Skill 8.5)

12. **In the fictional country of Nacirema the government controls the means of production and directs resources. It alone decides what will be produced. As a result, there is an abundance of capital and military goods but a scarcity of consumer goods. What type of economy is this?**

    A. Market economy

    B. Centrally planned economy

    C. Market socialism

    D. Capitalism

(Average) (Skill 9.2)

13. **The international organization established to work for world peace at the end of the Second World War is the:**

    A. League of Nations

    B. United Federation of Nations

    C. United Nations

    D. United World League

(Average) (Skill 9.2)

14. **How did the labor force change after 1830?**

    A. Employers began using children

    B. Employers began hiring immigrants

    C. Employers began hiring women

    D. Employers began hiring nonimmigrant men

(Rigorous) (Skill 9.2)

15. **One of the political parties that developed in the early 1790s was led by:**

    A. Thomas Jefferson

    B. George Washington

    C. Aaron Burr

    D. John Quincy Adams

(Rigorous) (Skill 9.2)

16. **The post–Civil War years were a time of low public morality, and a time of greed, graft, and dishonesty. Which one of the reasons listed would not be accurate?**

    A. The war itself, because of the money and materials needed to carry on the war

    B. The very rapid growth of industry and big business after the war

    C. The personal example set by President Grant

    D. Unscrupulous heads of large impersonal corporations

(Average) (Skill 10.4)

17. **A political scientist might use all of the following EXCEPT:**

    A. Investigation of government documents

    B. A geological timeline

    C. Voting patterns

    D. Polling data

(Rigorous) (Skill 10.4)

18. **A geographer wishes to study the effects of a flood on subsequent settlement patterns. Which might he or she find most useful?**

    A. A film clip of the floodwaters

    B. Aerial photograph of the river's source

    C. Census data taken after the flood

    D. A soil map of the A and B horizons beneath the flood area

(Average) (Skill 10.5)

19. **For the historian studying ancient Egypt, which of the following would be least useful?**

    A. The record of an ancient Greek historian on Greek–Egyptian interaction

    B. Letters from an Egyptian ruler to his/her regional governors

    C. Inscriptions on stele of the Fourteenth Egyptian Dynasty

    D. Letters from a nineteenth-century Egyptologist to his wife

(Rigorous) (Skill 11.2)

20. **An economist investigates the spending patterns of low-income individuals. Which of the following would yield the most pertinent information?**

    A. Prime lending rates of neighborhood banks

    B. The federal discount rate

    C. Citywide wholesale distribution figures

    D. Census data and retail sales figures

Answer Key

1. A	11. A
2. C	12. B
3. D	13. C
4. A	14. B
5. D	15. A
6. B	16. C
7. D	17. B
8. D	18. C
9. C	19. D
10. D	20. D

Rigor Table

RIGOR TABLE	
Rigor level	**Questions**
Easy 15%	6, 8, 9
Average 40%	1, 2, 10, 13, 14, 17, 19
Rigorous 45%	3, 4, 5, 7, 11, 12, 15, 16, 18, 20

Sample Test Questions and Rationale: Historical and Social Scientific Awareness

(Average) (Skill 7.2)

1. **The major force in eighteenth- and nineteenth-century politics was:**

   A. Nationalism

   B. Revolution

   C. War

   D. Diplomacy

   Answer: A.

   Nationalism was the driving force in politics in the eighteenth and nineteenth century. Groups of people that shared common traits and characteristics wanted their own government and countries. This often led to revolution, war, and the failure of diplomacy.

(Average) (Skill 7.2)

2. **The end to hunting, gathering, and fishing of prehistoric people was due to:**

   A. Domestication of animals

   B. Building crude huts and houses

   C. Development of agriculture

   D. Organized government in villages

   Answer: C.

   Although the domestication of animals, the building of huts and houses, and the first organized governments were all very important steps made by early civilizations, it was the development of agriculture that ended the once dominant practices of hunting, gathering, and fishing among prehistoric people. The development of agriculture provided a more efficient use of time and for the first time a surplus of food. This greatly improved the quality of life and contributed to early population growth.

(Rigorous) (Skill 7.2)

3. **Which of these is NOT a true statement about Roman civilization?**

   A. Its period of *Pax Romana* provided long periods of peace during which travel and trade increased, enabling the spread of culture, goods, and ideas over the known world

   B. It borrowed the concept of democracy from the Greeks and developed it into a complex representative government

   C. It flourished in the arts with realistic approach to art and a dramatic use of architecture

   D. It developed agricultural innovations such as crop rotation and terrace farming

   Answer: D.

   China developed crop rotation and terrace farming.

(Rigorous) (Skill 7.2)

4. **How did the ideology of John Locke influence Thomas Jefferson in writing the Declaration of Independence?**

   A. Locke emphasized human rights and believed that people should rebel against governments who violated those rights

   B. Locke emphasized the rights of government to protect its people and to levy taxes

   C. Locke believed in the British system of monarchy and the rights of Parliament to make laws

   D. Locke advocated individual rights over the collective whole

Answer: A.

The Declaration of Independence is an outgrowth of both ancient Greek ideas of democracy and individual rights and the ideas of the European Enlightenment and the Renaissance, especially the ideology of the political thinker John Locke. Thomas Jefferson was the author of the Declaration and borrowed much from Locke's theories and writings. John Locke was one of the most influential political writers of the seventeenth century, and he put great emphasis on human rights and put forth the belief that when governments violate those rights people should rebel. He wrote the book *Two Treatises of Government* in 1690, which had tremendous influence on political thought in the American colonies and helped shape the U.S. Constitution and Declaration of Independence.

(Rigorous) (Skill 7.4)

5. **As a sociologist, you would be most likely to observe:**

   A. The effects of an earthquake on farmland

   B. The behavior of rats in sensory-deprivation experiments

   C. The change over time in Babylonian obelisk styles

   D. The behavior of human beings in television focus groups

Answer: D.

Predominant beliefs and attitudes within human society are studied in the field of sociology. The effects of an earthquake on farmland might be studied by a geographer. The behavior of rats in an experiment falls under the field of behavioral psychology. Changes in Babylonian obelisk styles might interest a historian. None of these answers fit easily within the definition of sociology. A focus group, where people are asked to discuss their reactions to a certain product or topic, would be the most likely method for a sociologist of observing and discovering attitudes among a selected group.

(Easy) (Skill 8.1)

6. **The U.S. Constitution:**

   A. Is an unwritten constitution

   B. Is a precise, formal, written document

   C. Does not allow states to be sovereign in their own affairs

   D. Can be amended on the vote of two-thirds of the states

Answer: B.

The U.S. Constitution is not an unwritten constitution. It is not true that the U.S. Constitution fails to allow states to be sovereign in their own affairs. It requires three-fourths of the states, not two-thirds, to amend the U.S. Constitution.

(Rigorous) (Skill 8.1)

7. **In 2002, then-president George W. Bush briefly transferred his presidential power to Vice President Dick Cheney for about an hour while undergoing a colonoscopy. Under what amendment was this covered?**

   A. The Nineteenth Amendment

   B. The Twentieth Amendment

   C. The Twenty-second Amendment

   D. The Twenty-fifth Amendment

Answer: D.

Presidential succession is the focus of the Twenty-fifth Amendment, which provides a blueprint of what to do if the president is incapacitated or killed. The long battle for voting rights for women ended in success with the passage of the Nineteenth Amendment. The date for the beginning of terms for the president and the Congress was changed from March to January by the Twentieth Amendment. The Twenty-second Amendment limited the number of terms that a president could serve to two.

(Easy) (Skill 8.2)

8. **Populism arises out of a feeling:**

   A. Of intense happiness

   B. Of satisfaction with the activities of large corporations

   C. That women should not be allowed to vote

   D. Perceived oppression

Answer: D.

Perceived oppression felt by average people toward the wealthy elite gave rise to Populism. Populists do not become prominent when people are happy, or when people are satisfied with the activities of large corporations. Populists and other progressives fought for, not against, voting rights for women.

(Easy) (Skill 8.5)

9. **Economics is best described as:**

   A. The study of how money is used in different societies

   B. The study of how different political systems produce goods and services

   C. The study of how human beings use limited resources to supply their necessities and wants

   D. The study of how human beings have developed trading practices through the years

Answer: C.

How money is used in different societies might be of interest to a sociologist or anthropologist. The study of how different political systems produce goods and services is a topic of study that could be included under the field of political science. The study of historical trading practices could fall under the study of history. Only is the best general description of the social science of economics as a whole.

(Average) (Skill 8.5)

10. **Capitalism and Communism are alike in that they are both:**

A. Organic systems

B. Political systems

C. Centrally planned systems

D. Economic systems

Answer: D.

While economic and political systems are often closely connected, capitalism and Communism are primarily economic systems. Capitalism is a system of economics that allows the open market to determine the relative value of goods and services. Communism is an economic system where the market is planned by a central state. Communism is a centrally planned system; this is not true of capitalism. Organic systems are studied in biology, a natural science.

(Rigorous) (Skill 8.5)

11. **Which of the following countries has historically operated in a market economy?**

A. Great Britain

B. Cuba

C. Yugoslavia

D. India

Answer: A.

A market economy is based on supply and demand and the use of markets. Although Great Britain may have socialized medicine, it operates a market economy. Cuba, with its ties to Communism, has a centrally planned economy. Historically, China has had a centrally planned economy but is now moving toward a market economy. Yugoslavia was a market socialist economy, but the country no longer exists—it has been split into Montenegro and Serbia.

(Rigorous) (Skill 8.5)

12. **In the fictional country of Nacirema the government controls the means of production and directs resources. It alone decides what will be produced. As a result, there is an abundance of capital and military goods but a scarcity of consumer goods. What type of economy is this?**

A. Market economy

B. Centrally planned economy

C. Market socialism

D. Capitalism

Answer: B.

In a planned economy, the means of production are publicly owned, with little, if any, private ownership. Instead of the "three questions" being solved by markets, there is a planning authority that makes the decisions. The planning authority decides what will be produced and how. Since most planned economies direct resources into the production of capital and military goods, there is little remaining for consumer goods; the result is often chronic shortages.

(Average) (Skill 9.2)

13. **The international organization established to work for world peace at the end of the Second World War is the:**

A. League of Nations

B. United Federation of Nations

C. United Nations

D. United World League

Answer: C.

The international organization established to work for world peace at the end of the Second World War was the United Nations. From the ashes of the failed League of Nations, established following the First World War, the United Nations continues to be a major player in world affairs today.

(Average) (Skill 9.2)

14. **How did the labor force change after 1830?**

A. Employers began using children

B. Employers began hiring immigrants

C. Employers began hiring women

D. Employers began hiring nonimmigrant men

Answer: B.

Employers began hiring immigrants who were arriving in large numbers. Children and women began entering the labor force prior to 1830. Employers had always used nonimmigrant men.

(Rigorous) (Skill 9.2)

15. **One of the political parties that developed in the early 1790s was led by:**

A. Thomas Jefferson

B. George Washington

C. Aaron Burr

D. John Quincy Adams

Answer: A.

George Washington warned against the creation of "factions." Aaron Burr is the man who killed Alexander Hamilton in a duel. John Quincy Adams was still a young man at that time.

(Rigorous) (Skill 9.2)

16. **The post–Civil War years were a time of low public morality, and a time of greed, graft, and dishonesty. Which one of the reasons listed would not be accurate?**

A. The war itself, because of the money and materials needed to carry on the war

B. The very rapid growth of industry and big business after the war

C. The personal example set by President Grant

D. Unscrupulous heads of large impersonal corporations

Answer: C.

The post–Civil War years were a particularly difficult time for the nation and public morale was especially low. The war had plunged the country into debt and ultimately into a recession by the 1890s. Racism was rampant throughout the South and the North where freed blacks were taking jobs for low wages. The rapid growth of industry and big business caused a polarization of rich and poor, workers and owners. Many people moved into the urban centers to find work in the new industrial sector, jobs were typically low-wage, long hours, and poor working conditions. The heads of large impersonal corporations were arrogant in treating their workers inhumanely and letting morale drop to a record low. The heads of corporations showed their greed and malice toward the workingman by trying to prevent and disband labor unions.

(Average) (Skill 10.4)

17. **A political scientist might use all of the following EXCEPT:**

A. Investigation of government documents

B. A geological timeline

C. Voting patterns

D. Polling data

Answer: B.

Political science is primarily concerned with the political and governmental activities of societies. Government documents can provide information about the organization and activities of a government. Voting patterns reveal the political behavior of individuals and groups. Polling data can provide insight into the predominant political views of a group of people. A geological timeline describes the changes in the physical features of the Earth over time and would not be useful to a political scientist.

(Rigorous) (Skill 10.4)

18. **A geographer wishes to study the effects of a flood on subsequent settlement patterns. Which might he or she find most useful?**

A. A film clip of the floodwaters

B. Aerial photograph of the river's source

C. Census data taken after the flood

D. A soil map of the A and B horizons beneath the flood area

Answer: C.

A film clip of the flood waters may be of most interest to a historian; an aerial photograph of the river's source, and soil maps tell little about the behavior of the individuals affected by the flood. Census surveys record the population for certain areas on a regular basis, allowing a geographer to tell if more or fewer people are living in an area over time. These would be of most use to a geographer undertaking this study.

(Average) (Skill 10.5)

19. **For the historian studying ancient Egypt, which of the following would be least useful?**

    A. The record of an ancient Greek historian on Greek–Egyptian interaction

    B. Letters from an Egyptian ruler to his/her regional governors

    C. Inscriptions on stele of the Fourteenth Egyptian Dynasty

    D. Letters from a nineteenth-century Egyptologist to his wife

Answer: D.

Historians use primary sources from the actual time they are studying whenever possible. Ancient Greek records of interaction with Egypt, letters from an Egyptian ruler to regional governors, and inscriptions from the Fourteenth Egyptian Dynasty are all primary sources created at or near the actual time being studied. Letters from a nineteenth century Egyptologist would not be considered primary sources, as they were created thousands of years after the fact and may not actually be about the subject being studied.

(Rigorous) (Skill 11.2)

20. **An economist investigates the spending patterns of low-income individuals. Which of the following would yield the most pertinent information?**

    A. Prime lending rates of neighborhood banks

    B. The federal discount rate

    C. Citywide wholesale distribution figures

    D. Census data and retail sales figures

Answer: D.

Local lending rates and the federal discount rate might provide information on borrowing habits, but not necessarily spending habits, and they give no information on income levels. Citywide wholesale distribution figures would provide information on the business activity of a city, but tell nothing about consumer activities. Census data records the income levels of households within a certain area and retail sales figures for that area would give an economist data on spending, which can be compared to income levels, making this the most pertinent source.

SAMPLE TEST

Artistic Expression and the Humanities

(Easy) (Skill 12.1)

1. **The term for rhythm that is measured and divided into equal parts is:**

   A. Harmony

   B. Consonance

   C. Meter

   D. Dissonance

(Easy) (Skill 12.1)

2. **A series of single tones that add up to a recognizable pattern is called a:**

   A. Cadence

   B. Rhythm

   C. Melody

   D. Sequence

(Average) (Skill 12.1)

3. **Creating movements in response to music helps students to connect music and dance in which of the following ways?**

   A. Rhythm

   B. Costuming

   C. Harmony

   D. Vocabulary skills

(Average) (Skill 12.3)

4. **Universal themes are those that:**

   A. Explain how the universe was created

   B. Explain the nature of the universe

   C. Can be experienced by all people

   D. Belong to specific groups of people

(Average) (Skill 13.1)

5. **The history of theater is important to describe how theater has evolved over time. In which of the following theatrical traditions were the two main forms of theater, tragedy and comedy, developed?**

   A. Roman drama

   B. Greek theater

   C. Medieval drama

   D. Renaissance theater

(Average) (Skill 13.1)

6. **In the visual arts, the terms *fauvism* and *surrealism* relate to which of the following periods?**

   A. Roman art

   B. Baroque art

   C. Ancient Greek art

   D. Twentieth-century art

(Average) (Skill 13.1)

7. **In the Middle Ages, the overwhelming majority of the art created had to do with:**

   A. Neoclassicism

   B. Individual expression

   C. Religious themes

   D. Social realism

(Average) (Skill 13.1)

8. **Impressionism in art and music was an attempt to:**
   A. Capture the transitory aspects of the world
   B. Impress the audience with a photographic view of the world
   C. Express heart-felt emotions about nature
   D. Portray the common people in a heroic light

(Rigorous) (Skills 13.1, 13.3, and 15.6)

9. **Twentieth-century themes in art and literature are marked by:**
   A. Practicality and utilitarianism
   B. Idealized figures and exotic destinations
   C. Harmony and balance
   D. Diversity of views and individualism

(Average) (Skill 13.4)

10. **Renaissance artists and writers highly valued the forms and ideas of:**
    A. Ancient China and India
    B. Medieval France
    C. Northern Europe
    D. Classical Greece and Ancient Rome

(Rigorous) (Skill 15.3)

11. **A fiction reader's enjoyment of a work usually involves:**
    A. Disputing the author's claims
    B. Reading the author's biography
    C. Suspension of disbelief
    D. Attention to facts

(Easy) (Skill 15.3)

12. **The following type of writing is NOT a form of nonfiction:**
    A. Newspaper
    B. Diary
    C. Bildungsroman
    D. Biography

(Rigorous) (Skill 15.3)

13. **Some literature of the Renaissance period:**
    A. Could be vulgar and appealed to the masses
    B. Was created solely for use in monasteries
    C. Was based on linear perspective
    D. Was formal, quiet, and restrained

(Average) (Skill 16.1)

14. **In the religion of Hinduism, the three aspects of the universal spirit are:**
    A. Brahma, Vishnu, and Shiva
    B. Nirvana, Vishnu, and the Buddha
    C. Veda, Ramayana, and the Buddha
    D. Rig-Veda, Rama, and Shiva

(Average) (Skill 16.1)

15. **Buddhism emphasizes:**
    A. Preoccupation with the supernatural
    B. Strict adherence to the caste system
    C. Ancestor worship
    D. Spiritual peace through righteous living

(Easy) (Skill 16.1)

16. **Judaism was the first of the world's great religions to:**

    A. Emphasize belief in an afterlife

    B. Evolve from folk traditions

    C. Practice belief in one God

    D. Promote worship of many deities

(Rigorous) (Skill 16.1)

17. **The schism within the Christian religion resulted in the creation of the following parts:**

    A. Saints and sinners

    B. The Roman Catholic Church and the Orthodox Church

    C. Protestants and Jesuits

    D. The Roman Catholic Church and the Irish Catholic Church

(Average) (Skill 16.1)

18. **The philosophy best associated with Lao-tse is:**

    A. Government should be a strong force in society

    B. Mankind should live in fear of the gods

    C. Mankind should live in harmony with nature

    D. Mankind should strive toward intellectual perfection

(Easy) (Skills 16.1 and 16.3)

19. **The world religion associated with the caste system is:**

    A. Buddhism

    B. Hinduism

    C. Sikhism

    D. Jainism

Answer Key

1. C	11. C
2. C	12. C
3. A	13. A
4. C	14. A
5. B	15. D
6. D	16. C
7. C	17. B
8. A	18. C
9. D	19. B
10. D	

Rigor Table

RIGOR TABLE	
Rigor level	**Questions**
Easy 25%	1, 2, 12, 16, 19
Average 55%	3, 4, 5, 6, 7, 8, 10, 14, 15, 18
Rigorous 20%	9, 11, 13, 17

Sample Test Questions and Rationale: Artistic Expression and the Humanities

(Easy) (Skill 12.1)

1. **The term for rhythm that is measured and divided into equal parts is:**

   A. Harmony

   B. Consonance

   C. Meter

   D. Dissonance

   Answer: C.

   When rhythm is measured and divided into parts of equal time value, it is called meter.

(Easy) (Skill 12.1)

2. **A series of single tones that add up to a recognizable pattern is called a:**

   A. Cadence

   B. Rhythm

   C. Melody

   D. Sequence

   Answer: C.

   The melody of a musical piece refers to the pattern of single tones in a composition that does more than simply reinforce rhythm or provide harmony. The melody of a musical piece is often considered the "horizontal" aspect of the piece that flows from start to finish.

(Average) (Skill 12.1)

3. **Creating movements in response to music helps students to connect music and dance in which of the following ways?**

   A. Rhythm

   B. Costuming

   C. Harmony

   D. Vocabulary skills

   Answer: A.

   Rhythm refers to the pattern of regular or irregular pulses in music that result from the melodic beats of the music. Simple techniques to teach and practice rhythm include clapping hands and tapping feet to the beat of the music. Teachers can also incorporate the use of percussion instruments to examine rhythmic patterns, which also increases students' awareness of rhythm.

(Average) (Skill 12.3)

4. **Universal themes are those that:**

   A. Explain how the universe was created

   B. Explain the nature of the universe

   C. Can be experienced by all people

   D. Belong to specific groups of people

   Answer: C.

   Universal themes are themes that reflect the human experience regardless of time period, location, social standing, economic considerations, or religious or cultural beliefs.

(Average) (Skill 13.1)

5. **The history of theater is important to describe how theater has evolved over time. In which of the following theatrical traditions were the two main forms of theater, tragedy and comedy, developed?**

   A. Roman drama

   B. Greek theater

   C. Medieval drama

   D. Renaissance theater

   Answer: B.

   The history of theater can be dated back to early sixth century in Greece. From the Greek dramatic tradition the two main forms of drama developed: tragedy typically involved conflict between characters, and comedy involved paradoxical relationships between humans and the gods.

(Average) (Skill 13.1)

6. **In the visual arts, the terms *fauvism* and *surrealism* relate to which of the following periods?**

   A. Roman art

   B. Baroque art

   C. Ancient Greek art

   D. Twentieth-century art

   Answer: D.

   Major artistic movements of the twentieth century include symbolism, art nouveau, fauvism, expressionism, cubism (both analytical and synthetic), futurism, nonobjective art, abstract art, surrealism, social realism, constructivism, pop and op art, and conceptual art.

(Average) (Skill 13.1)

7. **In the Middle Ages, the overwhelming majority of the art created had to do with:**

   A. Neoclassicism

   B. Individual expression

   C. Religious themes

   D. Social realism

   Answer: C.

   Although the time span is expansive, the major themes remain relatively constant. Since the Roman Catholic Church was the primary patron of the arts, most work was religious in nature. Specific themes varied from the illustration of Bible stories to interpretations of theological allegory, to lives of the saints, and to consequences of good and evil.

(Average) (Skill 13.1)

8. **Impressionism in art and music was an attempt to:**

   A. Capture the transitory aspects of the world

   B. Impress the audience with a photographic view of the world

   C. Express heart-felt emotions about nature

   D. Portray the common people in a heroic light

   Answer: A.

   The themes behind Impressionism were the constant flux of the universe and the immediacy of the moment.

(Rigorous) (Skills 13.1, 13.3, and 15.6)

9. **Twentieth-century themes in art and literature are marked by:**

   A. Practicality and utilitarianism

   B. Idealized figures and exotic destinations

   C. Harmony and balance

   D. Diversity of views and individualism

   Answer: D.

   Artists and writers explored expression of a multitude of themes through a wide variety of forms. There were so many disparate artistic movements in the twentieth century—the audience for art became increasingly diverse, and artists felt liberated.

(Average) (Skill 13.4)

10. **Renaissance artists and writers highly valued the forms and ideas of:**

   A. Ancient China and India

   B. Medieval France

   C. Northern Europe

   D. Classical Greece and Ancient Rome

   Answer: D.

   The Renaissance period was concerned with the rediscovery of the works of classical Greece and Rome. The art, literature, and architecture were inspired by classical orders, which tended to be formal, simple, and concerned with the ideal human proportions.

(Rigorous) (Skill 15.3)

11. **A fiction reader's enjoyment of a work usually involves:**

   A. Disputing the author's claims

   B. Reading the author's biography

   C. Suspension of disbelief

   D. Attention to facts

   Answer: C.

   Enjoying fiction depends upon the ability of readers to suspend belief. Readers make a deal with writers that for the time it takes to read the story, their own belief will be put aside and be replaced by the convictions and reality that the writer has presented in the story. This is not true in nonfiction.

(Easy) (Skill 15.3)

12. **The following type of writing is NOT a form of nonfiction:**

   A. Newspaper

   B. Diary

   C. Bildungsroman

   D. Biography

   Answer: C.

   A bildungsroman (from the German meaning "novel of formation") is a novel that traces the spiritual, moral, psychological, or social development and growth of the main character from childhood to maturity.

(Rigorous) (Skill 15.3)

13. **Some literature of the Renaissance period:**

A. Could be vulgar and appealed to the masses

B. Was created solely for use in monasteries

C. Was based on linear perspective

D. Was formal, quiet, and restrained

Answer: A.

The Renaissance saw the introduction of the inexpensive chapbooks, which were condensed versions of mythology and fairy tales. Designed for the common people, chapbooks could be vulgar and grammatically imperfect, but were immensely popular because of their adventurous contents.

(Average) (Skill 16.1)

14. **In the religion of Hinduism, the three aspects of the universal spirit are:**

A. Brahma, Vishnu, and Shiva

B. Nirvana, Vishnu, and the Buddha

C. Veda, Ramayana, and the Buddha

D. Rig-Veda, Rama, and Shiva

Answer: A.

In Hinduism, the universal soul assumes the three forms of Brahma (the creator), Vishnu (the preserver), and Shiva (the destroyer).

(Average) (Skill 16.1)

15. **Buddhism emphasizes:**

A. Preoccupation with the supernatural

B. Strict adherence to the caste system

C. Ancestor worship

D. Spiritual peace through righteous living

Answer: D.

Buddhists follow the "eightfold path" toward spiritual living. Nirvana (spiritual peace), may be reached even in one lifetime by righteous living. Buddhism opposes the worship of numerous deities, the Hindu caste system, and preoccupation with the supernatural.

(Easy) (Skill 16.1)

16. **Judaism was the first of the world's great religions to:**

A. Emphasize belief in an afterlife

B. Evolve from folk traditions

C. Practice belief in one God

D. Promote worship of many deities

Answer: C.

Judaism is the oldest of the eight great world religions and it was the first to teach and practice the belief in one God.

(Rigorous) (Skill 16.1)

17. **The schism within the Christian religion resulted in the creation of the following parts:**

A. Saints and sinners

B. The Roman Catholic Church and the Orthodox Church

C. Protestants and Jesuits

D. The Roman Catholic Church and the Irish Catholic Church

Answer: B.

A schism resulted in the Western (Roman Catholic) and Eastern (Orthodox) parts.

(Average) (Skill 16.1)

18. **The philosophy best associated with Lao-tse is:**

A. Government should be a strong force in society

B. Mankind should live in fear of the gods

C. Mankind should live in harmony with nature

D. Mankind should strive toward intellectual perfection

Answer: C.

Philosopher Lao-tse taught that because laws cannot improve man's lot, government should be a minimal force in man's life. Man should live passively in harmony with Tao (nature).

(Easy) (Skills 16.1 and 16.3)

19. **The world religion associated with the caste system is:**

A. Buddhism

B. Hinduism

C. Sikhism

D. Jainism

Answer: B.

Though forbidden today by law, a prominent feature of Hinduism in the past was a rigid adherence to, and practice of, the infamous caste system. The caste system, which is incredibly complicated and nuanced, prevailed as the social system of India until modern times. In 1000 BCE four principal castes existed: priests and scholars, rulers and warriors, artisans and merchants, and unskilled workers.

SAMPLE TEST

Written Analysis and Expression

DIRECTIONS: The passage below contains several errors. Read the passage. Then answer each test item by choosing the option that corrects an error in the underlined portion(s). No more than one underlined error will appear in each item. If no error exists, choose "No change is necessary."

Every job places different kinds of demands on their employees. For example, whereas such jobs as accounting and bookkeeping require mathematical ability; graphic design requires creative/artistic ability.

Doing good at one job does not usually guarantee success at another. However, one of the elements crucial to all jobs are especially notable: the chance to accomplish a goal.

The accomplishment of the employees varies according to the job. In many jobs the employees become accustom to the accomplishment provided by the work they do every day.

In medicine, for example, every doctor tests him self by treating badly injured or critically ill people. In the operating room, a team of Surgeons is responsible for operating on many of these patients. In addition to the feeling of accomplishment that the workers achieve, some jobs also give a sense of identity to the employees'. Professions like law, education, and sales offer huge financial and emotional rewards. Politicians are public servants: who work for the federal and state governments. President Obama is basically employed by the American people to make laws and run the country.

Finally; the contributions that employees make to their companies and to the world cannot be taken for granted. Through their work, employees are performing a service for their employers and are contributing something to the world.

(Rigorous) (Competency 22)

1. **Every job places different kinds of demands on their employees.**

   A. place

   B. its

   C. employes

   D. No change is necessary

(Average) (Competency 22)

2. **For example, whereas such jobs as accounting and bookkeeping require mathematical ability; graphic design requires creative/artistic ability.**

   A. For example

   B. whereas,

   C. ability,

   D. No change is necessary

(Rigorous) (Competency 22)

3. **Doing good at one job does not usually guarantee success at another.**

   A. well

   B. usualy

   C. succeeding

   D. No change is necessary

(Average) (Competency 22)

4. **However, one of the elements crucial to all jobs are especially notable: the accomplishment of a goal.**

   A. However

   B. is

   C. notable;

   D. No change is necessary

(Rigorous) (Competency 22)

5. **The accomplishment of the employees varies according to the job.**

   A. accomplishment,

   B. employee's

   C. vary

   D. No change is necessary

(Average) (Competency 22)

6. **In many jobs the employees become accustom to the accomplishment provided by the work they do every day.**

   A. became

   B. accustomed

   C. provides

   D. No change is necessary

(Average) (Competency 22)

7. **In addition to the feeling of accomplishment that the workers achieve, some jobs also give a sense of self-identity to the employees'.**

   A. acheive

   B. gave

   C. employees

   D. No change is necessary

(Easy) (Competency 22)

8. **Politicians are public servants: who work for the federal and state governments.**

   A. were

   B. servants who

   C. worked

   D. No change is necessary

Read the following passage and answer questions 9 to 17.

One of the most difficult problems plaguing American education is the assessment of teachers. No one denies that teachers ought to be answerable for what they do, but what exactly does that mean? The *Oxford American Dictionary* defines accountability as: the obligation to give a reckoning or explanation for one's actions.

Does a student have to learn for teaching to have taken place? Historically, teaching has not been defined in this restrictive manner; the teacher was thought to be responsible for the quantity and quality of material covered and the way in which it was presented. However, some definitions of teaching now imply that students must learn in order for teaching to have taken place.

As a teacher who tries my best to keep current on all the latest teaching strategies, I believe that those teachers who do not bother even to pick up an educational journal every once in a while should be kept under close watch. There are many teachers out there who have been teaching for decades and refuse to change their ways even if research has proven that their methods are outdated and ineffective. There is no place in the profession of teaching for these types of individuals. It is time that the American educational system clean house, for the sake of our children.

(Rigorous) (Competency 22)

9. **What is the organizational pattern of the second paragraph?**
   A. Cause and effect
   B. Classification
   C. Addition
   D. Explanation

(Average) (Competency 22)

10. **What is the main idea of the passage?**
    A. Teachers should not be answerable for what they do
    B. Teachers who do not do their job should be fired
    C. The author is a good teacher
    D. Assessment of teachers is a serious problem in society today

(Rigorous) (Competency 22)

11. **From the passage, one can infer that:**
    A. The author considers herself a good teacher
    B. Poor teachers will be fired
    C. Students have to learn for teaching to take place
    D. The author will be fired

(Average) (Competency 22)

12. **Teachers who do not keep current on educational trends should be fired. Is this a fact or an opinion?**
    A. Fact
    B. Opinion

(Average) (Competency 22)

13. **What is the author's purpose in writing this?**
    A. To entertain
    B. To narrate
    C. To describe
    D. To persuade

(Rigorous) (Competency 22)

14. **Is there evidence of bias in this passage?**
    A. Yes
    B. No

(Average) (Competency 22)

15. **The author's tone is one of:**
    A. Disbelief
    B. Excitement
    C. Support
    D. Concern

(Easy) (Competency 22)

16. **What is meant by the word "plaguing" in the first sentence?**
    A. Causing problems
    B. Causing illness
    C. Causing anger
    D. Causing failure

(Easy) (Competency 22)

17. **Where does the author get her definition of "accountability?"**
    A. *Webster's Dictionary*
    B. *Encyclopedia Brittanica*
    C. *Oxford American Dictionary*
    D. *World Book Encyclopedia*

(Rigorous) (Competency 22)

18. **A figure of speech in which someone absent or something inhuman is addressed as though present and able to respond describes:**

    A. Personification

    B. Synechdoche

    C. Metonymy

    D. Apostrophe

(Average) (Competency 22)

19. **A sixth-grade science teacher has given her class a paper to read on the relationship between food and weight gain. The writing contains signal words such as "because," "consequently," "this is how," and "due to." This paper has which text structure?**

    A. Cause and effect

    B. Compare and contrast

    C. Description

    D. Sequencing

(Average) (Competency 22)

20. **Which of the following is not a figure of speech (figurative language)?**

    A. Simile

    B. Euphemism

    C. Onomatopoeia

    D. Allusion

Answer Key

1. B	11. A
2. C	12. B
3. A	13. D
4. B	14. A
5. C	15. D
6. B	16. A
7. C	17. C
8. B	18. A
9. D	19. A
10. D	20. D

Rigor Table

RIGOR TABLE	
Rigor level	**Questions**
Easy 15%	8, 16, 17
Average 50%	2, 4, 6, 7, 10, 12, 13, 15, 19, 20
Rigorous 35%	1, 3, 5, 9, 11, 14, 18

Sample Test Questions and Rationale: Written Analysis and Expression

DIRECTIONS: The passage below contains several errors. Read the passage. Then answer each test item by choosing the option that corrects an error in the underlined portion(s). No more than one underlined error will appear in each item. If no error exists, choose "No change is necessary."

Every job places different kinds of demands on their employees. For example, whereas such jobs as accounting and bookkeeping require mathematical ability; graphic design requires creative/artistic ability.

Doing good at one job does not usually guarantee success at another. However, one of the elements crucial to all jobs are especially notable: the chance to accomplish a goal.

The accomplishment of the employees varies according to the job. In many jobs the employees become accustom to the accomplishment provided by the work they do every day.

In medicine, for example, every doctor tests him self by treating badly injured or critically ill people. In the operating room, a team of Surgeons is responsible for operating on many of these patients. In addition to the feeling of accomplishment that the workers achieve, some jobs also give a sense of identity to the employees'. Professions like law, education, and sales offer huge financial and emotional rewards. Politicians are public servants: who work for the federal and state governments. President Obama is basically employed by the American people to make laws and run the country.

Finally; the contributions that employees make to their companies and to the world cannot be taken for granted. Through their work, employees are performing a service for their employers and are contributing something to the world.

(Rigorous) (Competency 22)

1. **Every job <u>places</u> different kinds of demands on <u>their</u> <u>employees</u>.**

   A. place

   B. its

   C. employes

   D. No change is necessary

   Answer: B.

   The singular possessive pronoun *its* must agree with its antecedent *job*, which is singular also. Option A is incorrect because *place* is a plural form and the subject, *job*, is singular. Option C is incorrect because the correct spelling of *employees* is given in the sentence.

(Average) (Competency 22)

2. **<u>For example,</u> <u>whereas</u> such jobs as accounting and bookkeeping require mathematical <u>ability;</u> graphic design requires creative/artistic ability.**

   A. For example

   B. whereas,

   C. ability,

   D. No change is necessary

Answer: C.

An introductory dependent clause is set off with a comma, not a semicolon. Option A is incorrect because the transitional phrase *for example* should be set off with a comma. Option B is incorrect because the adverb *whereas* functions like *while* and does not take a comma after it.

(Rigorous) (Competency 22)

3. **Doing good at one job does not usually guarantee success at another.**

   A. well

   B. usualy

   C. succeeding

   D. No change is necessary

Answer: A.

The adverb *well* modifies the word *doing*. Option B is incorrect because *usually* is spelled correctly in the sentence. Option C is incorrect because *succeeding* is in the wrong tense.

(Average) (Competency 22)

4. **However, one of the elements crucial to all jobs are especially notable: the accomplishment of a goal.**

   A. However

   B. is

   C. notable;

   D. No change is necessary

Answer: B.

The singular verb is is needed to agree with the singular subject *one*. Option A is incorrect because a comma is needed to set off the transitional word *however*. Option C is incorrect because a colon, not a semicolon, is needed to set off an item.

(Rigorous) (Competency 22)

5. **The accomplishment of the employees varies according to the job.**

   A. accomplishment,

   B. employee's

   C. vary

   D. No change is necessary

Answer: C.

The singular verb *vary* is needed to agree with the singular subject *accomplishment*. Option A is incorrect because a comma after *accomplishment* would suggest that the modifying phrase *of the employees* is additional instead of essential. Option B is incorrect because *employees* is not possessive.

(Average) (Competency 22)

6. **In many jobs the employees become accustom to the accomplishment provided by the work they do every day.**

   A. became

   B. accustomed

   C. provides

   D. No change is necessary

Answer: B.

The past participle *accustomed* is needed with the verb *become*. Option A is incorrect because the verb tense does not need to change to the past *became*. Option C is incorrect because *provides* is the wrong tense.

(Average) (Competency 22)

7. **In addition to the feeling of accomplishment that the workers achieve, some jobs also give a sense of self-identity to the employees'.**

A. acheive

B. gave

C. employees

D. No change is necessary

Answer: C.

Option C is correct because *employees* is not possessive. Option A is incorrect because *achieve* is spelled correctly in the sentence. Option B is incorrect because *gave* is the wrong tense.

(Easy) (Competency 22)

8. **Politicians are public servants: who work for the federal and state governments.**

A. were

B. servants who

C. worked

D. No change is necessary

Answer: B.

A colon is not needed to set off the introduction of the sentence. In Option A, *were*, is the incorrect tense of the verb. In Option C, *worked*, is in the wrong tense.

Read the following passage and answer questions 9 to 17.

One of the most difficult problems plaguing American education is the assessment of teachers. No one denies that teachers ought to be answerable for what they do, but what exactly does that mean? The *Oxford American Dictionary* defines accountability as: the obligation to give a reckoning or explanation for one's actions.

Does a student have to learn for teaching to have taken place? Historically, teaching has not been defined in this restrictive manner; the teacher was thought to be responsible for the quantity and quality of material covered and the way in which it was presented. However, some definitions of teaching now imply that students must learn in order for teaching to have taken place.

As a teacher who tries my best to keep current on all the latest teaching strategies, I believe that those teachers who do not bother even to pick up an educational journal every once in a while should be kept under close watch. There are many teachers out there who have been teaching for decades and refuse to change their ways even if research has proven that their methods are outdated and ineffective. There is no place in the profession of teaching for these types of individuals. It is time that the American educational system clean house, for the sake of our children.

(Rigorous) (Competency 22)

9. **What is the organizational pattern of the second paragraph?**

A. Cause and effect

B. Classification

C. Addition

D. Explanation

Answer: D.

The meaning of this word is directly stated in the same sentence.

(Average) (Competency 22)

10. **What is the main idea of the passage?**

    A. Teachers should not be answerable for what they do

    B. Teachers who do not do their job should be fired

    C. The author is a good teacher

    D. Assessment of teachers is a serious problem in society today

Answer: D.

Most of the passage is dedicated to elaborating on why teacher assessment is such a problem.

(Rigorous) (Competency 22)

11. **From the passage, one can infer that:**

    A. The author considers herself a good teacher

    B. Poor teachers will be fired

    C. Students have to learn for teaching to take place

    D. The author will be fired

Answer: A.

The first sentence of the third paragraph alludes to this.

(Average) (Competency 22)

12. **Teachers who do not keep current on educational trends should be fired. Is this a fact or an opinion?**

    A. Fact

    B. Opinion

Answer: B.

There may be those who feel they can be good teachers by using old methods.

(Average) (Competency 22)

13. **What is the author's purpose in writing this?**

    A. To entertain

    B. To narrate

    C. To describe

    D. To persuade

Answer: D.

The author does some describing, but the majority of her statements seemed geared toward convincing the reader that teachers who are lazy or who do not keep current should be fired.

(Rigorous) (Competency 22)

14. **Is there evidence of bias in this passage?**

    A. Yes

    B. No

Answer: A.

The entire third paragraph is the author's opinion on the matter.

(Average) (Competency 22)

15. **The author's tone is one of:**

    A. Disbelief

    B. Excitement

    C. Support

    D. Concern

    Answer: D.

    The author appears concerned with the future of education.

(Easy) (Competency 22)

16. **What is meant by the word "plaguing" in the first sentence?**

    A. Causing problems

    B. Causing illness

    C. Causing anger

    D. Causing failure

    Answer: A.

    The first paragraph makes this definition clear.

(Easy) (Competency 22)

17. **Where does the author get her definition of "accountability?"**

    A. *Webster's Dictionary*

    B. *Encyclopedia Brittanica*

    C. *Oxford American Dictionary*

    D. *World Book Encyclopedia*

    Answer: C.

    This is directly stated in the third sentence of the first paragraph.

(Rigorous) (Competency 22)

18. **A figure of speech in which someone absent or something inhuman is addressed as though present and able to respond describes:**

    A. Personification

    B. Synechdoche

    C. Metonymy

    D. Apostrophe

    Answer: A.

    Personification gives human reactions and thoughts to animals, things, and abstract ideas alike. This figure of speech is often present in allegory: for instance, the Giant Despair in John Bunyon's *Pilgrim's Progress*. Also, fables use personification to make animals able to speak.

(Average) (Competency 22)

19. **A sixth-grade science teacher has given her class a paper to read on the relationship between food and weight gain. The writing contains signal words such as "because," "consequently," "this is how," and "due to." This paper has which text structure?**

    A. Cause and effect

    B. Compare and contrast

    C. Description

    D. Sequencing

Answer: A.

Cause and effect is the relationship between two things when one thing makes something else happen. Writers use this text structure to show order, inform, speculate, and change behavior. This text structure uses the process of identifying potential causes of a problem or issue in an orderly way. It is often used to teach social studies and science concepts. It is characterized by signal words such as because, so, so that, if… then, consequently, thus, since, for, for this reason, as a result of, therefore, due to, this is how, nevertheless, and accordingly.

(Average) (Competency 22)

20. **Which of the following is not a figure of speech (figurative language)?**

    A. Simile

    B. Euphemism

    C. Onomatopoeia

    D. Allusion

Answer: D.

Allusion is an implied reference to a person, event, thing, or a part of another text. A simile is an indirect comparison between two things. Euphemism is the substitution of an agreeable or inoffensive term for one that might offend. Onomatopoeia is a word that vocally imitates the meaning it denotes, some sound.

ASSESSMENT OF TEACHING SKILLS—PERFORMANCE (ATS-P)

What Is the ATS-P?

Developed as part of the New York State Teacher Certification Examinations (NYSTCE®), the Assessment of Teaching Skills—Performance (ATS-P) was developed by the New York State Education Department and Pearson's Evaluation Systems division to demonstrate teacher candidates' instruction aptitude in an actual classroom setting. Teacher candidates are encouraged to produce their 20 to 30 minute video-recorded sample once they have completed one or two years of experience to ensure they have the knowledge and ability to apply their teaching skills effectively. However, they should turn in the submission no later than one year before their provisional certificate expiration date. Once a candidate has registered for the ATS-P, he or she should ensure the video is submitted by the final submission deadline or risk having to reregister without a refund or credit.

The session must be filmed in a public or nonpublic Pre-K, elementary, middle, or secondary school where the candidate currently teaches. Those working in a team-teaching environment should record a lesson they primarily conduct. If he or she does not have a teaching engagement, a lesson can be arranged; however, the classroom must not be the candidate's student teaching assignment and should be within the teaching area in which the candidate seeks permanent certification. The candidate's lesson plan and submission must be his or her own original work. Submissions comparable to another candidate's will result in the validity of both being questioned.

What Should the Recorded Lesson Include?

The recorded session must demonstrate the candidate's knowledge and skills with regard to the established ATS-P objectives:

1. Comprehension of the principles and procedures involved with arranging and implementing lessons in a way that enables learners to construct meaning and obtain intended outcomes
2. Comprehension of multiple instruction methods to assist learning in a variety of situations
3. Comprehension of motivational principles and procedures implemented to increase student achievement and active engagement
4. Demonstrated ability to implement various communication modes to increase student learning and create trust and support within the classroom setting
5. Demonstrated ability to structure and manage a classroom to create a safe and productive learning environment

It is important to plan the lesson objectives and content to ensure it easily conveys the teaching skills described above. The session should have a planned beginning and end. For lessons longer than the allotted time, the recording should focus on the portion that best demonstrates the candidate's active, effective teaching and that provides students with direct, explicit instruction. While other teaching personnel or educational support staff may be present, they should not provide substantial instruction (no more than a minute). Candidates are also encouraged to limit administrative tasks such as taking attendance and collecting homework, as well as the use of instructional media (film, slide, audiotape presentation) to less than five minutes.

Essentially, the video should demonstrate actively engaged and motivated students; a structured environment that allows all students to communicate and excel; and various teaching methods that enable learner mastery and desired instructional outcomes. **Candidates are strongly encouraged to visit the official NYSTCE Web site at *www.nystce.nesinc.com* for further information on the ATS-P objectives and submission requirements and to ensure they have the most up-to-date information as requirements sometimes change.**

Additional requirements

In addition to meeting the required objectives, the recorded session must adhere to a minimum of 20 minutes and maximum of 30 minutes of continuous recording and include at least 10 minutes of non-whole-group instruction. Non-whole-group instruction requires the teacher to provide a framework and learning conditions to individual learners or small groups of learners, then oversee and monitor the experience as the learners actively participate in their learning. This instruction format, which is considered not primarily teacher-directed, allows the teacher to answer any questions or concerns as students create their own educational experience. Some examples of non-whole-group lessons include small-group projects, discussions or presentations, peer tutoring, or cooperative learning activities. As most effective teachers integrate various instructional strategies into their lessons, the non-whole-group instruction can be broken down into segments within the 30 minutes of video recording.

Recording the session

Most schools have the video equipment required to complete the ATS-P, but candidates are encouraged to purchase a new videotape or DVD to ensure the highest recording quality and that there is no additional material on the tape. Only the following formats are acceptable:

- Standard ½-inch VHS videotape
- DVD or mini DVD

Candidates can either prepare a self-recorded video or have someone in the school (teacher, teaching intern, paraprofessional, or student) serve as the camera operator. While the self-recorded session limits the field of view, the camera can be moved to a new position during the lesson; however, extreme care should be taken to avoid turning the camera off as that will automatically disqualify the taping. The recording should have no interruptions, even accidental ones, or it will receive a Requirements Not Met (RNM) designation. Please note that no modifications can be made to the tape—it must be continuous without any breaks or edits including removing audio, adding subtitles, freeze-frames, or other special effects. With camera-operated taping, the teacher can move about the classroom as the person recording can track movement and zoom in and out to capture the lesson and teaching. The recorder should be encouraged not to interact with the students or influence their behavior.

Tips for recording

Regardless of which method is used, the filming equipment should be stabilized on a tripod or other device and the electronic stabilization function should be turned on if available. As the quality of the battery life can impact the video recording quality, ensure the camera is connected to either an AC power source or a fully charged battery. Be sure to enunciate words, speak up, and encourage students to speak up to ensure the audio is adequately captured. Given that video microphones frequently amplify ambient sounds, such as air conditioners and street noises, try to record in a quiet location so that instruction and students' interactions and responses can be clearly heard. To capture the highest quality filming, the camera lens should be directed away from windows or other sources of light. Candidates are also encouraged to turn on the autofocus function and turn off the date/time stamp.

Lessons should be planned and camera positioning situated in a way that predominantly captures the candidate, making his or her instruction clearly visible and audible. If the audio and video production or the playback quality prevents the scorers from assessing the candidate, the tape will be deemed RNM. Any chalkboards, flipcharts, or overhead projectors essential to the lesson should be captured as well. To ensure the recording meets the timing requirements, including the 10 minutes of non-whole-group instruction, candidates are encouraged to use a stop watch or ask the camera operator to track recording time.

While candidates are encouraged to inform students in advance and conduct a few practice recorded sessions to test the equipment and help students adjust to being filmed, recording for the purpose of the ATS-P does not require parent/guardian permission as the tape is considered a confidential classroom assessment record. Recording a few lessons before creating the submission video may make the teacher, students, and camera operator more comfortable. In addition, candidates are strongly encouraged to show their video to multiple permanently certified teachers for feedback on whether their submission aligns with the ATS-P objectives.

Finalizing the submission video

When submitting a ½-inch VHS videotape, candidates should remove the record-enabling tab found on the tape's spine and completely rewind the tape. Those submitting a DVD or mini DVD must finalize the disc before it can be played on a standard DVD player. Refer to the instruction manual or technology support personnel for specific procedures. DVD finalization is crucial because DVDs that do not play are considered RNM. Comprehensive finalization details will be mailed to the candidate within the ATS-P Procedures Manual once he or she has registered for the ATS-P. As the submitted video will not be returned, candidates are advised to make a copy for their records.

Accompanying paperwork

In addition to the actual video recording, teachers will need to submit the Context of Instruction Form. While the form is not scored, care should be taken in completing it because it helps the scorers review the submission. Be sure to fill out the classroom level, as omitting that information results in returned materials. Candidates are also advised against submitting any additional sheets that are not requested. Another mandatory form is the Candidate Identification Form, which requires a witness to view a portion of the candidate's video and verify that the video recording and Candidate Identification Form accurately reflect the candidate's identity. The witness must either provide his or her own social security number or provide the Candidate Identification Form and identification to a notary who will complete the Notary Acknowledgment portion and provide an official notary seal. Additionally, the witness must meet the following criteria:

- Hold a permanent New York State teaching certificate and work in the same public or nonpublic school or school district to which the candidate is employed;
- Hold a permanent certificate in another state and work as a certified professional in the same public or nonpublic school or school district to which the candidate is employed; or
- Serve as a school administrator in the same public or nonpublic school to which the candidate is employed, but which is not a New York State school.

Receipt of submission and results

If the candidate's materials are deemed complete, he or she will be mailed a receipt acknowledgment. The ATS-P video will be assessed independently by qualified New York State educators based on a holistic rating scale (an overall judgment). While the teaching quality—not the audio or video quality—will be scored, the scorers must be able to hear and view the instructor's lesson and implementation.

To pass the ATS-P, teachers must meet all five established objectives, demonstrating a structured lesson that achieves acceptable application of principles and procedures and which helps students create meaning and attain desired goals. The various teaching methods must assist student learning, motivate, and engage. The candidate should use questioning and other communication practices to advance student learning and support respect—in both the students themselves and for others. Structured and adequately managed, the classroom environment should prove the teacher's ability to produce a suitable learning climate in which rules and proper behavior are upheld.

Submission checklist

- Approved format (VHS videotape, DVD, or mini DVD)
- Camera is secured on tripod or other stabilization device
- Camera is connected to power source or has fully charged battery
- Autofocus and electronic stabilization are turn on and date/time stamp is turned off
- Practice sessions have been conducted to adjust teacher and students to filming and ensure that equipment is properly functioning
- Permanently certified educators have been asked for input on previously recorded sessions
- Timer is in place to ensure teacher captures minimum of 20 minutes, maximum of 30 minutes
- Video includes 10 minutes of non-whole-group instruction
- Lesson and filming provide ample evidence of teaching skills according to ATS-P objectives
- Lesson reflects the candidate's original work in an actual teaching situation (not simulated or staged)
- Student actions and responses have not been scripted

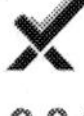

- Teacher is predominantly on-screen as are any essential visual elements (chalkboards, flipcharts, etc.)
- Recording has no breaks, interruptions, or edits (including special effects)
- Quality of audio and visual production as well as playback are adequate for scoring purposes
- Videotape has only the candidate's recorded session on the first 30 minutes
- Session focuses on candidate's teaching not administrative duties or presentations by others or media
- Copy of submission has been made for candidate's files
- Videotape has been rewound all the way or DVD has been finalized
- Properly completed Context of Instruction Form is included
- Properly completed (including witness and notary, if applicable) Candidate Identification Form is included

BONUS SAMPLE TEST

To provide you with even more value, we're including a free BONUS sample test with this guide.

The extra NYSTCE ATS-W Secondary Assessment of Teaching Skills - Written 91 will help you practice for the real exam with state-aligned questions. **XAMonline: dedicated to helping you succeed the first time.**

SAMPLE TEST

Student Development and Learning

DIRECTIONS: Read each item and select the best response.

(Average) (Skill 1.1)

1. **What developmental patterns should a professional teacher assess to meet the needs of the student?**

   A. Academic, regional, and family background

   B. Social, physical, and academic

   C. Academic, physical, and family background

   D. Physical, family, and ethnic background

(Average) (Skill 1.3)

2. **Louise is a first grade teacher. She is planning her instructional activities for the week. In considering her planning, she should keep in mind that activities for this age of child should change how often?**

   A. 25–40 minutes

   B. 30–40 minutes

   C. 5–10 minutes

   D. 15–30 minutes

(Rigorous) (Skill 2.1)

3. **What are the two types of performance that teaching entails?**

   A. Classroom management and questioning techniques

   B. Skill-building and analysis of outcomes

   C. Interaction with students and manipulation of subject matter

   D. Management techniques and levels of questioning

(Easy) (Skill 2.2)

4. **What are the two ways concepts can be taught?**

   A. Factually and interpretively

   B. Inductively and deductively

   C. Conceptually and inductively

   D. Analytically and facilitatively

(Rigorous) (Skill 2.2)

5. **What is one component of the instructional planning model that must be given careful evaluation?**

   A. Students' prior knowledge and skills

   B. The script the teacher will use in instruction

   C. Future lesson plans

   D. Parent participation

(Rigorous) (Skill 2.3)

6. **When using a kinesthetic approach, what would be an appropriate activity?**

   A. List

   B. Match

   C. Define

   D. Debate

(Rigorous) (Skill 2.3)

7. **Ms. Smith says, "Yes, exactly what do you mean by "It was the author's intention to mislead you." What does this illustrate?**

   A. Digression

   B. Restates response

   C. Probes a response

   D. Amplifies a response

(Average) (Skill 2.4)

8. **What are critical elements of instructional process?**

   A. Content, goals, teacher needs

   B. Means of getting money to regulate instruction

   C. Content, materials, activities, goals, learner needs

   D. Materials, definitions, assignments

(Rigorous) (Skill 2.4)

9. **According to Piaget, what stage is characterized by the ability to think abstractly and to use logic?**

   A. Concrete operations

   B. Preoperational

   C. Formal operations

   D. Conservative operational

(Easy) (Skill 2.4)

10. **How many stages of intellectual development does Piaget define?**

    A. Two

    B. Four

    C. Six

    D. Eight

(Easy) (Skill 2.4)

11. **Who developed the theory of multiple intelligences?**

    A. Bruner

    B. Gardner

    C. Kagan

    D. Cooper

(Average) (Skill 2.4)

12. **Students who can solve problems mentally have:**

    A. Reached maturity

    B. Physically developed

    C. Reached the preoperational stage of thought

    D. Achieved the ability to manipulate objects symbolically

(Rigorous) (Skill 2.5)

13. **Which description of the role of a teacher is no longer an accurate description?**

    A. Guide on the side

    B. Authoritarian

    C. Disciplinarian

    D. Sage on the stage

(Rigorous) (Skill 2.5)

14. **In the past, teaching has been viewed as _______ while in more current society it has been viewed as _________.**

    A. isolating, collaborative

    B. collaborative, isolating

    C. supportive, isolating

    D. isolating, supportive

(Rigorous) (Skill 2.6)

15. **The teacher states, "We will work on the first page of vocabulary words. On the second page we will work on the structure and meaning of the words. We will go over these together and then you will write out the answers to the exercises on your own. I will be circulating to give help if needed." What is this an example of?**

    A. Evaluation of instructional activity

    B. Analysis of instructional activity

    C. Identification of expected outcomes

    D. Pacing of instructional activity

(Rigorous) (Skill 2.6)

16. **If teachers attend to content, instructional materials, activities, learner needs, and goals in instructional planning, what could be an outcome?**

    A. Planning for the next year

    B. Effective classroom performance

    C. Elevated test scores on standardized tests

    D. More student involvement

(Rigorous) (Skill 2.6)

17. **When planning instruction, which of the following is an organizational tool to help ensure you are providing a well-balanced set of objectives?**

    A. Using a taxonomy to develop objectives

    B. Determining prior knowledge skill levels

    C. Determining readiness levels

    D. Ensuring you meet the needs of diverse learners

(Average) (Skill 3.4)

18. **What do cooperative learning methods all have in common?**

    A. Philosophy

    B. Cooperative task/cooperative reward structures

    C. Student roles and communication

    D. Teacher roles

(Average) (Skill 3.5)

19. **What is the definition of proactive classroom management?**

    A. Management that is constantly changing

    B. Management that is downplayed

    C. Management that gives clear and explicit instructions and rewarding compliance

    D. Management that is designed by the students

(Rigorous) (Skill 3.7)

20. **According to recent studies, what is the estimated number of adolescents that have physical, social, or emotional problems related to the abuse of alcohol?**

    A. Less that one million

    B. 1–2 million

    C. 2–3 million

    D. More than four million

(Rigorous) (Skill 4.1)

21. **Abigail has had intermittent hearing loss from the age of 1 through age 5 when she had tubes put in her ears. What is one area of development that may be affected by this?**

    A. Math

    B. Language

    C. Social skills

    D. None

(Rigorous) (Skill 4.1)

22. **Active listening is an important skill for teachers to utilize with both students and teachers. Active listening involves all of the following strategies except...**

    A. Eye contact

    B. Restating what the speaker has said

    C. Clarification of speaker statements

    D. Open and receptive body language

(Rigorous) (Skill 4.3)

23. **Students who are learning English as a second language often require which of the following to process new information?**

    A. Translators

    B. Reading tutors

    C. Instruction in their native language

    D. Additional time and repetitions

(Easy) (Skill 4.3)

24. **Many of the current ESOL approaches used in classrooms today are based on which approach?**

    A. Social Learning Methods

    B. Native Tongue Methods

    C. ESOL Learning Methods

    D. Special Education Methods

(Easy) (Skill 4.3)

25. **Which of the following is the last stage of second language acquisition according to the theories of Stephen Krashen?**

    A. The affective filter hypothesis

    B. The input hypothesis

    C. The natural order hypothesis

    D. The monitor hypothesis

(Average) (Skill 4.4)

26. **If a student has a poor vocabulary, the teacher should recommend that:**

    A. The student read newspapers, magazines, and books on a regular basis

    B. The student enroll in a Latin class

    C. The student write the words repetitively after looking them up in the dictionary

    D. The student use a thesaurus to locate synonyms and incorporate them into her vocabulary

(Rigorous) (Skill 4.4)

27. **All of the following are true about phonological awareness EXCEPT:**

    A. It may involve print

    B. It is a prerequisite for spelling and phonics

    C. Activities can be done by the children with their eyes closed

    D. Starts before letter recognition is taught

(Easy) (Skill 4.4)

28. **The arrangement and relationship of words in sentences or sentence structure best describes:**

    A. Style

    B. Discourse

    C. Thesis

    D. Syntax

(Easy) (Skill 4.4)

29. **Which of the following is not a technique of prewriting?**

    A. Clustering

    B. Listing

    C. Brainstorming

    D. Proofreading

(Rigorous) (Skill 4.5)

30. **One of the many ways in which a child can demonstrate comprehension of a story is by:**

    A. Filling in a strategy sheet

    B. Retelling the story orally

    C. Retelling the story in writing

    D. All of the above

(Easy) (Skill 4.5)

31. **Greg Ball went to an author signing where Faith Ringgold gave a talk about one of her many books. He was so inspired by her presence and by his reading of her book *Tar Beach* that he used the book for his reading and writing workshop activities. His supervisor wrote in his plan book that he was pleased that Greg had used the book as an/a _______ book.**

    A. basic

    B. feature

    C. anchor

    D. focus

(Easy) (Skill 5.1)

32. **Which of the following is an example of a restriction within the affective domain?**

    A. Unable to think abstractly

    B. Inability to synthesize information

    C. Inability to concentrate

    D. Inability complete physical activities

(Average) (Skill 5.2)

33. **What is a good strategy for teaching ethnically diverse students?**

    A. Don't focus on the students' culture

    B. Expect them to assimilate easily into your classroom

    C. Imitate their speech patterns

    D. Include ethnic studies in the curriculum

(Easy) (Skill 5.2)

34. **Which of the following is an accurate description of ESL students?**
    A. Remedial students
    B. Exceptional education students
    C. Are not a homogeneous group
    D. Feel confident in communicating in English when with their peers

(Rigorous) (Skill 5.2)

35. **What is an effective way to help a non-English speaking student succeed in class?**
    A. Refer the child to a specialist
    B. Maintain an encouraging, success-oriented atmosphere
    C. Help them assimilate by making them use English exclusively
    D. Help them cope with the content materials you currently use

(Average) (Skill 5.2)

36. **How can text be modified for low-level ESOL students?**
    A. Add visuals and illustrations
    B. Let students write definitions
    C. Change text to a narrative form
    D. Have students write details out from the text

(Rigorous) (Skill 5.2)

37. **Etienne is an ESOL student. He has begun to engage in conversation, which produces a connected narrative. In what developmental stage for second language acquisition is he?**
    A. Early production
    B. Speech emergence
    C. Preproduction
    D. Intermediate fluency

(Rigorous) (Skill 5.2)

38. **What is a roadblock to second language learning?**
    A. Students are forced to speak
    B. Students speak only when ready
    C. Mistakes are considered a part of learning
    D. The focus is on oral communication

(Average) (Skill 5.2)

39. **Why is praise for compliance important in classroom management?**
    A. Students will continue deviant behavior
    B. Desirable conduct will be repeated
    C. It reflects simplicity and warmth
    D. Students will fulfill obligations

(Average) (Skill 5.4)

40. **Which of the following is not a communication issue that is related to diversity within the classroom?**

A. Learning disorder

B. Sensitive terminology

C. Body language

D. Discussing differing viewpoints and opinions

(Rigorous) (Skill 6.2)

41. **Mr. Ryan has proposed to his classroom that the students may demonstrate understanding of the unit taught in a variety of ways including: taking a test, writing a paper, creating an oral presentation, or building a model or project. Which of the following areas of differentiation has Mr. Ryan demonstrated?**

A. Synthesis

B. Product

C. Content

D. Product

(Average) (Skill 6.2)

42. **When creating and selecting materials for instruction, teachers should complete which of the following steps:**

A. Make them relevant to the prior knowledge of the students

B. Allow for a variation of learning styles

C. Choose alternative teaching strategies

D. All of the above

(Rigorous) (Skill 6.4)

43. **Mr. Weiss understands that it is imperative that students who are struggling with acquiring concepts at a specific grade level can still benefit from participating in whole classroom discussions and lessons. In fact, such students should be required to be present for whole classroom lessons. Mr. Weiss's beliefs fall under which of the following principles?**

A. Self-fulfilling prophecy

B. Partial participation

C. Inclusion

D. Heterogeneous grouping

Instruction and Assessment

(Rigorous) (Skill 7.1)

44. **Reducing off-task time and maximizing the amount of time students spend attending to academic tasks is closely related to which of the following?**

A. Using whole class instruction only

B. Business-like behaviors of the teacher

C. Dealing only with major teaching functions

D. Giving students a maximum of two minutes to come to order

(Easy) (Skill 7.1)

45. **While teaching, three students cause separate disruptions. The teacher selects the major one and tells that student to desist. What is the teacher demonstrating?**

    A. Deviancy spread

    B. Correct target desist

    C. Alternative behavior

    D. Desist major deviance

(Average) (Skill 7.2)

46. **What must occur for seatwork to be effective?**

    A. All seatwork is graded immediately

    B. All seatwork should be explained by another student for clarification

    C. The teacher should monitor and provide corrective feedback for seatwork

    D. Seatwork should be a review of the previous day's lesson

(Rigorous) (Skill 7.2)

47. **Mrs. Peck wants to justify the use of personalized learning community to her principal. Which of the following reasons should she use?**

    A. They build multiculturalism

    B. They provide a supportive environment to address academic and emotional needs

    C. They builds relationships between students that promote lifelong learning

    D. They are proactive in their nature

(Rigorous) (Skill 7.2)

48. **Mrs. Potts has noticed an undercurrent of an unsettled nature in her classroom. She is in the middle of her math lesson but still notices that many of her students seem to be having some sort of difficulty. Mrs. Potts stops class and decides to have a class meeting. She understands that even though her math objectives are important, it is equally important to address whatever is troubling her classroom. What is it Mrs. Potts knows?**

    A. Discipline is important

    B. Social issues can impact academic learning

    C. Maintaining order is important

    D. Social skills instruction is important

(Average) (Skill 7.2)

49. **Which of the following could be an example of a situation that could have an effect on a student's learning and academic progress?**

    A. Relocation

    B. Abuse

    C. Both of the above

    D. Neither of the above

(Rigorous) (Skill 7.2)

50. **Mrs. Graham has taken the time to reflect, completed observations, and asked for feedback about the interactions between her and her students from her principal. It is obvious by seeking this information out that Mrs. Graham understands which of the following?**

    A. The importance of clear communication with the principal

    B. She needs to analyze her effectiveness of classroom interactions

    C. She is clearly communicating with the principal

    D. She cares about her students

(Rigorous) (Skill 7.3)

51. **What has been established to increase student originality, intrinsic motivation, and higher-order thinking skills?**

    A. Classroom climate

    B. High expectations

    C. Student choice

    D. Use of authentic learning opportunities

(Easy) (Skill 7.3)

52. **Which of the following can be measured utilizing the following types of assessments: direct observation, role playing, context observation, and teacher ratings?**

    A. Social skills

    B. Reading skills

    C. Math skills

    D. Need for specialized instruction

(Average) (Skill 7.5)

53. **What would improve planning for instruction?**

    A. Describe the role of the teacher and student

    B. Evaluate the outcomes of instruction

    C. Rearrange the order of activities

    D. Give outside assignments

(Average) (Skill 7.5)

54. **How can student misconduct be redirected at times?**

    A. The teacher threatens the students

    B. The teacher assigns detention to the whole class

    C. The teacher stops the activity and stares at the students

    D. The teacher effectively handles changing from one activity to another

(Rigorous) (Skill 7.5)

55. **What have recent studies regarding effective teachers concluded?**

    A. Effective teachers let students establish rules

    B. Effective teachers establish routines by the sixth week of school

    C. Effective teachers state their own policies and establish consistent class rules and procedures on the first day of class

    D. Effective teachers establish flexible routines

(Average) (Skill 7.5)

56. **To maintain the flow of events in the classroom, what should an effective teacher do?**

   A. Work only in small groups

   B. Use only whole class activities

   C. Direct attention to content rather than focusing the class on misbehavior

   D. Follow lectures with written assignments

(Rigorous) (Skill 7.5)

57. **The concept of efficient use of time includes which of the following?**

   A. Daily review, seatwork, and recitation of concepts

   B. Lesson initiation, transition, and comprehension check

   C. Review, test, and review

   D. Punctuality, management transition, and wait time avoidance

(Average) (Skill 7.5)

58. **What is a sample of an academic transition signal?**

   A. How do clouds form?

   B. Today we are going to study clouds.

   C. We have completed today's lesson.

   D. That completes the description of cumulus clouds. Now we will look at the description of cirrus clouds.

(Average) (Skill 8.1)

59. **When is utilization of instructional materials most effective?**

   A. When the activities are sequenced

   B. When the materials are prepared ahead of time

   C. When the students choose the pages to work on

   D. When the students create the instructional materials

(Rigorous) (Skill 8.1)

60. **When considering the development of the curriculum, which of the following accurately describes the four factors that need to be considered?**

   A. Alignment, Scope, Sequence, and Design

   B. Assessment, Instruction, Design, and Sequence

   C. Data, Alignment, Correlation, and Score

   D. Alignment, Sequence, Design, and Assessment

(Average) (Skill 8.2)

61. **What should be considered when evaluating textbooks for content?**

   A. Type of print used

   B. Number of photos used

   C. Free of cultural stereotyping

   D. Outlines at the beginning of each chapter

(Easy) (Skill 9.1)

62. **Which of the following is a presentation modification?**

    A. Taking an assessment in an alternate room

    B. Providing an interpreter to give the test in American Sign Language

    C. Allowing dictation of written responses

    D. Extending the time limits on an assessment

(Average) (Skill 9.2)

63. **What should a teacher do when students have not responded well to an instructional activity?**

    A. Reevaluate learner needs

    B. Request administrative help

    C. Continue with the activity another day

    D. Assign homework on the concept

(Average) (Skill 9.2)

64. **What is the best definition for an achievement test?**

    A. It measures mechanical and practical abilities

    B. It measures broad areas of knowledge that are the result of cumulative learning experiences

    C. It measures the ability to learn to perform a task

    D. It measures performance related to specific, recently acquired information

(Average) (Skill 9.2)

65. **How are standardized tests useful in assessment?**

    A. For teacher evaluation

    B. For evaluation of the administration

    C. For comparison from school to school

    D. For comparison to the population on which the test was normed

(Rigorous) (Skill 9.2)

66. **Which of the following test items is not objective?**

    A. Multiple choice

    B. Essay

    C. Matching

    D. True or false

(Rigorous) (Skill 9.2)

67. **Which of the following is NOT used in evaluating test items?**

    A. Student feedback

    B. Content validity

    C. Reliability

    D. Ineffective coefficient

(Average) (Skill 9.2)

68. **Safeguards against bias and discrimination in the assessment of children include:**

    A. The testing of a child in standard English

    B. The requirement for the use of one standardized test

    C. The use of evaluative materials in the child's native language or other mode of communication

    D. All testing performed by a certified, licensed psychologist

(Average) (Skill 9.3)

69. **On intelligence quotient scales, what is the average intelligence score?**

    A. 100–120

    B. 60–80

    C. 90–110

    D. 80–100

(Easy) (Skill 9.3)

70. **On what is evaluation of the instructional activity based?**

    A. Student grades

    B. Teacher evaluation

    C. Student participation

    D. Specified criteria

(Average) (Skill 9.3)

71. **What is an example of formative feedback?**

    A. The results of an intelligence test

    B. Correcting the tests in small groups

    C. Verbal behavior that expresses approval of a student response to a test item

    D. Scheduling a discussion before the test

(Easy) (Skill 9.3)

72. **What does the validity of a test refer to?**

    A. Its consistency

    B. Its usefulness

    C. Its accuracy

    D. The degree of true scores it provides

(Rigorous) (Skill 9.3)

73. **Which of the following describes why it is important and necessary for teachers to be able to analyze data on their students?**

    A. To provide appropriate instruction

    B. To make instructional decisions

    C. To communicate and determine instructional progress

    D. All of the above

(Easy) (Skill 9.4)

74. **When a teacher wants to utilize an assessment that is subjective in nature, which of the following is the most effective method for scoring?**

    A. Rubric

    B. Checklist

    C. Alternative Assessment

    D. Subjective measures should not be utilized

(Rigorous) (Skill 9.5)

75. **What steps are important in the review of subject matter in the classroom?**

    A. A lesson-initiating review, topic, and a lesson-end review

    B. A preview of the subject matter, an in-depth discussion, and a lesson-end review

    C. A rehearsal of the subject matter and a topic summary within the lesson

    D. A short paragraph synopsis of the previous day's lesson and a written review at the end of the lesson

(Rigorous) (Skill 9.5)

76. **The teacher states that the lesson the students will be engaged in will consist of a review of the material from the previous day, demonstration of the scientific of an electronic circuit, and small group work on setting up an electronic circuit. What has the teacher demonstrated?**

A. The importance of reviewing

B. Giving the general framework for the lesson to facilitate learning

C. Giving students the opportunity to leave if they are not interested in the lesson

D. Providing momentum for the lesson

(Average) (Skill 9.5)

77. **What is an effective way to prepare students for testing?**

A. Minimize the importance of the test

B. Orient the students to the test by telling them of the purpose, how the results will be used, and how it is relevant to them

C. Use the same format for every test are given

D. Have them construct an outline to study from

(Average) (Skill 9.5)

78. **How will students have a fair chance to demonstrate what they know on a test?**

A. When the examiner has strictly enforced rules for taking the test

B. When the examiner provides a comfortable setting free of distractions and positively encourages the students

C. When the examiner provides frequent stretch breaks to the students

D. When the examiner stresses the importance of the test to the overall grade

(Rigorous) (Skill 9.5)

79. **Which of the following is the correct term for the alignment of the curriculum across all grades K-12?**

A. Data-based decision making

B. Curriculum mapping

C. Vertical integration

D. Curriculum alignment

(Average) (Skill 9.5)

80. **Which of the following information can NOT be gained by examining school level data in an in-depth manner?**

A. Teacher effectiveness

B. Educational trends within a school

C. Student ability to meet state and national goals and objectives

D. Ways to improve student learning goals and academic success

(Average) (Skill 10.1)

81. **Which of following is NOT the role of the teacher in the instructional process:**

    A. Instructor

    B. Coach

    C. Facilitator

    D. Follower

(Rigorous) (Skill 10.2)

82. **Discovery learning is to inquiry as direct instruction is to...**

    A. Scripted lessons

    B. Well-developed instructions

    C. Clear instructions that eliminate all misinterpretations

    D. Creativity of teaching

(Rigorous) (Skill 10.6)

83. **When developing lessons it is imperative teachers provide equity in pedagogy so:**

    A. Unfair labeling of students will not occur

    B. Student experiences will be positive

    C. Students will achieve academic success

    D. All of the above

(Average) (Skill 10.6)

84. **Which of the following is a good reason to collaborate with a peer:**

    A. To increase your knowledge in areas where you feel you are weak, but the peer is strong

    B. To increase your planning time and that of your peer by combining the classes and taking more breaks

    C. To have fewer lesson plans to write

    D. To teach fewer subjects

(Rigorous) (Skill 10.6)

85. **Which of the following are ways a professional can assess her teaching strengths and weaknesses?**

    A. Examining how many students were unable to understand a concept

    B. Asking peers for suggestions or ideas

    C. Self-evaluation/reflection of lessons taught

    D. All of the above

(Rigorous) (Skill 10.6)

86. **Mr. German is a math coach. He is the only math coach in his building and, in fact, within his district. Mr. German believes it is imperative to seek out the support of colleagues to work in a more collaborative manner. Which of the following would be an appropriate step for him to take?**

    A. Collaborating with other teachers in his building regardless of their skill level knowledge in his area

    B. Asking for the administration to find colleagues with whom he can collaborate

    C. Joining a professional organization such as the National Council of Teachers of Mathematics (NCTM)

    D. Searching the Internet for possible collaboration opportunities

(Average) (Skill 11.1)

87. **Why is it important for a teacher to pose a question before calling on students to answer?**

    A. It helps manage student conduct

    B. It keeps the students as a group focused on the class work

    C. It allows students time to collaborate

    D. It gives the teacher time to walk among the students

(Rigorous) (Skill 11.1)

88. **What is an example of a low order question?**

    A. Why is it important to recycle items in your home?

    B. Compare how glass and plastics are recycled.

    C. What items do we recycle in our county?

    D. Explain the importance of recycling in our county.

(Rigorous) (Skill 11.1)

89. **What would be espoused by Jerome Bruner?**

    A. Thought depends on the acquisition of operations

    B. Memory plays a significant role in cognitive growth

    C. Genetics is the most important factor for cognitive growth

    D. Enriched environments have significant effects on cognitive growth

(Easy) (Skill 11.1)

90. **When asking questions of students it is important to:**

    A. Ask questions the students can answer

    B. Provide numerous questions

    C. Provide questions at various levels

    D. Provide only a limited amount of questions

(Rigorous) (Skill 11.4)

91. **With the passage of the No Child Left Behind Act (NCLB), schools are required to develop action plans to improve student learning. Which of the following is not a part of this action plan?**

    A. Clearly defined goals for school improvement

    B. Clearly defined assessment plan

    C. Clearly defined timelines

    D. Clearly defined plans for addressing social skills improvement

(Rigorous) (Skill 12.1)

92. **Mr. Smith is introducing the concept of photosynthesis to his class next week. In preparing for this lesson, he considers that this concept will be new to many of his students. Mr. Smith understands that his students' brains are like filing cabinets and that there is currently no file for photosynthesis in those cabinets. What does Mr. Smith need to do to ensure his students acquire the necessary knowledge?**

    A. Help them create a new file

    B. Teach the students the information; they will organize it themselves in their own way

    C. Find a way to connect the new learning to other information they already know

    D. Provide many repetitions and social situations during the learning process

(Rigorous) (Skill 12.1)

93. **Curriculum mapping is an effective strategy because it:**

    A. Provides an orderly sequence to instruction

    B. Provides lesson plans for teachers to use and follow

    C. Ties the curriculum into instruction

    D. Provides a clear map so all students receive the same instruction across all classes

(Rigorous) (Skill 13.1)

94. **Mrs. Grant is providing her students with many extrinsic motivators in order to increase their intrinsic motivation. Which of the best explains this relationship?**

    A. This relationship is good and will increase intrinsic motivation

    B. The relationship builds animosity between the teacher and the students

    C. Extrinsic motivation does not in itself help to build intrinsic motivation

    D. There is no place for extrinsic motivation in the classroom

(Average) (Skill 13.5)

95. **What is one way of effectively managing student conduct?**

    A. State expectations about behavior

    B. Let students discipline their peers

    C. Let minor infractions of the rules go unnoticed

    D. Increase disapproving remarks

(Rigorous) (Skill 13.5)

96. **How can mnemonic devices be used to increase achievement?**

    A. They help the child rehearse the information

    B. They help the child visually imagine the information

    C. They help the child to code information

    D. They help the child reinforce concepts

(Rigorous) (Skill 13.5)

97. The success-oriented classroom is designed to ensure students are successful at attaining new skills. In addition, mistakes are viewed as _______ in this type of classroom.

A. motivations to improve

B. a natural part of the learning process

C. ways to improve

D. building blocks

(Easy) (Skill 13.6)

98. Which statement is an example of specific praise?

A. John, you are the only person in class not paying attention.

B. William, I thought we agreed that you would turn in all of your homework.

C. Robert, you did a good job staying in line. See how it helped us get to music class on time?

D. Class, you did a great job cleaning up the art room.

(Average) (Skill 13.6)

99. What is one way a teacher can supplement verbal praise?

A. Help students evaluate their own performance and supply self-reinforcement

B. Give verbal praise more frequently

C. Give tangible rewards such as stickers or treats

D. Have students practice giving verbal praise

(Average) (Skill 13.6)

100. What is a frequently used type of feedback to students?

A. Correctives

B. Simple praise–confirmation

C. Correcting the response

D. Explanations

(Rigorous) (Skill 13.6)

101. The teacher responds, "Yes, that is correct" to a student's answer. What is this an example of?

A. Academic feedback

B. Academic praise

C. Simple positive response

D. Simple negative response

(Average) (Skill 13.6)

102. Which of the following is not a characteristic of effective praise?

A. Praise is delivered in front of the class so it will serve to motivate others

B. Praise is low-key

C. Praise provides information about student competence

D. Praise is delivered contingently

(Average) (Skill 14.1)

103. What is NOT a way that teachers show acceptance and give value to a student response?

A. Acknowledging

B. Correcting

C. Discussing

D. Amplifying

(Average) (Skill 14.1)

104. Which of the following is a definition of an intercultural communication model?

A. Learning how different cultures engage in both verbal and nonverbal modes to communicate meaning

B. Learning how classmates engage in both verbal and nonverbal modes to communicate meaning

C. Learning how classmates engage in verbal dialogues

D. Learning how different cultures engage in verbal modes to communicate meaning

(Average) (Skill 14.2)

105. How can the teacher establish a positive climate in the classroom?

A. Help students see the unique contributions of individual differences

B. Use whole group instruction for all content areas

C. Help students divide into cooperative groups based on ability

D. Eliminate teaching strategies that allow students to make choices

(Average) (Skill 14.4)

106. Wait-time has what effect?

A. Gives structure to the class discourse

B. Fewer chain and low-level questions are asked with more higher-level questions included

C. Gives the students time to evaluate the response

D. Gives the opportunity for in-depth discussion about the topic

(Rigorous) (Skill 14.4)

107. When is optimal benefit reached when handling an incorrect student response?

A. When specific praise is used

B. When the other students are allowed to correct that student

C. When the student is redirected to a better problem-solving approach

D. When the teacher asks simple questions, provides cues to clarify, or gives assistance for working out the correct response

(Average) (Skill 14.4)

108. What is an effective amount of "wait time?"

A. 1 second

B. 5 seconds

C. 15 seconds

D. 10 seconds

(Easy) (Skill 14.4)

109. Which of the following can impact the desire of students to learn new material?

A. Assessments plan

B. Lesson plans

C. Enthusiasm

D. School community

(Average) (Skill 14.6)

110. **When are students more likely to understand complex ideas?**

A. If they do outside research before coming to class

B. Later when they write out the definitions of complex words

C. When they attend a lecture on the subject

D. When they are clearly defined by the teacher and are given examples and nonexamples of the concept

(Easy) (Skill 15.1)

111. **How can DVDs be used in instruction?**

A. Students can use the DVD to create pictures for reports

B. Students can use the DVD to create a science experiment

C. Students can use the DVD to record class activities

D. Students can use the DVD to review concepts studied

(Easy) (Skill 15.1)

112. **How can students use a computer desktop publishing center?**

A. To set up a classroom budget

B. To create student-made books

C. To design a research project

D. To create a classroom behavior management system

(Average) (Skill 15.1)

113. **Which of the following is NOT a part of the hardware of a computer system?**

A. Storage device

B. Input devices

C. Software

D. Central processing unit

(Rigorous) (Skill 15.2)

114. **What is one benefit of amplifying a student's response?**

A. It helps the student develop a positive self-image

B. It is helpful to other students who are in the process of learning the reasoning or steps in answering the question

C. It allows the teacher to cover more content

D. It helps to keep the information organized

(Average) (Skill 15.3)

115. **Which of the following statements is true about computers in the classroom?**

A. Computers are simply a glorified game machine and just allow students to play games

B. The computer should replace traditional research and writing skills taught to school-age children

C. Computers stifle the creativity of children

D. Computers allow students to access information they may otherwise be unable to

(Average) (Skill 15.3)

116. **While an asset to students, technology is also important for teachers. Which of the following can be taught using technology to students?**

 A. Cooperation skills

 B. Decision-making skills

 C. Problem solving skills

 D. All of the above

(Easy) (Skill 15.3)

117. **As a classroom teacher, you have data on all of your students that you must track over the remainder of the school year. You will need to keep copies of the scores students receive and then graph their results to share progress with the parents an administrators. Which of the following software programs will be most useful in this manner?**

 A. Word processing program

 B. Spreadsheet

 C. Database

 D. Teacher utility and classroom management tools

(Average) (Skill 15.3)

118. **Which of the following statements is NOT true?**

 A. Printing and distributing material off of the Internet breaks the copyright law

 B. Articles are only copyrighted when there is a © in the article

 C. E-mail messages that are posted online are considered copyrighted

 D. It is not legal to scan magazine articles and place on your district Web site

(Easy) (Skill 15.5)

119. **The use of technology in the classroom allows for:**

 A. More complex lessons

 B. Better delivery of instruction

 C. Variety of instruction

 D. Better ability to meet more individual student needs

The Professional Environment

(Easy) (Skill 16.5)

120. **A district superintendent's job is to:**

 A. Supervise senior teachers in the district

 B. Develop plans for school improvement

 C. Allocate community resources to individual schools

 D. Implement policies set by the board of education

(Average) (Skill 16.5)

121. **Teacher's unions are involved in all of the following EXCEPT:**

 A. Updating teachers on current educational developments

 B. Advocating for teacher rights

 C. Matching teachers with suitable schools

 D. Developing professional codes and practices

(Average) (Skill 17.1)

122. What is a benefit of frequent self-assessment?

A. Opens new venues for professional development

B. Saves teachers the pressure of being observed by others

C. Reduces time spent on areas not needing attention

D. Offers a model for students to adopt in self-improvement

(Average) (Skill 17.1)

123. Which of the following could be used to improve teaching skills?

A. Developing a professional development plan

B. Use of self-evaluation and reflection

C. Building professional learning communities

D. All of the above

(Rigorous) (Skill 17.2)

124. Which of the following is NOT a sound educational practice for expanding the professional development opportunities for teachers?

A. Looking at multiple methods of classroom management strategies

B. Training teachers in understanding and applying multiple assessment formats and implementations in curriculum and instruction

C. Having the students complete professional development assessments on a regular basis

D. Teaching teachers how to disaggregate student data in improving instruction and curriculum implementation for student academic equity and access

(Rigorous) (Skill 17.3)

125. What would happen if a school utilized an integrated approach to professional development?

A. All stakeholders needs are addressed

B. Teachers and administrators are on the same page

C. High-quality programs for students are developed

D. Parents drive the curriculum and instruction

(Average) (Skill 17.4)

126. What must be a consideration when a parent complains that hc can't control a child's behavior?

A. Consider whether the parent gives feedback to the child

B. Consider whether the parent's expectations for control are developmentally appropriate

C. Consider how much time the parent spends with the child

D. Consider how rigid the rules are that the parent sets

(Average) (Skill 18.1)

127. Which of the following should NOT be a purpose of a parent-teacher conference?

A. To involve the parent in their child's education

B. To establish a friendship with the child's parents

C. To resolve a concern about the child's performance

D. To inform parents of positive behaviors by the child

(Easy) (Skill 18.1)

128. **Mr. Brown wishes to improve his parent communication skills. Which of the following is a strategy he can utilize to accomplish this goal?**

A. Hold parent-teacher conferences

B. Send home positive notes

C. Have parent nights where the parents are invited into his classroom

D. All of the above

(Easy) (Skill 18.1)

129. **Tommy is a student in your class, and his parents are deaf. Tommy is struggling with math and you want to contact the parents to discuss the issues. How should you proceed?**

A. Limit contact because of the parents' inability to hear

B. Use a TTY phone to communicate with the parents

C. Talk to your administrator to find an appropriate interpreter to help you communicate with the parents personally

D. Both B and C

(Easy) (Skill 18.1)

130. **When communicating with parents for whom English is not the primary language you should:**

A. Provide materials whenever possible in their native language

B. Use an interpreter

C. Provide the same communication as you would to native English speaking parents

D. All of the above

(Rigorous) (Skill 19.1)

131. **Which of the following increases appropriate behavior more than 80 percent?**

A. Monitoring the halls

B. Having class rules

C. Having class rules, giving feedback, and having individual consequences

D. Having class rules and giving feedback

(Average) (Skill 19.1)

132. **A 16-year-old girl who has been looking sad writes an essay in which the main protagonist commits suicide. You overhear her talking about suicide. What do you do?**

A. Report this immediately to school administration, talk to the girl, letting her know you will talk to her parents about it

B. Report this immediately to authorities

C. Report this immediately to school administration, make your own report to authorities if required by protocol in your school, and do nothing else

D. Just give the child some extra attention, as it may just be that's all she's looking for

(Rigorous) (Skill 19.1)

133. **Jeanne, a bright, attentive student is in her first hour English class. She is quiet, but very alert, often visually scanning the room in random patterns. Her pupils are dilated, and she has a slight but noticeable tremor in her hands. She fails to note a cue given from her teacher. At odd moments, she will act as if responding to stimuli that aren't there by suddenly changing her gaze. When spoken to directly, she has a limited response, but her teacher has a sense she is not herself. What should the teacher do?**

A. Ask the student if she is all right, then let it go, as there are not enough signals to be alarmed

B. Meet with the student after class to get more information before making a referral

C. Send the student to the office to see the nurse

D. Quietly call for administration, remain calm, and be careful not to alarm the class

(Average) (Skill 19.1)

134. **Which is true of child protective services?**

A. They have been forced to become more punitive in their attempts to treat and prevent child abuse and neglect

B. They have become more a means for identifying cases of abuse and less an agent for rehabilitation because of the large volume of cases

C. They have become advocates for structured discipline within the school

D. They have become a strong advocate in the court system

(Average) (Skill 19.1)

135. **In successful inclusion of students with disabilities:**

A. A variety of instructional arrangements are available

B. School personnel shift the responsibility for learning outcomes to the student

C. The physical facilities are used as they are

D. Regular classroom teachers have sole responsibility for evaluating student progress

(Average) (Skill 19.1)

136. **How may a teacher use a student's permanent record?**

A. To develop a better understanding of the needs of the student

B. To record all instances of student disruptive behavior

C. To brainstorm ideas for discussing with parents at parent-teacher conferences

D. To develop realistic expectations of the student's performance early in the year

(Rigorous) (Skill 19.1)

137. You receive a phone call from a person who indicates she is now tutoring a student in your class. She would like you to provide an overview of the academic areas which the student is having difficulties. What is the first thing you should do?

A. Find a time and talk with the tutor about issues you see within the classroom

B. Call the parents

C. Put together a packet of information to share with the tutor

D. Offer to invite the tutor in to have a discussion and observe the child

(Rigorous) (Skill 19.2)

138. Marcus is a first grade boy of good developmental attainment. His learning progress is good the first half of the year. He shows no indicators of emotional distress. After the holiday break, he returns much changed. He is quieter, sullen even, tending to play alone. He has moments of tearfulness, sometimes almost without cause. He avoids contact with adults as often as he can. Even play with his friends has become limited. He has episodes of wetting not seen before and often wants to sleep in school. What approach is appropriate for this sudden change in behavior?

A. Give him some time to adjust; the holiday break was probably too much fun to come back to school from

B. Report this change immediately to administration; do not call the parents until administration decides a course of action

C. Document his daily behavior carefully as soon as you notice such a change, report to administration the next month or so in a meeting

D. Make a courtesy call to the parents to let them know he is not acting like himself, being sure to tell them he is not making trouble for others

(Rigorous) (Skill 19.2)

139. Andy shows up to class abusive and irritable. He is often late, sleeps in class, sometimes slurs his speech, and has an odor of alcohol. What is the first intervention to take?

A. Confront him, relying on a trusting relationship you think you have

B. Do a lesson on alcohol abuse, making an example of him

C. Do nothing; it is better to err on the side of failing to identify substance abuse

D. Call administration, avoid conflict, and supervise others carefully

(Average) (Skill 19.4)

140. **A parent has left an angry message on the teacher's voicemail. The message relates to a concern about a student and is directed at the teacher. The teacher should:**

A. Call back immediately and confront the parent

B. Cool off, plan what to discuss with the parent, then call back

C. Question the child to find out what set off the parent

D. Ignore the message, since feelings of anger usually

Answer Key

ANSWER KEY								
1. B	18. B	35. B	52. A	69. C	86. C	103. B	120. D	137. B
2. D	19. C	36. A	53. B	70. D	87. B	104. A	121. C	138. B
3. C	20. D	37. D	54. D	71. C	88. C	105. A	122. A	139. D
4. B	21. B	38. A	55. C	72. B	89. D	106. B	123. D	140. B
5. A	22. B	39. B	56. C	73. D	90. C	107. C	124. C	
6. B	23. D	40. A	57. D	74. A	91. D	108. B	125. C	
7. C	24. A	41. B	58. D	75. A	92. C	109. C	126. B	
8. C	25. A	42. D	59. A	76. B	93. A	110. D	127. B	
9. C	26. A	43. B	60. A	77. B	94. C	111. D	128. D	
10. B	27. A	44. B	61. C	78. B	95. A	112. B	129. D	
11. B	28. D	45. D	62. B	79. C	96. B	113. C	130. D	
12. D	29. D	46. C	63. A	80. A	97. B	114. B	131. C	
13. D	30. D	47. B	64. B	81. D	98. C	115. D	132. C	
14. A	31. C	48. B	65. D	82. C	99. A	116. D	133. D	
15. B	32. C	49. C	66. B	83. D	100. B	117. B	134. B	
16. B	33. D	50. B	67. D	84. A	101. C	118. B	135. A	
17. A	34. C	51. C	68. C	85. D	102. A	119. D	136. A	

Rigor Table

RIGOR TABLE	
Rigor level	**Questions**
Easy 20%	4, 10, 11, 24, 25, 28, 29, 31, 32, 34, 45, 52, 62, 70, 72, 74, 90, 98, 109, 111, 112, 117, 119, 120, 128, 129, 130
Average 40%	1, 2, 8, 12, 18, 19, 26, 33, 36, 39, 40, 42, 46, 49, 53, 54, 56, 58, 59, 61, 63, 64, 65, 68, 69, 71, 77, 78, 80, 81, 84, 87, 95, 99, 100, 102, 103, 104, 105, 106, 108, 110, 113, 115, 116, 118, 121, 122, 123, 126, 127, 132, 134, 135, 136, 140
Rigorous 40%	3, 5, 6, 7, 9, 13, 14, 15, 16, 17, 20, 21, 22, 23, 27, 30, 35, 37, 38, 41, 43, 44, 47, 48, 50, 51, 55, 57, 60, 66, 67, 73, 75, 76, 79, 82, 83, 85, 86, 88, 89, 91, 92, 93, 94, 96, 97, 101, 104, 107, 114, 124, 125, 131, 133, 137, 138, 139

Sample Test with Rationales: Student Development and Learning

DIRECTIONS: Read each item and select the best response.

(Average) (Skill 1.1)

1. **What developmental patterns should a professional teacher assess to meet the needs of the student?**

   A. Academic, regional, and family background

   B. Social, physical, and academic

   C. Academic, physical, and family background

   D. Physical, family, and ethnic background

   Answer: B. Social, physical, and academic

   The effective teacher applies knowledge of physical, social, and academic developmental patterns and individual differences to meet the instructional needs of all students in the classroom. The most important premise of child development is that all domains of development (physical, social, and academic) are integrated. The teacher has a broad knowledge and thorough understanding of the development that typically occurs during the student's current period of life. More important, the teacher understands how children learn best during each period of development. An examination of the student's file coupled with ongoing evaluation assures a successful educational experience for both teacher and students.

(Average) (Skill 1.3)

2. **Louise is a first grade teacher. She is planning her instructional activities for the week. In considering her planning, she should keep in mind that activities for this age of child should change how often?**

   A. 25–40 minutes

   B. 30–40 minutes

   C. 5–10 minutes

   D. 15–30 minutes

   Answer: D. 15–30 minutes

   For young children, average activities should change about every twenty minutes.

(Rigorous) (Skill 2.1)

3. **What are the two types of performance that teaching entails?**

   A. Classroom management and questioning techniques

   B. Skill-building and analysis of outcomes

   C. Interaction with students and manipulation of subject matter

   D. Management techniques and levels of questioning

   Answer: C. Interaction with students and manipulation of subject matter

   The effective teacher develops her skills in both areas. Manipulation of subject matter begins with planning but is constantly tested and adjusted in the classroom. Even if she is very good at that, if she does not develop her skills for interacting with students successfully, she will not be successful.

(Easy) (Skill 2.2)

4. **What are the two ways concepts can be taught?**

   A. Factually and interpretively

   B. Inductively and deductively

   C. Conceptually and inductively

   D. Analytically and facilitatively

   Answer: B. Inductively and deductively

   Induction is reasoning from the particular to the general—that is, looking at a feature that exists in several examples and drawing a conclusion about that feature. Deduction is the reverse; it's the statement of the generality and then supporting it with specific examples.

(Rigorous) (Skill 2.2)

5. **What is one component of the instructional planning model that must be given careful evaluation?**

   A. Students' prior knowledge and skills

   B. The script the teacher will use in instruction

   C. Future lesson plans

   D. Parent participation

   Answer: A. Students' prior knowledge and skills

   The teacher will, of course, have certain expectations regarding where the students will be physically and intellectually when he plans for a new class. However, there will be wide variations in the actual classroom. If he doesn't make the extra effort to understand where there are deficiencies and where there are strengths in the individual students, the planning will probably miss the mark, at least for some members of the class. This information can be obtained through a review of student records, by observation, and by testing.

(Rigorous) (Skill 2.3)

6. **When using a kinesthetic approach, what would be an appropriate activity?**

   A. List

   B. Match

   C. Define

   D. Debate

   Answer: B. Match

   Brain lateralization theory emerged in the 1970s and demonstrated that the left hemisphere appeared to be associated with verbal and sequential abilities, whereas the right hemisphere appeared to be associated with emotions and with spatial, holistic processing. Although those particular conclusions continue to be challenged, it is clear that people concentrate, process, and remember new and difficult information under very different conditions. For example, auditory and visual perceptual strengths, passivity, and self-oriented or authority-oriented motivation often correlate with high academic achievement, whereas tactual and kinesthetic strengths, a need for mobility, nonconformity, and peer motivation often correlate with school underachievement (Dunn & Dunn, 1992, 1993). Understanding how students perceive the task of learning new information differently is often helpful in tailoring the classroom experience for optimal success.

(Rigorous) (Skill 2.3)

7. **Ms. Smith says, "Yes, exactly what do you mean by "It was the author's intention to mislead you." What does this illustrate?**

   A. Digression

   B. Restates response

   C. Probes a response

   D. Amplifies a response

   Answer: C. Probes a response

   From ancient times, notable teachers such as Socrates and Jesus have employed oral-questioning to enhance their discourse, stimulate thinking, and stir emotion among their audiences. Educational researchers and practitioners virtually all agree that teachers' effective use of questioning promotes student learning. Effective teachers continually develop their questioning skills.

(Average) (Skill 2.4)

8. **What are critical elements of instructional process?**

   A. Content, goals, teacher needs

   B. Means of getting money to regulate instruction

   C. Content, materials, activities, goals, learner needs

   D. Materials, definitions, assignments

Answer: C. Content, materials, activities, goals, learner needs

Goal setting is a vital component of the instructional process. The teacher will, of course, have overall goals for her class, both short-term and long-term. However, perhaps even more important than that is the setting of goals that take into account the individual learner's needs, background, and stage of development. Making an educational program child-centered involves building on the natural curiosity children bring to school and asking children what they want to learn. Student-centered classrooms contain not only textbooks, workbooks, and literature, but they also rely heavily on a variety of audiovisual equipment and computers. There are tape recorders, language masters, filmstrip projectors, and DVD players to help meet the learning styles of the students. Planning for instructional activities entails identification or selection of the activities the teacher and students will engage in during a period of instruction.

(Rigorous) (Skill 2.4)

9. **According to Piaget, what stage is characterized by the ability to think abstractly and to use logic?**

   A. Concrete operations

   B. Preoperational

   C. Formal operations

   D. Conservative operational

   Answer: C. Formal operations

   The four development stages are described in Piaget's theory:

   1. *Sensorimotor* stage: from birth to age 2 years (children experience the world through movement and senses)
   2. *Preoperational stage*: from ages 2 to 7 (acquisition of motor skills)
   3. *Concrete operational stage*: from ages 7 to 11 (children begin to think logically about concrete events)
   4. *Formal operational stage*: after age 11 (development of abstract reasoning)

   These chronological periods are approximate and, in light of the fact that studies have demonstrated great variation between children, cannot be seen as rigid norms. Furthermore, these stages occur at different ages, depending upon the domain of knowledge under consideration. The ages normally given for the stages reflect when each stage tends to predominate even though one might elicit examples of two, three, or even all four stages of thinking at the same time from one individual, depending upon the domain of knowledge and the means used to elicit it.

(Easy) (Skill 2.4)

10. **How many stages of intellectual development does Piaget define?**

    A. Two

    B. Four

    C. Six

    D. Eight

    Answer: B. Four

    The stages are:

    1. *Sensorimotor stage*: from birth to age 2 years (children experience the world through movement and senses)
    2. *Preoperational stage*: from ages 2 to 7 (acquisition of motor skills)
    3. *Concrete operational stage*: from ages 7 to 11 (children begin to think logically about concrete events)
    4. *Formal operational stage*: after age 11 (development of abstract reasoning)

(Easy) (Skill 2.4)

11. **Who developed the theory of multiple intelligences?**

    A. Bruner

    B. Gardner

    C. Kagan

    D. Cooper

Answer: B. Gardner

Howard Gardner's most famous work is probably *Frames of Mind*, which details seven dimensions of intelligence (visual/spatial intelligence, musical intelligence, verbal intelligence, logical/mathematical intelligence, interpersonal intelligence, intrapersonal intelligence, and bodily/kinesthetic intelligence). Gardner's claim that pencil and paper IQ tests do not capture the full range of human intelligences has garnered much praise within the field of education but has also been met with criticism, largely from psychometricians. Since the publication of *Frames of Mind*, Gardner has additionally identified the eighth dimension of intelligence, naturalist intelligence, and is still considering a possible ninth—existentialist intelligence.

(Average) (Skill 2.4)

12. **Students who can solve problems mentally have:**

A. Reached maturity

B. Physically developed

C. Reached the preoperational stage of thought

D. Achieved the ability to manipulate objects symbolically

Answer: D. Achieved the ability to manipulate objects symbolically

When students are able to solve mental problems, it is an indication to the teacher that they have achieved the ability to manipulate objects symbolically and should be instructed to continue to develop their cognitive and academic skills.

(Rigorous) (Skill 2.5)

13. **Which description of the role of a teacher is no longer an accurate description?**

A. Guide on the side

B. Authoritarian

C. Disciplinarian

D. Sage on the stage

Answer: D. Sage on the stage

The old phrase of describing a teacher as a sage on the stage is no longer accurate. It is not the responsibility of the teacher to impart his or her knowledge on students. Teachers do not, nor should it be thought that they, have all of the answers. In contrast, it is the responsibility of the teacher to guide students through the learning process.

(Rigorous) (Skill 2.5)

14. **In the past, teaching has been viewed as ________ while in more current society it has been viewed as __________.**

A. isolating, collaborative

B. collaborative, isolating

C. supportive, isolating

D. isolating, supportive

Answer: A. isolating, collaborative

In the past, teachers often walked into their own classrooms and closed the door. They were not involved in any form of collaboration and were responsible for only the students within their classrooms. However, in today's more modern schools, teachers work in collaborative teams and are responsible for all of the children in a school setting.

(Rigorous) (Skill 2.6)

15. **The teacher states, "We will work on the first page of vocabulary words. On the second page we will work on the structure and meaning of the words. We will go over these together and then you will write out the answers to the exercises on your own. I will be circulating to give help if needed." What is this an example of?**

A. Evaluation of instructional activity

B. Analysis of instructional activity

C. Identification of expected outcomes

D. Pacing of instructional activity

Answer: B. Analysis of instructional activity

The successful teacher carefully plans all activities to foresee any difficulties in executing the plan. This planning also ensures that the directions being given to students will be clear, avoiding any misunderstanding.

(Rigorous) (Skill 2.6)

16. **If teachers attend to content, instructional materials, activities, learner needs, and goals in instructional planning, what could be an outcome?**

A. Planning for the next year

B. Effective classroom performance

C. Elevated test scores on standardized tests

D. More student involvement

Answer: B. Effective classroom performance

Another outcome will be teacher satisfaction in a job well done and in the performance of her students. Her days will have far fewer disruptions and her classroom will be easy to manage.

(Rigorous) (Skill 2.6)

17. **When planning instruction, which of the following is an organizational tool to help ensure you are providing a well-balanced set of objectives?**

A. Using a taxonomy to develop objectives

B. Determining prior knowledge skill levels

C. Determining readiness levels

D. Ensuring you meet the needs of diverse learners

Answer: A. Using a taxonomy to develop objectives

The use of a taxonomy, such as Bloom's, allows teachers to ensure that the students are receiving instruction at a variety of different levels. It is important that students are able to demonstrate skills and knowledge at a variety of different levels.

(Average) (Skill 3.4)

18. **What do cooperative learning methods all have in common?**

A. Philosophy

B. Cooperative task/cooperative reward structures

C. Student roles and communication

D. Teacher roles

Answer: B. Cooperative task/cooperative reward structures.

Cooperative learning situations, as practiced in today's classrooms, grew out of searches conducted by several groups in the early 1970s. Cooperative learning situations can range from very formal applications such as STAD (Student Teams-Achievement Divisions) and CIRC (Cooperative Integrated Reading and Composition) to less formal groupings known variously as "group investigation," "learning together," and "discovery groups." Cooperative learning as a general term is now firmly recognized and established as a teaching and learning technique in American schools. Because cooperative learning techniques are so widely diffused in the schools, it is necessary to orient students in the skills by which cooperative learning groups can operate smoothly and thereby enhance learning. Students who cannot interact constructively with other students will not be able to take advantage of the learning opportunities provided by the cooperative learning situations and will furthermore deprive their fellow students of the opportunity for cooperative learning.

(Average) (Skill 3.5)

19. **What is the definition of proactive classroom management?**

A. Management that is constantly changing

B. Management that is downplayed

C. Management that gives clear and explicit instructions and rewarding compliance

D. Management that is designed by the students

Answer: C. Management that gives clear and explicit instructions and rewards compliance

Classroom management plans should be in place when the school year begins. Developing a management plan takes a proactive approach—that is, decide what behaviors will be expected of the class as a whole, anticipate possible problems, and teach the behaviors early in the school year. Involving the students in the development of the classroom rules lets the students know the rationale for the rules and allows them to assume responsibility in the rules because they had a part in developing them.

(Rigorous) (Skill 3.7)

20. **According to recent studies, what is the estimated number of adolescents that have physical, social, or emotional problems related to the abuse of alcohol?**

A. Less that one million

B. 1–2 million

C. 2–3 million

D. More than four million

Answer: D. More than four million

Because of the egregious behavioral problems encountered in the teenage world today that have nothing to do with substance abuse but mimic its traits, discrimination is difficult. Predisposing behaviors indicating a tendency toward the use of drugs and alcohol usually are behaviors that suggest low self-esteem and as such might be indicated by academic failure, social maladaptation, antisocial behavior, truancy, disrespect, chronic rule breaking, aggression and anger, and depression. The student tending toward the use of drugs and alcohol will exhibit losses in social and academic functional levels that were previously attained. He may begin to experiment with substances.

(Rigorous) (Skill 4.1)

21. **Abigail has had intermittent hearing loss from the age of 1 through age 5 when she had tubes put in her ears. What is one area of development that may be affected by this?**

A. Math

B. Language

C. Social skills

D. None

Answer: B. Language

Frequent ear infections and intermittent hearing loss can significantly impair the development of language skills.

(Rigorous) (Skill 4.1)

22. **Active listening is an important skill for teachers to utilize with both students and teachers. Active listening involves all of the following strategies except…**

A. Eye contact

B. Restating what the speaker has said

C. Clarification of speaker statements

D. Open and receptive body language

Answer: B. Restating what the speaker has said

While it is often taught that it is important to restate conversations during meetings, when you are active listening it is more appropriate to seek clarification rather than simply restating.

(Rigorous) (Skill 4.3)

23. **Students who are learning English as a second language often require which of the following to process new information?**

A. Translators

B. Reading tutors

C. Instruction in their native language

D. Additional time and repetitions

Answer: D. Additional time and repetitions

While there are varying thoughts and theories on the most appropriate instruction for ESOL students, much ground can be gained by simply providing additional repetitions and time for new concepts. It is important to include visuals and the other senses into every aspect of this instruction.

(Easy) (Skill 4.3)

24. **Many of the current** ESOL **approaches used in classrooms today are based on which approach?**

A. Social Learning Methods

B. Native Tongue Methods

C. ESOL Learning Methods

D. Special Education Methods

Answer: A. Social Learning Methods

Placing students in mixed groups and pairing them with native speakers, ESOL students are given the opportunities to practice English in a more natural setting.

(Easy) (Skill 4.3)

25. **Which of the following is the last stage of second language acquisition according to the theories of Stephen Krashen?**

A. The affective filter hypothesis

B. The input hypothesis

C. The natural order hypothesis

D. The monitor hypothesis

Answer: A. The affective filter hypothesis

According to Stephen Krashen's theories the five principles are:

1. The acquisition-learning hypothesis
2. The monitor hypothesis
3. The natural order hypothesis
4. The input hypothesis
5. The affective filter hypothesis

(Average) (Skill 4.4)

26. **If a student has a poor vocabulary, the teacher should recommend that:**

A. The student read newspapers, magazines, and books on a regular basis

B. The student enroll in a Latin class

C. The student write the words repetitively after looking them up in the dictionary

D. The student use a thesaurus to locate synonyms and incorporate them into her vocabulary

Answer: A. The student read newspapers, magazines, and books on a regular basis

It is up to the teacher to help the student choose reading material, but the student must be able to choose where she will search for the reading pleasure indispensable for enriching vocabulary.

(Rigorous) (Skill 4.4)

27. **All of the following are true about phonological awareness EXCEPT:**

A. It may involve print

B. It is a prerequisite for spelling and phonics

C. Activities can be done by the children with their eyes closed

D. Starts before letter recognition is taught

Answer: A. It may involve print

The key word here is EXCEPT, which will be highlighted in upper case on the test as well. All of the options are correct aspects of phonological awareness except the first one, because phonological awareness *does not* involve print.

(Easy) (Skill 4.4)

28. **The arrangement and relationship of words in sentences or sentence structure best describes:**

    A. Style

    B. Discourse

    C. Thesis

    D. Syntax

    Answer: D. Syntax

    Syntax is the grammatical structure of sentences.

(Easy) (Skill 4.4)

29. **Which of the following is not a technique of prewriting?**

    A. Clustering

    B. Listing

    C. Brainstorming

    D. Proofreading

    Answer: D. Proofreading

    Proofreading cannot be a method of prewriting, because it is done on already written texts only.

(Rigorous) (Skill 4.5)

30. **One of the many ways in which a child can demonstrate comprehension of a story is by:**

    A. Filling in a strategy sheet

    B. Retelling the story orally

    C. Retelling the story in writing

    D. All of the above

    Answer: D. All of the above

    All of the choices provided show different ways in which students can demonstrate the comprehension of a story.

(Easy) (Skill 4.5)

31. **Greg Ball went to an author signing where Faith Ringgold gave a talk about one of her many books. He was so inspired by her presence and by his reading of her book *Tar Beach* that he used the book for his reading and writing workshop activities. His supervisor wrote in his plan book that he was pleased that Greg had used the book as an/a _______ book.**

    A. basic

    B. feature

    C. anchor

    D. focus

    Answer: C. anchor

    A book that is used to teach reading and writing is called an anchor book.

(Easy) (Skill 5.1)

32. **Which of the following is an example of a restriction within the affective domain?**

    A. Unable to think abstractly

    B. Inability to synthesize information

    C. Inability to concentrate

    D. Inability complete physical activities

Answer: C. Inability to concentrate

The affective domain refers to such things as concentration, focus, lack of participation, inability to express one's self, and inconsistent behavior. Areas of the affective domain may affect other domains such as the cognitive or physical.

(Average) (Skill 5.2)

33. **What is a good strategy for teaching ethnically diverse students?**

A. Don't focus on the students' culture

B. Expect them to assimilate easily into your classroom

C. Imitate their speech patterns

D. Include ethnic studies in the curriculum

Answer: D. Include ethnic studies in the curriculum

Exploring a student's own cultures increases their confidence levels in the group. It is also a very useful tool when students are struggling to develop identities that they can feel comfortable with. The bonus is that this is good training for living in the world.

(Easy) (Skill 5.2)

34. **Which of the following is an accurate description of ESL students?**

A. Remedial students

B. Exceptional education students

C. Are not a homogeneous group

D. Feel confident in communicating in English when with their peers

Answer: C. Are not a homogeneous group

Because ESL students are often grouped in classes that take a different approach to teaching English than those for native speakers, it's easy to assume that they all present with the same needs and characteristics. Nothing could be further from the truth, even in what they need when it comes to learning English. It's important that their backgrounds and personalities be observed just as with native speakers. It was very surprising several years ago when Vietnamese children began arriving in American schools with little training in English and went on to excel in their classes, often even beyond their American counterparts. In many schools, there were Vietnamese merit scholars in the graduating classes.

(Rigorous) (Skill 5.2)

35. **What is an effective way to help a non-English speaking student succeed in class?**

A. Refer the child to a specialist

B. Maintain an encouraging, success-oriented atmosphere

C. Help them assimilate by making them use English exclusively

D. Help them cope with the content materials you currently use

Answer: B. Maintain an encouraging, success-oriented atmosphere

Anyone who is in an environment where his language is not the standard is likely to feel embarrassed and inferior. The student who is in that situation expects to fail. Encouragement is even more important for these students. They need many opportunities to succeed.

(Average) (Skill 5.2)

36. **How can text be modified for low-level ESOL students?**

    A. Add visuals and illustrations

    B. Let students write definitions

    C. Change text to a narrative form

    D. Have students write details out from the text

Answer: A. Add visuals and illustrations

No matter what name we put on it, a book is a book. If students can see the object, not only will they be able to compare their own word for it, a useful tool in learning a new language, but the object can serve as a mnemonic device. The teacher might use actual objects in a classroom to facilitate learning the new language.

(Rigorous) (Skill 5.2)

37. **Etienne is an ESOL student. He has begun to engage in conversation, which produces a connected narrative. In what developmental stage for second language acquisition is he?**

    A. Early production

    B. Speech emergence

    C. Preproduction

    D. Intermediate fluency

Answer: D. Intermediate fluency

Attaining total fluency usually takes several years, although the younger the learner, the shorter the time it takes.

(Rigorous) (Skill 5.2)

38. **What is a roadblock to second language learning?**

    A. Students are forced to speak

    B. Students speak only when ready

    C. Mistakes are considered a part of learning

    D. The focus is on oral communication

Answer: A. Students are forced to speak

It's embarrassing for anyone who is in a foreign language environment to be forced to expose his inability to use that language before she is ready. Being flexible with these students until they're ready to try their wings will shorten the time it will take to approach fluency.

(Average) (Skill 5.2)

39. **Why is praise for compliance important in classroom management?**

    A. Students will continue deviant behavior

    B. Desirable conduct will be repeated

    C. It reflects simplicity and warmth

    D. Students will fulfill obligations

Answer: B. Desirable conduct will be repeated

The tried-and-true principle that behavior that is rewarded will be repeated is demonstrated here. If other students laugh at a child's misbehavior, that child will repeat it. On the other hand, if the teacher rewards the behaviors she wants to see repeated, it is likely to happen.

(Average) (Skill 5.4)

40. **Which of the following is not a communication issue that is related to diversity within the classroom?**

    A. Learning disorder

    B. Sensitive terminology

    C. Body language

    D. Discussing differing viewpoints and opinions

    Answer: A. Learning disorders

    Learning disorders, while they may have a foundation in the specific communication skills of a student, are not in and of themselves a communication issue related to diversity within the classroom.

(Rigorous) (Skill 6.2)

41. **Mr. Ryan has proposed to his classroom that the students may demonstrate understanding of the unit taught in a variety of ways including: taking a test, writing a paper, creating an oral presentation, or building a model or project. Which of the following areas of differentiation has Mr. Ryan demonstrated?**

    A. Synthesis

    B. Product

    C. Content

    D. Product

    Answer: B. Product

    There are three ways to differentiate instruction: content, process, and product. In the described case, Mr. Ryan has chosen to provide the students with alternate opportunities to produce knowledge; therefore, the product is the area being differentiated.

(Average) (Skill 6.2)

42. **When creating and selecting materials for instruction, teachers should complete which of the following steps:**

    A. Make them relevant to the prior knowledge of the students

    B. Allow for a variation of learning styles

    C. Choose alternative teaching strategies

    D. All of the above

    Answer: D. All of the above

    It is imperative that when creating and selecting materials for instruction that teachers consider many different factors; this makes the planning for instruction a difficult and somewhat time consuming process. Numerous factors must be balanced in order to deliver the most appropriate and beneficial instruction to students.

(Rigorous) (Skill 6.4)

43. **Mr. Weiss understands that it is imperative that students who are struggling with acquiring concepts at a specific grade level can still benefit from participating in whole classroom discussions and lessons. In fact, such students should be required to be present for whole classroom lessons. Mr. Weiss's beliefs fall under which of the following principles?**

    A. Self-fulfilling prophecy

    B. Partial participation

    C. Inclusion

    D. Heterogeneous grouping

Answer: B. Partial participation

The concept of partial participation indicates that children, even those struggling, can participate in complex concepts at least to a partial degree. While they may not be able to complete all of the requirements of a lesson objective, they may be able complete portions of the objective and will benefit from that additional learning in a positive manner.

Sample Test with Rationales: Instruction and Assessment

(Rigorous) (Skill 7.1)

44. **Reducing off-task time and maximizing the amount of time students spend attending to academic tasks is closely related to which of the following?**

A. Using whole class instruction only

B. Business-like behaviors of the teacher

C. Dealing only with major teaching functions

D. Giving students a maximum of two minutes to come to order

Answer: B. Business-like behaviors of the teacher

The effective teacher continually evaluates his own physical/mental/social/emotional well-being with regard to the students in his classroom. There is always the tendency to satisfy social and emotional needs through relationships with the students. A good teacher genuinely likes his students, and that's a positive thing. However, if students are not convinced that the teacher's purpose for being there is to get a job done, the atmosphere in the classroom becomes difficult to control. This is the job of the teacher. Maintaining a business-like approach in the classroom yields many positive results. It's similar to a benevolent boss.

(Easy) (Skill 7.1)

45. **While teaching, three students cause separate disruptions. The teacher selects the major one and tells that student to desist. What is the teacher demonstrating?**

A. Deviancy spread

B. Correct target desist

C. Alternative behavior

D. Desist major deviance

Answer: D. Desist major deviance

When the teacher attempts to desist a deviancy, what she says and how it is said directly influence the probability of stopping the misbehavior. The effective teacher demonstrates awareness of what the entire class is doing and is in control of the behavior of all students even when she is working with only a small group of children. In an attempt to prevent student misbehaviors, the teacher makes clear, concise statements about what is happening in the classroom, directing attention to content and the students' accountability for their work rather than focusing the class on the misbehavior. It is also effective for the teacher to make a positive statement about the appropriate behavior that is observed. If deviant behavior does occur, the effective teacher will specify who the deviant is, what the student is doing wrong, and why this is unacceptable conduct or what the proper conduct would be. When more than one student is disrupting the class, it is wise to focus on the one that is causing the greatest problem. This is usually sufficient to bring the others into line. This can be a difficult task to accomplish, as the teacher must maintain academic focus and flow while addressing and desisting misbehavior. The teacher must make clear, brief statements about the expectations without raising her voice and without disrupting instruction.

(Average) (Skill 7.2)

46. **What must occur for seatwork to be effective?**

A. All seatwork is graded immediately

B. All seatwork should be explained by another student for clarification

C. The teacher should monitor and provide corrective feedback for seatwork

D. Seatwork should be a review of the previous day's lesson

Answer: C. The teacher should monitor and provide corrective feedback for seatwork

This period should not be seen as free time for the teacher when she can plan tomorrow's class or grade papers. She should be circulating among the students, observing what they are doing, and commenting in positive ways so that the time is spent profitably by the class in achieving the goals for that particular lesson.

(Rigorous) (Skill 7.2)

47. **Mrs. Peck wants to justify the use of personalized learning community to her principal. Which of the following reasons should she use?**

A. They build multiculturalism

B. They provide a supportive environment to address academic and emotional needs

C. They builds relationships between students that promote lifelong learning

D. They are proactive in their nature

Answer: B. They provide a supportive environment to address academic and emotional needs

While professional learning communities do provide all of the choices, this question asks for a justification statement. The best justification of those choices provided for implementing a personalized learning community in a classroom is to provide a supportive environment to help address the academic and emotional needs of her students.

(Rigorous) (Skill 7.2)

48. **Mrs. Potts has noticed an undercurrent of an unsettled nature in her classroom. She is in the middle of her math lesson but still notices that many of her students seem to be having some sort of difficulty. Mrs. Potts stops class and decides to have a class meeting. She understands that even though her math objectives are important, it is equally important to address whatever is troubling her classroom. What is it Mrs. Potts knows?**

A. Discipline is important

B. Social issues can impact academic learning

C. Maintaining order is important

D. Social skills instruction is important

Answer: B. Social issues can impact academic learning

Mrs. Potts understands that as long as there is a social situation or issue in the classroom, it is unlikely that any academics she presents will be learned. All of those areas instructed are important; however, it is this understanding of the fact that the academics will be impacted that is important in this particular situation as she is interrupting her math instruction.

(Average) (Skill 7.2)

49. **Which of the following could be an example of a situation that could have an effect on a student's learning and academic progress?**

A. Relocation

B. Abuse

C. Both of the above

D. Neither of the above

Answer: C. Both of the above

An unlimited number of situations can affect a student's learning. Teachers need to keep these situations in mind when teaching. Students are whole people and, just as stress affects us as adults, children experience the same feelings. They usually do not have the same toolbox that adults have to deal with the feelings and may require some additional guidance.

(Rigorous) (Skill 7.2)

50. **Mrs. Graham has taken the time to reflect, completed observations, and asked for feedback about the interactions between her and her students from her principal. It is obvious by seeking this information out that Mrs. Graham understands which of the following?**

    A. The importance of clear communication with the principal

    B. She needs to analyze her effectiveness of classroom interactions

    C. She is clearly communicating with the principal

    D. She cares about her students

    Answer: B. She needs to analyze her effectiveness of classroom interactions

    Utilizing reflection, observations, and feedback from peers or supervisors, teachers can help to build their own understanding of how they interact with students. In this way, they can better analyze their effectiveness at building appropriate relationships with students.

(Rigorous) (Skill 7.3)

51. **What has been established to increase student originality, intrinsic motivation, and higher-order thinking skills?**

    A. Classroom climate

    B. High expectations

    C. Student choice

    D. Use of authentic learning opportunities

    Answer: C. Student choice

    While all of the descriptors are good attributes for students to demonstrate, research has shown that providing student choice can increase all of the described factors.

(Easy) (Skill 7.3)

52. **Which of the following can be measured utilizing the following types of assessments: direct observation, role playing, context observation, and teacher ratings?**

    A. Social skills

    B. Reading skills

    C. Math skills

    D. Need for specialized instruction

    Answer: A. Social skills

    Social skills can be measured using the listed types of assessments. They can also be measured using sociometric measures including peer nomination, peer rating, and paired-comparison.

(Average) (Skill 7.5)

53. **What would improve planning for instruction?**

    A. Describe the role of the teacher and student

    B. Evaluate the outcomes of instruction

    C. Rearrange the order of activities

    D. Give outside assignments

Answer: B. Evaluate the outcomes of instruction

Important as it is to plan content, materials, activities, and goals and then taking into account learner needs in order to base what goes on in the classroom on the results of that planning, it makes no difference if students are not able to demonstrate improvement in the skills being taught. An important part of the planning process is for the teacher to constantly adapt all aspects of the curriculum to what is actually happening in the classroom. Planning frequently misses the mark or fails to allow for unexpected factors. Evaluating the outcomes of instruction regularly and making adjustments accordingly will have a positive impact on the overall success of a teaching methodology.

(Average) (Skill 7.5)

54. **How can student misconduct be redirected at times?**

A. The teacher threatens the students

B. The teacher assigns detention to the whole class

C. The teacher stops the activity and stares at the students

D. The teacher effectively handles changing from one activity to another

Answer: D. The teacher effectively handles changing from one activity to another

Appropriate verbal techniques include a soft nonthreatening voice void of undue roughness, anger, or impatience regardless of whether the teacher is instructing, providing student alerts, or giving a behavior reprimand. Verbal techniques that may be effective in modifying student behavior include simply stating the student's name and explaining briefly and succinctly what the student is doing that is inappropriate and what the student should be doing. Verbal techniques for reinforcing behavior include both encouragement and praise delivered by the teacher. In addition, for verbal techniques to positively affect student behavior and learning, the teacher must give clear, concise directives while implying her warmth toward the students.

(Rigorous) (Skill 7.5)

55. **What have recent studies regarding effective teachers concluded?**

A. Effective teachers let students establish rules

B. Effective teachers establish routines by the sixth week of school

C. Effective teachers state their own policies and establish consistent class rules and procedures on the first day of class

D. Effective teachers establish flexible routines

Answer: C. Effective teachers state their own policies and establish consistent class rules and procedures on the first day of class

The teacher can get ahead of the game by stating clearly, on the first day of school, exactly what the rules are. These should be stated firmly but unemotionally. When one of those rules is broken, he can then refer to the rules, rendering enforcement much easier to achieve. It's extremely difficult to achieve goals with students who are out of control. Establishing limits early and consistently enforcing them enhances learning. It is also helpful for the teacher to prominently display the classroom rules. This will serve as a visual reminder of the students' expected behaviors. In a study of classroom management procedures, it was established that the combination of conspicuously displayed rules, frequent verbal references to the rules, and appropriate consequences for appropriate behaviors led to increased levels of on-task behavior.

(Average) (Skill 7.5)

56. **To maintain the flow of events in the classroom, what should an effective teacher do?**

A. Work only in small groups

B. Use only whole class activities

C. Direct attention to content rather than focusing the class on misbehavior

D. Follow lectures with written assignments

Answer: C. Direct attention to content rather than focusing the class on misbehavior

Students who misbehave often do so to attract attention. Focusing the attention of the misbehaver as well as the rest of the class on the real purpose of the classroom sends the message that misbehaving will not be rewarded with class attention to the misbehaver. Engaging students in content by using the various tools available to the creative teacher goes a long way in ensuring a peaceful classroom.

(Rigorous) (Skill 7.5)

57. **The concept of efficient use of time includes which of the following?**

A. Daily review, seatwork, and recitation of concepts

B. Lesson initiation, transition, and comprehension check

C. Review, test, and review

D. Punctuality, management transition, and wait time avoidance

Answer: D. Punctuality, management transition, and wait time avoidance

The "benevolent boss" applies here. One who succeeds in managing a business follows these rules; so does the successful teacher.

(Average) (Skill 7.5)

58. **What is a sample of an academic transition signal?**

    A. How do clouds form?

    B. Today we are going to study clouds.

    C. We have completed today's lesson.

    D. That completes the description of cumulus clouds. Now we will look at the description of cirrus clouds.

Answer: D. That completes the description of cumulus clouds. Now we will look at the description of cirrus clouds.

Transitions are language bridges between one topic and another. The teacher should thoughtfully plan transitions when several topics are going to be presented in one lesson to be sure that students are carried along. Without transitions, sometimes students are still focused on a previous topic and are lost in the discussion.

(Average) (Skill 8.1)

59. **When is utilization of instructional materials most effective?**

    A. When the activities are sequenced

    B. When the materials are prepared ahead of time

    C. When the students choose the pages to work on

    D. When the students create the instructional materials

Answer: A. When the activities are sequenced

Most assignments will require more than one educational principle. It is helpful to explain to students the proper order in which these principles must be applied to complete the assignment successfully. Subsequently, students should also be informed of the nature of the assignment (i.e., cooperative learning, group project, individual assignment). This is often done at the start of the assignment.

(Rigorous) (Skill 8.1)

60. **When considering the development of the curriculum, which of the following accurately describes the four factors that need to be considered?**

    A. Alignment, Scope, Sequence, and Design

    B. Assessment, Instruction, Design, and Sequence

    C. Data, Alignment, Correlation, and Score

    D. Alignment, Sequence, Design, and Assessment

Answer: A. Alignment, Scope, Sequence, and Design

When developing curriculum, it is important to first start with alignment. Alignment to state, national, or other standards is the first step. Next, the scope of the curriculum involves looking at the amount of material covered within a grade level or subject. Next, the sequence of material needs to be considered. Finally, it is important to look at the design of the units individually from beginning to end.

(Average) (Skill 8.2)

61. **What should be considered when evaluating textbooks for content?**

    A. Type of print used

    B. Number of photos used

    C. Free of cultural stereotyping

    D. Outlines at the beginning of each chapter

    Answer: C. Free of cultural stereotyping

    While textbook writers and publishers have responded to the need to be culturally diverse in recent years, a few texts are still being offered that don't meet these standards. When teachers have an opportunity to be involved in choosing textbooks, they can be watchdogs for the community in keeping the curriculum free of matter that reinforces bigotry and discrimination.

(Easy) (Skill 9.1)

62. **Which of the following is a presentation modification?**

    A. Taking an assessment in an alternate room

    B. Providing an interpreter to give the test in American Sign Language

    C. Allowing dictation of written responses

    D. Extending the time limits on an assessment

    Answer: B. Providing an interpreter to give the test in American Sign Language

    There are numerous types of modifications that can be provided to students in the classroom and for assessments. All of the described choices are appropriate modifications, but the only one that affects the presentation of the items is the one related to providing an interpreter.

(Average) (Skill 9.2)

63. **What should a teacher do when students have not responded well to an instructional activity?**

    A. Reevaluate learner needs

    B. Request administrative help

    C. Continue with the activity another day

    D. Assign homework on the concept

    Answer: A. Reevaluate learner needs

    The value of teacher observations cannot be underestimated. It is through the use of observations that the teacher is able to informally assess the needs of the students during instruction. These observations will drive the lesson and determine the direction that the lesson will take based on student activity and behavior. After a lesson is carefully planned, teacher observation is the single most important component of an instructional presentation. If the teacher observes that a particular student is not on-task, she will change the method of instruction accordingly. She may change from a teacher-directed approach to a more interactive approach. Questioning will increase in order to increase the participation of the students. If appropriate, the teacher will introduce manipulative materials to the lesson. In addition, teachers may switch to a cooperative group activity, thereby removing the responsibility of instruction from the teacher and putting it on the students.

(Average) (Skill 9.2)

64. **What is the best definition for an achievement test?**

    A. It measures mechanical and practical abilities

    B. It measures broad areas of knowledge that are the result of cumulative learning experiences

    C. It measures the ability to learn to perform a task

    D. It measures performance related to specific, recently acquired information

Answer: B. It measures broad areas of knowledge that are the result of cumulative learning experiences

The ways that a teacher uses test data is a meaningful aspect of instruction and may increase the motivation level of the students especially when this information is available in the form of feedback to the students. This feedback should indicate to the students what they need to do in order to improve their achievement. Frequent testing and feedback is most often an effective way to increase achievement.

(Average) (Skill 9.2)

65. **How are standardized tests useful in assessment?**

    A. For teacher evaluation

    B. For evaluation of the administration

    C. For comparison from school to school

    D. For comparison to the population on which the test was normed

Answer: D. For comparison to the population on which the test was normed.

While the efficacy of the standardized tests that are being used nationally has come under attack recently, they are actually the only device for comparing where an individual student stands with a wide range of peers. They also provide a measure for a program or a school to evaluate how their own students are doing as compared to the populace at large. Even so, they should not be the only measure upon which decisions are made or evaluations drawn. There are many other instruments for measuring student achievement that the teacher needs to consult and take into account.

(Rigorous) (Skill 9.2)

66. **Which of the following test items is not objective?**

A. Multiple choice

B. Essay

C. Matching

D. True or false

Answer: B: Essay

Because you need to use a rubric and there are various interpretations of this type of assessment, it is not objective.

(Rigorous) (Skill 9.2)

67. **Which of the following is NOT used in evaluating test items?**

A. Student feedback

B. Content validity

C. Reliability

D. Ineffective coefficient

Answer: D. Ineffective coefficient

The purpose for testing the students is to determine the extent to which the instructional objectives have been met. Therefore, the test items must be constructed to achieve the desired outcome from the students. Gronlund and Linn advise that effective tests begin with a test plan that includes the instructional objectives and subject matter to be tested, as well as the emphasis each item should have. Having a test plan will result in valid interpretation of student achievement.

(Average) (Skill 9.2)

68. **Safeguards against bias and discrimination in the assessment of children include:**

A. The testing of a child in standard English

B. The requirement for the use of one standardized test

C. The use of evaluative materials in the child's native language or other mode of communication

D. All testing performed by a certified, licensed psychologist

Answer: C. The use of evaluative materials in the child's native language or other mode of communication

The law requires that the child be evaluated in his native language or mode of communication. The idea that a licensed psychologist evaluate the child does not meet the criteria if it is not done in the child's normal mode of communication.

(Average) (Skill 9.3)

69. **On intelligence quotient scales, what is the average intelligence score?**

A. 100–120

B. 60–80

C. 90–110

D. 80–100

Answer: C. 90–110

The use of a general index of cognitive ability raises technical issues that have attracted the attention of developmental researchers for many years. These issues are:

1. Whether IQ is an important developmental construct that is predictive of significant life outcomes
2. Whether IQ is changeable and whether changes in IQ are meaningful
3. Whether these changes are due primarily to error or are systematic
4. The degree, if any, to which there is continuity or discontinuity in IQ during different developmental stages
5. Whether other individual-difference variables are predictive of those life-quality indicators that are traditionally linked to IQ

These issues are relevant for the teacher, who should be cautioned to pay attention to the reported IQs of her students but not to take them as the final word for a particular student's capabilities. As we all know, tests can often err badly for all kinds of reasons, not the least of which is the state of mind of the subject at the time of the test. The teacher's own observations are more important in determining where to start with a particular student.

(Easy) (Skill 9.3)

70. **On what is evaluation of the instructional activity based?**

    A. Student grades

    B. Teacher evaluation

    C. Student participation

    D. Specified criteria

Answer: D. Specified criteria

The way that a teacher uses test data is a meaningful aspect of instruction and may increase the motivation level of the students, especially when this information takes the form of feedback to the students. However, in order for a test to be an accurate measurement of student progress, the teacher must know how to plan and construct tests. Perhaps the most important caveat in creating and using tests for classroom purposes is the old adage to test what you teach. Actually, it is better stated that you should teach what you plan to test. This second phrasing more clearly reflects the need for thorough planning of the entire instructional program. Before you begin instruction, you should have the assessment planned and defined. One common method of matching the test to the instruction is to develop a table of specifications, a two-way grid in which the objectives of instruction are listed on one axis and the content that has been presented is listed on the other axis. Then the individual cells are assigned percentages that reflect the focus and extent of instruction in each area. The final step is to distribute the number of questions to be used on the test among the cells of the table in proportion to the identified percentages.

(Average) (Skill 9.3)

71. **What is an example of formative feedback?**

    A. The results of an intelligence test

    B. Correcting the tests in small groups

    C. Verbal behavior that expresses approval of a student response to a test item

    D. Scheduling a discussion before the test

Answer: C. Verbal behavior that expresses approval of a student response to a test item

Standardized testing is currently under great scrutiny, but educators agree that any test that serves as a means of gathering and interpreting information about children's learning and that can provide accurate, helpful input for nurturing children's further growth is acceptable. All testing must be formative in nature. Formative evaluation is the basic, everyday kind of assessment that teachers continually do to understand students' growth and to help them learn further.

(Easy) (Skill 9.3)

72. **What does the validity of a test refer to?**

    A. Its consistency

    B. Its usefulness

    C. Its accuracy

    D. The degree of true scores it provides

Answer: B. Its usefulness

The joint technical standards for educational and psychological testing (APA, AERA, NCME, 1985) states: "Validity is the most important consideration in test evaluation. The concept refers to the appropriateness, meaningfulness, and usefulness of the specific inferences made from test scores. Test validation is the process of accumulating evidence to support such inferences. A variety of inferences may be made from scores produced by a given test, and there are many ways of accumulating evidence to support any particular inference. Validity, however, is a unitary concept. Although evidence may be accumulated in many ways, validity always refers to the degree to which that evidence supports the inferences that are made from test scores."

(Rigorous) (Skill 9.3)

73. **Which of the following describes why it is important and necessary for teachers to be able to analyze data on their students?**

    A. To provide appropriate instruction

    B. To make instructional decisions

    C. To communicate and determine instructional progress

    D. All of the above

Answer: D. All of the above

Especially in today's high stakes environment, it is critical teachers have a complete understanding of the process involved in examining student data in order to make instructional decisions, prepare lessons, determine progress, and report progress to stakeholders.

(Easy) (Skill 9.4)

74. **When a teacher wants to utilize an assessment that is subjective in nature, which of the following is the most effective method for scoring?**

A. Rubric

B. Checklist

C. Alternative Assessment

D. Subjective measures should not be utilized

Answer: A. Rubric

Rubrics are the most effective tool for assessing items that can be considered subjective. They provide the students with a clearer picture of teacher expectations and provide the teacher with a more consistent method of comparing this type of assignment.

(Rigorous) (Skill 9.5)

75. **What steps are important in the review of subject matter in the classroom?**

A. A lesson-initiating review, topic, and a lesson-end review

B. A preview of the subject matter, an in-depth discussion, and a lesson-end review

C. A rehearsal of the subject matter and a topic summary within the lesson

D. A short paragraph synopsis of the previous day's lesson and a written review at the end of the lesson

Answer: A. A lesson-initiating review, topic, and a lesson-end review

The effective teacher utilizes all three of these together with comprehension checks to make sure the students are processing the information. Lesson-end reviews are restatements (by the teacher or teacher and students) of the content of discussion at the end of a lesson. Subject matter retention increases when lessons include an outline at the beginning of the lesson and a summary at the end of the lesson. This type of structure is used in successful classrooms. Moreover, when students know what is coming next, and what is expected of them, they feel more a part of their learning environment and deviant behavior is lessened.

(Rigorous) (Skill 9.5)

76. **The teacher states that the lesson the students will be engaged in will consist of a review of the material from the previous day, demonstration of the scientific of an electronic circuit, and small group work on setting up an electronic circuit. What has the teacher demonstrated?**

    A. The importance of reviewing

    B. Giving the general framework for the lesson to facilitate learning

    C. Giving students the opportunity to leave if they are not interested in the lesson

    D. Providing momentum for the lesson

Answer: B. Giving the general framework for the lesson to facilitate learning

If children know where they're going, they're more likely to be engaged in getting there. It's important to give them a road map whenever possible for what is coming in their classes.

(Average) (Skill 9.5)

77. **What is an effective way to prepare students for testing?**

    A. Minimize the importance of the test

    B. Orient the students to the test by telling them of the purpose, how the results will be used, and how it is relevant to them

    C. Use the same format for every test are given

    D. Have them construct an outline to study from

Answer: B. Orient the students to the test by telling them of the purpose, how the results will be used, and how it is relevant to them

If a test is to be an accurate measure of achievement, it must test the information, not the format of the test itself. If students know ahead of time what the test will be like, why they are taking it, what the teacher will do with the results, and what it has to do with them, the exercise is more likely to result in a true measure of what they've learned.

(Average) (Skill 9.5)

78. **How will students have a fair chance to demonstrate what they know on a test?**

    A. When the examiner has strictly enforced rules for taking the test

    B. When the examiner provides a comfortable setting free of distractions and positively encourages the students

    C. When the examiner provides frequent stretch breaks to the students

    D. When the examiner stresses the importance of the test to the overall grade

Answer: B. When the examiner provides a comfortable setting free of distractions and positively encourages the students

Taking a test is intimidating to students at best. In addition, some students are unable to focus when there are distractions. Feeling that the teacher is on their side helps students relax and truly demonstrate what they have learned on a test.

(Rigorous) (Skill 9.5)

79. **Which of the following is the correct term for the alignment of the curriculum across all grades K-12?**

A. Data-based decision making

B. Curriculum mapping

C. Vertical integration

D. Curriculum alignment

Answer: C. Vertical integration

Curriculum mapping is the process of taking the curriculum and deciding when the information needs to be taught throughout the school year. Curriculum alignment involves the process of connecting the curriculum to something else (typically standards) to ensure that all areas are being taught. Vertical integration is the process of ensuring that the curriculum flows in an appropriate manner from the lowest levels to the highest levels in a logical and responsible manner.

(Average) (Skill 9.5)

80. **Which of the following information can NOT be gained by examining school level data in an in-depth manner?**

A. Teacher effectiveness

B. Educational trends within a school

C. Student ability to meet state and national goals and objectives

D. Ways to improve student learning goals and academic success

Answer: A. Teacher effectiveness

While to some degree student progress can provide information on the effectiveness of a teacher, looking only at statistical information may not provide a clear and accurate representation of the effectiveness of a teacher. For example, data showing that 75 percent of the students achieved the state goals may indicate that the teacher was not very effective. However, if in the previous year, only 10 percent of these same students achieved the state goals, the same data would provide a completely different picture on the effectiveness of this teacher.

(Average) (Skill 10.1)

81. **Which of following is NOT the role of the teacher in the instructional process:**

A. Instructor

B. Coach

C. Facilitator

D. Follower

Answer: D. Follower

The teacher demonstrates a variety of roles within the classroom. Teachers, however, should not be followers. They must balance all of their roles in an efficient way to ensure that instruction is delivered to meet the needs of his or her students.

(Rigorous) (Skill 10.2)

82. **Discovery learning is to inquiry as direct instruction is to…**

    A. Scripted lessons

    B. Well-developed instructions

    C. Clear instructions that eliminate all misinterpretations

    D. Creativity of teaching

    Answer: C. Clear instructions that eliminate all misinterpretations

    Direct instruction is a technique that relies on carefully, well-developed instructions and lessons that eliminate misinterpretations. In this manner, all students have the opportunity to acquire and learn the skills presented to the students. This approach limits teacher creativity to some extent, but has a good solid research-based following with much ability to replicate its results.

(Rigorous) (Skill 10.6)

83. **When developing lessons it is imperative teachers provide equity in pedagogy so:**

    A. Unfair labeling of students will not occur

    B. Student experiences will be positive

    C. Students will achieve academic success

    D. All of the above

    Answer: D. All of the above

    Providing equity of pedagogy allows for students to have positive learning experiences, achieve academic success, and helps to prevent the labeling of students in an unfair manner.

(Average) (Skill 10.6)

84. **Which of the following is a good reason to collaborate with a peer:**

    A. To increase your knowledge in areas where you feel you are weak, but the peer is strong

    B. To increase your planning time and that of your peer by combining the classes and taking more breaks

    C. To have fewer lesson plans to write

    D. To teach fewer subjects

    Answer: A. To increase your knowledge in areas where you feel you are weak, but the peer is strong

    Collaboration with a peer allows teachers to share ideas and information. In this way, the teacher is able to improve his skills and share additional information.

(Rigorous) (Skill 10.6)

85. **Which of the following are ways a professional can assess her teaching strengths and weaknesses?**

    A. Examining how many students were unable to understand a concept

    B. Asking peers for suggestions or ideas

    C. Self-evaluation/reflection of lessons taught

    D. All of the above

    Answer: D. All of the above

    It is important for teachers to involve themselves in constant periods of reflection and self-reflection to ensure they are meeting the needs of the students.

(Rigorous) (Skill 10.6)

86. **Mr. German is a math coach. He is the only math coach in his building and, in fact, within his district. Mr. German believes it is imperative to seek out the support of colleagues to work in a more collaborative manner. Which of the following would be an appropriate step for him to take?**

A. Collaborating with other teachers in his building regardless of their skill level knowledge in his area

B. Asking for the administration to find colleagues with whom he can collaborate

C. Joining a professional organization such as the National Council of Teachers of Mathematics (NCTM)

D. Searching the Internet for possible collaboration opportunities

Answer: C. Joining a professional organization such as the National Council of Teachers of Mathematics (NCTM)

Joining a professional organization, such as NCTM, would provide Mr. German with the ability to learn and update his own knowledge specifically in his field of study and also open up the opportunity for him to interact with colleagues in his field from across the country.

(Average) (Skill 11.1)

87. **Why is it important for a teacher to pose a question before calling on students to answer?**

A. It helps manage student conduct

B. It keeps the students as a group focused on the class work

C. It allows students time to collaborate

D. It gives the teacher time to walk among the students

Answer: B. It keeps the students as a group focused on the class work

It doesn't take much distraction for a class's attention to become diffused. Once this happens, effectively teaching a principle or a skill is very difficult. The teacher should plan presentations that will keep students focused on the lesson. A very useful tool is to use effective, well thought-out, pointed questions.

(Rigorous) (Skill 11.1)

88. **What is an example of a low order question?**

A. Why is it important to recycle items in your home?

B. Compare how glass and plastics are recycled.

C. What items do we recycle in our county?

D. Explain the importance of recycling in our county.

Answer: C. What items do we recycle in our county?

Remember that the difference between specificity and abstractness is a continuum. The most specific is something that is concrete and can be seen, heard, smelled, tasted, or felt, such as cans, bottles, and newspapers. At the other end of the spectrum is an abstraction, such as importance. Lower-order questions are on the concrete end of the continuum; higher-order questions are on the abstract end.

(Rigorous) (Skill 11.1)

89. **What would be espoused by Jerome Bruner?**

A. Thought depends on the acquisition of operations

B. Memory plays a significant role in cognitive growth

C. Genetics is the most important factor for cognitive growth

D. Enriched environments have significant effects on cognitive growth

Answer: D. Enriched environments have significant effects on cognitive growth

In "Selecting and Applying Learning Theory to Classroom Teaching Strategies," by Donald R. Coker and Jane White in *Education* (1993), they write: "Jerome Bruner poises the ultimate question for teachers when he asked, 'How do you teach something to a child, arrange a child's environment if you will, in such a way that he can learn something with some assurance that he will use the material that he has learned appropriately in a variety of situations?' When presented with this query, most teachers have difficulty responding even though their days are spent trying to accomplish this very purpose. Why do those of us who teach have such an apparent inability to define the nature of our instructional activities in terms of lasting benefit to the learner? Perhaps this dilemma results from confusion regarding basic concepts of how children learn.

When we honestly examine our own learning, the information we crammed into our heads for Friday's spelling test or Wednesday's history quiz is long gone. What remains with us is typically learning we personally wanted or learning that actively involved us in the process, i.e., typing, sewing, woodworking, drama, acting, drafting, computers, writing, etc. A reflection on our own learning allows us to see what made the process work:

- Being taught by a teacher who knew more than we,
- Being interested and active in the learning process
- Learning to focus on ideas, concepts, and being encouraged to generalize
- Being teased into new areas of insight by teachers who encouraged risks, making mistakes, and learning from them
- Seeing connections between the new information and what we already knew
- Being taught by a mentor who expected us to succeed
- Being taught in an atmosphere of support, not anxiety and fear
- Seeing, talking, and doing made the task easier, while sitting quietly and listening was difficult
- Being allowed to choose from a variety of appropriate classroom activities
- Being responsible for our own learning

As teachers, we should examine our own teaching strategies and check them against criteria such as these in an effort to answer the question, 'Does my classroom allow for all of these conditions?'"

(Easy) (Skill 11.1)

90. **When asking questions of students it is important to:**

A. Ask questions the students can answer

B. Provide numerous questions

C. Provide questions at various levels

D. Provide only a limited amount of questions

Answer: C. Provide questions at various levels

Providing questions at various levels is essential to encourage deeper thinking and reflective thought processes.

(Rigorous) (Skill 11.4)

91. **With the passage of the No Child Left Behind Act (NCLB), schools are required to develop action plans to improve student learning. Which of the following is not a part of this action plan?**

A. Clearly defined goals for school improvement

B. Clearly defined assessment plan

C. Clearly defined timelines

D. Clearly defined plans for addressing social skills improvement

Answer: D. Clearly defined plans for addressing social skills improvement

The school action plan as related to NCLB should address all of the following areas:

- Clearly defined goals and objectives for student learning and school improvement
- Clear alignment of goals and objectives
- Developing clear timelines and accountability for goal implementation steps
- Constructing an effective evaluation plan for assessing data around student performance and established objectives for student learning outcomes
- Defining a plan B in case plan A falls short of meeting the goals and objectives for student achievement and school improvement

(Rigorous) (Skill 12.1)

92. **Mr. Smith is introducing the concept of photosynthesis to his class next week. In preparing for this lesson, he considers that this concept will be new to many of his students. Mr. Smith understands that his students' brains are like filing cabinets and that there is currently no file for photosynthesis in those cabinets. What does Mr. Smith need to do to ensure his students acquire the necessary knowledge?**

A. Help them create a new file

B. Teach the students the information; they will organize it themselves in their own way

C. Find a way to connect the new learning to other information they already know

D. Provide many repetitions and social situations during the learning process

Answer: C. Find a way to connect the new learning to other information they already know

While behavioral theories indicate that it is through socialization and multiple repetitions that students acquire new information, new research into the brain and how it works indicates that students learn best by making connections There-fore, it is imperative when teaching new concepts that teachers find a way to connect new information to previously learned material.

(Rigorous) (Skill 12.1)

93. **Curriculum mapping is an effective strategy because it:**

A. Provides an orderly sequence to instruction

B. Provides lesson plans for teachers to use and follow

C. Ties the curriculum into instruction

D. Provides a clear map so all students receive the same instruction across all classes

Answer: A. Provides an orderly sequence to instruction

Curriculum mapping is a strategy used to tie the actual curriculum with the support materials (textbooks) being utilized to support the teaching of said curriculum. Mapping is usually done to the month or quarter and provides a logical sequence to instruction so that all necessary skills and topics are covered in an appropriate fashion.

(Rigorous) (Skill 13.1)

94. **Mrs. Grant is providing her students with many extrinsic motivators in order to increase their intrinsic motiva-tion. Which of the best explains this relationship?**

A. This relationship is good and will increase intrinsic motivation

B. The relationship builds animosity between the teacher and the students

C. Extrinsic motivation does not in itself help to build intrinsic motivation

D. There is no place for extrinsic motiva-tion in the classroom

Answer: C. Extrinsic motivation does not in itself help to build intrinsic motivation

There are some cases where it is necessary to utilize extrinsic motivation; however, the use of extrinsic motivation is not alone a strategy to use to build intrinsic motivation. Intrinsic motivation comes from within the student themselves, while extrinsic motivation comes from outside parties.

(Average) (Skill 13.5)

95. **What is one way of effectively managing student conduct?**

A. State expectations about behavior

B. Let students discipline their peers

C. Let minor infractions of the rules go unnoticed

D. Increase disapproving remarks

Answer: A. State expectations about behavior

The effective teacher demonstrates awareness of what the entire class is doing and is in control of the behavior of all students even when the teacher is working with only a small group of children. In an attempt to prevent student misbehaviors, the teacher makes clear, concise statements about what is happening in the classroom, directing attention to content and the students' accountability for their work rather than focusing the class on the misbehavior. It is also effective for the teacher to make a positive statement about the appropriate behavior that is observed. If deviant behavior does occur, the effective teacher will specify who the deviant is, what he or she is doing wrong, and why this conduct is unacceptable or what the proper conduct would be. This task can be difficult to accomplish because the teacher must maintain academic focus and flow while addressing and desisting misbehavior. The teacher must make clear, brief statements about the expectations without raising his voice and without disrupting instruction.

(Rigorous) (Skill 13.5)

96. **How can mnemonic devices be used to increase achievement?**

A. They help the child rehearse the information

B. They help the child visually imagine the information

C. They help the child to code information

D. They help the child reinforce concepts

Answer: B. They help the child visually imagine the information

Mnemonics are verbal cues, something such as a very short poem or a special word used to help a person remember something, particularly lists. Mnemonics rely not only on repetition to remember facts but also on associations between easy-to-remember constructs and lists of data, based on the principle that the humanistic mind much more easily remembers insignificant data attached to spatial, personal, or otherwise meaningful information than that occurring in meaningless sequences. The sequences must make sense, though. If a random mnemonic is made up, it is not necessarily a memory aid.

(Rigorous) (Skill 13.5)

97. **The success-oriented classroom is designed to ensure students are successful at attaining new skills. In addition, mistakes are viewed as ______ in this type of classroom.**

A. motivations to improve

B. a natural part of the learning process

C. ways to improve

D. building blocks

Answer: B. a natural part of the learning process

In the success-oriented classroom, mistakes are viewed as a natural part of learning. In this way, mistakes continue the learning. Students have the ability to continually improve their grades or learning by correcting mistakes, rather than the mistake being a penalty.

(Easy) (Skill 13.6)

98. **Which statement is an example of specific praise?**

    A. John, you are the only person in class not paying attention.

    B. William, I thought we agreed that you would turn in all of your homework.

    C. Robert, you did a good job staying in line. See how it helped us get to music class on time?

    D. Class, you did a great job cleaning up the art room.

    Answer: C. Robert, you did a good job staying in line. See how it helped us get to music class on time?

    Praise is a powerful tool in obtaining and maintaining order in a classroom. In addition, it is an effective motivator. It is even more effective if the positive results of good behavior are included.

(Average) (Skill 13.6)

99. **What is one way a teacher can supplement verbal praise?**

    A. Help students evaluate their own performance and supply self-reinforcement

    B. Give verbal praise more frequently

    C. Give tangible rewards such as stickers or treats

    D. Have students practice giving verbal praise

    Answer: A. Help students evaluate their own performance and supply self-reinforcement

    While praise is useful in maintaining order in a classroom and in motivating students, it's important for the teacher to remember at all times that one major educational objective is that of preparing students to succeed in the world once the supports of the classroom are gone. Self-esteem and lack of it are often barriers to success. An important lesson and skill for students to learn is how to bolster one's own self-esteem and confidence.

(Average) (Skill 13.6)

100. **What is a frequently used type of feedback to students?**

    A. Correctives

    B. Simple praise–confirmation

    C. Correcting the response

    D. Explanations

    Answer: B. Simple praise–confirmation

    Even if the student's answer is not perfect, there are always ways to praise her and to make use of her answer unless, of course, she was deliberately answering wrongly. When a behavior is praised, it is likely to be repeated.

(Rigorous) (Skill 13.6)

101. **The teacher responds, "Yes, that is correct" to a student's answer. What is this an example of?**

A. Academic feedback

B. Academic praise

C. Simple positive response

D. Simple negative response

Answer: C. Simple positive response

Academic praise is a group of specific statements that give information about the value of the response or its implications. For example, a teacher using academic praise would respond, "That is an excellent analysis of Twain's use of the river in *Huckleberry Finn*." Whereas a simple positive response to the same question would be:"That's correct."

(Average) (Skill 13.6)

102. **Which of the following is not a characteristic of effective praise?**

A. Praise is delivered in front of the class so it will serve to motivate others

B. Praise is low-key

C. Praise provides information about student competence

D. Praise is delivered contingently

Answer: A. Praise is delivered in front of the class so it will serve to motivate others

The reason for praise in the classroom is to increase the desirable in order to eliminate the undesirable in both conduct and academic focus. It further states that effective praise should be authentic, it should be used in a variety of ways, and it should be low-key.

(Average) (Skill 14.1)

103. **What is NOT a way that teachers show acceptance and give value to a student response?**

A. Acknowledging

B. Correcting

C. Discussing

D. Amplifying

Answer: B. Correcting

There are ways to treat every answer as worthwhile even if it happens to be wrong. The objective is to keep students involved in the dialogue. If their efforts to participate are "rewarded" with what seems to them to be a rebuke or that leads to embarrassment, they will be less willing to respond the next time.

(Average) (Skill 14.1)

104. **Which of the following is a definition of an intercultural communication model?**

A. Learning how different cultures engage in both verbal and nonverbal modes to communicate meaning

B. Learning how classmates engage in both verbal and nonverbal modes to communicate meaning

C. Learning how classmates engage in verbal dialogues

D. Learning how different cultures engage in verbal modes to communicate meaning

Answer: A. Learning how different cultures engage in both verbal and nonverbal modes to communicate meaning

This process lets students begin to understand the process of communicating with each other in a multicultural manner, which helps them better understand their own learning. It provides for a more global learning process for all students.

(Average) (Skill 14.2)

105. **How can the teacher establish a positive climate in the classroom?**

A. Help students see the unique contributions of individual differences

B. Use whole group instruction for all content areas

C. Help students divide into cooperative groups based on ability

D. Eliminate teaching strategies that allow students to make choices

Answer: A. Help students see the unique contributions of individual differences

In the first place, an important purpose of education is to prepare students to live successfully in the real world, and this is an important insight and understanding for them to take into that world. In the second place, the most fertile learning environment is one in which all viewpoints and backgrounds are respected and where everyone has equal respect.

(Average) (Skill 14.4)

106. **Wait-time has what effect?**

A. Gives structure to the class discourse

B. Fewer chain and low-level questions are asked with more higher-level questions included

C. Gives the students time to evaluate the response

D. Gives the opportunity for in-depth discussion about the topic

Answer: B. Fewer chain and low-level questions are asked with more higher-level questions included

One part of the questioning process for the successful teacher is wait time: the time between the question and either the student response or your follow-up. Many teachers vaguely recommend some general amount of wait-time (until the student starts to get uncomfortable or is clearly perplexed), but we focus here on wait-time as a specific and powerful communicative tool that speaks through its structured silences. Embedded in wait-time are subtle clues about your judgments of a student's abilities and your expectations of individuals and groups. For example, the more time you allow a student to mull through a question, the more you trust his or her ability to answer that question without getting flustered. As a rule, the practice of prompting is not a problem. Giving support and helping students reason through difficult conundrums is part of being an effective teacher.

(Rigorous) (Skill 14.4)

107. When is optimal benefit reached when handling an incorrect student response?

A. When specific praise is used

B. When the other students are allowed to correct that student

C. When the student is redirected to a better problem-solving approach

D. When the teacher asks simple questions, provides cues to clarify, or gives assistance for working out the correct response

Answer: C. When the student is redirected to a better problem-solving approach

It's important that students feel confident and comfortable in making responses, knowing that even if they give a wrong answer, they will not be embarrassed. If a student is ridiculed or embarrassed by an incorrect response, the student my shut down and not participate thereafter in classroom discussion. One way to respond to the incorrect answer is to ask the child, "Show me from your book why you think that." This gives the student a chance to correct the answer and redeem himself or herself. Another possible response from the teacher is to use the answer as a nonexample. For example, after discussing the characteristics of warm-blooded and cold-blooded animals, the teacher asks for some examples of warm-blooded animals. A student raises his or her hand and responds, "A snake." The teacher could then say, "Remember, snakes lay eggs; they do not have live births. However, a snake is a good nonexample of a mammal." The teacher then draws a line down the board and under a heading of "nonexample" writes "snake." This action conveys to the child that even though the answer was wrong, it still contributed positively to the class discussion. Notice how the teacher did not digress from the task of listing warm-blooded animals, which in other words is maintaining academic focus, and at the same time allowed the student to maintain dignity.

(Average) (Skill 14.4)

108. What is an effective amount of "wait time?"

A. 1 second

B. 5 seconds

C. 15 seconds

D. 10 seconds

Answer: B. 5 seconds

In formal training, most preservice teachers are taught the art of questioning. One part of the questioning process is wait time: the time between the question and either the student response or your follow-up. Many teachers vaguely recommend some general amount of wait-time (until the student starts to get uncomfortable or is clearly perplexed), but we focus here on wait-time as a specific and powerful communicative tool that speaks through its structured silences. Embedded in wait-time are subtle clues about your judgments of a student's abilities and your expectations of individuals and groups. For example, the more time you allow a student to mull through a question, the more you trust his or her ability to answer that question without getting flustered. As a rule, the practice of prompting is not a problem. Giving support and helping students reason through difficult conundrums is part of being an effective teacher.

(Easy) (Skill 14.4)

109. **Which of the following can impact the desire of students to learn new material?**

A. Assessments plan

B. Lesson plans

C. Enthusiasm

D. School community

Answer: C. Enthusiasm

The enthusiasm a teacher exhibits can have positive effects on students' desire to learn, as well as on on-task behaviors.

(Average) (Skill 14.6)

110. **When are students more likely to understand complex ideas?**

A. If they do outside research before coming to class

B. Later when they write out the definitions of complex words

C. When they attend a lecture on the subject

D. When they are clearly defined by the teacher and are given examples and nonexamples of the concept

Answer: D. When they are clearly defined by the teacher and are given examples and nonexamples of the concept

Several studies have been carried out to determine the effectiveness of giving examples as well as the difference in effectiveness of various types of examples. It was found conclusively that the most effective method of concept presentation included giving a definition along with examples and nonexamples and also providing an explanation of them. These same studies indicate that boring examples were just as effective as interesting examples in promoting learning. Additional studies have been conducted to determine the most effective number of examples that will result in maximum student learning. These studies concluded that a few thoughtfully selected examples are just as effective as many examples. It was determined that the actual number of examples necessary to promote student learning was relative to the learning characteristics of the learners. It was again ascertained that learning is facilitated when examples are provided along with the definition.

(Easy) (Skill 15.1)

111. **How can DVDs be used in instruction?**

A. Students can use the DVD to create pictures for reports

B. Students can use the DVD to create a science experiment

C. Students can use the DVD to record class activities

D. Students can use the DVD to review concepts studied

Answer: D: Students can use the DVD to review concepts studied

The teacher's arms are never long enough to render all the help that is needed when students are learning new concepts and practicing skills. Audiovisual aids such as the DVD extend her arms. Students who need more time to master a skill can have that without the teacher having to work one-on-one with a single student or with a classroom of students.

(Easy) (Skill 15.1)

112. **How can students use a computer desktop publishing center?**

A. To set up a classroom budget

B. To create student-made books

C. To design a research project

D. To create a classroom behavior management system

Answer: B. To create student-made books

By creating a book, students gain new insights into how communication works. Suddenly, the concept of audience for what they write and create becomes real. They also have an opportunity to be introduced to graphic arts, an exploding field. In addition, just as computers are a vital part of the world they will be entering as adults, so is desktop publishing. It is universally used by businesses of all kinds.

(Average) (Skill 15.1)

113. **Which of the following is NOT a part of the hardware of a computer system?**

A. Storage device

B. Input devices

C. Software

D. Central processing unit

Answer: C. Software

Software is not a part of the hardware of a computer, but instead consists of all of the programs that allow the computer to run. Software is either an operating system or an application program.

(Rigorous) (Skill 15.2)

114. **What is one benefit of amplifying a student's response?**

A. It helps the student develop a positive self-image

B. It is helpful to other students who are in the process of learning the reasoning or steps in answering the question

C. It allows the teacher to cover more content

D. It helps to keep the information organized

Answer: B. It is helpful to other students who are in the process of learning the reasoning or steps in answering the question

Not only does the teacher show acceptance and give value to student responses by acknowledging, amplifying, discussing, or restating the comment or question, she also helps the rest of the class learn to reason. If a student response is allowed, even if it is blurted out, it must be acknowledged and the student made aware of the quality of the response. A teacher acknowledges a student response by commenting on it. For example, the teacher states the definition of a noun and then asks for examples of nouns in the classroom. A student responds, "My pencil is a noun." The teacher answers, "Okay, let us list that on the board." By this response and the action of writing "pencil" on the board, the teacher has just incorporated the student's response into the lesson. A teacher may also amplify the student response through another question directed to either the original student or to another student. For example, the teacher may say, "Okay," giving the student feedback on the quality of the answer, and then add, "What do you mean by 'run' when you say the battery runs the radio?" Another way of showing acceptance and value of student response is to discuss the student response. For example, after a student responds, the teacher would say, "Class, let us think along that line. What is some evidence that proves what Susie just stated?" The teacher may also restate the response. For example, the teacher might say, "So you are saying the seasons are caused by the tilt of the earth. Is this what you said?"

(Average) (Skill 15.3)

115. **Which of the following statements is true about computers in the classroom?**

A. Computers are simply a glorified game machine and just allow students to play games

B. The computer should replace traditional research and writing skills taught to school-age children

C. Computers stifle the creativity of children

D. Computers allow students to access information they may otherwise be unable to

Answer: D. Computers allow students to access information they may otherwise be unable to

Computers, particularly those connected to the Internet, provide students with the ability to research information school libraries might otherwise be unable to provide because of funding issues. It opens the doors and pathways for students to increase the amount of information they acquire in school.

(Average) (Skill 15.3)

116. **While an asset to students, technology is also important for teachers. Which of the following can be taught using technology to students?**

A. Cooperation skills

B. Decision-making skills

C. Problem solving skills

D. All of the above

Answer: D. All of the above

Having students work together on a project using the technology available to you within your school not only teaches the content you wish them to learn but can also provide them with skills in cooperation, decision making, and problem solving.

(Easy) (Skill 15.3)

117. **As a classroom teacher, you have data on all of your students that you must track over the remainder of the school year. You will need to keep copies of the scores students receive and then graph their results to share progress with the parents an administrators. Which of the following software programs will be most useful in this manner?**

A. Word processing program

B. Spreadsheet

C. Database

D. Teacher utility and classroom management tools

Answer: B. Spreadsheet

Spreadsheets help a teacher to organize numeric information and can easily take that data and transfer it into a graph for a visual representation to administrators or parents.

(Average) (Skill 15.3)

118. **Which of the following statements is NOT true?**

A. Printing and distributing material off of the Internet breaks the copyright law

B. Articles are only copyrighted when there is a © in the article

C. E-mail messages that are posted online are considered copyrighted

D. It is not legal to scan magazine articles and place on your district Web site

Answer: B. Articles are only copyrighted when there is a © in the article

Articles, even without the symbol, are considered copyrighted material. This includes articles from newspapers, magazines, or even posted online.

(Easy) (Skill 15.5)

119. **The use of technology in the classroom allows for:**

A. More complex lessons

B. Better delivery of instruction

C. Variety of instruction

D. Better ability to meet more individual student needs

Answer: D. Better ability to meet more individual student needs

The utilization of technology provides the teacher with the opportunity to incorporate more than one learning style into a lesson. In this way, the teacher is better able to meet the individual needs of his or her students.

Sample Test with Rationales: The Professional Environment

(Easy) (Skill 16.5)

120. **A district superintendent's job is to:**

A. Supervise senior teachers in the district

B. Develop plans for school improvement

C. Allocate community resources to individual schools

D. Implement policies set by the board of education

Answer: D. Implement policies set by the board of education

A district superintendent is the chief officer of the school district and has the responsibility of overseeing that the policies set forth by the Board of Education are implemented by the schools in the district. He does not have the responsibility of directly supervising teachers or students or developing individual school improvement plans.

(Average) (Skill 16.5)

121. **Teacher's unions are involved in all of the following EXCEPT:**

A. Updating teachers on current educational developments

B. Advocating for teacher rights

C. Matching teachers with suitable schools

D. Developing professional codes and practices

Answer: C. Matching teachers with suitable schools

The role of teacher's unions is to work with teachers to develop and improve the profession of teaching by advocating for higher wages and improved conditions for teachers, developing professional codes and practices, and keeping teachers up to date on current educational developments. It is not the role of unions to find suitable employment for teachers.

(Average) (Skill 17.1)

122. **What is a benefit of frequent self-assessment?**

A. Opens new venues for professional development

B. Saves teachers the pressure of being observed by others

C. Reduces time spent on areas not needing attention

D. Offers a model for students to adopt in self-improvement

Answer: A. Opens new venues for professional development

When a teacher is involved in the process of self-reflection and self-assessment, one of the common outcomes is that the teacher comes to identify areas of skill or knowledge that require more research or improvement on her part. She may become interested in overcoming a particular weakness in her performance or may decide to attend a workshop or consult with a mentor to learn more about a particular area of concern.

(Average) (Skill 17.1)

123. **Which of the following could be used to improve teaching skills?**

A. Developing a professional development plan

B. Use of self-evaluation and reflection

C. Building professional learning communities

D. All of the above

Answer: D. All of the above

Creating a personalized plan for increasing your professional development, using self reflection, and working with other teachers in a professional learning community are all excellent strategies for improving ones teaching skills.

(Rigorous) (Skill 17.2)

124. **Which of the following is NOT a sound educational practice for expanding the professional development opportunities for teachers?**

A. Looking at multiple methods of classroom management strategies

B. Training teachers in understanding and applying multiple assessment formats and implementations in curriculum and instruction

C. Having the students complete professional development assessments on a regular basis

D. Teaching teachers how to disaggregate student data in improving instruction and curriculum implementation for student academic equity and access

Answer: C. Having the students complete professional development assessments on a regular basis

Giving teachers tests on a regular basis, while providing information on what knowledge they may have, does not expand the professional development opportunities for teachers.

(Rigorous) (Skill 17.3)

125. **What would happen if a school utilized an integrated approach to professional development?**

A. All stakeholders needs are addressed

B. Teachers and administrators are on the same page

C. High-quality programs for students are developed

D. Parents drive the curriculum and instruction

Answer: C. High-quality programs for students are developed

The implementation of an integrated approach to professional development is a critical component to ensuring success of programs for students. It involves teachers, parents, and other community members working together to develop appropriate programs to ensure students are receiving the necessary instruction to be successful in the future workforce.

(Average) (Skill 17.4)

126. **What must be a consideration when a parent complains that he can't control a child's behavior?**

A. Consider whether the parent gives feedback to the child

B. Consider whether the parent's expectations for control are developmentally appropriate

C. Consider how much time the parent spends with the child

D. Consider how rigid the rules are that the parent sets

Answer: B. Consider whether the parent's expectations for control are developmentally appropriate

The teacher is the expert when it comes to developmental expectations. This is one area where a concerned and helpful teacher can be invaluable in helping a family through a crisis. Parents often have unrealistic expectations about their children's behavior simply because they don't know what is normal and what is not. Some stages tend to be annoying, especially if they are not understood. A teacher can help to defuse the conflicts in these cases.

(Average) (Skill 18.1)

127. **Which of the following should NOT be a purpose of a parent-teacher conference?**

A. To involve the parent in their child's education

B. To establish a friendship with the child's parents

C. To resolve a concern about the child's performance

D. To inform parents of positive behaviors by the child

Answer: B. To establish a friendship with the child's parents

The purpose of a parent teacher conference is to involve parents in their child's education, address concerns about the child's performance, and share positive aspects of the student's learning with the parents. It would be unprofessional to allow the conference to degenerate into a social visit to establish friendships.

(Easy) (Skill 18.1)

128. **Mr. Brown wishes to improve his parent communication skills. Which of the following is a strategy he can utilize to accomplish this goal?**

A. Hold parent-teacher conferences

B. Send home positive notes

C. Have parent nights where the parents are invited into his classroom

D. All of the above

Answer: D. All of the above

Increasing parent communication skills is important for teachers. All of the listed strategies are methods a teacher can utilize to increase his skills.

(Easy) (Skill 18.1)

129. **Tommy is a student in your class, and his parents are deaf. Tommy is struggling with math and you want to contact the parents to discuss the issues. How should you proceed?**

A. Limit contact because of the parents' inability to hear

B. Use a TTY phone to communicate with the parents

C. Talk to your administrator to find an appropriate interpreter to help you communicate with the parents personally

D. Both B and C

Answer: D. Both B and C

You should never avoid communicating with parents for any reason; instead you should find strategies to find an effective way to communicate in various methods, just as you would with any other student in your classroom.

(Easy) (Skill 18.1)

130. **When communicating with parents for whom English is not the primary language you should:**

A. Provide materials whenever possible in their native language

B. Use an interpreter

C. Provide the same communication as you would to native English speaking parents

D. All of the above

Answer: D. All of the above

When communicating with non-English speaking parents, it is important to treat them as you would any other parent and utilize any means necessary to ensure they have the ability to participate in their child's educational process.

(Rigorous) (Skill 19.1)

131. **Which of the following increases appropriate behavior more than 80 percent?**

A. Monitoring the halls

B. Having class rules

C. Having class rules, giving feedback, and having individual consequences

D. Having class rules and giving feedback

Answer: C. Having class rules, giving feedback, and having individual consequences

Clear, consistent class rules go a long way to preventing inappropriate behavior. Effective teachers give immediate feedback to students regarding their behavior or misbehavior. If there are consequences, they should be as close as possible to those they would receive in the outside world, especially for adolescents. Consistency, especially with adolescents, reduces the occurrence of power struggles and teaches them that predictable consequences follow for their choice of actions.

(Average) (Skill 19.1)

132. **A 16-year-old girl who has been looking sad writes an essay in which the main protagonist commits suicide. You overhear her talking about suicide. What do you do?**

A. Report this immediately to school administration, talk to the girl, letting her know you will talk to her parents about it

B. Report this immediately to authorities

C. Report this immediately to school administration, make your own report to authorities if required by protocol in your school, and do nothing else

D. Just give the child some extra attention, as it may just be that's all she's looking for

Answer: C. Report this immediately to school administration, make your own report to authorities if required by protocol in your school, and do nothing else

A child who is suicidal is beyond any help that can be offered in a classroom. The first step is to report the situation to administration. If your school protocol calls for it, the situation should also be reported to authorities.

(Rigorous) (Skill 19.1)

133. **Jeanne, a bright, attentive student is in her first hour English class. She is quiet, but very alert, often visually scanning the room in random patterns. Her pupils are dilated, and she has a slight but noticeable tremor in her hands. She fails to note a cue given from her teacher. At odd moments, she will act as if responding to stimuli that aren't there by suddenly changing her gaze. When spoken to directly, she has a limited response, but her teacher has a sense she is not herself. What should the teacher do?**

A. Ask the student if she is all right, then let it go, as there are not enough signals to be alarmed

B. Meet with the student after class to get more information before making a referral

C. Send the student to the office to see the nurse

D. Quietly call for administration, remain calm, and be careful not to alarm the class

Answer: D. Quietly call for administration, remain calm, and be careful not to alarm the class

These behaviors are indicative of drug use. The best thing a teacher can do in this case is call for help from administration.

(Average) (Skill 19.1)

134. **Which is true of child protective services?**

A. They have been forced to become more punitive in their attempts to treat and prevent child abuse and neglect

B. They have become more a means for identifying cases of abuse and less an agent for rehabilitation because of the large volume of cases

C. They have become advocates for structured discipline within the school

D. They have become a strong advocate in the court system

Answer: B. They have become more a means for identifying cases of abuse and less an agent for rehabilitation because of the large volume of cases

Nina Bernstein, who wrote *The Lost Children of Wilder*, told of a long-running lawsuit in New York City that attempted to hold the city and its child-care services responsible for meeting the needs of abused children. Unfortunately, while it is an extreme case, it is not atypical of the plight of children all across the country. The only thing a teacher can do is attempt to provide a refuge of concern and stability during the time such children are in her care, hoping that they will, somehow, survive.

(Average) (Skill 19.1)

135. **In successful inclusion of students with disabilities:**

A. A variety of instructional arrangements are available

B. School personnel shift the responsibility for learning outcomes to the student

C. The physical facilities are used as they are

D. Regular classroom teachers have sole responsibility for evaluating student progress

Answer: A. A variety of instructional arrangements are available

Here are some support systems and activities that are in evidence where successful inclusion has occurred:

Attitudes and beliefs

- The regular teacher believes the student can succeed
- School personnel are committed to accepting responsibility for the learning outcomes of students with disabilities
- School personnel and the students in the class have been prepared to receive a student with disabilities

Services and physical accommodations

- Services needed by the student are available (e.g., health, physical, occupational, or speech therapy)
- Accommodations to the physical plant and equipment are adequate to meet the students' needs (e.g., toys, building and playground facilities, learning materials, or assistive devices)

School support

- The principal understands the needs of students with disabilities
- Adequate numbers of personnel, including aides and support personnel, are available
- Adequate staff development and technical assistance, based on the needs of the school personnel, are being provided (e.g., information on disabilities, instructional methods, awareness and acceptance activities for students and team-building skills)
- Appropriate policies and procedures for monitoring individual student progress, including grading and testing are in place

Collaboration

- Special educators are part of the instructional or planning team
- Teaming approaches are used for program implementation and problem solving
- Regular teachers, special education teachers, and other specialists collaborate (e.g., co-teach, team teach, or work together on teacher assistance teams)

Instructional methods

- Teachers have the knowledge and skills needed to select and adapt curricular and instructional methods according to individual student needs
- A variety of instructional arrangements is available (e.g., team teaching, cross-grade grouping, peer tutoring, or teacher assistance teams)
- Teachers foster a cooperative learning environment and promote socialization

(Average) (Skill 19.1)

136. **How may a teacher use a student's permanent record?**

A. To develop a better understanding of the needs of the student

B. To record all instances of student disruptive behavior

C. To brainstorm ideas for discussing with parents at parent-teacher conferences

D. To develop realistic expectations of the student's performance early in the year

Answer: A. To develop a better understanding of the needs of the student

The purpose of a student's permanent record is to give the teacher a better understanding of the student's educational history and provide him with relevant information to support the student's learning. Permanent records may not be used to arrive at preconceived judgments or to build a case against the student. Above all, the contents of a student's permanent record are confidential.

(Rigorous) (Skill 19.1)

137. **You receive a phone call from a person who indicates she is now tutoring a student in your class. She would like you to provide an overview of the academic areas which the student is having difficulties. What is the first thing you should do?**

A. Find a time and talk with the tutor about issues you see within the classroom

B. Call the parents

C. Put together a packet of information to share with the tutor

D. Offer to invite the tutor in to have a discussion and observe the child

Answer: B. Call the parents

Before you share any information with anyone about a student, you should always secure parental permission in writing.

(Rigorous) (Skill 19.2)

138. **Marcus is a first grade boy of good developmental attainment. His learning progress is good the first half of the year. He shows no indicators of emotional distress. After the holiday break, he returns much changed. He is quieter, sullen even, tending to play alone. He has moments of tearfulness, sometimes almost without cause. He avoids contact with adults as often as he can. Even play with his friends has become limited. He has episodes of wetting not seen before and often wants to sleep in school. What approach is appropriate for this sudden change in behavior?**

A. Give him some time to adjust; the holiday break was probably too much fun to come back to school from

B. Report this change immediately to administration; do not call the parents until administration decides a course of action

C. Document his daily behavior carefully as soon as you notice such a change, report to administration the next month or so in a meeting

D. Make a courtesy call to the parents to let them know he is not acting like himself, being sure to tell them he is not making trouble for others

Answer: B. Report this change immediately to administration; do not call the parents until administration decides a course of action

Anytime a child's disposition, attitude, or habits change significantly, teachers and parents need to seriously consider the existence of emotional difficulties. Emotional disturbances in childhood are not uncommon and take a variety of forms. Usually these problems show up in the form of uncharacteristic behaviors. Most of the time, children respond favorably to brief treatment programs of psychotherapy. At other times, disturbances may need more intensive therapy and are harder to resolve. All stressful behaviors need to be addressed, and any type of chronic antisocial behavior needs to be examined as a possible symptom of deep-seated emotional upset. In a case where the change is sudden and dramatic, administration needs to become involved.

(Rigorous) (Skill 19.2)

139. **Andy shows up to class abusive and irritable. He is often late, sleeps in class, sometimes slurs his speech, and has an odor of alcohol. What is the first intervention to take?**

A. Confront him, relying on a trusting relationship you think you have

B. Do a lesson on alcohol abuse, making an example of him

C. Do nothing; it is better to err on the side of failing to identify substance abuse

D. Call administration, avoid conflict, and supervise others carefully

Answer: D. Call administration, avoid conflict, and supervise others carefully

Educators are not only likely to, but often do, face students who are high on something. Of course, they are not only a hazard to their own safety and those of others, but their ability to be productive learners is greatly diminished, if not nonexistent. They show up instead of skip, because it's not always easy or practical for them to spend the day away from home but not in school. Unless they can stay inside, they are at risk of being picked up for truancy. Some enjoy being high in school, getting a sense of satisfaction by putting something over on the system. Some just don't take drug use seriously enough to think usage at school might be inappropriate. The first responsibility of the teacher is to assure the safety of all of the children. Avoiding conflict with the student who is high and obtaining help from administration is the best course of action.

(Average) (Skill 19.4)

140. **A parent has left an angry message on the teacher's voicemail. The message relates to a concern about a student and is directed at the teacher. The teacher should:**

A. Call back immediately and confront the parent

B. Cool off, plan what to discuss with the parent, then call back

C. Question the child to find out what set off the parent

D. Ignore the message, since feelings of anger usually

Answer: B. Cool off, plan what to discuss with the parent, then call back

It is professional for a teacher to keep her head in the face of emotion and respond to an angry parent in a calm and objective manner. The teacher should give herself time to cool off and plan the conversation with the parent with the purpose of understanding the concern and resolving it, rather than putting the parent in their place. Above all, the teacher should remember that parent-teacher interactions should aim to benefit the student.

Sample Written Assignment

Instructions: Write an answer of 300–600 words that addresses the topic described below.

- You need to identify the grade level involved and provide information about the purpose of your approach, the strategies you would employ, and the rationale or reasoning behind your plan of action.
- Imagine the intended reader of this essay to be another educator.
- Take your time and think through what you want to write before you start.
- You may want to outline the essay before you actually start writing.

YOUR ASSIGNMENT

Your school district is barely meeting the AYP standards of No Child Left Behind in several areas. Although there are no official external goals that must be met, the faculty, administration, and parents want to improve student achievement across the board and prevent any difficulties with AYP scores. A joint task force has been formed to identify methods to help all students improve their performance. To this end, they have asked teachers to submit ideas for consideration. **Describe a plan that you believe would positively impact student achievement in multiple subject areas.**

A good response by an elementary teacher

This plan is designed for third graders.

Student achievement is affected by many factors. These include the teacher's style and attitude, the curriculum and instructional methods, the atmosphere of the classroom and the school, the home environment from which students come, students' unique learning styles, individual student needs and/or limitations, cultural and linguistic diversity, and prior learning experiences. In spite of individual differences and needs, all students can be supported to learn and grow in the academic environment with the right attention and approach. A commitment to an inclusive classroom, where students of all achievement levels work together and diversity is honored and supported, goes a long way to ensuring student success. Attending to students' individual academic and psychosocial needs and working collaboratively with parents and community supports are also essential in helping to ameliorate or remove obstacles to student achievement.

Another major element in student achievement is student motivation. My plan is to implement instructional approaches that will increase student motivation, thereby raising student achievement. I would recommend focusing on two areas: child-centered learning methodologies and an integrated curriculum. The advantages of the integrated curriculum is that it mirrors the real world, where learning crosses "subject" lines such as reading, science, the arts, math, social studies, and language arts. This is especially effective for young children as their worldview is not broken down into discrete "subjects." An integrated curriculum feels familiar to them and engages their natural curiosity, enhancing their motivation to learn.

Using child-centered instructional techniques increase the likelihood that students will enjoy learning. When they enjoy the process of learning, they are more highly motivated to complete tasks, to take risks to learn new things, and to consider new ideas. By capitalizing on young children's innate urge to discover and explore, as well as their use of play to attain mastery, child-centered approaches for young children can yield a high level of engagement and motivation to learn.

Specific child-centered learning methodologies could include the following:

- Generating a list of questions that students want to answer on a specific topic; these questions can be posted in the classroom with space for the answers to be added as the class learns about the topic. The teacher will develop activities across subjects to help student address these questions.
- Using integrated subject learning stations that the students can choose from, as long as they complete three out of five within a given time frame.
- Incorporating play activities into the classroom that access content-related material across subject areas. An example might be to put on a play about the animals that live in the forests and the fields.
- Being attuned to and utilizing teachable moments as they occur in classroom activities as well as on the playground.
- Creating small group activities where the students have the chance to make choices as a group about what and how they are going to study. For example, in groups of three or four, students have a worksheet with five key words related to the topic under study. The task is to learn three things about each of the key words. They can ask their parents/guardians for information, go to the library and ask for help, look in books in the classroom, or share information they already know. They may use the Internet, draw a picture of the key word, or create a pantomime. Each group can then share or post their information for the entire class.

A good response by a secondary teacher

This plan is designed for eleventh graders.

Student achievement is affected by many factors. These include the teacher's style and attitude, the curriculum and instructional methods, the atmosphere of the classroom and the school, the home environment from which students come, students' unique learning styles, individual student needs and/or limitations, cultural and linguistic diversity, and prior learning experiences. In spite of individual differences and needs, all students can be supported to learn and grow in the academic environment with the right attention and approach. A commitment to an inclusive classroom, where students of all achievement levels work together and diversity is honored and supported, goes a long way to ensuring student success. Attending to students' individual academic and psychosocial needs and working collaboratively with parents and community supports are also essential in helping to ameliorate or remove obstacles to student achievement.

Another major element in student achievement is student motivation. My plan is to implement instructional approaches that will increase student motivation by engaging them in self-chosen topics, thereby raising student achievement. I would use two strategies to improve student achievement with eleventh graders: using self-directed study and informational interviewing. These could be incorporated in various subject courses, such as English, social studies, science, and the arts. The intent behind both of these strategies is to engage students in active exploration of topics relevant to them and to help them to take responsibility for their learning process in and out of the classroom.

In both of these strategies, I would provide some guidelines and a rubric for assessment. The specific goals to be evaluated by the rubric would be part of the student's process of determining their topic and the learning approaches they will employ.

Self-directed study involves students picking a topic among those included in a specific curriculum and determining what they want to learn about that topic. They establish goals, learning strategies, and intended outcomes. There are checkpoints built in so they can receive feedback as they work on their project to ensure that they have crafted a workable plan and benefit from the teacher's input. They can utilize a wide range of methods (such as using the arts to describe scientific ideas or concepts) and sources (creative nonfiction, the Internet, professionals in the field, as well as textbooks). Outcomes can be equally varied.

Informational interviewing can be incorporated into a self-directed study project or can stand on its own as a strategy to engage students. The key is to generate interest in students to find a topic or profession about which they are curious. It can be a particular job, a scientific theory, a method of manufacture, or a form of artistic expression. The goal is for students to identify key questions that need to be asked in order to answer their general inquiry, identify informants (e.g., someone who performs a certain job or someone who works in the field of study), conduct the interview(s), and then create a report about the topic. The report must meet certain criteria per the teacher-derived rubric, but students have a lot of freedom in how the report is created (e.g., written text, artistic expression, multimedia presentation).

Both of these approaches can be part of a larger strategy to engage students in learning by drawing on interactions with real-world information and to take learning beyond the classroom. This learning can be brought back into the classroom through "poster sessions" (as is used at professional conferences) or in discussion groups or public speaking activities. All of these activities provide opportunities for the student to develop self-responsibility and a positive self-concept, also factors in increasing student motivation and achievement.

Guidelines for Crisis Management and Emergency Response

Increasingly, teachers are faced with emergency and crisis situations that demand careful, coordinated, and immediate response. These situations are challenging for many reasons. These guidelines address some of these reasons as well as the core concepts involved in effective crisis management, including the importance of preparedness.

Emergency response planning

To ensure student and personnel safety, various levels of planning must be implemented in an effort to anticipate a range of situations. At their most basic, plans must exist for ensuring safety in different scenarios. Local natural disasters must be accounted for, as should plans for ensuring safety when, for example, the police are searching for a loose criminal in the surrounding neighborhood or the community is faced with a health crisis such as a flu pandemic. Many schools may even have to consider safety plans for local terrorist attacks, particularly if the school is located near a strategic or popular site.

Plans should include methods for getting students to a safe area, as well as for communication among everyone involved. Strategies for dealing with crisis reactions also need to be in place. (Communication and intervention strategies are addressed in the next section.)

In planning for evacuation, routes should be drawn so that each hallway has the least amount of students walking through it as possible, with no student having to walk too far. The quickest route out of a building may clog a hallway, thereby making the route much slower. However, it would also be unwise to have a whole classroom full of students walk far around a particular hallway and still be in a potentially dangerous location. Often, fire departments or safety consultants can assist in designing solid, quality evaluation plans.

A lockdown plan is the opposite of an evacuation plan and consists of various rules and procedures for getting or keeping all students in a secure location, such as a classroom. Often communication suffers during a lockdown, so many schools now insist that school personnel look at their e-mail accounts as soon as a lock-down occurs, to give the administration an efficient way to communicate to many people quickly.

The next level of ensuring safety concerns communicating those plans to staff, parents, students, and the district. Clear directions should be posted all over campus for clarification when events occur. Directions and procedures should be mailed home to parents annually, as well.

Crisis Management and Intervention Planning

Crisis and emergency situations are events beyond the realm of every day life. They always involve some degree of surprise, shock, loss, and emotion. Crises include death, natural disasters such as earthquakes and hurricanes, vehicular and other accidents, health concerns such as flu pandemics, school shootings, and other forms of extreme violence. The unpredictability of crises, the experience of loss that invariably accompanies such situations, and the strong feelings that are evoked all make crisis and emergency events particularly potent and challenging for everyone involved.

The value of being prepared

As noted, preplanning is essential. Equally important, specialized training in crisis management skills can be extremely helpful in responding effectively. Although the events themselves may be unpredictable, there is a body of information about how people react to crisis and what responders can do to ameliorate and manage the aftermath of crisis. This is important in school settings, where there are a large number of people congregated in one place and contagion is a concern. Anxiety and misinformation can spread like wildfire, exacerbating the short- and long-term effects of traumatic events.

Designating and training a crisis response team is essential in well-functioning schools. Ideally, the crisis response team includes some administrators, counselors, teachers, and the school nurse. Comprehensive crisis management training and ongoing refresher courses are necessary for a team to function well. A clearly defined leader (not the principal or assistant principal, as he or she will have enough to do in any crisis situation) facilitates the work of the crisis team. The leader may be a teacher or other member of the team. The important skills the leader must possess are the ability to remain calm, think clearly, and have excellent communication skills. He or she will be responsible for "thinking on one's feet" with some decisions, although the larger decisions will be made by administrators.

In addition to a crisis team, school districts need to have clearly defined crisis response plans, including the evacuation and lockdown plans discussed previously. They should include as much detail as possible, with specific recommendations for different situations as needed, although a general plan is applicable in many circumstances. At minimum, the plan should incorporate the following:

- Delineate the school's goals in crisis situations (such as maintaining as normal a school day as possible, or providing timely information)
- Identify key players on the crisis response team, including a team leader and a backup leader
- Specify how communication will be handled
- Discuss how decisions will be made regarding the need to bring in outside resources
- Describe what interventions will be used with students
- Note how interactions and referrals to outside agencies will be managed
- Describe the process for decision-making regarding disclosures to the media
- Detail what follow-up is needed after each event

The plan should also include information from the Center for Disease Control and Prevention regarding health and natural disaster–related crises. Notes about local contacts with the Red Cross and other disaster response teams as well as the local police can be incorporated into the plan.

Further, it helps to have handouts about traumatic stress reactions available for teachers and parents, sample letters to parents and guardians, sample press releases, and other useful documents ready prior to any event.

The need for information

Everyone who experiences a traumatic event needs to be aware of the normal reactions and common feelings of survivors, as well as receive accurate information about the event itself (when this is not known publicly). They also need to know what the school is doing in response. This means that the district needs to make clear decisions about the actions the school is taking, including what parents and guardians need to know and do, and communicate these plans succinctly and in a timely manner to all in the school community. Information also needs to flow to the larger community. Specific, to-the-point information is valuable; avoid all rumors.

Intervention for students

Most commonly, school counselors, teachers, and other school personnel will be available for crisis counseling and support in a designated room for a day or two after a traumatic event. Some districts will invite local experts in traumatic stress response or grief counseling to come to the school to aid school personnel. Interventions include listening, normalizing the reactions of students, offering to call parents and guardians, and making arrangements for the student to go home early when needed. Referrals to outside professionals may also be made.

Self-care during and after the event

Part of a school crisis plan should spell out how responders and other school personnel will receive and give support during the implementation of the crisis management plan. Further, crisis team members need to get rest and support after doing crisis response work. This work is very demanding, and the effects on responders may not be immediately apparent. Secondary post-traumatic stress is a concern, particularly when the crisis response team has multiple or ongoing situations to manage. Adequate administrative and personal support, time off, and sufficient training and debriefing are essential.

Follow-up planning

After events that compromise safety or involve crisis, school leaders must do a few things. Reporting to district administrators, local police, parents, students, and sometimes media should be spelled out as part of the crisis management plan. Sometimes this reporting happens during the course of the event; other times it occurs after the fact. Regardless, reporting needs to happen as soon as possible. Once the situation is stabilized but before too much time has passed, the team and school administrators must sit down with other staff members and discuss the performance of the school community in responding to the crisis. From that discussion, the team can then make informed modifications to the plans. New plans, of course, must then be communicated to all school community members.

The following Web sites have information about emergency response, school crisis management, traumatic stress reactions, and related topics:

www.nctsnet.org/nccts/nav.do?pid=ctr_aud_schlmeans that part of the crisis response

www.cdc.gov/niosh/unp-trinstrs.html

www.aaets.org/trresp.htm

www.apa.org/practice/traumaticstress.html

www.ed.gov/admins/lead/safety/training/responding/crisis_pg11.html?exp=2.

For information on assessing your school's risk during a crisis event see the Web site of the National Clearinghouse for Educational Facilities:

http://www.ncef.org/pubs/mitigating_hazards.pdf.

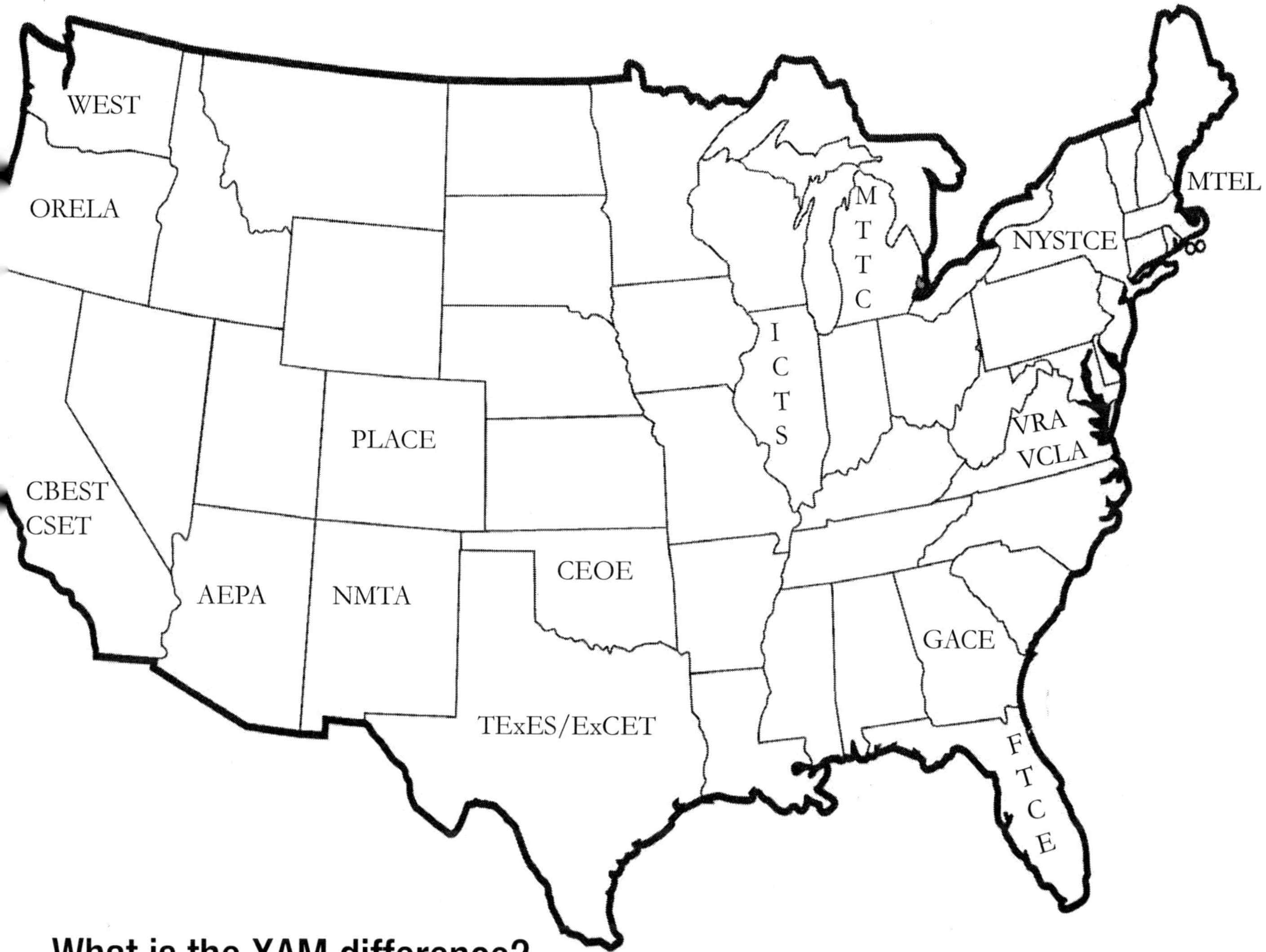

Want an enhanced study experience? You need the IntelliGuide™, XAMonline's advanced technology product.

Experience the XAM difference, demo IntelliGuide, our new online platform that transforms the traditional eBook experience into an enhanced study and test practice session through innovative tools such as sticky notes and flashcards. Available for the **NYSTCE Multi-Subject 002**, the IntelliGuide technology product is in full color and includes the same comprehensive content as the print guide but features:

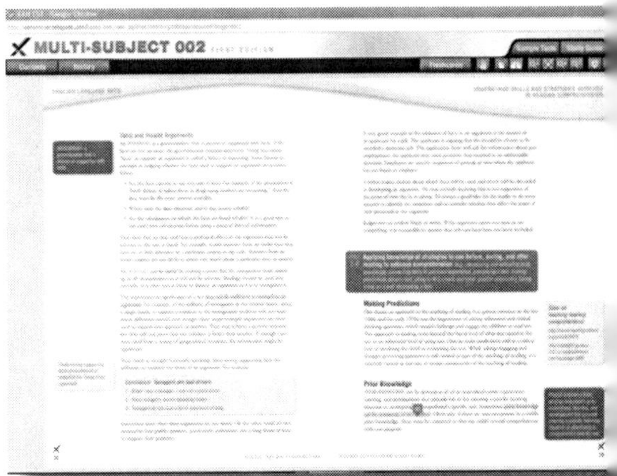

Easy Navigation and Full Color

Previously viewed content can be quickly recalled using the "History" tab. This saves time and prevents frustration as you can easily flip back and reference a previous page or topic you recently viewed. IntelliGuide, which is in full color, features more vocabulary call out boxes.

eStickynotes

Allows you to write digital notes anywhere in the study guide, then combine and print out all your notes for easy, "on-the-go" studying.

In-text Search and Highlight

Where was that topic mentioned? This feature enables you to quickly locate the content you need. Simply type in the search term and the IntelliGuide lists the page numbers and highlights where in the page the reference occurs. Mark text for later review using the digital highlighter.

eFlashcards

XAMonline's digital flashcards enable you to study pre-made cards or create your own. The "Hide" function allows you to skip cards you already know, creating a customized study experience.

More Sample Tests

Additional timed and scored practice tests assess how much you know and help identify the areas you need to focus on. Timed and scored to mirror the real test or pause the timer to flip back and reference specific skills or competencies.

Experience the XAMonline difference with our free IntelliGuide™ demo:

www.XAMonline.com/IntelliGuide

Interested in saving some  **?**

Use code NYIG at XAMonline.com

XAMonline.com

CPSIA information can be obtained at www.ICGtesting.com
225755LV00001B/11/P

9 781607 870197